NO-BODY HOMICIDE CASES

A Practical Guide to Investigating, Prosecuting, and Winning Cases When the Victim Is Missing

NO-BODY HOMICIDE CASES

A Practical Guide to Investigating, Prosecuting, and Winning Cases When the Victim Is Missing

Thomas A. (Tad) DiBiase

CRC Press
Taylor & Francis Group
Boca Raton London New York

CRC Press is an imprint of the
Taylor & Francis Group, an **informa** business

CRC Press
Taylor & Francis Group
6000 Broken Sound Parkway NW, Suite 300
Boca Raton, FL 33487-2742

First issued in paperback 2021

ISBN 13: 978-0-367-77919-1 (pbk)
ISBN 13: 978-1-4822-6006-9 (hbk)

Library of Congress Cataloging-in-Publication Data

DiBiase, Thomas A. (Tad), author.
No-body homicide cases : a practical guide to investigating, prosecuting, and winning cases when the victim is missing / Thomas A. (Tad) DiBiase.
pages cm
Includes bibliographical references and index.
ISBN 978-1-4822-6006-9 (hardback)
1. Criminal investigation--United States. 2. Criminal procedure--United States. 3. Murder--Investigation--United States. 4. Trials (Murder)--United States. 5. Homicide investigation--United States. 6. Victims of crimes--United States. 7. Evidence, Criminal--United States. 8. Forensic sciences--United States. I. Title.

KF9619.D53 2014
345.73'02523--dc23 2014039483

Visit the Taylor & Francis Web site at
http://www.taylorandfrancis.com

and the CRC Press Web site at
http://www.crcpress.com

The fact that a murderer may successfully dispose of the body of a victim should not entitle him to an acquittal. That is one form of success for which society should have no reward.

***People v. Charles Manson*, 71 Cal. App. 3d. 1, 42 (1975)**

Contents

Acknowledgments

Matt DiBiase, Joanna DiBiase, Sophie DiBiase, the Honorable Garen Horst, Detective Don Murchison, Paula Moore, Tom Baudhuin, Amanda Rasmussen, Steve Blake, and special thanks to Erika Maskal, who did a great job writing flawless summaries. And last but not least, to my wife, Jenny, a woman with the patience of Job and the fortitude to listen to me discuss these cases.

Figure 0.1 Closing arguments in *California v. Mario Garcia*. Prosecuting and Winning Cases When the Victim Is Missing. Courtesy of Vicki Behringer, Courtroomartist.com.

Introduction

"How can you prosecute a murder without the body?" I cannot count the number of times I have been asked this question over the past ten years. My answer has always been the same: "Yes, it can be done and has been done, more times than you think." If murder is the ultimate crime, then a "no-body" murder is the ultimate murder. In our nation's history there have been just under 400 no-body murder trials, that is, trials where the victim's body has never been found. Now, for the first time ever, this book will provide a practical guide for police and prosecutors facing the challenges in these cases. This book takes an expansive look at both the history of no-body murder cases and the best methods to solve and try them. I will take the reader step by step from the first days of a homicide investigation through the trial of a case involving the ultimate law enforcement challenge: proving someone guilty of murder when the best piece of evidence, the victim's body, is missing. In doing so, I examine the history of no-body cases and discuss why these cases are so difficult to investigate and prosecute. All of this is through the lens of my own experience investigating and trying a no-body case and having consulted on scores of no-body murder cases with police and prosecutors across the country.

Exploring the history of confessions, jailhouse snitches, and CSI-style forensics, *"No-Body" Homicide Cases: A Practical Guide to Investigating, Prosecuting, and Winning Cases When the Victim Is Missing* offers an insider's view of modern homicide investigative techniques. The book analyzes the type of defendant who not only murders someone but also then successfully hides or destroys his victim's body in an attempt to escape justice and deny his victim's family and friends any closure for their loved one's death. Often gory but never boring and relentlessly practical, *"No-Body" Homicide Cases* catalogues the myriad methods defendants have used to dispose of bodies and the clever investigative techniques police must use to catch these most devious killers. For any police investigator faced with a no-body murder case, this book is an indispensable resource for the successful closure of such a case. For any prosecutor about to try a no-body case, this book provides a roadmap to a conviction.

Background and Overview

No-body murder cases are unique. Unique legally. Unique factually. Unique in their effect on the victim's family, friends, and loved ones. It is this uniqueness that poses a significant challenge for police and prosecutors investigating and prosecuting these cases. In the United States, records of no-body or bodiless cases go back to the 1840s, but in total, as of this writing in February of 2014, there have been fewer than 400 no-body trials nationwide. By comparison, according to the FBI, in 2010 there were just under 13,000 murders nationwide.* The national closure rate was 62 percent, meaning there were arrests or closures (which could mean the death of a suspect before an arrest or a justifiable homicide with no arrest) in 10,394 cases. If only 10 percent of these cases go to trial, then at least 1,000 murder trials occur per year across the nation. Moreover, the number of murders in 2010 was well below many prior years so, conservatively, there could be an average of 1,500 murder trials per year. In the last twenty years alone, that would mean more than 30,000 trials. Thus, even with the advent of modern forensics, no-body cases that go to trial remain incredibly rare.

And for good reason. The victim's body remains the single most important piece of evidence in any murder case. Consider the amount of useful information a body provides. First, it can reveal the cause of death. Was the victim shot, stabbed, strangled, or poisoned? A body can potentially tell you. A skilled medical examiner, and not all are skilled, can measure the spread of powder deposits left on the skin (soot and stipple) to determine the distance between the muzzle of a gun and the victim's body. Recovering either a bullet or shell casing from in or near a body means a ballistics expert can identify not only the caliber of the weapon used but also the exact weapon if the gun is also recovered. Poisoning can be detected through advanced toxicology tests. Was the victim strangled? If so, contusions may appear on the neck. Minute bleeding in the eyelids, called petechial hemorrhaging, may also be present. The hyoid bone, a small horseshoe-shaped bone attached to the tongue, can break when someone is strangled. Today forensic pathologists can determine the length of a knife as well as the width and shape of its blade by the marks left behind on severed flesh and cut bone. Of course one of the best forensic clues, body fluids such as blood and semen used to conduct DNA tests, is not available when the body is gone or the scene of the crime is a mystery. Evidence of bite marks, blunt force trauma, and even fingerprints is simply not present when a body is permanently disposed of.

Without a body, it is impossible to calculate the victim's time of death (also known as the postmortem interval, or PMI). In recent decades, important

* From http://www.fbi.gov/about-us/cjis/ucr/crime-in-the-u.s/2010/crime-in-the-u.s.-2010/tables/10shrtbl08.xls. Last accessed on March 2, 2013.

scientific advances and a broader variety of forensic methods have improved the ability to determine time of death. At death, the human body begins a process of shutting down, and a cycle called rigor mortis begins. Rigor mortis, in a nutshell, occurs as the body's muscles break down and produce lactic acid—the same lactic acid that causes a marathoner's legs to stiffen at the end of a race. This buildup of acid occurs in a predictable fashion, first in the smaller muscles, and then it gradually moves to the larger muscles during the next six to twelve hours. Therefore, when a body is first discovered, a trained police officer can test the state of rigor mortis by checking to see which of the victim's muscles are stiff. Full rigor mortis can last from six to twelve hours and begins to recede over a final six- to twelve-hour cycle. The entire cycle is highly dependent upon the environment a body is in. A body in a closed, unair-conditioned room in Washington, D.C., in August is going to travel through the cycle and begin decomposing much more quickly than a body outdoors in January in Fairbanks, Alaska.

While science has long known of rigor mortis and its importance as a death clock, recently, modern science has added more arrows to the time-of-death quiver. Body temperature, known as algor mortis, is a more accurate predictor of time of death because the body cools in a predictable fashion. By measuring a corpse's temperature in the liver, ear, or rectum, a comparison with the living temperature of 98.6 degrees Fahrenheit can be made, and through backward calculation an accurate time of death can be determined.

Similarly, discoloration of the skin occurs as a body decomposes, providing valuable clues about time of death. Livor mortis occurs as red and white blood cells separate and begin to settle in the body as gravity takes over. This settling leads to a purplish color forming where the body is lowest and begins to spread over the entire body. By viewing the advancement of livor mortis, forensic pathologists can work backward and determine the PMI.

Other methods of pinpointing the time of death include measuring vitreous eye fluid and examining insect activity on the body. By measuring levels of certain chemicals found in the vitreous fluid in the eyeball, a calculation can be made to determine with reasonable accuracy the time of death.* Similarly, the level of insect activity on a body can also determine the time when a victim was killed. Beginning in the 1980s, forensic pathologists began to realize that the maggots and insects found on a dead body could provide clues about a victim's time of death. Different insects preferred to—and there's no delicate way to say this—feast on human flesh at different intervals. Different species of blow flies, also known as blue or green bottle flies, lay eggs from which maggots hatch. By determining the species of blow

* http://medind.nic.in/jal/t04/i4/jalt04i4p136.pdf. Last accessed on March 9, 2013.

fly and the stage of growth, scientists can determine how long the insect or maggot has been living on a dead body.*

Given these medical advances, a medical examiner's failure either to test or observe any of these changes in a body, when you have a body, can be fodder for attacking a prosecution's time-of-death estimate. At the scene of a spousal murder case I once tried, a forensic pathologist responded to the crime scene inside the victim's house. The victim was in her bed upstairs with her throat cut so badly that her head was nearly severed. It is rare in DC for a medical examiner to respond to a crime scene, but because the date and time of the victim's murder was critical, the detective on the scene wisely summoned an experienced medical examiner. At the scene, the medical examiner was able to test the victim's level of rigor mortis, examine the lividity of her skin, and examine evidence at the scene that helped determine her time of death. At trial, however, the doctor was attacked during cross-examination for failing to have used a thermometer to record the victim's temperature. (He testified he did not have a thermometer.) By using the victim's body temperature and the room temperature, the time of death can be calculated to a fairly exact time by counting backward from a normal body temperature.

Luckily, the doctor had sufficient other evidence of the time of death that his failure to take a body temperature did not lead to an acquittal. But a defense attorney's attack on the government's case for failing to perform a forensic test is a common technique and even has a name among police and prosecutors: the *CSI* effect.† *CSI*, for a long time the nation's most watched television show, has led millions of viewers to believe that forensic science is an even more powerful crime-fighting tool than it actually is. In the DC US Attorney's Office where I worked we often joked that if they ever added *CSI: Washington* to the lineup, viewership would plummet because, given the DC Police Department's less-than-stellar reputation back then, each episode would end with the crime scene officers running out of powder to lift latent fingerprints or light bulbs to light their fluorescent DNA detection lamps.

Determination of the PMI is highly dependent on the environment a body is in. Not having a body often means there is no crime scene. Without a crime scene, most of the aforementioned investigative techniques or those that detectives use at a scene are worthless. Blood spatter pattern analysis, which analyzes blood patterns at a scene to determine how a murder occurred, cannot be done if you do not know where the murder occurred and therefore do not know where to locate any spatter. Nor can you conduct scene-specific searches for trace evidence, such as minute pieces of hair and fiber left behind with every contact between a suspect and an object if you do

* *Corpse: Nature, Forensics and the Struggle to Pinpoint Time of Death,* Jessica Synder Sachs, Perseus Publishing, 2001.

† http://www.people.com/people/article/0,,626076,00.html. Last accessed on March 9, 2013.

not know where your murder scene is. Investigators also cannot use crime scene reconstruction or tracking dogs if the location of the scene is unknown.

Historically, the previous problems often meant that a murderer's ability to successfully dispose of a body meant he (and in no-body cases 91 percent of the time the murderer is a he*) would get away with murder. Some of the earliest no-body murder cases involved only the most obvious murders: ships returning from sea minus their captains or crewmembers. The earliest trial I have uncovered in my research is from 1839 involving the ship *Braganza*. The crew, led by Cornelius Wilhelms, mutinied against the captain and officers and killed them and two women aboard, tossing all of them overboard. In 1893, three sailors were found guilty for murdering and tossing overboard a fellow shipmate.†

Missing persons who did not go missing at sea were not so lucky. In the days before nearly instantaneous communication via telephone, a murderer would simply tell friends and families of the missing party that she had skipped town or was vacationing overseas or had moved. Not only was trying to locate such a person nearly impossible given the primitive communication facilities, proving they were truly dead was just as difficult. Today we take for granted the electronic trail we leave behind, but up until forty to fifty years ago one could simply disappear without a trace. Although I have found nearly 400 no-body murder trials since the mid-1800s, I have no idea how many no-body murders have taken place where the killer was not caught. Certainly in the time before the advent of modern criminal detection techniques, such as DNA and trace evidence, most no-body murderers got away with their crimes.

Today, thankfully for our investigative purposes, truly disappearing is nearly impossible. Every day each of us leaves in our wake an incredibly accurate electronic trail. From the time we wake up in the morning to the time we go to bed, we touch an endless number of electronic "processes" that leave an indelible mark in the ether. From Facebook to Twitter to Instagram to ATMs to E-ZPass to GPS locators in our cars and phones, we leave a trail as indelible as footprints in cement. There are closed-circuit cameras that monitor our vehicle speed, our adherence to stoplights, our purchases, and whether and when we show up to work or steal supplies from the supply closet. We are watched, recorded, surveilled, and downloaded scores of times per day. Putting aside whatever privacy concerns one may legitimately have, as an investigator, these data are a gold mine and are the main reason (aside from such forensic advances as DNA) that building a no-body case is easier today than ever before. All of these data, such as cell phone records, credit

* Statistics gathered by Paula Moore, Henderson Police Department (Nevada), based upon website www.nobodymurdercases.com, e-mail to author dated March 9, 2013.

† http://nobodymurdercases.com/cases.html.

card transactions, or time clocks at work, are the mother's milk of any investigation. The key to any no-body investigation is to know what information to get, how to get it, and where to get it and then getting it quickly before it disappears.

The challenge of a no-body murder case is that it is a 100-meter sprint where the murderer starts at the 30-meter mark. Not having a body, as shown above, is a huge handicap, but a handicap that can be overcome through methodical, patient, and creative investigation. A no-body murder case will doubtlessly be the most challenging case of your career. There are two appendices in this book that I hope will assist you in this challenge. Appendix A is a checklist of investigative tasks for no-body cases that are covered in detail in this book. Appendix B is a summary of every no-body case that has gone to trial in the United States through February 2014. You can use that appendix both to find no-body cases from your jurisdiction or state and to find cases that may be similar to yours in terms of the evidence the police and prosecutors had for trial.

Since it is an advantage to the murderer to dispose of the body, there is no end to the creativity shown by such fiends to do so. Killers have thrown bodies out of airplanes into the ocean, pushed them off ships into the sea, and dumped them into canals. They have buried bodies deep in the woods, thrown them into landfills, and dumped them on the ground where they are left to rot. Defendants have burned bodies in furnaces, in the victim's own home, and on wooden pyres. They have sawed bodies apart with chainsaws, ripped them apart with wood chippers, and fed bodies to pigs. One defendant tried to eliminate his victim by using sulfuric acid, while another boiled his wife in his sausage plant. (Think about that the next time you gobble down a breakfast link.) Dumpsters, landfills, and large bodies of water are perennial resting places for victims. Damien Lamb, who beat a man to death with a shovel, found perhaps the most unusual hiding place: hiding his victim's body in a beaver lodge on his stepfather's property.

Luckily, a body is not easy to get rid of. Disposing of 150 pounds of flesh, bones, teeth, and hair is a lot harder than it seems. One need only look at the forearms of an assistant in most medical examiners' offices to understand that cutting up a body, even with the sharpest of instruments, is hard work. The most common way to dispose of bodies is to bury them, but digging a hole in the ground big enough to completely cover a body and make it deep enough to escape detection from both man and beast is difficult. And forget about it if the murder happens in the winter when the ground is frozen. Before the advent of backhoes and other mechanical digging machines, most cemeteries did not bury bodies in the winter because it was too difficult to manually dig a hole. Throwing an unweighted body into water does not always work as a disposal method because as a body decomposes it releases gases, which bloat the body and cause it to float.[*] Interestingly, compared with burying a body in winter, a body in extremely cold water may remain submerged and not float to the surface.[†] Burning a body completely requires temperatures of at least 1,400 to 1,800 degrees Fahrenheit, and even then bone fragments can remain behind.[‡]

Because of the difficulty of disposing of a body, an investigator must move very quickly when it is first discovered that a person may be dead, not just missing. Indeed, one of the biggest mistakes made in a no-body investigation is to treat the case like a missing persons case for too long. A study in England showed that 1 in 7,400 missing persons cases end in homicide, but 1 in 34 homicides starts as a missing persons case.[§] Obviously, not every missing persons case turns into a homicide case; indeed, the vast majority do not. But many homicide cases start off as missing persons cases, and in any case where there is a suspicion that a person may be dead and not just missing, err on the side of treating it as a homicide case. It is better to have your missing person turn up alive during a homicide investigation than to learn your victim is dead during a missing persons investigation. The scope of these two investigations is vastly different in terms of the resources called upon, methods used, and the skill level of the investigator assigned to the case.

[*] http://7-11.imascientist.org.uk/2012/07/why-does-a-dead-body-float-and-an-alive-body-sink. Last accessed January 2014

[†] http://users.skynet.be/lilith/english/deathtodust.html. Last accessed January 20, 2014.

[‡] http://www.nfda.org/planning-a-funeral/cremation/160.html#hot. Last accessed March 3, 2013.

[§] Centrex, Developing Policing Excellence, NCOF, Operational Support Section, Missing Persons, Suggested Lines of Enquiry in Suspicious Missing Person Investigations, Version 3, September 2003.

Author Biography

Thomas A. (Tad) DiBiase is a native New Yorker, born in Elmira and raised in Westchester County. He received a B.A. in politics from Wake Forest University in 1987 and a J.D. from Brooklyn Law School in 1991. Mr. DiBiase joined the Washington office of the Wall Street firm Shearman & Sterling where he practiced corporate litigation for nearly four years. After turning down a clerkship with a federal district court judge in Texas, Mr. DiBiase joined the United States Attorney's Office for the District of Columbia in 1995. He began prosecuting homicides in 1998 and during his time there tried twenty homicide cases. Although he was a federal prosecutor, Mr. DiBiase spent most of his career in the far grittier world of D.C.'s Superior Court, one of the nation's busy urban courthouses. Mr. DiBiase specialized in domestic violence and forensic homicide cases. His high-profile homicide cases included *United States v. Harold Austin*, the city's second "no-body" murder case ever, and *United States v. Sydney Smith*, where the main piece of evidence against Smith, a Metro employee who murdered his wife, was a cigarette the defendant left behind at the scene. Other cases he successfully prosecuted include *United States v. John Williamson*, a murder-for-hire case, and *United States v. James Stewart*, an attempted murder case involving a man who fired an AK-47 rifle down a street filled with children.

At various times he served as the deputy chief of the Misdemeanor Section, chief of the Third District Homicide/Major Crimes Section, special counsel to the U.S. Attorney for Professional Development and Training, and deputy chief of the Homicide Section. He is the nation's leading expert on no-body homicide cases and has a website that tracks and discusses these cases at www.nobodymurdercases.com. He consults with police and prosecutors throughout the country on no-body murder cases and has formally consulted on more than two dozen no-body murder cases. He has appeared on television numerous times and has been quoted widely in newspapers throughout the country.

The Early Investigative Phase

1

Introduction

The A&E television series *The First 48* looks at real-life detectives during the crucial first forty-eight hours of a homicide investigation. According to the show, the chances of solving a murder drop by half if a lead is not found during the first forty-eight hours after a murder is committed.* I do not know whether this can be empirically proven, but I do know that the first forty-eight hours of a no-body case are critical. The problem, of course, is that it is the rare no-body case where you know the person who is missing is actually dead within forty-eight hours of his or her death. Despite this handicap time is of the essence, and the faster an investigator can gather clues, the greater the chance of finding the victim's body and making an arrest. Note that all of these techniques are useful even if the victim is merely missing and not actually dead.

One of the most important aspects of a no-body case is that, unlike a traditional murder investigation, the investigation of a no-body murder is a two-pronged investigation. The first prong is to find the killer while also making sure to eliminate any other suspects. (More on this later.) The second prong is equally important and does not exist in a traditional homicide case: You must prove the victim is dead and was murdered. As we walk through some of the following investigative techniques keep in mind that you cannot forget that second prong. Interviewing a victim's family member may not lead to a suspect, but it will certainly help prove that the victim is dead. ("She used to call me every Sunday but I haven't heard from her in two weeks. That's not like her at all.") A trial of a no-body case is about both of these prongs: proving the victim is dead and proving the defendant did it.

Searching for the Victim

Typically an investigator will not immediately know whether a missing person is dead or merely missing. As noted already, however, if the victim is someone who you would not ordinarily expect to suddenly be missing for any period of time—for example, a mother of young children, a child, or

* Episode viewed on March 7, 2012, on A&E at 9 p.m. EST.

someone with preexisting plans that have been missed such as work, school, or other event—it makes sense to treat the case as a possible homicide.

One of the key elements of a no-body murder investigation is "victimology." In any murder investigation, the victimology, that is, what type of person is this victim, is essential in solving the case. An investigation of a known street prostitute or drug addict is much different from the investigation of a hard-working mother of three. (Note that I did not say that one investigation is more important than the other. All murder victims deserve the same level of investigation, resources, and dedication no matter who they were or what their stature was in life.) Knowledge of victimology is critical to keep your investigation on the right track. In a no-body case, victimology is even more important because, again, your investigation focuses on not only who committed the murder but also proving that a murder occurred.

Your victim's victimology can make proving the fact of her murder more difficult. A missing drug addict is much more likely to be thought of as dying from an overdose or simply disappearing than a young mother with no history of drug abuse. By studying and knowing your victim's victimology you will know what types of evidence will persuade a jury that your victim is indeed dead. Remember that every victim has a victimology that can help prove she is dead. While it is easy to prove the death of most individuals who have a well-worn path of obligations such as families, jobs, and friends, even the most downtrodden victim has habits and patterns, family and friends. The absence of these patterns can demonstrate just as conclusively that a person is dead as someone missing work or an important family milestone. In the no-body case I tried, my victim was an alcoholic and possible drug user who was not employed. The initial detective assigned to the case even dismissed her sister as a "crackhead" in a written report. In fact, she had five children for whom she cared deeply and we demonstrated that she had missed their birthdays and holidays when she had never done so before. This was proof to a jury that she was dead. One of the most poignant moments of my trial was the testimony of the victim's twelve-year-old daughter, who testified that her mother had never missed her birthday or Christmas until after she went missing.

The fact that the person is presumed dead and not merely missing can also lead to your pool of suspects. I will discuss the common personality type of a no-body murderer, but as a matter of logic, a no-body murder does not lead itself to a certain type of defendant. A burglar who breaks into a home and is surprised by the owner who he then shoots and kills is not going to hang around to dispose of the body. Disposing of a body takes time, and that is not something an accidental killer, such as a burglar, robber, or carjacker, is typically willing to risk. There are certainly stranger-on-stranger no-body murders, but those cases typically involve the murderer deliberating seeking a victim for the thrill of the killing, such as child predators. They want to cover up their crimes in order to get away with it. In cases of accidental murders where the body is hidden, there is almost always a preexisting relationship between the killer and his victim. Classic examples are a coworker killing another coworker over a work dispute or two business associates having a falling out that results in one killing the other. These types of murders occur on familiar grounds for the killer, often the workplace, and the murderer can take the time to dispose of the body, safe in the knowledge that no one is likely to surprise him at the workplace. Since a no-body murder requires time and effort, by far the most common suspect is a person known to the victim.

I offer these tips on searching for a body not because it may be the first thing an investigator does but because, despite the success in prosecuting no-body murder cases, it is always preferable to have the body both from an investigative standpoint and for the victim's family. Thus, whether looking for the body is the first thing you do or occurs at a later point, it cannot be overemphasized enough that finding the body if possible is the most important part of your investigation.

As noted already, burying is the most common method of hiding a body. Determine if there are ways to get into the air to survey the area and look for recent disturbances in the earth. Can you get a local pilot to fly you over the area if you are looking in a rural or suburban area? Is it winter, when any disturbance to the earth is going to be very noticeable? Talk to those who go out into the woods, such as hikers, hunters, and trail runners. Ask them if they've seen anything out of the ordinary or recently disturbed areas.

Investigate what hobbies your suspect has to help determine where he might go to bury a body. Is he a hunter? Where does he hunt? A birdwatcher? Camper? Cross-country skier? As always, put yourself in his shoes and ask yourself, if I need to get rid of a body and needed some time to do it, where would I go? It is unlikely you would go somewhere you did not know well and risk detection since you would not know the potential "traffic" at the location.

When bodies are found in murder cases, they are often found in locations either near or familiar to the murderer. As detailed, search warrants or consent searches should be executed on any suspect's car, home, or workplace. (When searching his car, do not forget to see how much gas he has in the tank. A full tank may mean he recently filled up after a long trip, so check with local gas stations to see if they have a record of his visit through credit cards and interviews.) But when disposing of a body a murderer will try not to be too obvious. Thus, while he may have murdered his victim in his own home, he will not necessarily hide the body there. It is still critical to search his home for clues to the murder, but you must also search areas outside his home: his property, nearby properties, particularly if they are wooded or belong to entities other than private citizens, such as government-owned property or property owned by commercial interests such as factories or farms. Concealing a body on private property can be dangerous because a suspect will stand out while on the property and will be afraid that someone else may discover the body by accident. Burying a body on his own land, land owned by an absentee owner, or land that is unoccupied at night is a much safer bet.

In connection with burying, it is common to see bodies dismembered as well. A thorough search of the suspect's house must be conducted for signs of this grisly process. Because of the time and effort involved in cutting up a body, it is often conducted indoors, and, needless to say, it is messy. Drains in sinks, bathtubs, and washing machines must be removed and checked for signs of blood. Basements and crawl spaces are common places to both cut up the body and hide the tools used to do so. It is also extremely common to see signs of a cleanup throughout a house, and often this is the best evidence not only that a murder did occur but also that it is where the murder took place. Evidence of a cleanup can include finding cleaning products such as bleach and carpet cleaners, the removal of carpets, rugs, or furniture, and even the running of fans to get rid of a smell.

Instruments that could have been used to cut up a body must be searched for, and with no-body cases, what is missing is often as important as what is present. Are knives missing from the house? Saws or other cutting implements? Family members and friends are often familiar with what was in a house, apartment, or toolbox. In a case in Massachusetts, the evidence against the defendant included flesh and bone recovered from a power saw.[*] One of the first cases that brought forensic criminologist Henry Lee to fame was a Connecticut case where the defendant fed his wife through a wood chipper during a snowstorm. Pieces of her bone and hair were recovered, which helped lead to Richard Crafts' conviction.[†]

As the nation becomes more urbanized, disposing of bodies in dumpsters that go to landfills or landfills themselves has become increasingly common. Obviously in any urban location, nearby dumpsters must be carefully checked, not just for a body or body part but also evidence of a cleanup or evidence of the victim's clothes or other possessions being disposed of. Once the dumpster has been removed to the landfill, however, it becomes much more difficult to search for a body, but it can be done. Searching a landfill is not only difficult but also can be extremely dangerous due to hazardous materials and the buildup up of dangerous gases from the decay of waste, such as methane and carbon dioxide. There are actually experts on conducting landfill searches, and consulting with such an expert and working closely

[*] http://mercuryservices.hubpages.com/video/No-Body-Trials-Locking-Up-Murderers-When-the-Victims-Corpse-Is-Missing. Last accessed on March 9, 2013.

[†] http://www.trutv.com/library/crime/notorious_murders/family/woodchipper_murder/10.html. Last accessed on March 9, 2013.

with the landfill owners or operators is essential.[*] Landfills often track where trash came from and where it is placed in the landfill, so having close cooperation from the landfill owners, whether private or public, is critical.[†] In any event, searching a landfill can be extremely expensive and even cost too much given the difficulties of finding anything. In a recent case in DC, the police and prosecutors opposed a defendant's request to search a landfill—even though the defendant had confessed to putting the body into a dumpster that was delivered to the landfill—because of the prohibitive cost and low probability of recovering the body. Apparently, the defense hoped that recovery of the body would lead to evidence that would show that the defendant had not committed the murder or that the lack of a body would show that the confession was false.[‡]

Recent advances in geophysical tools may lead to a greater ability to search landfills and other places where bodies might be buried. According to a recent article in *Science Live*, British researchers are conducting experiments with buried pigs to test ground-penetrating radars and other geophysical methods. (Pig skin is very similar to human skin.) Although their research is in the early stages, these techniques could prove to be a real boon to investigators searching for a missing body.[§]

Searches for the body are often conducted by private citizens. These private searches are often a good way for the family and friends of the victim to get involved in a positive and productive way. While it is preferable that a member of the investigative team go along on these searches, in all cases the searches performed should be maintained in a logbook keeping track of when the search occurred, the location and areas searched, the resources used, and man hours spent searching. All of this can be very useful at trial to demonstrate the immense effort that went into finding the victim.

It is also essential that any unidentified bodies in the area are carefully checked to make sure that a medical examiner's (ME) office does not have your victim's body but does not know who it is. Statistics from the Department of Justice show that ME's offices nationwide will receive 4,400 unidentified bodies each year.[¶] Of those 4,400 bodies, an average of 1,000 remain unidentified after one year.[**] One of the best ways to identify a body is

[*] See http://www.policechiefmagazine.org/magazine/index.cfm?fuseaction=display&article_id=2270&issue_id=122010, which profiles Ron Olive of Naval Criminal Investigative Services (NCIS) and his expertise in searching landfills. Last accessed March 17, 2013.

[†] http://www.letsk9professionals.org/landfills.html. Last accessed March 17, 2013.

[‡] http://homicidewatch.org/2011/04/27/judge-wont-compel-search-for-latisha-fraziers-body/. Last accessed on March 17, 2013.

[§] "Hidden Graves Revealed with Geophysical Tools," http://www.livescience.com/31982-hidden-bodies-found-using-geophysics.html. Last accessed May 17, 2013.

[¶] Driscoll, D., "Resolving Missing and Unidentified Person Cases Using Today's Technology," *The Police Chief*, May 2013.

[**] Ibid.

by using the National Missing and Unidentified Persons System (NAMUS). NAMUS "assists law enforcement in their investigations of missing and unidentified person cases."* NAMUS has three databases: Missing Persons, Unidentified Persons, and Unclaimed Persons. The Missing Persons database contains information on missing persons entered by law enforcement. The information is verified before being entered into the system. The Unidentified Persons database contains information entered by medical examiners and coroners on unidentified bodies. The Unclaimed Persons database contains information entered by medical examiners and coroners about persons who have been identified but not claimed by family.

NAMUS also provides a number of free forensic services including DNA testing and anthropology and odontology services. NAMUS provides analytical services that assist law enforcement with solving missing and unidentified cases. Analysts have access to multiple law enforcement databases including Accurint for Law Enforcement and Consolidated Lead Evaluation and Reporting (CLEAR). The NAMUS analysts can also research the National Crime Information Center (NCIC) database. Additionally, NAMUS analysts are experts in using social media to search for missing people, something critical in a no-body murder. They can review sites such as Facebook, Spokeo, Google, and Ancestry.com to determine whether the missing person is posting information. This evidence (or lack thereof) can prove critical to proving a person is not missing but is actually dead. It is important to exhaustively search both government and private databases to ensure both yourself and a jury that the victim is not somehow secretly living somewhere else.

If you have the victim's DNA, it should be entered into the FBI's Combined DNA Index System (CODIS). CODIS contains DNA from persons convicted of crimes, DNA profiles taken from crime scenes, profiles from unidentified human remains, and DNA samples from the families of missing persons.†

In many no-body cases, psychics contact the investigators offering "tips" or their visions of the case. No matter what your view of psychics, it is best to determine how they are going to be handled. If they are documented, then you must decide whether to try to follow up on any of their leads. At trial, the issue of psychics may come up and, as with tips from any less-than-credible sources, you must be prepared to explain exactly how this information was handled and why. In a no-body case, you simply cannot afford to say you did not track a lead or did not follow up without providing a solid basis for why you did so.

* Ibid. All of the information in this paragraph and the next are from this article. See also http://www.namus.gov.

† Behavioral Analysis Unit, National Center for the Analysis of Violent Crime, "Serial Murder, Multi-Disciplinary Perspectives for Investigators," p. 37.

Cell Phones

Today's cell phones/smartphones have a wealth of information, and their widespread use in today's society makes them a valuable source of information. Other than forensic evidence such as DNA, cell phones probably provide more evidence in successful no-body cases than any other item. An investigator, often with the help of a subpoena issued by the prosecutor's office, should get the records from the victim's phone and see who the victim was calling, when the calls stopped, and who called after the outgoing calls stopped. You should check the frequency of the calls to help determine who was close to the victim and find anyone with whom the victim had lengthy calls. It is essential to obtain the cell phone records of anyone the victim was in a relationship with, such as a boyfriend or husband or lover, and that person should also have his records checked as well. (You may not need a subpoena to do this if the person agrees to cooperate. If they do not agree, you need to dig deeper to figure out why they are not cooperating.)

When examining the cell phone records of a potential suspect, note if there are any gaps in the times calls were made when a suspect could have been committing a murder. Do not let the sheer number of cell phone records overwhelm you. Look for patterns: Whom did the victim call most often? Who called the victim? At what times was the phone used? All of these calls can lead to subjects who will be interviewed for both leads to a suspect but also information that can help prove the victim is really dead. Focus on the lengthier calls first and move to other calls after that. Do not forget to check voicemail, text messages, photos, and address lists in phones, although you probably need a search warrant for this information. Get a warrant and send the phone to your district attorney's office or your department's forensic ID unit, which can search for the entire contents of the phone including deleted information.

Cell phones utilize cell towers to make calls, and obtaining cell tower records can tell you where a call (and thus a caller) was coming from. Indeed, the cell towers to which a phone sends a signal can change during the duration of a call, so police can track the path of the victim. However, phone companies keep cell tower records for very limited periods, often only twenty to thirty days, so you must move quickly to get these records. Again, you may need a subpoena. Of course, all of these techniques apply to potential suspects as well, and having cell tower records of your suspect can be very powerful evidence against him if a body is eventually found.

Recently I have encountered cases where suspects have turned their phones off during the time of the murder. Obviously the existence of cell towers and the wide spread use of GPS has made even criminals aware of the possible hazards of keeping their phones on, but some phones will leave a cell tower trail even when turned off so always check even if you are initially told the phone was off.

In addition to the cell tower location feature, most phones now have a GPS feature and can be "pinged" in the real time by the company. Typically a cell phone company will provide pinging or other information without a court order or subpoena if it is a bona fide emergency. I know of one case where the police were looking for a suspect in a case where he threatened to kill his wife. The ping told the police he was at a casino in Connecticut and he was caught there after the casino was informed of his presence. While it does not always work—if the phone is off, for instance, it will not work—but it is a great technique and can locate the subject within a few feet. You will have to send a court order after the fact, but the phone companies will give the information upon the completion of a form as long as it is an emergency. Officers should have the emergency forms before they need them to save time.

Social Media

Obtain the passwords to all social media used by the victim, either through a search warrant or the family's cooperation. You will be able to view stored messages and the victim's postings on Facebook, Twitter, Tumblr, or other media. Given the ubiquity of social media, it is essential that any interviews of friends and families include questions about what social media the victim used. It is also necessary that, if you are not conversant with these technologies, you find someone who is. The face of social media changes rapidly, as shown by the rise and fall of sites such as MySpace. As of this writing, Facebook, Twitter, Tumblr, and Instagram reign supreme. However, a year from now the popular sites could be completely different. Do not let any tech phobia you may have hinder your investigation. Get help if needed.

It is critical that you have a skilled forensic examiner review the victim or suspect's computer history. This is important not only so you do not miss any important clues but also so that your search is preserved and can be provided to the defense in event of a trial.

You should also consider whether using social media in an undercover capacity could further your investigation. Can you reach out to the suspect through Facebook, establish a friendship, and insert an undercover that could get him to talk? Meeting online is so common today that it might be the best way to draw out a suspect, and people tend to let down their guard more readily online.

Interviews

In virtually every homicide case your best evidence is going to be people. This is true even if you are lucky enough to have forensic evidence such as

DNA. No-body cases are no different from traditional homicides with one big exception: Most no-body murders are committed without any witnesses. No-body murder defendants still confess to others, however, and even in cases where there are not confessions, no-body suspects often make damning statements to others. One of my favorites is the suspect who asked a friend if his brother, who was an attorney, would represent him. When the friend said his brother probably would not represent him, the suspect replied, "Can you ask him if you can be prosecuted for murder if they don't have the body?"

You should immediately interview as many people who know the victim as possible. Close family members and friends must be interviewed in detail to gather information. Video or audiotaping these interviews is best because if the story changes down the road, the police have an accurate record of what was said initially. Any suspects should also be interviewed and their story thoroughly examined and confirmed so at trial an alibi cannot change. Note that an initial interview with a suspect may be a one-shot deal. It is very common for a suspect, such as a husband or boyfriend, to initially be cooperative with the police because he believes he can avoid suspicion by doing so. Also, as discussed further, the classic no-body defendant believes he is smarter than everyone else so he believes he can outsmart the police. But typically after initially cooperating, a defendant will see it is a mistake to keep talking to the police and will either hire an attorney or simply refuse to speak to the police any further. Therefore, any initial interview with a possible suspect is critical, and getting it on video or audio is helpful to impeach the defendant in court if he later changes his story. Also, using a video or audio system is helpful because it keeps the interview fresh in your memory for later review. In addition, sometimes what was said makes sense only after further investigation or not at all afterward. When conducting an interview, if possible have another detective watch the video feed from another room so the interviewer can step out for a minute and check with the other detective to see if the interviewer is missing any visual cues or questions to be asked.

Make sure you are well-prepared for all of your interviews. You should keep photos of the victim and suspect handy. Preferably several different shots and ones that are recent, not necessarily ones the family gave you when the suspect or victim looked their best. While the prom shot is nice, that may not be what the victim looked like a month ago. Having the photo of the suspect is helpful when you are interviewing people who may not know him or may not know that they know him, for example, when inquiring in a hardware store to see if your suspect recently purchased shovels, tarps, and plastic.

Interviews and interrogations will be treated in more detail following, but one important element is to build a bond with the suspect. Interviews or even interrogations should never be conducted from behind a desk. You should be next to or facing the interviewee with nothing in the space between the two of you. Interviewing someone from behind a desk conveys the wrong image of power and intimidation, and it is the rare interview where you want your subject to be intimidated or uncomfortable. A relaxed, informal, and noncoercive environment is always the best and most effective method of obtaining useful information.

In the no-body case I tried, the lead detective interviewed the defendant over the course of five hours. He brought the defendant barbequed chicken and apple pie in order to win his confidence. (Although tellingly, the defendant never touched any of the food.) At the beginning of the interview the detective was seated across the table from the defendant. By the end of the interview when the defendant finally confessed to grabbing a gun out of his girlfriend's hand and shooting her with it, the detective was seated next to the defendant with his hand on his shoulder convincing him to confess. That confession would not have been won by browbeating the suspect, a very experienced criminal.

When dealing with a possible suspect, be cautious about making judgments about the level of grief displayed by a suspect or loved one. People grieve very differently, and it can be dangerous to ascribe guilt or innocence based upon a suspect's reaction during the early stages of an investigation. Focus on what the suspect or subject says, not as much on how he says it. Any detail he offers must be carefully checked out, and have him repeat his story, particularly his alibi, if any, to see if he trips up and forgets or changes anything.

Be particularly alert to statements made by the victim to friends regarding any fears the victim had because it may be possible to use these statements down the road at trial. In most jurisdictions, statements by the victim are not going to be admitted as evidence at trial because of hearsay rules. Many jurisdictions, however, have specific rules that permit these statements, often as a state-of-mind exception. It is essential to collect these statements and then work with the prosecutor to determine if these statements can be entered into evidence. Obviously, any statements about actual violence between the suspect and the victim are extremely valuable. These statements must be accurately recorded and preserved. Also, in looking for people to interview, do not overlook the old-fashioned, door-to-door canvassing: "Yeah, I heard a blood-curdling scream by a woman at about midnight last night, now that I think about it."

It is important to lock in testimony that is helpful as quickly as possible and before witnesses get cold feet. This can be done through video or audio recording, but also consider putting the person into the grand jury in jurisdictions that use grand juries. One of the best uses of the grand jury is to preserve statements made by witnesses. If these witnesses try to change their statements at trial, they can be impeached or contradicted with what they said in the grand jury. In some jurisdictions, since grand jury testimony is under oath, the statements made in the grand jury can be used as substantive evidence against the defendant, not merely as impeaching evidence.

If you are not recording what a witness said but simply writing it down, do not wait too long before writing down what witnesses said. First, you might forget what was said if it is only from your memory; or second, the witness may forget or change his or her story before you have an opportunity to have him or her adopt the statement. Having reviewed many no-body investigation files over the years, I am amazed how some investigators record every single action and interaction they have on a case while others barely record interviews of suspects.

Be sure to keep track of any lies the suspects tell. Lies are powerful pieces of evidence to show to a judge or jury down the road as evidence of a defendant's guilt, and being able to show that the suspect lied about anything, even if not directly connected to the investigation, is persuasive evidence against him. Jurors tend to harshly judge defendants who lie, particularly those who have a relationship with the missing person, since there rarely is a good reason for a person not involved in the disappearance to lie to those trying to solve the case. However, recall Congressman Gary Condit, who initially lied about his relationship with missing intern Chandra Levy. He was not her murderer, but it appears his lies may have led investigators to focus on him as a suspect for far too long.*

Search Warrants

In numerous cases over the years, I have witnessed the difficulties police have in getting search warrants for suspects' houses or other possible scenes in missing persons cases. Thus, it is critical to aggressively pursue consent searches, if possible. You should search the victim's home, place of work, and places where the victim hung out, including boyfriend's house, and relatives' homes. (Again, these are consent searches, so a red flag should go up if someone asked does not cooperate.) If obtaining consent fails, you should try to get a search warrant. There's nothing wrong with including information in a search explaining that the police suspect foul play and that the victim's characteristics are inconsistent with having simply left town, for example, has left behind children, is a child, has not accessed bank accounts, or failed to show up to work. Citing other cases of missing persons from your jurisdiction who were later found dead or were never found increases the chances the judge reviewing the warrant will agree the victim may be dead which will increase the chances of a warrant being served.

Getting inside a suspect's house often leads to very valuable scientific evidence. Any search should include a cadaver dog. You would be amazed at how

* *Finding Chandra*, by Scott Higham and Sari Horwitz, Scribner 2010.

often suspects bury a body nearby, sometimes temporarily until they can move it to another, safer location. A cadaver dog can "alert" on a scent even if the body is no longer present. By carefully examining the site of the dog "alert" you may find physical evidence of the body's previous presence, such as jewelry, clothing, or forensic evidence that was left behind after a body was moved.

You should be aware of the issues surrounding the use of cadaver dogs and the admissibility of their "testimony" in court. The training of the dog is key and must be well-documented. A recent Supreme Court case dealt with drug-sniffing dogs, but the logic is applicable to cadaver dogs as well.* In *Florida v. Harris*, the court rejected a lower court's checklist of requirements that a drug-detecting dog must have fulfilled before its "testimony" will be accepted in court or its "hit" be found to be probable cause. If a dog has been trained and has a certificate from a training school, that may be enough for officers to search a location after a positive hit. Therefore, while extensive training requirements are probably not required for a cadaver dog, it will still be important to be able to demonstrate that the dog has been well-trained.

It is important to get search warrants for the victim and suspect's computers as well. A victim's computer can contain a wealth of information about the victim's state of mind, which aids in undercutting an argument that she ran away, and can also reveal her feelings toward the suspect. Also, in this day and age of Internet communications, you may find communications between the victim and a stranger on the Internet that none of her other friends or family are aware of.

Obtaining a search warrant for a suspect's computer is obvious and should be done very early in the investigation. As noted previously with victims, do not overlook a suspect's work computer. Again, it is important to have a trained forensic examiner look at the computer so there are no issues at trial with getting what was found into evidence. Typically, a mirror image of the hard drive is made so that the original hard drive remains intact and there are no questions about what was originally on the computer. Making a copy for the defense should also be done early on in the case.

When conducting any search be aware of what is missing as well as what's present. Are a victim's personal effects there, such as a purse, car keys, or wallet? If the victim supposedly left town, do the missing items match that supposition? Are keys, luggage, clothes, and money gone? There was a no-body murder case where the suspect claimed the victim, his wife, had left to go on a trip. With the help of the victim's family, the police were able to prove that although there were some clothes missing as if she had packed for a trip, the victim had failed to pack any bras, something she would not have done. (This was also an indication that a man had "packed" the victim's

* *Florida v. Harris*, 568 U.S. ___ (2013).

bag.) Are there "prized possessions" that a missing person who left or fled would not have left behind, perhaps photographs of loved ones or similar precious items? Remember that the investigation of a no-body murder is a two-tracked one: proving she is dead and proving who did it. Being able to argue that the victim is certainly dead because she would not have left her children's photos behind is powerful evidence of her murder.

During the execution of a search warrant, be sure to get any items of the victim that may have the victim's DNA on it for identification purposes, such as towels, toothbrush, and hairbrush. If a body is never recovered, it will be essential to have the victim's DNA to compare with any forensic evidence uncovered at the scene.

It is also essential to get DNA samples from family members of the victim. If you never find the victim or recover any DNA you can be certain is hers, your next step is to compare any DNA you do discover with the DNA from a family member. In the no-body case I tried in DC, the victim was in the process of moving her family to another home when she was murdered. The defendant, who was dating the victim, managed to get the family to move while she was still missing and in the process threw out many of her possessions. As a result, we did not have any item of the victim's that we were confident had her DNA. We ended up getting DNA from the victim's mother and made comparisons with that DNA to the blood recovered from the victim's bed. We had one additional challenge, however. With the known DNA from the mother, the FBI could type the blood found in the victim's bed only as having come from a female descendant of the mother's. However, the victim had four sisters, one of whom was deceased. Since the DNA could have been from any of them as well as from the victim, we had to have each sister testify at trial that they had not bled in their sister's bed. Fortunately, the deceased sister had died many years before so their defense could not argue the blood was hers. We were also fortunate that we had taken the mother's DNA well before trial because she died several months before the trial.

Electronic Trail

Credit card, bank, and employment records must all be reviewed to see if there is any indication they were accessed. This access could be by either the victim or a suspect. When was the last time a computer (work and home) was signed onto? This review must continue over weeks and months. In the case I prosecuted, the defendant made a false accident claim using the victim's name weeks after he murdered her. We tracked down the insurance claim, which led to a valuable witness against him. Put a fraud alert on as many accounts as possible so the company will contact you if someone tries to access the account. Do not forget about Social Security accounts (particularly if the victim has children who might be receiving benefits), welfare, food stamps, and child support payments. It is highly unlikely someone who fled and is not missing or dead would forgo an opportunity to receive money due to him or her.

There are many other examples of electronic trails we leave behind, but it is also important to check these trails to prevent a defendant from arguing that by not checking these things, the prosecution was not thorough. Imagine at trial if a detective was asked if he checked with the State Department to see if the victim had used a passport to fly overseas and this was not checked. The Advanced Passenger Information System (APIS) used by U.S. Customs and Border Protection can tell you whether someone traveled overseas and when. Similarly, highway toll systems such as E-ZPass and SunPass should be checked to see if the victim (or the suspect, for that matter) went through any of those checkpoints with a pass, or even without, since these systems have license plate readers to catch those who do not pay.

Do not overlook any surveillance cameras that might have filmed either the victim or the suspect at any point. Go over the various travel paths of both suspect and victim and look very carefully to see if there are any cameras in place. Acting quickly is absolutely critical here because most recording systems, even if they are digital, do not keep footage beyond thirty days.

As of 2012, 75 percent of police departments use license plate readers, so it is important to check with all area departments to see if there has been a recent license plate hit on your victim or your suspect's car.* These cameras, either stationary or mounted on patrol cars, record every license plate that comes into its view. It can be a rich source of information if you are looking to see whether the victim or suspect's car was in a certain area. There are increasing privacy concerns so retention of this information varies greatly from department to department, but it is worth running the tags of any vehicles you are interested in through these systems.†

Pressure Suspect

If there is an obvious suspect, investigative pressure must be applied. Through effective interrogation techniques, a suspect will often confess early on since the guilt is fresh and the suspect's story is not quite thought out yet. There is an excellent book on the interview and interrogation of witnesses and

* http://www.washingtonpost.com/local/despite-cuccinellis-advice-nva-police-still-maintaining-databases-of-license-plates/2014/01/16/055ec09a-7e38-11e3-9556-4a4bf7bcbd84_story.html. Last accessed January 20, 2014.

† http://edition.cnn.com/2013/07/18/us/license-plate-readers/index.html?hpt=hp_t3. Last accessed July 20, 2013.

suspects called *Practical Aspects of Interview and Interrogation,* by David E. Zulawski and Douglas Wicklander. (Full disclosure: The authors sent me this book for free but have not asked me to plug or review it.) Their book is not easily summarized, but in a nutshell they are strong and effective advocates for the bonding type of interview, not the harsh, confrontational method used by many police departments (and prosecutors). Among the topics they cover in their book are nonverbal clues to behavior, false confessions, establishing creditability with a subject, and using rationalizations to make it easier for a suspect to confess. Both men are recognized experts in their field and train police officers and private investigators on the methods they believe have the greatest chance of garnering confessions and incriminating testimony. I strongly recommend this book to police and prosecutors faced with difficult interrogations, which almost every no-body case has. To quote my brother, a detective in New York for more than twenty years, "The bonding interview technique cannot be stressed enough. I can't tell you how many times people have confessed to me and in conversations later I usually inquire as to why they ended up talking to me. Invariably they say something along the lines of it was because they believed that I was not judging them or that I understood why they did it. Only lazy or inexperienced detectives use any other method (in most cases)." The Reid method, perhaps the best known bonding interrogation technique, is another classic in this field.*

One of the most important interrogation techniques is to shut up and listen. Too often officers and prosecutors try to fill silence with questions rather than letting the silence "sit" and make suspects or interviewees uncomfortable and force him or her to talk. This is a skill that requires training and patience, but it is often during those silent moments that they chime in to explain themselves, leading to a damaging statement. Before the interrogation in my case, the lead detective met with investigators from the Navy Criminal Investigations Services (NCIS) to discuss approaches to the suspect. In addition to telling the detective to play to his ego (more on this later), they advised using silence as a technique to force him to talk. During the interrogation (which was videotaped), the detective used this technique very effectively. At one point, he sat silently for over two and a half minutes in order to let the suspect speak. Eventually, the suspect did confess, and the detective's patience was a big reason that he confessed.

Suspects should be placed under surveillance to see if they return to the crime scene or where the body was disposed of. Advances in GPS technology have led police to placing GPS tracking devices on a suspect's car and using the information to see where the suspect goes. This is a rapidly advancing area of the law, however, as evidenced by a recent Supreme Court case that discusses

* http://www.reid.com/. Last accessed May 4, 2013.

when police must obtain a warrant to place a GPS on a car.* It is essential to consult the prosecutor before this investigative step is taken so as to avoid problems at trial with getting the evidence admitted. Indeed, the New Jersey Supreme Court recently held that police must obtain a warrant before tracking data from a cell phone. This is the first time a state supreme court has so held.†

Motive

The prosecution is never required legally to prove a motive at trial. That does not mean, however, that you should not try to figure out what motivated the defendant or suspect to kill and dispose of your victim. Not only will a juror wonder, which is human nature, but also figuring out a motive can often lead to the murderer himself. Motive in no-body murder cases, which are often domestic murders, are no different from other murder cases: scorned love, bad marriage, or money to be gained by the victim's death. It is important to look for life insurance policies because the beneficiaries of these policies are not always obvious. Even relatively small policies can provide a motive for murder. Many employers have life insurance policies for their employees, so do not overlook them. You can often find unknown insurance policies by contacting insurance investigators—often former detectives—for the larger insurers. Another resource is the National Insurance Crime Bureau (www.nicb.org), a not-for-profit association run by member insurance companies that assists law enforcement with the identification, detection and prosecution of insurance criminals. Family and friends can also be sources of information about life insurance policies. When children with large life insurance policies go missing, parental involvement must be checked first.

Since many no-body murder cases are also domestic violence cases, look for a triggering event, that is, a recent event that could have made the suspect angry. Common triggering events are a divorce being made final, a court order to pay alimony or child support, a fight between the victim and the suspect, or any event where the victim asserts her independence from the suspect. Domestic abuse is usually about power, so any indication that the balance of power is shifting from the suspect to the victim can act as a trigger for murder. Finding a triggering event can often lead to the likely suspect. In a domestic violence murder I once prosecuted, the defendant and the victim were in the middle of a contentious divorce. The Tuesday before the Friday murder the defendant nearly came to blows with the victim's attorney during a court-ordered mediation. The defendant had to be removed from the

* 132 S.Ct. 945 (2012) Jones v. U.S..

† http://www.nj.com/politics/index.ssf/2013/07/police_need_warrants_to_track_cell-phone_data_nj_supreme_court_rules.html. Last accessed July 20, 2013.

session, and this could have been the last straw for a man who was about to lose custody of his children. The defendant staged the murder to look like a burglary gone wrong, but the presence of the triggering event plus additional evidence pointing at the defendant enabled us to focus our case on him. However, we made sure to thoroughly investigate the possibility of a burglary so as to prevent that argument from being made at trial by the defense.

Think Creatively

Do not treat the case like a missing persons case; treat it like a homicide where the best evidence of the crime is missing: the body. Police must think outside the box. In one case, the family had not heard from the missing victim for some time but was receiving letters allegedly written by the victim. The family, suspicious that the victim was actually dead, wrote back and reminded the victim to send the money he owed to another family member and to not forget that same family member's birthday. A few days letter a birthday card arrived along with a check for $25. Of course, the victim did not owe that family member any money and it was not his birthday, so the family knew that it was not the victim writing the letters. This is just one example of police and a family thinking creatively to ensnare a killer.

Someone with the ability to conceal a body is not a criminal who is likely to make stupid mistakes, like the bank robber who writes a stickup note on his own deposit slip. These cases are huge law enforcement challenges and require creative solutions and investigative techniques.

Consider wiring up a close friend of the suspect to get admission from the suspect. If the suspect is incarcerated, consider talking to all of his cellmates to see what he may have said.

Finally, do not hesitate to ask for help. In my brother's jurisdiction in New York, a small town an hour north of New York City, the New York State Police Department usually offers its help. It has huge resources and will send as many people as are needed to do the job and will not steal the case. Detectives should know beforehand whom they can call and what they can get. Most police departments in the United States have fewer than ten officers.* Departments with fewer than 100 officers could reasonably handle a major case without help. Besides, the help is free, so why not use it, even if it is only to run down the bogus leads that come in any no-body murder investigation? The FBI's Behavioral Analysis Unit does a great job at both profiling who the possible killer might be and suggesting approaches to a suspect during an interview or interrogation.

* http://www.fop.net/labor/icpra/3TheFutureofLawEnforcementintheUnitedStatesofAmerica.pdf. Last accessed January 20, 2014.

As noted already, the NCIS does the same, although it is typically looking for a naval or armed forces connection.

Missing Children

Investigations for missing children are often very different from those of missing adults. With children of a certain age, there is typically no discussion that the child ran away. Children who are old enough to actually run away are typically reunited with their families very quickly. According to a *Washington Post* article, although nearly 800,000 children are reported missing each year, 98.5 percent are returned to their families.[*] Those children who are not returned are typically kidnapped by family members or people known to them, such as babysitters, neighbors, or family friends.[†] True stranger-on-stranger kidnappings of children are very rare, about 110 to 115 cases per year, according to Robert G. Lowery Jr. of the National Center for Missing and Exploited Children.[‡] The advent of Amber Alerts and the use of cell phones even by young children have enabled missing children to be discovered much more quickly.[§]

What does this mean for you as an investigator? If a child is not located within the first twenty-four to forty-eight hours, the odds greatly increase that their disappearance may mean a case of murder rather than a case of a runaway child. Given the relatively low number of stranger-on-stranger abductions, any initial investigation should focus on family, friends, and those with regular access to the child. Children of all ages now leave tracks on the same social media that adults use and those must be thoroughly searched, since it is not uncommon for teenagers and preteens to have online relationships of which parents are completely unaware. Close friends of the child must also be closely interviewed, since they may have information that is also not known to the parents and that they may be reluctant to reveal. Using a skilled and experienced child interview specialist is usually a good idea, since they know how to successfully interview a child.

* "Technology has improved victims' odds in abductions," *Washington Post*, May 10, 2013, http://www.washingtonpost.com/national/technology-thwarts-many-kidnappers/2013/05/08/76ba0b24-b7ea-11e2-aa9e-a02b765ff0ea_story.html. Last accessed May 12, 2013.

† Ibid.

‡ Ibid. NCMEC, www.missingkids.com, works closely with law enforcement and has a variety of resources at their disposal, including creating missing children posters, training programs, and information on child trafficking groups.

§ "5 Myths about missing children," *Washington Post*, May 12, 2013, http://www.washingtonpost.com/opinions/five-myths-about-missing-children/2013/05/10/efee398c-b8b4-11e2-aa9e-a02b765ff0ea_story.html. Last accessed May 12, 2013. This same article notes that FBI statistics show that missing person cases of all kinds are down 31 percent from 1997 to 2011.

Traditionally, police departments treated cases of missing teenagers as runaways and did little initial investigation. While the previously cited numbers support the idea that most children who are missing are not going to end up harmed, it is important to carefully listen to the family and determine whether the child fits the profile of a runaway. Has the child done this before? Was the child in school and doing well? Has the child recently undergone any type of personality changes or major life changes, such as a divorce, death, move, or other significant experience?

Proving the Victim Is Dead

To a layperson, the biggest challenge in a no-body case is proving that the victim is dead. I have found in most cases, this is less difficult than it appears. The true challenge of most cases is figuring out who killed the victim. Indeed, in this age of instant communication, it is much easier to prove that someone is dead and not just missing than was true even ten years ago. That said, it is still an essential part of any no-body investigation and trial to prove that the victim is dead and not just missing.

There are two ways to prove a victim is dead: through physical evidence or through the lack of evidence of life. Physical evidence that can prove a victim is dead can include a scene that is so bloody (and the blood is tied to the victim) that a forensic pathologist could opine that no one could lose that much blood and survive. This is the most common method in which evidence is used to prove that the person has died. Absent this type of evidence, however, the most common way death is proven in a no-body case is by the lack of evidence of life. All of the aforementioned evidence can be used to show that the victim has died: no contact with the family or friends, no use of bank accounts, cell phones, or social media. The more of this evidence you can put before the jury, the better. Often half of the evidence presented at a no-body trial is evidence that the victim is dead. Because no-body trials remain rare, there will always be some understandable skepticism that the victim is truly dead, and the more evidence you can put forth that she is dead the stronger your case. By the close of your case, you do not want any juror doubting that the victim is dead. The more evidence you can compile of missed anniversaries, birthdays, holidays, and the like, the better the proof that the victim is really dead. Be sure to contact the victim's doctors to see if she had scheduled appointments that she neither attended nor rescheduled. (See the discussion in the section on trials on how to ensure that anyone who could not find a defendant guilty in a no-body case should be eliminated from the jury pool.)

Eliminating Other Suspects

As noted already, any no-body investigation is a two-pronged investigation. In addition to figuring out who the suspect is, you must also be able to eliminate any other suspects. Although the issue of "the real killer" occurs in non-no-body cases, it is very common in no-body cases to have a defense of another killer. As discussed in the trial section, if you fail to eliminate other suspects by the time of trial, it may be too late. Having to deal with a named suspect at trial can be a disaster, since it puts reasonable doubt in a juror's mind. The time to find and eliminate other possible suspects is during the investigative phase, not at trial.

Ideally your investigative efforts result in the defense not even arguing that some other named suspect committed the murder or that the court keeps any mention of this person out of the trial. The next best thing is to be able to demonstrate at the trial why the other person could not be or is not a likely suspect. This is one reason it is essential to videotape as many interviews as possible because you may end up at trial showing the jury an interview with the "other killer" as your best evidence that this person was not likely to be the suspect. Of course, confirming his alibi for the time of the murder (if known) is best and effort should be made to do this early in the case. Trying to confirm an alibi a year or two after the fact is difficult when people's memories fade, and evidence that can support the alibi, such as cell phone records and other electronic evidence, may be long gone.

The Later Investigative Phase

2

Using the Media

It is essential to use the media to your advantage. The media can be a help or a hindrance to an investigation, depending on how you relate to them. The media can help keep the case in the spotlight, which can lead to witnesses coming forward with information. (On the flip side, any high-profile case tends to attract a number of loony bins who want publicity for themselves and insert themselves into the case.) Police who fear the media rarely use them wisely and end up being the subject of stories pointing out how little is seemingly being done on the investigation or how incompetent the police are. Most journalists will respect a police request to keep information out of the media, and by speaking to media on background or off the record, you can get out your side of the story without compromising the investigation.

Do not overlook blogs, social media, and other new media as a way to keep the case in people's minds. The more people who are aware of the case, the greater the chances are of getting a break through a previously unknown witness and of keeping the pressure on the defendant.

Using social media is also a way for the family to stay involved. Setting up a Facebook page or Twitter feed about the case serves to keep the case alive, keeps family and friends productively involved, and may even lead to your killer. Once the social media content has been online for some time, obtain a list of the IP addresses that have viewed the site. If you have a suspect's IP address, you can see how often he is accessing the site or even track down who the suspect is through sites such as whois.net.

Remember the Anniversaries

One of the ways to keep the case in the media is to note the anniversaries of the disappearance or the victim's missed birthday or wedding anniversary. This is a natural hook for the media and, again, keeps the pressure on any suspects. This is also another good way to keep the family involved and apprised of the investigation and its status, and it is often the best avenue for clues and leads. You or the family should organize searches on the anniversaries. Are you likely to find anything? Probably not, but again, it keeps the case in the media and increases the chances of a witness coming forward. Also, at trial, it is another point to make to the jury that shows how thorough the investigation has been.

Go back to reinterview witnesses and suspects. As years pass, people's memories change, and it is always good to keep memories fresh by having witnesses repeat what they have previously said (which you duly recorded in some fashion the first time they told you), see if they have any new memories, and keep the word out there that the case has not languished. Interviewing suspects also tells them you're not going away, either. Guilt is a powerful emotion, and you would be surprised at how it eats away at some people and can lead to a confession years later. Also, you never know what new witnesses you might find to whom the suspect confessed because he felt safe so many years after the murder. Always be alert for new friends/girlfriends of the suspect who you can interview. The number one rule of both cold cases and no-body murder cases is simple: Never, ever give up.

If You Have a Suspect

Having a suspect in a no-body case can make for advantages and disadvantages. It is obviously easier to focus your resources when there is one strong suspect in mind. Eliminating other suspects is easier as well, because you can treat nonsuspects differently than suspects. Having a "good" suspect, however, can also be a disadvantage if it leads to tunnel vision. Focusing on just one suspect can lead an investigation to overlook other viable suspects. Not eliminating other suspects, as noted earlier, can cause problems at trial as the defense points out leads not followed up on, clues ignored, and potential killers missed. In *People v. Garcia*, the victim's boyfriend had a history of domestic violence against her. He had actually been arrested for assaulting her seven months before her disappearance. The investigators quickly checked out his alibi, however, and believed it. Their focus turned to someone the victim had met in a local casino. If they had simply focused on the boyfriend to the exclusion of other, they might have missed gathering valuable surveillance evidence from the casino that turned out to be the key to solving the case.

That said, having a suspect is better than not having one. When dealing with a suspect, examine how he reacts to the status of the case. How does he react to the fact that the victim is missing? Was he the one who originally reported the victim as missing? Does he cooperate with any search? Does he cooperate with the police? How does he react on the anniversary? Does your suspect talk to the media or shun them? Does he contact the police to keep up on the status of the case? Does he move in with someone new too soon, or does he dispose of the victim's things too early? Are there any changes to his car or house, such as being remodeled or changed in a significant way? Do any lifestyle changes become apparent?

Jailhouse Informants: A Cautionary Tale

The use of jailhouse informants truly merits an entirely separate book. For purposes of a no-body case, however, certain guidelines for using jailhouse informants or "snitches" bear repeating. The use of jailhouse informants is not uncommon in no-body murder cases. As noted previously, committing a no-body murder with another or having witnesses to such a murder is quite rare. Thus, codefendants or eyewitnesses to these murders are a rare breed at trial. However, it is not uncommon in no-body murder trials for jailhouse informants to testify to statements made by the defendant when the defendant was in jail prior to his trial. There are many rules surrounding the use of jailhouse informants because of the Sixth Amendment, which provides for a right to counsel. If a jailhouse informant is acting as an agent for you, there could be serious problems with any statement obtained from the defendant/suspect if he already has an attorney. If the informant obtained the information on his own accord, however, the statement may be able to be used. Thus, this is ground that must be trod on carefully, and it is essential that the prosecutor be involved in any discussion regarding the use of an informant.

Often a jailhouse informant comes to light when he informs an investigator that he has a statement from the defendant. A statement from a defendant delivered through an informant is worthless at trial unless it can be corroborated by separate evidence. It was always my practice to confirm with separate evidence every bit of evidence I received from an informant, or I did not use the informant or that part of the statement. Any half-decent defense attorney will shred an informant in court if his statements are not corroborated by other independent evidence. Using an informant at trial remains a double-edged sword, given the deals that must often be struck with an informant in exchange for their testimony. (Hopefully it goes without saying that any such deal must be disclosed to the defense counsel and should be brought out at trial to the jury.) Jurors are predisposed not to like most cooperators, hence the pejorative "snitch" label that is attached to them. But an informant who is corroborated can be a powerful witness against a defendant. It is not uncommon for no-body murderers to confess to jail cellmates, because of either guilt or pride in what they did.

In the case I tried, we had an interesting and involved jailhouse informant issue. While we were investigating the murder, our suspect committed an armed robbery and was arrested. Since he was on parole for an earlier crime, his armed robbery arrest resulted in him being shipped from DC to a federal detention center in Philadelphia for his parole hearing. While incarcerated in Philadelphia, he admitted to a fellow inmate that he had murdered someone and thrown her in the "Baltimore Lake" (there is no such lake). The man he confessed to told the prosecutor on his case, who in turn contacted us. We travelled to Philadelphia and debriefed the informant. He was credible, and, although the details of the story told by our suspect did not quite fit, the informant had enough facts that we knew he had spoken to our suspect. Also, since our case had not been in the news, we knew he could not have gotten the details from the media. This is essential. You must be able to prove at trial that the information the informant reveals came from the defendant, not from another source. We also reviewed the discovery that had been sent to the defendant in his robbery and parole cases to make sure there was no information in there that the informant was simply parroting.

Armed with this information, we needed to determine what to do. The informant came across as credible but was facing an enormous amount of federal time for gun running. Having him testify would probably mean we would have to promise him a reduced sentence on his charges, and that is always a risk in front of a jury since it affects their evaluation of his credibility. In addition, the story he gave us from our defendant was similar to what we believed happened but was not exactly the same and it did not help us locate the body. However, one odd thing the informant told us enabled us to pursue another investigative lead with his information.

While talking to the informant, our suspect freely admitted that he had murdered the victim. The suspect told the informant to tell his attorney about the confession and that the attorney would then inform the police and prosecutors. The informant would cooperate with the authorities, help convict the suspect of the murder, and get off on his own charges. When the informant was free, he could then send money to the suspect to use at the jail canteen. (Yes, not a brilliant plan.) Apparently, the suspect felt that the combination of his parole hit and his armed robbery arrest were going to get him sent back to prison for such a long time that he might as well make the best of it.

Based on this, we decided to have the informant tell the suspect he had done as requested and told his lawyer. The informant would tell the suspect that before his attorney would inform the police, however, he wanted his own investigator to interview the suspect to determine if the story was true. In fact, the informant's "investigator" was actually an undercover detective we had selected to play that role.

We transferred our suspect from Philadelphia to the DC jail so we could send in our undercover more easily. However, we had one concern. The suspect had already been charged and arraigned on his armed robbery case. Therefore, his Sixth Amendment right to counsel had attached. Would we be violating that right by putting an undercover police officer into the visitor's area with the suspect in order to talk about a murder he had committed? After extensive discussions with our appellate chief, we concluded that having the undercover officer speak to the suspect would not violate his right to counsel. First, the right to counsel is case specific, so having counsel assigned in one matter (the armed robbery and the parole cases) does not mean he is assigned counsel for any other criminal matter (such as a murder case). Second, the right to counsel means that a defendant cannot be compelled to speak to law enforcement without his attorney being present. Here, however, the suspect would not know that he was speaking to law enforcement but would believe he was speaking to an investigator for the informant. Thus, even though he actually was speaking to law enforcement, he would not know that he was and therefore his right to counsel was not violated. This seemed a little odd to me, but our appellate chief was very well-respected on these issues. (Indeed, he went on to become a judge on DC's highest appellate court.)

Once the suspect was in the DC jail we sent in our undercover complete with a wire so he could record the entire conversation with the suspect. Unfortunately, things did not go as planned. The suspect freely talked to our detective but blamed the murder on a man I'll call Lawrence Whittington. In this telling of the story to our undercover investigator, the suspect was simply a witness to Whittington murdering our victim. He told the undercover detective many of the details that we believed matched the actual murder but blamed everything on Whittington. Even worse for us: Whittington was a real person and knew the suspect.

The real Lawrence Whittington was a well-established Washington businessman. He owned several residential rental properties around DC and had both rented an apartment to the suspect as well as hired him as a handyman a few times. So now we had a real person whom the suspect had accused of the murder and no confession from the defendant.

We proceeded to do a background check on Lawrence Whittington, including getting his cell phone records for the relevant time period. We were able to determine that he had had no calls with the suspect during the relevant time frame and had very little contact with the defendant at all. He had no connection to the victim and certainly no motive to kill her. Ultimately, we interviewed Whittington and convinced ourselves that the suspect had invented the story out of whole cloth. We revealed all of this information to the defense and convinced the court not to let any of this information into evidence. (Of course, the suspect could have brought this out at trial by taking the stand in his own defense, but he did not.) We did not use the informant at trial either, even though his testimony about what the suspect told him was pretty close to what we believed actually happened. Given the problems with using jailhouse informants and the fact that the information did not exactly match what we believed happened, we decided we could win a conviction without this evidence, and we did.

Cold Case

3

A no-body case can often take many years to solve. It can take so long that the original detectives on the case retire or move into other assignments and the case, now maybe years old, is assigned to a brand-new set of eyes. The benefit of new eyes is that they look at the file with no preconceived notions about the case. Every piece of paper in the file must be carefully reviewed to see if any lead was missed or not completely investigated. Remember that very often, the murderer's name is in the file and the key is finding out which name it is.

It is important to stay close to the family because they hear things about the case. People who would never go to the police with information often go to the family instead. Even if the family is frustrated with the pace or results of the investigation to date, and they often are, it is imperative to try to maintain cordial relationships with the family so that you can both get information from them and have them assist you in sifting through any new information or leads.

Reexamine everything in the file, including all physical evidence. Advances in DNA mean that smaller and smaller samples can be tested, so search evidence bins to see if anything has been overlooked. Advances in alternate light sourcing mean that evidence that may have previously gone undetected may now be detected. The older the case, the more carefully physical evidence must be reevaluated in light of modern forensic technologies. Physical locations must also be searched, even if many years later. While the possibility of recovering evidence may be slim, if there is a trial you will be able to show a jury that you at least tried.

In my own no-body case a nearly overlooked piece of evidence ended up becoming key to the defendant's conviction. In all of my homicide investigations and trials, I created lengthy and all encompassing to-do lists, much to the bane of my investigators who were constantly on the receiving end of my endless lists. In my no-body case, we were near the end of the investigation and about to get the final vote from the grand jury and have an indictment in hand. There was one item that had sat on my to-do list for months: contacting the mother of my suspect's one child. My suspect had had a daughter with a woman with whom he had had a very brief relationship about thirteen years before the murder. The woman and her daughter now lived in New York City and seemingly had very little contact with my suspect. Sitting in my office with my lead detective, we decided, almost on a lark, to call the suspect's daughter's mother. Hardly believing we had the correct number, I dialed it and the suspect's old girlfriend, whom I will call Portia Hancock, answered almost immediately. I told her who I was and that I was calling to ask her about my suspect. Ms. Hancock then said, "Oh, did he really kill that girl?" Picking my jaw up off the floor, I asked her what she meant. She proceeded to tell me that around the time of my victim's disappearance the suspect had called Ms. Hancock twice, first to complain about the victim and how she was acting. During that call Ms. Hancock actually spoke to the victim, who told her that the suspect had a gun in his hand. Ms. Hancock told the victim she should leave him because he was violent. Ms. Hancock told us that a day or two later, the suspect called her again and claimed he had shot the victim. Ms. Hancock did not believe him and ended the conversation fairly quickly. The next time she heard anything about this was when we had called. We could hardly believe our luck.

Through her cell phone records we were able to confirm that the calls had taken place and around the time of the murder. We put Ms. Hancock in the grand jury and eventually called her at the trial. Although she was quite a character and her story seemed almost too good to be true, the confirmation of the telephone records was key and seemingly convincing to the jury. This evidence only came to light because we wanted to leave no stone or investigative lead unturned. You do the same. In the end, according to Joe Kennedy of the Navy Criminal Investigation Services, cases are solved through time, technology, and tenacity, all of which must be supplied by you.

4 Trial

Pretrial Preparation

No-body murder trials tend to be longer and involve more witnesses and evidence than other murder trials. This is partially because with no body, the prosecution must spend a lot of time proving that the victim is dead. Therefore, it is essential that you make the case as easy for the jury to follow as possible. One way to do this is to create a timeline to use at trial. Having a clear timeline is essential to trying a no-body case. It makes it easier for the jury to follow events that may cover many years. Using either a large poster board or PowerPoint that enables you to add each event as the testimony and evidence is admitted gives the jury the feel of solving the case along with you. The timeline must be clear and easy to follow, so consider using color coding based on type of fact (e.g., events related to victim, events related to suspect, forensic evidence, investigation, etc.). I once tried a case with an enormous amount of evidence. I used a large poster board on which was written a timeline and with key points of evidence and testimony written on small cards that were mounted on the board with Velcro. As each witness testified or evidence was entered, I attached the card to the poster board timeline. I also left the poster board in the jury's view during the entire trial, and for some reason the defense never moved it. I noticed the jury looking at it throughout the trial and was able to enter it into evidence and have it sent back with them during deliberations. I am sure they relied on this timeline during their deliberations, which is exactly what you want your jury to do.

Voir Dire

When picking a jury, you or the judge (depending on who conducts voir dire), must ask each juror if they could find a defendant guilty of murder even if the government does not produce a body or a cause of death. Despite the increasing frequency that no-body cases are being prosecuted, they are still exceedingly rare, and it is not uncommon to encounter laypeople who refuse to believe that a person can be convicted if there is no body. Anyone who states that they could not convict without a body should be eliminated by the court or, failing that, by the prosecutor. You simply cannot have a juror who will not convict if you do not have a body.

It is essential to use a written questionnaire to test receptivity to circumstantial evidence/lack of body. Many laypeople assume that a circumstantial evidence case is worse than a case with direct evidence. Putting aside whether that's true as a factual matter (most prosecutors would prefer a DNA-based case versus an eyewitness case), the law clearly treats circumstantial and direct evidence as equal. The jury must know this and know this very early on. Although it borders on argument, I suggest getting this in front of the jury in openings. Ask the court if you can present the jury instruction that informs the jury that circumstantial evidence should be treated the same as direct evidence. In closing arguments it is important to demonstrate to the jurors that they use circumstantial evidence every day and accept it as if they had seen something with their own eyes. An argument I used many times went as follows:

> The court will instruct you that circumstantial evidence is to be treated the same as direct. At first this may not make sense. We are used to thinking of circumstantial evidence as less powerful, "Oh man, all they have against me is circumstantial evidence." But if you think about it we rely on circumstantial evidence every day. If last night you looked out your window and saw it was snowing, that is direct evidence that it snowed. If, on the other hand, when you went to bed last night, it was not snowing but then when you woke up this morning, you looked out your window and saw your lawn or sidewalk covered in snow, you also know it snowed even though you did not see it snow. That is circumstantial evidence. Is it possible that a Hollywood production team came and dumped snow all over your house and yard? Sure. Is it reasonable to believe that? No. There is no difference between direct and circumstantial evidence, and you know this not just because the judge tells you that is so, but because your own life experience tells you so as well.

What type of juror are you looking for? The answer to this question varies greatly from jurisdiction to jurisdiction. Generally, as police and prosecutors, we want conservative, law-abiding, mature citizens. You'll find a million books on jury selection, some useful, most not. In any murder case, I sought to have mature, thoughtful, and intelligent jurors, ones who could follow the evidence and not be distracted by red herrings thrown out by the defense. Although the Supreme Court has made certain rules about the basis for eliminating a juror—for example, a peremptory challenge cannot be based on race or gender—most jurisdictions permit juror strikes based on age. In my experience, and certainly in no-body cases, I have a preference for older, more mature jurors. Making a decision in a murder case, let alone a murder case without a body, is difficult work. I have found older jurors better able to reach a conclusion based upon the evidence than younger jurors who tend to have a harder time making a decision, not surprising since they have generally had to make fewer important decisions in their lives. I have also found that younger jurors tend to see the world less as black and white and more gray, which is not a good thing when you are trying to prove something beyond a reasonable doubt.

Hearsay

As in domestic homicides generally, statements by the victim can be a huge help to the prosecution if you can get them admitted. It is critical to be sure of your nonhearsay basis (or exception to the hearsay rule) that gets the statement in and be prepared to prove it to the judge, often through use of a trial memorandum. Do not ever assume any statement is coming in unless you are certain.

Puzzle Argument

Having used a PowerPoint or chart to have the various pieces of the puzzle of the murder put together, you need to pull all of the evidence together in closing arguments. One of the main problems with a no-body case is that evidence is often missing or certain questions that cannot be answered at the time of trial. I have used the following argument many times when my case has some "holes" in it, and you can modify to fit your own circumstances:

> I have an older sister, and like every good little brother, I tried to be as much of a pest as possible when we were growing up. One of the things my sister loved to do when we were young was jigsaw puzzles, and she would take days to complete these huge 500- to 1,000-piece puzzles of beach scenes, a park, the U.S. Capitol, whatever. They would take like a week to complete. Because I was a pest I would always steal two to three pieces and hide them under my mattress. Thus, I was secure in the knowledge that she would never, ever completely finish the puzzle and I had ruined her fun.
>
> But you know what? My sister never cared. She would finish the puzzle, minus the two to three pieces I had hidden, and she could still tell exactly what the scene was. She knew I had the missing pieces, but she didn't care. It was still a picture of the beach, the park, the U.S. Capitol.
>
> Now in this case, there are some missing pieces. (Go over them now.) And I wish I could tell you I have the missing puzzle pieces under my bed. But I don't. Because real life doesn't work that way, and this defendant wanted there to be missing pieces. But you know what, ladies and gentlemen, you can still see the whole puzzle here even without those pieces. (Then review each piece of evidence that has been admitted.)

In the case of *People v. Mario Garcia*,* the prosecutor, Garen Horst, used an effective method in his closing argument to bring home to the jury the power of a circumstantial case:

> In the Garcia case, this was done during closing argument by enlarging and mounting two photos side-by-side: one of the victim and the other of the defendant (Figure 4.1). Important facts that helped to show the death of the victim, such as "no contact with her family and friends," "left behind personal effects," "no e-mails," "no phone use," "no financial activity," were written on the side of her photo. The last fact written here that helped to establish her death was the "investigation of the defendant." The word "murdered" was printed across her picture. When the closing began, the defendant's photo was completely covered with puzzle pieces, and each piece had a key fact written on it that was used to show his guilt. The pieces were made of stiff cardboard and had double-sided tape on their backside that could peel off and stick like a Post-it note.
>
> During the closing argument, each fact used to ultimately show the death of the victim was discussed. When the last one, "investigation of the defendant" was referenced, the focus shifted to the other side of the board. As each fact of the investigation was discussed, that puzzle piece was peeled off and placed on the victim's photo. By the end of closing arguments, the defendant's photo was almost completely exposed, except for two pieces that still covered part of his picture. Those pieces represented facts that were unknown (i.e., the method of murder and the location of the body). Although the whole photo was not uncovered, the jurors still knew that it was a photo of the defendant (Figure 4.2).
>
> By contrast, the victim's photo was almost completely covered with those same puzzle pieces of the investigation—illustrating her death. Because two of the pieces were still stuck on the defendant's photo, those empty spaces of the victim's photo were strategically located to maximize impact and theme. One empty space exposed the word 'murdered' written on the victim's photo, and the other exposed her right eye. At the end of the closing, this exhibit faced the jury box, and the jurors were told [the victim] was the silent witness of the case. Even though she was not physically present to testify, she left behind injuries on the defendant to tell of her struggle him and her DNA in his vehicle to tell how she was inside the car and tried to escape.
>
> Those same techniques and strategies that were effective in the Garcia trial can be employed in many cases that rely primarily on circumstantial evidence. A circumstantial case can be quite powerful and compelling if presented properly. From jury selection, to case presentation, to closing argument, jurors can be convinced of the power of circumstantial evidence and persuaded to arrive at the just verdict."†

* Super. Ct., Sacramento County 2006, No. 62-55517. The murder happened in Placer County, California, but was moved to Sacramento County due to a change of venue motion.

† Horst, G., "The Power of Circumstantial Evidence: Techniques Used in a No-Body Homicide Prosecution," *Prosecutor's Brief* Vol. 30, No. 1, reprinted with permission.

Figure 4.1 Prosecuting and Winning Cases When the Victim Is Missing. (From Horst, G. *The Power of Circumstantial Evidence: Techniques Used In a No-Body Homicide Prosecution*. Prosecutor's Brief. Fall 2007. With permission from Laura Bell [lbell@cdaa.org].)

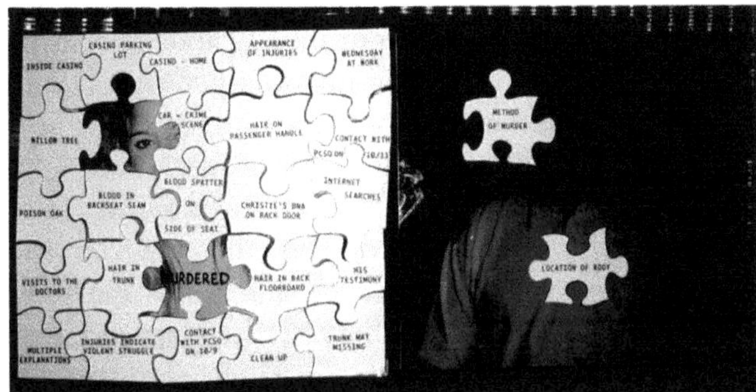

Figure 4.2 Prosecuting and Winning Cases When the Victim Is Missing. (From Horst, G. *The Power of Circumstantial Evidence: Techniques Used In a No-Body Homicide Prosecution*. Prosecutor's Brief. Fall 2007. With permission from Laura Bell [lbell@cdaa.org].)

Rope vs. Chain Analogy

Another common argument in no-body murder cases is that the prosecution needs to prove every part of the case and that if one "link" is missing then the case is "broken" and the defendant should be acquitted. This is, of course, absurd. There are many issues in a murder case that do not have to be proven by the prosecution: motive, exactly how the victim died (except to show it was murder and not an accident), where the victim died, when the victim died, etc.

The best way to rebut this argument is what I call the rope versus chain analogy. The defendant is arguing that the government's case is like a chain: break one link and the chain breaks. In fact, any prosecution, particularly a no-body case, is much more like a rope: A rope is made up of many smaller, thinner strands wrapped together. If one strand breaks, the rope is still strong. Indeed, you can break many strands and the rope will still stay together. A no-body murder prosecution is typically made up of many pieces of evidence, the puzzle pieces we talked of above. You argue to the jury that even if they discount certain pieces of evidence, the overall case remains strong and is not broken by one particular piece of evidence that is missing or one unresolved issue.

SODDI

The most common defense to a no-body murder case is that the victim is not dead. This is the most stupid argument a defendant can make. Another common defense is one seen in other murder cases: someone else committed the murder. In courtroom parlance this is known as the SODDI defense: Some Other Dude Did It. If you have done your investigation properly, the defense will have a very difficult time arguing that another person committed the crime, particularly if the other person is a named suspect. Be prepared to exonerate specific people through alibi, lack of motive, or opportunity or however they can be eliminated. Ideally, by filing a motion in limine, basically a pretrial request to the court, you keep the jury from hearing about evidence of a named person at all. Your pretrial motions will hopefully eliminate any argument from the defense that the defendant did not murder the victim but in fact John Jones did. If not, you will need to spend time in your case in chief, "proving" to the jury that Jones did not commit the offense. I say "proving" because, of course, you do not need to prove it beyond a reasonable doubt as you would for a defendant, but any jury is going to need to be convinced that the third party is not guilty of the offense to a fairly high standard of proof.

Even if the defense is unable or is not permitted to name a particular person as the "true" killer, the defendant will always be permitted to argue that someone else, unknown to everyone, was the killer. I call this the "Killer X" theory.

If that evidence is going to be admitted, however, you must also be prepared to eliminate Killer X. Often this can be done by focusing on "victimology," that is, put on evidence about your victim that makes it unlikely he or she would be subjected to random violence that, by the way, also caused her body to be hidden so effectively. Understanding your victim can often mean understanding your killer. Does a random robber/mugger/burglar kill someone and then hide the body? Who would want to kill a mother/nurse/professional? Obviously, if your victimology is not good this becomes harder, but on "clean" victims it can be powerful evidence if the suspect is connected to the victim in some fashion.

Use the thoroughness of your investigation as a shield against the attack that someone else murdered the victim. By putting on evidence of the thoroughness of your investigation, you knock out claims that investigative leads were overlooked and make it more difficult for defendants to argue that someone else committed the murder. This is also why it is essential to try to track down every lead, no matter how far fetched. Many a no-body trial has had the specter of the defense witness who says they saw the victim well after the time of the murder. The witness may be obviously crazy to you, but you need to be able to show this to a jury and it is much easier to knock down a crazy witness during the investigative phase than during the stress of a trial.

Why Arguing the Victim Is Not Dead Is a Defendant's Worst Enemy

The most common defense in any no-body trial is that the victim is not dead or that the prosecution has not proven that the victim is dead. This happens because, despite the increasing number of no-body prosecutions and the advent of DNA testing, most laypeople (our jurors) still believe that proving a no-body case is so difficult because you cannot demonstrate that someone is truly dead without a body.

This is a poor defense for a number of reasons, and arguing it actually benefits the prosecution. First, it forces the prosecution to prove the victim is dead, which generally means putting on a wealth of evidence about the victim. You will put on evidence about her lifestyle, her habits, and her ties to her family, her work, and her community. Unlike an ordinary murder case where there is very little information about the victim put forth at trial, in a no-body trial there is the opportunity to put in all sorts of positive information about the victim. Use this to your advantage to paint a very positive portrayal of the victim so that the jury sympathizes with your victim. Your goal should be to get a juror to say, "Gee, she seemed like a nice person. What sort of monster would kill her and hide her body?"

In addition, in today's society it is not too difficult to show someone is dead given the number of ties both human and electronic most of us have. Thus, the defense is making an argument that is usually not only easy to defeat but ends up hurting their case. The best defense would be to concede that the victim has died or even was murdered but that this defendant had nothing to do with her death. Then the prosecution would be forced to forgo most of its proof of death and forced to admit only evidence that the defendant murdered the victim. Of course, given the skepticism of most jurors, a court may permit evidence that the victim is dead, even if the defense does not contest this, in order to allow the prosecution to "prove" this fact to a jury. Indeed, a bold defendant might actually offer to stipulate that the victim was murdered and force the prosecutor to avoid putting on any proof along the lines just discussed. However, since a stipulation must be agreed upon by both parties, you should never agree to this so you can present this evidence.

5 No-Body Murder Case Statistics

In looking at both historic and recent no-body cases, some interesting patterns emerge. On my website, www.nobodymurdercases.com, I have collected every no-body murder trial in the United States that I can find. As of the writing of this book, (March 2014), there were 399 trials. As Figures 5.1, 5.2, and 5.3 demonstrate, some conclusions about the "typical" no-body murder can be gleaned from these trials.

Of the cases that went to trial, as shown in Figure 5.2, 59.3 percent of the victims were female. The suspects, however, as shown in Figure 5.1, were overwhelmingly male, 90.4 percent. The analysis of where cases went to trial also reveals some surprises: While such populous states as California, New York, Texas, and Florida have the largest number of cases, some less-populous states such as Colorado and Michigan have had quite a few cases as well. As of this writing, only Idaho and New Hampshire have not had any no-body murder trials (see Figure 5.3).* As noted throughout this book, most no-body murders are committed by someone known (and usually well-known) to the victim, and the statistics bear this out. My research has revealed that of the cases that have gone to trial, more than 54 percent have involved domestic relationships in one form or another. These relationships include husband and wife, boyfriend/girlfriend, ex-husbands and wives and boyfriends and

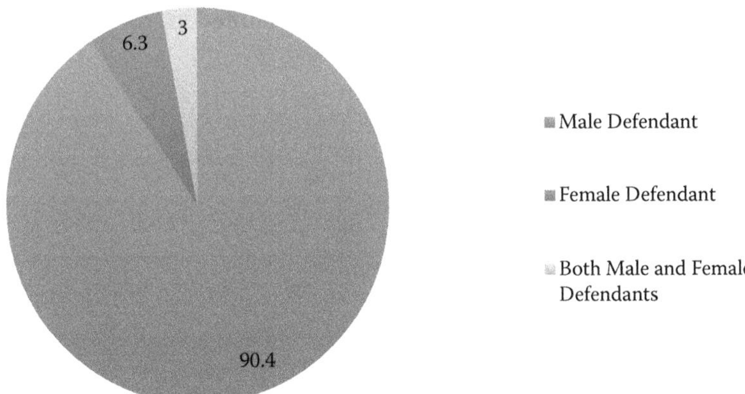

Figure 5.1 Proportion of Male and Female Defendants (9.3 percent of all cases had multiple male defendants, and 5 percent were multiple female defendants).

* Thanks to Paula Moore, Henderson (Nevada) Police Department, for her analysis of this data, current as of April 30, 2014.

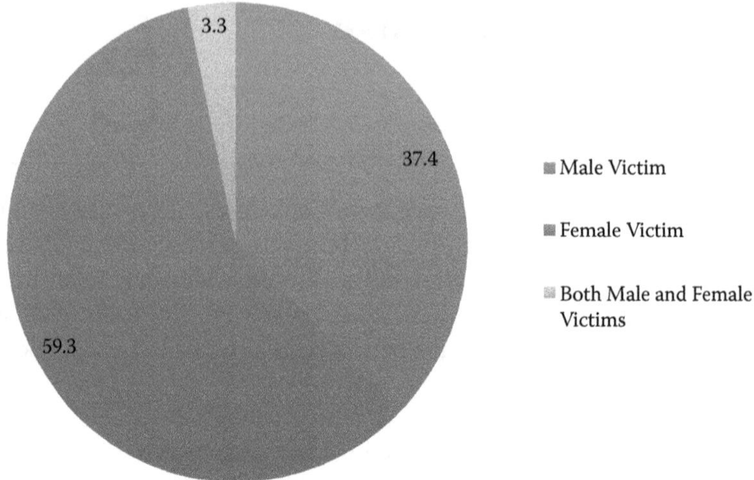

Figure 5.2 Proportion of Male and Female Victims (2.5 percent of all cases had multiple male victims, and 3 percent were multiple female victims).

girlfriends, parents killing their children, sons-in-law killing mothers-in-law, and boyfriends killing ex-boyfriends and husbands. Note that I have defined domestic relationships broadly, including even brief dating relationships such as a murderer picking up someone at a bar. Given that these are the cases that went to trial, and thus presumably had some evidentiary weaknesses in the eyes of the defendant, I suspect the domestic relationship percentage is even higher in cases that plead before trial. Finally, in what I think is an example of juries never being quite sure someone is really dead, of the 399 cases that have gone to trial, only 25 have resulted in the death penalty.

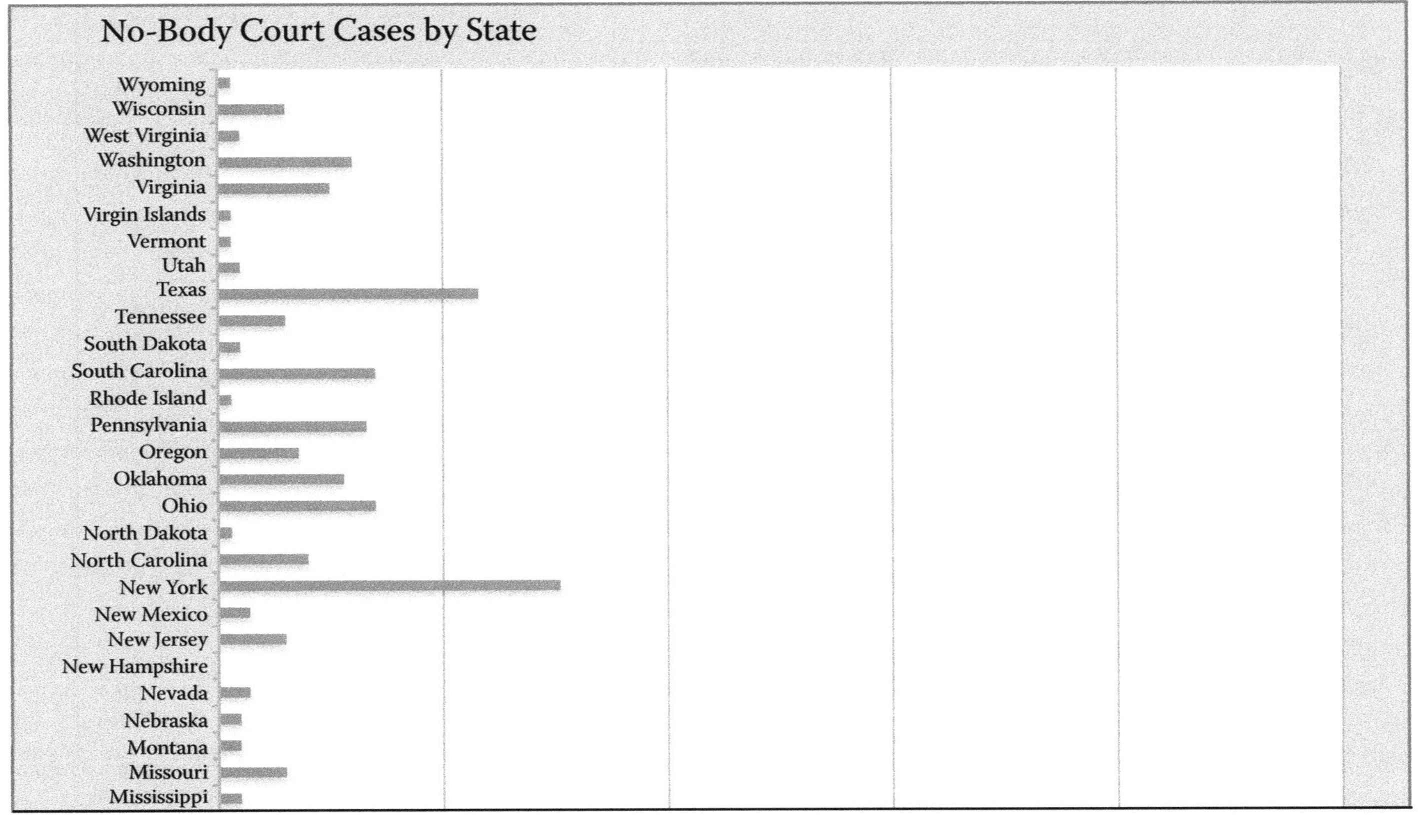

Figure 5.3 No-body court cases by state. *(continued)*

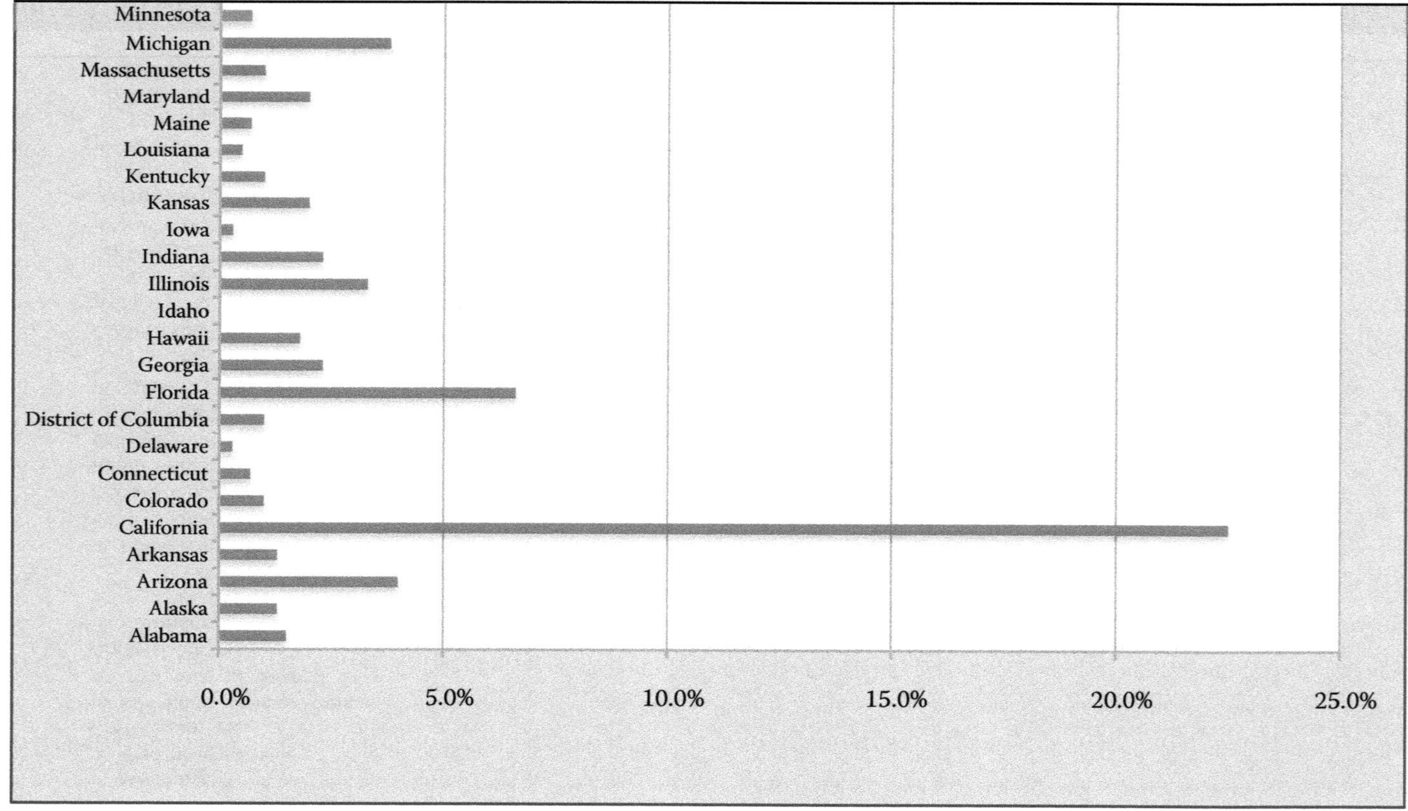

Figure 5.3 (Continued) No-body court cases by state.

Personality of a Murderer

6

Most no-body murder cases (54 percent by my count) are domestic violence cases, a husband killing his wife or lover, a boyfriend killing a girlfriend, and parent killing a child.* Most domestic homicides start with a history of domestic abuse between the defendant and the victim. Most domestic abusers are obsessed with power and control. It is critical to their self-worth that they be in control or appear to be in control. A no-body murderer takes this control to the extreme: By getting rid of the victim's body, he retains ultimate control over her because no one else knows where she is hidden. When you have a suspect who is in (or was in) a domestic relationship with the victim, particularly a marriage or a dating or sexual relationship, you must keep this idea of power in mind. A domestic abuser is about control, controlling his victim, controlling what happens to her, controlling the investigation. You can use this need for control to your benefit in your investigation. A control freak wants to know what is going on with the investigation when it involves him, so use that to entice him to talk. Perhaps by holding out the promise of giving him some information, you may get information, intentionally or not, from him. As noted already, suspects often want to know the status of an investigation so they may revisit where the body is buried or may keep it buried closer to them than might be wise in order to be able to track how close the police are getting to finding the body. In interviewing a domestic abuser, it is important to play to his ego and downplay his culpability. As odious as it may seem, when interrogating a suspect, the best plan is often to blame the victim in order to form a bond with the suspect and make him feel more comfortable in confessing. Remember that browbeating a suspect rarely leads to a confession in real life.

* Note that this number applies only to cases that went to trial. I suspect the percentage of domestic no-body murders that either plead or were undetected is actually higher, since cases where the suspect is more obvious, such as a domestic murder, plead at a higher rate than stranger homicide cases.

Future

7

I am often asked what the future holds for no-body murder cases. A few trends are obvious. First, there have been many, many more cases in the last ten years than the ten years before that or the ten years before that. This trend is accelerating. Of the nearly 400 no-body cases that have gone to trial since 1839, exactly half have gone to trial since 2000.* I expect this trend to continue as technology improves and makes it easier to find small traces even the most careful suspect failed to detect. Advances in ground-penetrating radar, DNA, and trace evidence will make it easier to find bodies or at least find evidence of a crime. In addition, as more of these cases are brought and more convictions obtained, it is easier for subsequent juries to understand that "no-body" does not equal "not guilty." Another trend is that the time frame between disappearance, arrest, and trial is being greatly reduced. Given all of the modern ways that we keep track of one another—social media, credit cards, surveillance cameras—it is no longer necessary to wait a year, seven years, or a decade to be certain the victim is dead. My own experience has shown that police and prosecutors are much more willing to arrest suspects and bring cases to trial more quickly than in the past because they can prove with more certainty that the victim is dead and not just missing. Finally, as more cases are brought to a close by a guilty plea or conviction, police and prosecutors are becoming more aggressive about not only bringing more cases to trial but going through their cold cases to see if they have older no-body cases that can be reinvestigated and closed.

Currently, the conviction rate of no-body cases that have gone to trial is 88 percent. I see this rate as probably staying about the same for two reasons. First, as more jurors get comfortable with the idea of convicting a defendant even when there is no body, the conviction rate would conceivably rise. Conversely, however, I believe police and prosecutors are becoming more willing to bring cases that they would not have brought in the past, cases that are not as strong as prior cases. This is a laudable thing, since it may mean justice for families that were unable to achieve it before. But this also means the cases may be weaker and it may make it more difficult to garner convictions. Therefore, the 88 percent conviction rate probably is not going to change significantly. In any event, I suspect that ten years from now, no-body murder cases, while still a challenge, will be much less the rare birds they remain today.

* All statistics in this section taken from the Table of No-Body Murder cases at http://www.nobodycases.com/no_body2.pdf.

Indices

The following keywords can be used in conjunction with the cases listed in Appendix B to search for cases with evidence similar to your case. I have categorized all of the cases by one of more of the following ten keywords: codefendant testimony; confession to friends and family; confession to police, death penalty; eyewitness; forensics evidence: DNA; forensics evidence: Other (such as fiber, fingerprints, etc.), informant; life or not applicable (meaning none of the prior categories apply).

Keyword Index

Codefendant Testimony

Confession to Friends and Family

Salado, Salas, Sax, Schubert, Scott (Albert Raymond), Sedlak, Shepherd, Stanley, Stephenson, Stewart (Bryan), Suleski, Sullivan, Teigen, Thrift, Tjelveit, Torres, Trussell, Walker (Leslie), Watkins, Watson, White (Charles Thomas), Wills, Wilson, Wright, York, Zarinsky, Zavala

Confession to Police

Abercrombie, Adamson, Asher, Austin, Awana, Bach, Barnes, Basham, Bell, Bennett, Bingham, Blom, Campbell (Carl), Clark (Hadden), Cowell, Cunningham, Dahmer, Derring, Eby, Fish, Flagner, Forsberg, Frey, Gacy, Gaudenzi, Gilbert, Gonzales, Guilford, Heiges, Jaggers, James (Reggie Carnell), Janto, Johnson (Brandon), Jones (Michelle), Kimes, Kretz, Lamb (George H.), Lankford, Lawrence, Leftridge, Lemons, Lent, Lerch, Lettrich, Levine, Lewis (Carson), Lipsky, Lodmell, Lung, MacPhee, Malinski, Marquez, McIlwain, McMonigle, Merola, Modelski, Monie, Moore (Larry), O'Shields, Oakes, Oelerich, Owens (Alvin), Payne, Pyle, Quillin, Ream, Reddish, Reiser, Robinson (Buddy), Rodriguez, Roger, Shepherd, Smith (Billy D.), Scout, Stabler, Stanley, Swartout, Tjelveit, Trejos, Trussell, Vega, Vickery, Warmke, Whitesides, Williams (Augustus), Yakovlev, Zapata, Zarabozo, Zarif, Zarinsky

Death Penalty

Allen (Clarence), Anderson (Richard), Anthony, Ballard, Basham, Brown (Cornelius), Cole, Crew, Dalton, Davis, Derring, Fish, Gacy, Hicks (Ellias), McDuff, McMonigle, Meyers, Ng, Payne, St. Clair, Thomas (William), Thompson (Raymond Michael), Walker (Charles Anthony), Watson, Wilhelms

Eyewitness

Alviso, Anderson (Terry), Arnold, Austin, Bondurant, Brown, (Cornelius), Bulger, Campbell (John), Carrasco, Clamp, Crafts, Crew, Crews, Dianovsky, Docherty, Dudley, Duvall, Elliott, Evans (Randy), Fannings, Faulkner, Fawaz, Ferrell, Forsythe, Gibson (Larry), Grabbe, Graham, Grayer, Griffin, Harmon, Hicks (James), Hurley, Jaggers, Jaime, James (Reggie Carnell), Kiffe, King (Ervin), King (Jack Lee), Kirby, Lamb (Damien James), Lankford, Lawrence, Lewis (Carson), Lindesy, Luetgert, Morales, Mason, Marquez, McMonigle, Meeks, Merola, Montano, Moore (Antonio), Nauss, Nowicki, Oakes, Orona, Pann, Pizzonia, Price, Prion, Quick, Racz, Rader, Ramsammy, Ream, Rebeterano, Rice, Rivera, Roberson, Robinson (Gary Lee), Robinson (Tamara), Rutan, Sandoval, Scharf, Scott (Albert Raymond), Sedlak, Seifert, Shawkey, Shepherd, Sherer, Skaggs, Smith (Larry David), Sochor, Srout,

Forensics: DNA

Forensics: Other

Informant

Abbott, Mora, Adamson, Anderson (Richard), Ballard, Boorn, Brown (Cornelius), Bruce, Bulger, Bustamante, Caracappa, Clark (Hadden), Doan, Estrella, Fountain, Graham, Halcomb, Hall (Henry William), Harshman, Hummel, Johnson (Gary), MacPhee, Malinski, Owens (Alvin), Persico, Rawlings, Rickman, Rivera, Rodriguez, Sax, Smith (Jerry T.), Stewart (Bryan), Thomas (Leonard Bryce), Thompson (Drew), Wills

Life

Abbott, Abercrombie, Abdur Rashid, Allen (Merritt Arnold), Bailey, Bell, Blom, Bolinski, Boorn, Brasic, Bruce, Burns, Bustamante, Campos, Campano, Caracappa, Corean, Coronel, Dailey, Deleon, Doan, Dorsey, Duvall, Eby, Elliott, Elmore, Epperly, Fannings, Faulkner, Ferrell, Flagner, Fontenot, Ford, Fountain, Freeby, Frey, Gambrell, Garner, Gilchrist, Grabbe, Grayer, Grissom, Guilford, Hall (Freddie), Haris (Raphello), Heflin, Henning, Hicks (Gary), Hinton, Hunt, James (Elijah), James (Reggie Carnell), Janto, Johnson (Gary), Koblan, Konigsberg, Kutz, Lamb (Damien James), Lankford, Leniart, Lentz, Lerch, Lettrich, Levine, Lewis (Carson), Luetgert, Lynch, MacKerley, Maner, Manson, March, Martell, Marquez, Mason, McDonald, McIlwain, Meeks, Merrow, Messick, Meyers, Mihajson, Miller, Montano, Moore (Antonio), Mora, Nauss, Neslund, Nowicki, O'Shields, Orona, Ouedraogo, Owens (Alvin), Owens (Rodney), Pann, Parker, Peel, Peeler, Phillips, Pyle, Ramsammy, Rawlings, Ream, Reddish, Rice, Riggins, Rivera, Rodriguez, Romano, Russell, Rutan, Salado, Scott (Albert Raymond), Shawkey, Smith (Jerry T.), Smith (Larry David), Sochor, Srout, Stephenson, Stewart (Doug), Suleski, Sullivan, Teigen, Tjeltveit, Tocker, Torres, Tovar, Trussell, Vickery, White (Steven Wayne), Wills, Zarabozo, Zarif, Zarinsky

Not Applicable

Baker, Bierenbaum, Clark (Michael Lubahn), Dickens, Dunford, Fisher (Jerry), Green, Head (Gary), Lesko, Libertowski, Mahaney, Martinez, Mays, Nelson, Rulloff, Scott (Robert Leonard Ewing), Smith (Eugene Marvin), Stobaugh

State Index

Cases are listed by defendant's last name. Note that all codefendants are listed, so the number of defendants does not equal the number of no-body trials held in that state.

Alabama

Cole, Glichrist, Gonzalez, Lewis (Carson), O'Shields, York

Alaska

Ibach, Kerwin, McDonald, Seaman, Smith (Billy D.)

Arizona

Anthony, Bach, Hall (Henry William), Ingersoll, Kiles, Payne, Philip, Prion, Roberts, Skaggs, Srout, Stewart (Bryan), Tocker, Velentini, Wilson, Zochowski

Arkansas

Derring, Hudspeth, Merrow, Peeler, Younger

California

Alcantara, Allen (Clarence), Alviso, Anderson (Craig), Anderson (Robert), Bannister, Barnes, Bechler, Beckett, Bennett, Bolinski, Bustamante, Carlotto, Carrasco, Clamp, Clark (Everett Drew), Clark (Kevin), Clark (Michael), Covain, Cowell, Crew, Cruz, Cullen, Cunningham, Dailey, Dalton, Davis (Bruce), Deleon, Demery, Dimascio, Fassler, Ford, Forsberg, Freeman, Garcia, Green, Grogan, Hansen, Herring, Hicks (Gary), Hunt, Jackson, Johnson (Gary), Jones (Jeffrey), Junt, Kennedy, Kent, Kirby, Koklich, Kovacich, Kretz, Levine, Lisowski, Mahaney, Manson, Martinez, Marquez, McMonigle, Mihajson, Monie, Mora, Morales, Ng, Nivarez, Prentice, Racz, Rader, Reiser, Scharf, Skuba, Roberson, Robinson (Tamara), Scott (Albert Raymond), Scott (Leonard Ewing), Shawkey, Smith (Larry David), Sparf, St. Clair, Stanley, Thomas (Bryce), Tibon, Tovar, Valot, Vasquez, Vickery, Von Vilas, Watson, Witte, York

Colorado

Sandoval, Smith (Eugene Marvin), Thompson (Aaron), Watter

Connecticut

Crafts, Estrella, Leniart

Delaware

Campano

District of Columbia

Austin, Barnett, Ruff, Sweet

Florida

Allen (Jason), Anderson (Richard), Ballard, Barrow, Crain, Crews, Docherty, Ezzell, Graham, Holt, James (Elijah), Koblan, Lewin, Mackerley, Meyers, Peel, Phillips, Ramsammy, Rodriguez, Roger, Sax, Sochor, Thomas (William), Thompson (Michael), White (Steven Wayne), Zarabozo

Georgia

Farraj, Fawaz, Grayer, Hinton, Lesko, McIlwain, Parker, Thrift, Wallace, White (Charles Thomas)

Hawaii

Awana, Coronel, Elmore, Janto (Frank), Lankford, Lawrence, Torres

Idaho

No trials

Illinois

Bailey, Campbell (John), Casciaro, Dianovsky, Faulkner, Gacy, Gilbert, Grabbe, Luetgert, Lyng, Montano, Nowicki, Null

Indiana

Campbell (Carl), Halcomb, Head (Gary), Jones (Michelle), Libertowski, Malinski, Mays, Vega, Whitesides

Iowa

Anderson (Terry)

Kansas

Kentucky

Louisiana

Maine

Maryland

Massachusetts

Michigan

Minnesota

Mississippi

Missouri

Montana

Martell, Moore (Larry)

Nebraska

Edwards, Stabler

Nevada

Messick, Tjeltveit, Watson

New Hampshire

No trials

New Jersey

Evans (Lee), Johnson (Brandon), Reddish, Watkins, Zarinsky

New Mexico

Gilliland, Lee (Oliver), Henning

New York

Adamson, Bierenbaum, Baker (David), Caracappa, Chrysler, Curro, DiCongilio, Eppolito, Fish, Guilford, Harris (Calvin), Hicks (Elias), Kimes, Konigsberg, Lent, Lewis (Martin), Lippe, Lipsky, Margolies, Nash, Persico, Pizzonia, Popal, Provenzano, Ruloff, Seifert, Weygandt, Wilhelms, Yaklvlev, Zarif

North Carolina

Abercrombie, Adams, Head (John), Mayse, Quick, Walker (Charles Anthony), Ward (Estil), Williams (Robert T.)

North Dakota

Bell

Ohio

Arnold, Barker (Harold), Bruce, Carroll, Christman, Doan, Dudley, Flagner, Forsythe, Kilbane, Nicely, Noser, Robinson (Gary), Williams (Augustus)

Oklahoma

Allen (Merritt Arnold), Brown (Nettie), Crider, Elliott, Fontenot, Leftridge, Meek, Rawlings, Rutan, Salado, Ward (Thomas Jesse)

Oregon

Abbott, Al-Wadud, Brown (Cornelius Lemonza), Gibson (Larry), Heflin, Lerch, Miller

Pennsylvania

Bradfield, Burns, Freeby, Frey, Harshman, Jones (Earl), Lettrich, Nause, Rivera, Sedlak, Smith (Jay C.), Swartout, Williams (Daniel Norman)

Rhode Island

Merola

South Carolina

Basham, Campbell, Carson, Fulks, Jones (Leon), Gambrell, Harmon, Lynch, Maner, McCullough, Richardson, Stephenson, Sullivan, Weston

South Dakota

Corean, Teigan

Tennessee

Bondurant, Dickens, James (Reggie Carnell), Lindsey, March, Rimmer

Texas

Bigham, Campos, Cearley, Fisher (Thomas), Fountain, Griffin, Hamilton, Jaggers, King (Jack Lee), McDuff, Munn, Negri, Orona, Owens, Shepherd, Smith (Jerry T.), Smith (Timothy), Stobaugh, Trejos, Williams (Jimmy Russell), Winder, Wynn, Zavala

Utah

Lodmell, Rebeterano

Vermont

Boorn

Virgin Islands

Harris (Raphello)

Virginia

Barker (Glenn), Dunford, Epperly, Gaudenzi, Hall (Freddie Lee), Hughes, Lentz, Russell, Schmerhorn, Wills

Washington

Eby, Hummel, Kemp, Lung, Mason, Neslund, Oakes, Price, Quillin, Schubert, Sherer, Thompson (Drew)

West Virginia

Ferrell, MacPhee

Wisconsin

Dahmer, Homberg, Kutz, Oelerich, Rickman, Zapata

Wyoming

Bush

Closing arguments in *California v. Hans Reiser.* (Courtesy of Vicki Behringer, Courtroomartist.com.)

Appendix A

No-Body Homicide Investigative Checklist*

Investigative Model

- ☐ Put in place an investigative team made up of both prosecutors and investigators.
- ☐ Methodology of investigating crime should be intelligence driven, and investigating officer should be able to clearly articulate the methodology on the witness stand.
- ☐ Quick response and clear delegation of investigator assignments according to each individual's strengths.
- ☐ Frequent, open communication and full disclosure between investigators and prosecutors.
- ☐ Designate a case manager to keep all of the paperwork and files for the case; frequently a case manager is a paralegal in the district attorney's office or administrative person in the detective's office.
- ☐ Conduct frequent briefings involving all key players in investigation to encourage free flow of information and leads.
- ☐ Meetings should be brief and to the point.
- ☐ Be open to brainstorming with all key personnel to encourage initiative.
- ☐ Be open to outsourcing tasks and asking for assistance from other agencies.
- ☐ Remember that personal animosity and petty rivalries must give way to the good of the case.
- ☐ Be unified in your communications with the victim's family.
- ☐ Understand that there will not always be agreement between team members or the investigative and prosecution teams. Often the best way to move forward emerges through discussion and respect for one another's knowledge and experience.
- ☐ Make sure all team members keep current on reports.

* Many thanks to the Honorable Garen Horst, Superior Court of California, and Detective Don Murchison, Placer County Sheriff's Office, for drafting the original versions of these lists. They investigated and prosecuted the case of *People v. Mario Garcia* in 2007 and have remained interested in no-body homicides ever since.

Circumstances of Disappearance

- ☐ Was it sudden? Was it suspicious?
- ☐ Was it normal pattern of behavior for victim?

Immediate Time-Sensitive Issues

- ☐ Canvass area for witnesses, evidence.
- ☐ Canvass immediate area and entrance/egress points for video surveillance. (Footage may be erased or overwritten daily.)
- ☐ Contact victim's cell phone company immediately to track cell phone, which may be with victim, via "pinging." (Pinging information may be available for only hours.)
- ☐ Contact appropriate company if victim's vehicle is equipped with LoJack, OnStar, BMW Assist, or other GPS tracking abilities.
- ☐ Obtain a recent photograph of the victim to use on search posters and in the media. Be certain to use a photograph that best resembles the victim today even if the family wants a more endearing or "nicer" picture.

Search Effort for Victim

- ☐ Create a master plan for search efforts for both private and public efforts.
- ☐ Consider use of canines, helicopters, and mounted patrol.
- ☐ Create a master search log and keep track of times, locations, areas searched, and resources used, including man hours.
- ☐ Areas searched should be based on evidence.
- ☐ Send out press release on anniversary of victim's disappearance.
- ☐ Use TV, radio, and print media to help locate victim.
- ☐ Use Internet web pages such as YouTube, Facebook, and missing persons websites with pictures of victim and links to law enforcement websites.
- ☐ Keep a file with articles, stories, and logs of the times stories on victim are aired on TV and radio.
- ☐ Develop a protocol for taking tips and following up on leads from the public. It is essential that all tips be tracked, and follow up on those tips recorded.
- ☐ Develop a system for dealing with psychics
  Should they all be documented? Should any be followed up on?
- ☐ Use a tracking program to track tips and link them together.

Contact Victim's Work, Friends, Family, and People Significant to the Victim

- ☐ Contact spouse, significant other, previous partners.
- ☐ Interview people victim worked with, ask about the victim's job, routine, behavior. Has the victim missed work before?
- ☐ Identify friends, family, and other significant people and contact them.
- ☐ Were there people, belongings, or pets that the victim cared about and wouldn't leave?
- ☐ How often did victim remain in contact with those people?
- ☐ How often did victim communicate with these people, e-mail, text, home or cell phone calls, Sprint Direct Connect, face to face, instant message, voice over Internet protocol (VOIP), and letters or notes?
- ☐ Was it unusual for victim to disappear without communication?
- ☐ How frequent did victim remain in contact, and is it unusual for them not to hear from victim?
- ☐ Contact everyone in victim's address book, e-mail lists, home phone directory, cell phone directory, and instant message list.
- ☐ Ask everyone you contact to notify you immediately if they hear from victim and provide them with your contact information.

State-of-Mind Evidence

- ☐ Identify those in contact with victim leading up to disappearance.
- ☐ Ask for and obtain any recent voice messages, e-mails, letters and notes, and instant messages from victim prior to disappearance.
- ☐ Obtain and examine victim's personal calendar, Blackberry, smartphone, diary, and computer.
- ☐ Interview victim's neighbors regarding their recent observations, habits of victim, and anything unusual.
- ☐ What were victim's activities leading up to disappearance?
- ☐ What was victim's demeanor, mental state, intentions, plans?
- ☐ What events in the future was the victim planning for?
- ☐ What steps did the victim take towards his/her plans toward the future?
- ☐ Document any significant missed events that victim missed post-disappearance.
- ☐ Was there any indication that victim was suicidal?
- ☐ Was there any indication victim wanted to disappear, assume a new identity?
- ☐ Was there any indication victim was scared, threatened, or running away from someone?

- ☐ Obtain any recent photos, recordings, video evidence of victim that reflects on mental state.

Personal Items Left Behind

- ☐ What everyday items were left behind, such as wallet, purse, car, medicine, clothes, toiletries, eyeglasses, contacts, and important documents? If so, photograph and collect.
- ☐ Obtain items such as hairbrushes, toothbrushes, curling irons or any other items that may contain the victim's DNA for comparison at a later date if needed. (Have a different detective than the one processing the crime scene collect the above items to minimize contamination or transfer of evidence arguments at trial.)
- ☐ Determine if any treasured items, such as photos, pets, heirlooms, and good luck charms, any things important to the victim have been left behind and if so, document and photograph.

Telephone Records

- ☐ Examine cell phone if found for recent incoming/outgoing calls or Direct Connects, texts, instant messages, internet activity, or e-mails.
- ☐ Obtain a search warrant to examine phone records to include incoming/outgoing calls, texts, Direct Connect communications, internet browsing, instant messages, and cell tower information.
- ☐ Call everyone on phone list leading up to disappearance.
- ☐ Obtain phone records at least six months prior to disappearance to review patterns of communication and to aid in determining frequency of calls, persons called or calling locations where victim frequently visited through cell tower records.
- ☐ Consider keeping the victim's cell phone account active to monitor incoming voice messages and monitor incoming call history.

Financial Information and Records

- ☐ Identify all sources of income, bank accounts, credit cards, and access to funds.
- ☐ Make contact with an individual at any of victim's financial institutions who can monitor activity for you.
- ☐ Obtain search warrant and examine records for any activity and consider going back at least six months for historical information.
- ☐ Consider keeping account open with limited funds to track potential location of victim or suspect information.

- ☐ Did victim have access to significant funds to disappear?
- ☐ Any evidence that funds were taken out upon disappearance?
- ☐ Was money left behind in the account?
- ☐ Does the victim have any unclaimed assets left behind, such as workers' compensation, retirement, disability, bank account proceeds, tax return refund, and ownership in real estate?
- ☐ Obtain credit reports from all three major credit agencies.

E-Mail Accounts

- ☐ Obtain a search warrant and examine records for any logging in by account holder post disappearance, keep accounts current through trial.
- ☐ Obtain search warrants for e-mails before victim's disappearance and after.
- ☐ Review contacts list for addresses to contact.
- ☐ Have a skilled computer forensic expert examine the victim's computer to determine if the victim had any "secret" e-mail accounts not know to family and friends.

Obtain Victim's Computer

- ☐ Begin forensic analysis for e-mails, content documents, and websites visited, instant messaging.
- ☐ Any indication that victim was attempting to disappear, or change identity?
- ☐ Any indication of threats, enemies, or problems?
- ☐ Examine for state of mind evidence.

Missing Persons Investigation

- ☐ APBs, BOLOs: document all activities done.
- ☐ Critical reach bulletins with current picture of victim—distribute and document.
- ☐ Be sure distribution lists are documented and complete, confirm receipt.
- ☐ Check all hospitals (medical and psychiatric), jails, shelters in area.
- ☐ Check local and nearby coroner's offices for possible unidentified dead bodies.
- ☐ Run victim in DMV and state law enforcement databases such as WALES, and CLETS.
- ☐ Enter victim information in NCIC.

- ☐ Procure evidence that could contain victim's DNA and also obtain DNA from close relatives particularly mother and father if possible (e.g., toothbrush, hairbrush, comb, workout clothes, gloves, water bottles, mouthwash bottles).
- ☐ Submit victim's DNA to CODIS.
- ☐ Consider making and storing a scent pad for possible canine tracking.
- ☐ Develop contacts in U.S. Department of Homeland Security to access their databases.
- ☐ Determine if any record of travel by victim in taxis, airline (AFIS), and ocean liner.
- ☐ Contact State Department for passport information.
- ☐ Ask family and friends if victim had a passport, driver's license, or other forms of identification.
- ☐ Notify private missing persons organizations of disappearance, such as North American Missing Person Network, National Center for Missing Adults, and The Carol Sund/Carrington Memorial Reward Foundation.
- ☐ Run victim in private databases such as Accurint, or Lexis/Nexis.
- ☐ Contact local employment bureaus for to see if victim took new job and is paying state taxes.

Do a Complete Victimology

- ☐ Obtain employment, residence, and schooling history.
- ☐ What financial obligations did the victim have?
- ☐ What were victim's habits, hobbies, rituals, personality, and strengths and weaknesses?
- ☐ Contact medical providers for information.
- ☐ Identify and interview victim's physician, therapist, and counselor.

Appendix B

One of the most common questions I get from police and prosecutors is whether I know of any successful no-body cases that have facts like mine. Although I have had a table of no-body trials for many years listed on my website, www.nobody-murdercases.com, the table provides only a brief description of each case and does not contain enough information about the quantum of evidence put forth at trial. In order to help investigators and prosecutors find cases that are similar to ones they are investigating, with this appendix I have greatly expanded on the table by summarizing and attempting to list the evidence that was used in each trial. By reviewing the cases, you can look for cases similar to the case you are investigating and look at prior cases in your jurisdiction and state. In addition, I have added categories to each case so that you can more quickly look for cases similar to yours by looking at all cases with confessions, for example. Any case that has no keywords (N/A) means it was a case with little traditional evidence and might prove to be especially useful if you have a similarly tough case. One cautionary note: These brief reviews may not capture all of the evidence put forth at a trial. Also, I was limited by what I could find either online, in appellate cases, talking to the police and prosecutors about that particular case, or from my own knowledge of the case. Any case that seems similar to yours should be researched in depth (starting by using the listed sources) to see how closely it fits with your case. I hope these summaries can narrow the universe of cases closest to yours and help you focus only on the cases that have similar fact patterns and evidence.

Note that when Wikipedia or Murderpedia is cited as a source, you search for that particular case by the defendant's name. However, if the Charley Project is listed as a source, you search for that case by the victim's name at www.charleyproject.org. It is hard to overstate what a phenomenal source of information the Charley Project is on cold cases and no-body murders. Meaghan Good is amazing, and I am proud to call her a friend.

Categories

The following keywords can be used to search for cases with evidence similar to your case. (Cases are organized by keyword in the keyword index.) I have categorized all of the case by one or more of the following ten keywords: codefendant testimony, confession to friends and family, confession to police, death penalty, eyewitness, forensics evidence: DNA, forensics. Others include (fiber and fingerprints, etc.), informant, life or not applicable (meaning none of the prior categories apply).

Codefendant testimony
Confession to friends and family
Confession to police
Death penalty
Eyewitness
Forensic evidence: DNA
Forensic evidence: Other
Informant
Life
Not applicable (N/A)

No-Body Murder Trials: Case Summaries (399)

Defendant: **First Name Last Name**
Victim: First Name Last Name
Trial: Month, Year Jurisdiction: County or City, State
Murder: Exact date if known
Evidence: Concise summary of evidence admitted at trial. Verdict and sentence.
Sources: Author's last name, first initial, "Title of the story or headline," *Name of publication*, Date
Keywords: **From list above**

Case 1

Defendant: **Joel Terrence Abbott**
Victim: Carolann Payne
Trial: March 1993 Jurisdiction: Oregon
Murder: August 1985
Evidence: Grandmother of victim, who was defendant's girlfriend, testified that she had not heard from the victim since early 1985. Victim did not have a fixed address, bank accounts, or credit cards. Prosecutor proved victim was dead by showing victim had not had any run-ins with law enforcement, her Social Security number had never been used, and she had made no financial transactions. Friends and acquaintances of defendant testified that he had a violent temper with women. A friend of defendant was a police informant and secretly tape-recorded defendant saying that he had shot victim with a rifle in the back and head and buried her where no one would find her. Defendant also confessed to his ex-wife. Defendant sentenced to 25 years to life.
Sources: Bolt, G., "Murder charges approved," *The Bulletin*, September 11, 1992; Bolt, G., "Family says victim has disappeared," *The Bulletin*, February 26, 1993
Keywords: **Informant, Confession to friends and family, Life**

Case 2

Defendant: **Donald Lewis Abercrombie**
Victims: Hoyle Smith and Margie Shaw
Trial: February 1997 Jurisdiction: Lee County, North Carolina
Murder: November 4, 1995
Evidence: Victims Smith and Shaw were boyfriend and girlfriend. Blood found in Smith's house tied defendant to the murders. House was burglarized and defendant pleaded guilty to burglary before being charged with murder. Defendant confessed to murder. Victims were supposedly buried in woods. Defendant convicted of first-degree murder. Death penalty sought but given life.
Sources: Charley Project; Briansdreams.com (Under victim Hoyle Smith)
Keywords: **Forensic evidence: DNA, Confession to police, Life**

Case 3

Defendants: **Hobart Adams, Lori Mayse, Estil Ward**
Victim: Robert Mayse
Trial: 1988 Jurisdiction: Alexander County, North Carolina
Murder: November 1986
Evidence: Mayse and Ward testified against Adams and all three were convicted. Body was allegedly thrown in dumpster. Ward supposedly practiced satanic rituals, which was why murder occurred.
Sources: "Ward Sentence: Life plus 12," *Daily News*, January 13, 1988; "Mayse Trial Delayed," *The Dispatch*, October 15, 1987
Keywords: **Codefendant testimony**

Case 4

Defendant: **Stacy Adamson**
Victim: Daniel Jamison
Trial: April 2004 Jurisdiction: Schenectady, New York
Murder: February 1, 2003
Evidence: Defendant was pimp and met victim when he came to have sex with teenaged prostitute. When victim could not perform, defendant and prostitute beat him to death and dumped body in Queens. During the prolonged beating, defendant used victim's car and cell phone. Police retrieved garbage bags full of bloodied evidence, and the house had signs of bleach cleaning. Defendants fled to Texas and were located through defendant's GPS. Defendant apparently believed victim was a cop and wanted to have evidence he had sex with teen to prove he was not a cop. Both the prostitute and defendant's wife testified against him. All three confessed to varying levels of culpability. Defendant convicted of first-degree murder.
Source: fightcrimecase.com, *People v. Stacey J. Adamson*, NY State Supreme Court, (3d. Dept. 2007)
Keywords: **Informant, Confession to police, Forensic evidence: Other**

Case 5

Defendant: **Al-Wadud Abdur Rashid**
Victim: Yolanda Panek
Trial: March 1996 Jurisdiction: Portland, Oregon

Murder: July 1995

Evidence: Defendant and victim were married at common law and their 2-year-old son was found in victim's car near bus and train depot. Defendant and victim had checked into motel and blood-stained sheets were found in room. There was a prior history of domestic abuse and defendant had threatened to slit throat of victim. Defendant arrested one week after disappearance in California. Defendant convicted of first-degree murder and sentenced to life.

Source: "Man arraigned in death of girlfriend," *Eugene Register-Guardian*, July 23, 1995

Keywords: **Forensic evidence: DNA, Life**

Case 6

Defendant: **John Alcantara**

Victim: Robert Bennett

Trial: March 2008 Jurisdiction: Whittier, California

Murder: February 1983

Evidence: Victim was last seen in his truck with coworker defendant. Large amount of victim's blood was found near sanitation plant where they worked, on shovel, and in dump truck. Victim and defendant had clashed before, and victim had denied defendant a promotion to foreman, which angered defendant. Defendant threatened another coworker, and the threat was reported to victim the day before his disappearance. Victim had said he would confront defendant the day before murder. Prosecutors lacked evidence in case until coworker came forward in 2004 and said defendant had confessed to murder in 2000. Defendant's ex-wife also said he confessed. Defendant is believed to have shot victim in head and dismembered him. A third coworker, who died in 1997, is alleged to have dumped body in landfill. Searches of landfills were unsuccessful. Defendant convicted of first-degree murder.

Sources: Charley Project; Gonzales, R., "Jury finds John Alcantara guilty in '83 slaying," *Whittier Daily News*, March 11, 2008

Keywords: **Confession to friends and family**

Case 7

Defendant: **Clarence Allen**

Victim: Mary Kitts

Trial: November 1977 Jurisdiction: Fresno, California

Murder: June 29, 1974

Evidence: Defendant ordered the murder of victim because he believed she was "snitching" on him regarding a burglary of a store he had committed. Defendant strangled victim and threw her body into the Friant-Kern Canal. The store owner's son testified against defendant at trial and stated that the keys to the store had been taken from his pocket before the burglary while he was swimming at the defendant's house. Victim later confessed to this witness that defendant had burgled the store. The witness confronted defendant's son, who admitted that he and his father had committed the crime. Defendant then ordered the murder of victim. Defendant convicted of first-degree murder and was given the death penalty for three other murders of witnesses who had testified against him in the Kitts trial.

Sources: Wikipedia; Charley Project

Keywords: **Death penalty**

Case 8

Defendant: **Jason Allen**

Victim: Yalitza Garcia

Trial: October 2013 Jurisdiction: Broward County, Florida

Murder: July 4/5, 2009

Evidence: Defendant and victim were dating and had a 2-year-old son. After victim disappeared, defendant was found at her apartment by coworkers of victim looking for her. Large amounts of victim's blood and clean up efforts were also discovered. Also found at her apartment, where she had moved due to fights with defendant, were her wallet, phone, purse and keys. There was also evidence that the couple had fought over custody of their son. Victim had $20,000 in her bank account from an insurance settlement that had been deposited the day before. Defendant admitted withdrawing $1,400 from the account after her disappearance. Defendant was convicted of second-degree murder.

Sources: Olmeda, R., "Man convicted of killing missing girlfriend," *Sun-Sentinel*, October 11, 2013; http://www.sheriff.org/posts/post.cfm?id=2b8b9971-2ded-452d-bd44-a0105f1eefc6

Keywords: **Forensic evidence: DNA**

Case 9

Defendant: **Merritt Arnold Allen**

Victim: Henry Copeland

Trial: 1985 Jurisdiction: Wagoner County, Oklahoma

Murder September 11, 1984

Evidence: Victim was the boyfriend of defendant's stepdaughter. Witness heard loud sounds described as car doors slamming or pots banging on day of disappearance. Defendant borrowed ex-wife's car and later she saw him at his father's property near lake covered in blood and dirt. Car was eventually sold after being in storage and was missing seat fabric, door panel, and floor mats, and carpet in trunk had been removed. Defendant did not show up for work for two days after victim went missing. Defendant told ex-wife he had shot and killed victim and asked her to help with getting rid of body. Defendant showed stepdaughter a spent bullet and said victim would not bother her anymore. (Victim had history of abuse toward stepdaughter.) Defendant admitted to both ex-wife and stepdaughter he had shot victim six times with a .38 when victim was sleeping in his car. Ex-wife spoke to police and permitted them to "bug" her house. Defendant again admitted what he had done. Defendant allegedly burned body. Defendant was convicted of first-degree murder and given life.

Source: *Allen v. State*, 803 P.2d 1145 (1990)

Keywords: **Confession to friends and family, Life**

Case 10

Defendants: **Jose Maria Alviso and Pacheco Alviso**
Victim: John Ruhland
Trial: 1879 Jurisdiction: Monterey County, California
Murder: February 1879
Evidence: Defendants were brothers who came to victim's house in February 1839. Victim was living with another man named Juan Valdez. Defendants came looking for victim and told Valdez to leave because they were "taking a bad step." As Valdez was packing to leave, victim arrived and Jose Maria confronted him with a pistol. Jose Maria told his brother to tie the victim up but victim ran. As his brother ran to catch him, Jose Maria shot victim in the eye and back. Defendants told Valdez to leave and told him not to tell anyone. Later that day, two boys walking past victim's house saw a large fire near his cabin and saw both defendants. One of the defendants told his wife that victim had given him and his brother sheep. They put sheep in the mountains and sold the wool. The men were arrested and Pacheco told his wife that Jose Maria had shot victim and burned the body. He also admitted that he had seen Valdez and the two boys passing by the cabin. A search of a scorched tree revealed small bones that could not be identified as human. Pacheco lied about where victim was when he and his brother sheared the sheep and sold the wool. Both men were convicted of murder.
Source: *California v. Alviso*, 55 Cal. 230 (1880)
Keywords: **Eyewitness, Confession to friends and family, Forensic evidence: Other**

Case 11

Defendant: **Craig Anderson**
Victim: Denise Redlick
Trial: May 1986 Jurisdiction: San Mateo, California
Murder: November 11, 1985
Evidence: Defendant was engaged to victim before she broke it off. He rented a van to follow her and abducted her outside a restaurant where she had had lunch with a friend. Blood found in the van was same type as victim's blood. Defendant claimed he had cut himself in the van. (Note this was before the existence of DNA testing.) Janet Parker Back wrote a book on the case called *Too Good To Be True*. At first parole hearing in 2001, defendant confessed to murdering victim. Defendant convicted of first-degree murder and given 25 years to life.
Source: http://www.sanbrunobart.com/news/2007/05/01/denise-redlick-denied-parole
Keywords: **Forensic evidence: Other**

Case 12

Defendant: **Richard Anderson**
Victim: Robert Grantham
Trial: February 1988 Jurisdiction: Hillsborough County, Florida
Murder: May 7, 1987

Evidence: Defendant agreed to let victim spend one night with his girlfriend for $10,000 but planned to rob him instead. Defendant shot victim four times in head from back seat while victim was driving victim's car and defendant's girlfriend was in front seat. Two witnesses testified that defendant admitted scheme to them, and defendant's girlfriend testified against him. The .22 caliber casings found in victim's car matched gun recovered from river near bridge where girlfriend told police defendant had thrown murder weapon. Jailhouse informant testified that defendant offered him money to kill his girlfriend after he knew she was cooperating with police. Defendant was convicted of first-degree murder and sentenced to death.
Source: Murderpedia.org
Keywords: **Confession to friends and family, Forensic evidence: Other, Informant, Codefendant testimony, Death penalty**

Case 13

Defendant: **Robert Anderson**
Victim: Margaret Armstrong
Trial: May 1999 Jurisdiction: Eureka, California
Murder: 1994
Evidence: Defendant and codefendant kidnapped and killed victim because they thought she had molested two children. After being beaten by a mob, defendants put victim in sleeping bag bound with duct tape and put in trunk of codefendant's car. Witnesses saw defendant hand rock to codefendant, who hit victim with rock. Defendant then dropped small boulder on her head. Victim was thrown into ravine and codefendant told witness he had stepped on her neck until it "crunched." Codefendant testified against defendant. Defendant testified and blamed codefendant for murder but admitted he was present and participated in limited fashion. On appeal defendant argued he had committed murder under duress from codefendant, but California Supreme Court rejected this defense. Defendant was convicted of first-degree murder.
Source: *People v. Anderson*, 28 Cal. 4th 767 (2002)
Keywords: **Codefendant testimony**

Case 14

Defendant: **Terry Andersen**
Victim: Douglas Churchill
Trial: 1998 Jurisdiction: Council Bluffs, Iowa
Murder: January 1998
Evidence: Witnesses saw defendant shoot victim, and DNA belonging to victim was found near river. It is believed that victim was dismembered before being thrown into river. Defendant was convicted.
Sources: "Prosecuting Murder Without a Body," WOWT, March 20, 2007; http://projectjason.org/forums/topic/26-assumed-deceased-jessica-ogrady-ne-5102006/page-2
Keywords: **Forensic evidence: DNA, Eyewitness**

Case 15

Defendant: **David Anthony**
Victims: Donna Anthony, Danielle Romero, Richard Romero
Trial: April 2002 Jurisdiction: Phoenix, Arizona
Murder: July 2001
Evidence: Defendant accused of killing his wife and her two children from a previous marriage to cover up defendant's alleged sexual abuse of Danielle Romero. Danielle's blood and defendant's semen was found on mattress in defendant's home. Blood from all three victims also found in his house, including on master bedroom wall, a concrete slab under the carpet of the office, the doorframe of Danielle's bedroom, Danielle's bed, Richard's bed, and on the bed liner of Donna's pickup truck. Defendant lied to police about the state of his marriage and had engaged in financial misconduct in the business he and Donna owned. In the months before the murders, defendant moved large sums of money out of a joint account and into a private account and made threatening statements to others toward his wife and her children. Donna and children were supposed to fly from Phoenix to Ohio but never made flight. Shortly after, Donna's PIN for her bank account was changed, defendant arranged to buy a new truck, and defendant arranged for a carpet cleaner to come to the house. (Carpet cleaner helped the defendant remove an old mattress from the house and said defendant told him a dog had bled on carpet.) After murder, defendant bought new mattress and gave store false name and address. Defendant also purchased a new clothes washer, dryer, and vacuum cleaner. He also had house cleaners come to the house. Police recovered Pine-Sol, rubber surgical gloves, two knives, and a .38 revolver that were hidden in an air vent in the house. Both house and Donna's truck showed extensive evidence of a cleanup. The bodies of all three victims were found in trash drums hidden under trees 40 miles from Phoenix three years after trial. Defendant's initial conviction for first-degree murder in 2002 was reversed because prosecution improperly used child molestation evidence. Defendant was convicted again in August 2012 of first-degree murder and died of natural causes on death row in December 2012.
Sources: Murderpedia; *Arizona v. Anthony*, 189 P.3d 366 (AZ 2008)
Keywords: **Forensic evidence: DNA, Death penalty**

Case 16

Defendants: **Elias and Arthur Arnold**
Victim: Melvin Charles Horst
Trial: 1929 Jurisdiction: Orrville, Ohio
Murder: December 27, 1928
Evidence: Victim, who was 4 years old, was playing with friends when he announced he needed to go home and left. His house was one block away, but he never arrived, although a toy wagon he had had with him was found in his front yard. A massive search ensued and there was national publicity for the case. Defendant Elias, a bootlegger, and his son were arrested and charged with murder six days after the disappearance. The basis of arrest was that defendant, who had spent time in jail for bootlegging, had a grudge against the victim's uncle, who

was the town marshal and a strict enforcer of Prohibition, and that an 8-year-old and 9-year-old testified that they saw victim being lured into defendant's house, which was around the corner from victim's house. After defendant's conviction, authorities determined that one of the witnesses could not have seen what he said he saw, and the defendants were granted a new trial. Both were acquitted at second trial. Father of victim was later accused of murder and allegedly confessed to police, but confession was found to have been coerced by police. The murder was never officially solved.

Source: Charley Project

Keywords: **Eyewitness**

Case 17

Defendant: **Barbara Asher**

Victim: Mark Lord

Trial: January 2006 Jurisdiction: Quincy, Massachusetts

Murder: July 3, 2000

Evidence: Defendant was a professional dominatrix who was accused of manslaughter when victim suffered a heart attack while strapped to a replica medieval torture device. Defendant admitted to police victim had died and that she and her boyfriend had dismembered the body and thrown it into a dumpster. The boyfriend cut up the body in the bathtub with a hacksaw. Her confession was only evidence in case, as there was no DNA nor proof of disposal of body. There were phone records that showed contact between defendant and victim the day of the murder. A landfill was searched, but no evidence was found. Defendant was acquitted of manslaughter.

Source: Murderpedia

Keywords: **Confession to police**

Case 18

Defendant: **Harold Austin**

Victim: Marion Fye

Trial: January 2006 Jurisdiction: Washington, DC

Murder: November 2003

Evidence: Defendant shot victim, his girlfriend, during an argument in victim's house. Five children were in house at the time of murder, including three of victim's children. Children heard shots and one saw defendant cleaning a gun afterwards. Blood on victim's mattress was tied to victim through her mother's DNA, because prosecution did not have victim's DNA. Defendant also made fraudulent insurance claim while driving victim's car after her murder. Defendant confessed to police that he was in fight with victim, she pulled gun on him, and while wrestling it away from her, it went off and killed her. Defendant said he put her body in garbage bags and put her in a dumpster behind popular restaurant. Defendant convicted of second-degree murder and sentenced to 42 years in prison.

Source: Thomas A. (Tad) DiBiase

Keywords: **Confession to police, Forensic evidence: DNA, Eyewitness**

Case 19

Defendant: **Gregory Awana**
Victim: Yorck Woita
Trial: December 2004 Jurisdiction: Hawaii
Murder: August 2003
Evidence: Defendant was an investigator for the Honolulu Medical Examiner's Office and before that a deputy sheriff. Defendant and victim were partners in a marijuana business before defendant backed out to grow with other partners. During the course of an argument about profits victim felt defendant owed him, defendant shot him. Defendant eventually confessed to police, telling them that during the argument, victim grabbed a .22 Baretta pistol that defendant kept in a drawer. He threatened defendant, and a struggle over the gun ensued. Victim was shot in the head three times. Defendant then panicked and burned victim's car. Defendant borrowed a boat, weighed victim's body down with a chain, and tossed it, along with the Baretta, into a bay. Defendant cleaned house with Clorox and flushed two of the three shell casings down the toilet. Defendant found guilty of second-degree murder.
Source: *Hawaii v. Awana*, #27145, Intermediate Court of Appeals, April 13, 2007
Keywords: **Confession to police**

Case 20

Defendant: **Jeremy Bach**
Victim: Brad Hansen
Trial: November 1997 Jurisdiction: Phoenix, Arizona
Murder: November 10, 1995
Evidence: Defendant, who was 13 years old, was charged as an adult in killing of victim, also 13 years old. Defendant confessed to police, telling them that he had accidently shot victim in the chest when the two boys were playing with two guns that belonged to defendant's father. Police believe he actually shot victim on purpose over dispute over a girl, and defendant admitted it took over an hour for victim to die, during which he had not called for help. Defendant said he placed victim's body into 90-gallon trash container where it was picked up and emptied automatically by city trash truck. Police searched landfill for two months and $100,000 cost, but to no avail. Victim's blood was found in defendant's kitchen and a trash container, which had two inches of blood and body fluids. Two handguns were recovered as well. Defendant had told a cousin he had killed a boy. Before the murder, defendant told a teacher he was going to kill the victim for "stealing" his girl and asked questions about bleeding to death. Defendant, 15 years old at the time of trial, was found guilty of second-degree murder and sentenced to 22 years.
Sources: "Boy recounts to police how he shot friend with father's gun," *Arizona Daily Wildcat*, April 8, 1996; Charley Project
Keywords: **Confession to police, Forensic evidence: Other**

Case 21

Defendant: **Richard Bailey**
Victim: Helen Vorhees Brach
Trial: July 1994 Jurisdiction: Chicago, Illinois
Murder: February 21, 1977
Evidence: Victim was heir to the candy fortune of her deceased husband, Frank Brach. She disappeared when she was supposed to be flying from the Mayo Clinic in Minnesota to her home in Chicago. Her "houseman" said he picked her up at O'Hare Airport and then dropped her off there again four days later for a flight to Florida. The victim was a "telephone addict" but did not call anyone during those four days and she did not have any luggage with her for her trip to Florida. The houseman, an ex-con, cashed checks worth $15,000 that he alleged were written by victim, but when this was disproved, he said he had written them with her permission because she had injured her hand. Handwriting analysis showed he had not signed the checks. The houseman's wife told police a different story, saying her husband had waited in Illinois for the victim to return from the Mayo Clinic. During that period, the houseman had the carpeting replaced in one room of victim's house and had two rooms repainted. The pink Cadillac he drove for her was also cleaned, waxed, and the interior shampooed. He did not report her missing for two weeks and destroyed her diaries. Lie detector tests taken by the houseman were inconclusive. The houseman, however, was never charged with murder. The victim's "boyfriend," a n'er-do-well con man named Richard Bailey, was ultimately tried for numerous counts of fraud and conspiracy to commit murder. Bailey conned elderly women into buying horses as investments and swindled them. Police believe victim realized that the defendant was a con man and was about to expose him. She had hired an independent horse appraiser who had told her that she had overpaid for the horses she had invested in. Bailey was convicted of numerous counts, but not murder. He was sentenced to life, which was later reduced to 30 years.
Sources: Charley Project; Wikipedia
Keywords: **Life**

Case 22

Defendants: **David Baker aka William Brown, George Matthews, William Webster**
Victim: Walter A. Nicoll
Trial: December 1843 Jurisdiction: New York County, New York
Murder: July 14 or 15, 1843
Evidence: The victim was a ship's mate on the *Sarah Lavinia* who was tossed overboard. One of the earliest no body cases.
Source: *United States v. Brown*, Case No. 14,656a (SDNY)
Keywords: **N/A**

Case 23

Defendant: **Roy Ballard**
Victim: Autumn Marie Traub

Trial: July 2008 Jurisdiction: Zephyrhills, Florida
Murder: September 13, 2006
Evidence: Defendant murdered his stepdaughter who was trying to prevent him from getting custody of her 14-year-old daughter whom the defendant was allegedly abusing. Defendant met with victim on day of murder, and police found plastic bags with victim's blood on them and a roll of duct tape with blood. Police also found sex toys in defendant's car with DNA from the 14-year-old girl. Defendant admitted to cellmate that he had murdered victim, telling him he had hit her in head with pipe, broken her teeth, and put body in acidic water. Police recovered receipt from hardware store for 18-inch pipe and duct tape. Police also recovered a shovel that defendant said he needed in his job as a maintenance supervisor, but the dirt on shovel was not consistent with dirt from his workplace. Cell tower records showed defendant was in rural area the day before and the day of victim's disappearance. Defendant was convicted of first-degree murder and sentenced to death, but his sentence was later reduced to life without parole.
Sources: Geary, J., "Jury Urges Death for Ballard in Murder," *The Ledger*, July 25, 2008; Charley Project
Keywords: **Forensic evidence: DNA, Informant, Death penalty**

Case 24

Defendant: **William Bannister**
Victim: April Anne Cooper
Trial: December 1998 Jurisdiction: Rancho, California
Murder: December 1986
Evidence: Defendant was babysitting the victim, who was 6 years old, when she disappeared. Defendant said he gave her $5 and she went to an arcade. He showed up at his father's wedding the next day in dirty clothes and told people he had been participating in the search for April, something that was not true. The defendant left the wedding early and his father told his bride that "William has done it again." This was a reference to the defendant's previous conviction in 1978 for murdering his girlfriend. In 1995 he was charged with this victim's murder. His son testified that defendant told him victim was dead and that she had fallen and broken her neck while they were hiking. He was convicted of murder and sentenced to life without parole.
Source: Charley Project
Keywords: **Confession to friends and family**

Case 25

Defendant: **Glenn Barker**
Victim: Katherine Sybil Worsky
Trial: January 1983 Jurisdiction: Charlottesville, Virginia
Murder: July 12, 1982
Evidence: Victim, 12 years old, was sleeping over at a friend's house. Defendant had dated the mother of victim's friend, at whose house she was sleeping over. Defendant admitted to police he had been at house that night and said he had given victim and another girl some

beer. He told police he left the house after everyone had gone to bed. Police searched his house and found hidden wet blood-stained men's clothing. Some of the blood was the same as defendant's type and some was the same as victim's. (Victim's blood was typed from menstrual blood on her sheets.) Police also found in the defendant's sock drawer a rolled up pair of girl's underwear, which had a small stain of blood consistent with the area where victim injected insulin. Blood of victim's type was also found on the living room rug and on the coffee table of the house where victim had slept. Police believed defendant got victim drunk, molested her, and then killed her. Defendant was convicted of second-degree murder and sentenced to 18 years.

Source: Charley Project

Keywords: **Forensic evidence: Other**

Case 26

Defendant: **Harold Barker**

Victim: Shelly Turner

Trial: August 2009 Jurisdiction: Montgomery County, Ohio

Murder: September 30, 2006

Evidence: Defendant said he was with victim, his fiancée, when she started talking to a man named Bill. Victim got into car with Bill after handing defendant her engagement ring and he never saw her again. At trial, government presented evidence from two friends of defendant to whom he confessed murder. To one he said he punched victim in the throat by accident and then buried her in weeds and burned her clothes. To other he said he cut her up and buried her in a barrel. A bartender from where victim was last seen testified that shortly before victim's disappearance, defendant said he was going to do something bad that would send him back to jail. Evidence of death included that victim's bank account was untouched, she left behind all personal possession except for a bank card and was close to her family, including two young sons. Victim had future plans including finding a church to attend and had purchased pumpkins to carve for Halloween. Defendant convicted of felony murder.

Sources: Charley Project; *State v. Barker*, 191 Ohio App.3d 293 (2010)

Keywords: **Confession to friends and family**

Case 27

Defendant: **Michael John Barnes**

Victim: Dawn Renee Peitz

Trial: January 1999 Jurisdiction: Placerville, California

Murder: December 14, 1997

Evidence: Defendant's parents were initially charged with trying to destroy evidence of murder before defendant was charged with murder. Authorities believed defendant's car was used in murder and later cleaned by parents. Defendant testified at parent's trial and eventually admitted to murder. Mother was acquitted but father found guilty of being accessory to murder. Defendant then convicted of second-degree murder. Victim's purse was found on I-680. Victim's skull was found five years later one half mile from area where defendant had told police to search in effort to help his parents.

Source: Lee, H., and Stannard, B, "Skull confirms old murder verdict," SFgate.com, March 2, 2002

Keywords: **Confession to police**

Case 28

Defendant: **Terrence Barnett**

Victim: Yolanda Baker

Trial: March 2010 Jurisdiction: Washington, DC

Murder: July 31, 1999

Evidence: Defendant and victim had twin 5-year-olds together and a history of domestic violence. Victim was seeking child support from defendant at the time of her disappearance, and a court had ordered defendant to pay child support. Victim and defendant attended a party and then left together in the victim's car. Victim was never seen again, and defendant gave conflicting stories about her location and never reported her missing to police. Victim's car was discovered a week later, and victim's blood was found in the trunk and spare tire wheel well, but so was the DNA of two men who were caught driving her car. There was also a foul odor emanating from the trunk of car. Defendant's DNA was found mixed with victim's DNA on the walls, ceiling and floor of the house they shared along with the shirt defendant wore the night of the murder. The house also showed signs of having been cleaned, including the use of bleach and missing carpet in the master bedroom. At trial, a sister of victim testified that the night of the party she saw defendant removing a large trash bag from the trunk of victim's car while standing on a local bridge. Defendant was convicted of second-degree murder.

Sources: defrostingcoldcases.com; Alexander, K., "Boyfriend convicted of murder in '99 disappearance of D.C. woman," *Washington Post*, March 31, 2010

Keywords: **Forensic evidence: DNA**

Case 29

Defendant: **Mark Barrow**

Victim: Rae Meichelle Tener

Trial: August 2007 Jurisdiction: Palm Beach County, Florida

Murder: August 24, 2004

Evidence: The victim and her 13-year-old son lived in the same trailer park as defendant and his girlfriend. Defendant hosted a party at his trailer, and around 11 p.m., victim and defendant took victim's son back to victim's trailer and returned to defendant's trailer. Others at the party were asked by victim to leave, and both defendant and victim appeared to be intoxicated. The next day victim's son went looking for his mother and went to defendant's trailer, where he saw defendant asleep and saw his mother's cigars and lighter on the ground near defendant's trailer. All of victim's belongings were found in her trailer, including her driver's license and money, and her car was in her driveway. Defendant's girlfriend, who was not at the party, testified that defendant seemed angry after the party and that their van smelled oddly. She found victim's keys in the van. While cleaning a room in the trailer she smelled the same stench she smelled in the van and found a bag containing bloody jeans. Defendant then confessed to her that he had killed victim because she made a sexual advance toward him. He threw her out of the trailer and she hit her head. Fearful he would have to go back to jail for assaulting her, he ended up killing her with a rock and putting her body in a black trash bag. He then threw her body in a canal after breaking her neck. Blood was found in defendant's van, and DNA testing revealed that the blood came from the same donor. Victim's son could not be excluded as being related to the source of the DNA, but defendant was eliminated as the source. Defendant told the police a story inconsistent with what he had told his girlfriend. There was also evidence that victim did sometimes disappear for periods of time. Defendant was convicted of first-degree murder, but conviction was reversed and set for new trial based upon the trial court's failure to permit the jury to hear read backs of testimony.

Sources: *Barrow v. Florida*, No. 4D07-3420 (Fla.App.,2010); Musgrave, J., "Supreme Court: West Palm Beach Murder Deserves New Trial," *Palm Beach Post*, May 31, 2012

Keywords: **Forensic evidence: DNA, Confession to friends and family**

Case 30

Defendants: **Branden Basham, Chadrick Fulks**

Victims: Samantha Burns, Alice Donovan

Trial: September 2004 Jurisdiction: Conway, South Carolina

Murder: November 11 and 14, 2002

Evidence: Defendants escaped from a Kentucky jail one week before two separate abductions and murders. Basham was arrested shortly thereafter committing another abduction, and Fulks was arrested a few days later. Before being captured, both men committed several other crimes, including tying a man to a tree in freezing weather and shooting another man. Donovan's kidnapping from a Walmart was caught on a security camera. Defendants were linked to Burns' abduction through attempts to withdraw money from victim's ATM and because they burned victim's car. Basham admitted kidnapping both women but denied murdering them, even though he had possession of Burns' ring. Defendants also made successful withdrawals from Donovan's bank accounts. Fulks confessed to FBI but stated that Basham had committed both murders. Defendants admitted to crimes, and federal trial was for sentencing purposes only. Both men found guilty of kidnapping, carjacking, and other crimes, and both sentenced to death. Both cases upheld on appeal.

Sources: Project Jason; *United States v. Fulks*, 454 F.3d 410 (4th Cir. 2006)

Keywords: **Confession to police, Death penalty**

Case 31

Defendant: **Clarence Oliver Bean**

Victim: Diana Chorba

Trial: 2001 Jurisdiction: Luther, Michigan
Murder: May 24, 1979
Evidence: Victim was pregnant with defendant's second child when she disappeared. Defendant was married and told authorities that his girlfriend had been aboard American Airlines Flight 191, which crashed in Chicago, Illinois, on May 25, 1979. Authorities confirmed that victim was not on the flight by using dental and medical records of the victim. Defendant's wife testified that defendant had confessed to killing victim and came home to get his chainsaw. She then drove with defendant and defendant's young son (from victim) into the woods, where she saw victim's body. Defendant then cut a tree stump to cover up victim's body. She also testified of past domestic abuse by defendant. Case was broken in 1999 when defendant's wife admitted she had lied to the police in supporting defendant's story. Defendant was found guilty of second-degree murder and sentenced to 30 to 60 years.
Sources: Miller, J., "Jury: Bean guilty of second degree murder," *Ludington Daily News*, August 30, 2001; *Bean v. Ludwick*, No. 05-70361 (ED Mich. 2005)
Keywords: **Forensic evidence: Other, Confession to friends and family**

Case 32

Defendant: **Eric Bechler**
Victim: Pegye Bechler
Trial: March 2001 Jurisdiction: Orange County, California
Murder: July 7, 1997
Evidence: Defendant told authorities he was being pulled on a bodyboard by his wife in a speedboat when he hit a wave and was knocked under the water. When he surfaced, he said the boat was going in circles and his wife was gone. Given that victim was a swimming champion as a child and an experienced triathlete, authorities were immediately suspicious of defendant's story. Defendant was later recorded telling his new girlfriend that he had murdered his wife with a dumbbell and then threw her weighted body into the ocean. Defendant sought unsuccessfully to collect on a $2 million life insurance policy on his wife. There was no physical evidence found in the boat, such as blood. Defendant was convicted and sentenced to life without the possibility of parole.
Sources: Pfeifer, S., "Wife-killer Bechler gets life term" *Los Angeles Times*, March 17, 2001
Keywords: **Confession to friends and family**

Case 33

Defendants: **Robert Wayne Beckett, Senior and Junior**
Victim: Tracy Lea Stewart
Trial: August 1989/August 1995 Jurisdiction: Los Angeles, California
Murder: August 9, 1981
Evidence: Robert Jr. was the last person seen with victim, whom he had taken on a date. Victim had called her parents and told them she was on a date with someone named Robbie and would be home by 1 a.m. Robert Jr. testified against his father in the 1995 trial and said he had

taken victim to a bowling alley and then to the apartment he shared with his father. Together the two men raped and tortured victim for three days before strangling and clubbing her to death. They disposed of the body in a rural area. Both men were convicted.

Sources: "Tustin: Jury finds man guilty in '81 murder of woman" *Los Angeles Times*, August 18, 1989; Charley Project

Keyword: **Codefendant testimony**

Case 34

Defendant: **Kyle Kenneth Bell**

Victim: Jeanna Dale North

Trial: August 1999 Jurisdiction: Fargo, North Dakota

Murder: June 28, 1993

Evidence: Victim, 11 years old, was rollerblading with a friend at around 10:30 p.m. They were seen at a convenience store by a police officer, and victim's friend left her just a few blocks from the victim's house. Two years later, defendant, a convicted child molester, confessed to murdering victim in his garage after he sexually assaulted her. He told police he threw her body in the Sheyenne River. In 1996, police found a piece of rope and a cinder block in the river that matched items from defendant's home. Hairs found in defendant's truck matched victim's DNA. Defendant claimed that the death was accidental from victim slipping on her rollerblades. Defendant convicted of Class AA murder and given a life sentence.

Sources: Charley Project; Tellijohn, A., "Man guilty of killing girl, 11; Jeanna North's 'life has been avenged,' father says," *Star Tribune* (Minneapolis, Minnesota), August 21, 1999

Keywords: **Confession to police, Forensic evidence: Other, Forensic evidence: DNA, Life**

Case 35

Defendant: **Timothy Bennett**

Victim: Mary Jo Bennett

Trial: December 1974 Jurisdiction: Merced, California

Murder: October 18, 1972

Evidence: Defendant and victim were married and had a daughter. They had a stormy relationship, and eventually defendant said he would agree to a divorce if he could retain custody of their daughter. Victim refused and left the marital home with the daughter to live with her parents. Defendant was interviewed by the police three days after his wife's disappearance and was cooperative. He could not, however, account for two hours of his time on the date and time of his wife's disappearance. Defendant consented to a search of his van, during which blood, several strands of hair, leather gloves, and two knives were recovered. At one point during the consent search defendant asked the police, "Could I have killed Mary Jo?" A search of defendant's room uncovered letters to a girlfriend. Defendant told a psychiatrist at Stanford Medical School that he may not have amnesia regarding the missing two hours, that victim's family may have conspired against him, and various statements that he hated victim and she was a bad, immoral woman. Defendant admitted to the doctor that he had had two dreams involving victim's death, which the doctor, at trial, termed "wish fulfillment." Defendant was convicted, but the conviction was reversed because the prosecution failed to prove that the doctor has adequately Mirandized the defendant. Since the doctor was acting as an agent of the police during a custodial interview, the failure to Mirandize defendant led to the statements being thrown out.

Source: *California v. Bennett*, 58 Cal. App. 3d 230 (1976)

Keywords: **Confession to police**

Case 36

Defendant: **Christopher Bingham**

Victim: Lora Gabbert

Trial: April 1999 Jurisdiction: Pecos, Texas

Murder: December 1, 1997

Evidence: Victim was defendant's girlfriend and, according to defendant, she purchased a bus ticket on the date of her disappearance to travel to Dallas to visit a friend. Victim was never seen again, and the bus company denied she had ever purchased a ticket. Defendant then moved to Washington and returned two of victim's daughters to their fathers but kept her 13-year-old daughter. Defendant eventually confessed to shooting victim after claiming she pointed a gun at his back and he shot her in self-defense. He said he buried her at first near Pecos but later dug her up and put her into a barrel, burned the body, and threw the barrel into the Pecos River. Divers found a barrel matching defendant's description, which was tested and found to contain human remains. (While DNA testing was not possible, defendant testified that it was "very probable" that the bones in the barrel were victim's.) Victim's 13-year-old daughter stated that defendant told her that her mother committed suicide and that she saw her mother's remains in the barrel. Defendant was convicted and sentenced to 75 years.

Sources: Charley Project; Doe Network

Keywords: **Forensic evidence: Other, Confession to police**

Case 37

Defendant: **Robert Bierenbaum**

Victim: Gail Katz Bierenbaum

Trial: October 2000 Jurisdiction: New York, New York

Murder: July 7, 1985

Evidence: Defendant and victim had a troubled marriage. Defendant said his wife left their apartment to cool down in Central Park after a fight. Victim was never seen again. Defendant told friends and family she may have been mugged in park. Family of victim told police of domestic violence and that victim had said defendant had tried to kill her cat by dunking it in toilet. Police discovered defendant had taken his plane on a two-hour flight over the Atlantic on the day his wife disappeared yet never mentioned this to the police. He also tried to alter the flight log. At trial, prosecution showed no evidence of victim from Social Security, bank, or credit card records. Prosecution showed police reenactment of how duffel bag with body could be thrown from similar plane. Defendant found guilty of second-degree murder and sentenced to 20 years to life.

Source: Murderpedia

Keywords: **N/A**

Case 38

Defendant: **Donald Blom**

Victim: Katie Poirer

Trial: July 2000 Jurisdiction: Carlton, Minnesota

Murder: May 1999

Evidence: An unusual stranger-on-stranger no-body murder because defendant is seen on surveillance video kidnapping his 19-year-old victim from a convenience store by grabbing her around the neck. The video was played by the media, and defendant's coworkers recognized both defendant and his pickup truck. In addition, a witness had seen a partial tag from the truck, which matched defendant's tag. The coworkers noted that defendant had been absent from work the day after the abduction and that he had cut his hair as well. It turned out defendant had been using a false name at work and was suspected of prior abductions and sexual assaults. Defendant confessed to the police and said he had burned victim's body in the fire pit of his vacation home. Charred bones were found in the pit, but they could not be tied to victim. A tooth found in the pit was tied to victim by dental records related to her filling, but this was challenged at trial by a defense expert. Defendant recanted his confession at trial and said it was from the stress of solitary confinement and medications he was taking. Defendant was convicted of first-degree murder and sentenced to life.

Sources: "Blom gets life without parole for kidnapping and killing Poirier," Minnesota Public Radio, August 17, 2000; Ramsland, K., "Donald Blom: A repeat sex offender finally stopped," *Crime Library*

Keywords: **Confession to police, Forensic evidence: Other, Life**

Case 39

Defendant: **Dennis Ray Bolinski**

Victim: Paul Morrow Taylor

Trial: 1966 Jurisdiction: Palm Springs, California

Murder: August 20, 1965

Evidence: Victim was a relief manager for Western Union and worked at different locations all over California. He disappeared from the Western Union he was working at on August 20, 1965. Credit card receipts showed gas purchases at two different gas stations, one in victim's handwriting and one that was not. The credit card was used by defendant the next several days, and a witness said he paid for his meals with $2 bills, something victim collected. A police officer stopped defendant in victim's car but let him go since the car had not been reported stolen at that point. Defendant was eventually arrested and told police he was hitchhiking when he was picked up by victim. (Victim was known to have picked up hitchhikers.) Defendant said that victim ended up lending him both his credit card and his car and that he had dropped victim off at his house in Orange County. The police started asking questions about a revolver the defendant had been seen with and then recorded a phone call the defendant made to his sister asking her to lie about the whereabouts of the gun along with other incriminating statements. Defendant was convicted of first-degree murder and sentenced to life in prison.

Source: *California v. Bolinski*, 260 Cal. App. 2d 705 (1968)

Keywords: **Confession to friends and family, Life**

Case 40

Defendants: **Kenneth Patterson (Pat), Hugh Peter Bondurant**

Victim: Gwenn Dugger

Trial: March 1991 Jurisdiction: Giles County, Tennessee

Murder: 1986

Evidence: Defendants are twins, and they kidnapped and raped victim, a young mother. At trial, Pat's wife testified against both men and told how they had tortured victim, shot her, and then burned her body in a 55-gallon drum. They dumped the ashes in a creek near a rental farmhouse owned by Pat. Victim was partially identified by a part of a tennis shoe and pink baby pin. At trial, defendants, who did not testify, blamed Pat's wife, saying she had killed victim after discovering Pat having sex with her. Defendants admitting burning victim's body to try and hide the evidence of her death. They were both convicted and received 25-year sentences.

Sources: Kazek, K., "Vicious 1980s murders committed by Tennessee brothers, 'The Bondurant Boys,' to be featured on 'Evil Twins'," Al.com, September 5, 2013; http://www.redhawkreporter.com/articles/murder-murder.8894; "Jury finds twins guilty of murder," Rome (Ga.) *News-Tribune*, March 31, 1991

Keywords: **Eyewitness**

Case 41

Defendants: **Jesse Boorn, Stephen Boorn**

Victim: Richard Colvin

Trial: 1819 Jurisdiction: Manchester, Vermont

Murder: 1812

Evidence: This is an unusual case because it may be one of the very few cases where the victim was found alive after defendants' conviction. But it may also be that the so-called alive victim was not the actual victim after all. The victim, Russel Colvin, was married to defendants' sister. He was considered "feeble-minded" and often disappeared for months at a time. When he disappeared in May 1812, no one paid much attention, since this had happened before. This time, however, months changed to years, and suspicion focused on the Boorn brothers, who had not gotten along with victim. A neighbor had seen defendants arguing with victim the day he disappeared. The brothers' uncle had a dream in which victim told the uncle he had been killed and where his grave was. At some point the brothers' barn burned and it was suspected they burned it themselves to hide evidence. A dog found human bones near their property, and both brothers were arrested. While in prison, a cellmate of Jesse's came forward and testified that Stephen had confessed to killing victim. According to the informant, Jesse confessed that Stephen had struck victim in a fight but had not killed him. Jesse and another brother had carried victim to an old cellar, and the other brother, Barney, slit victim's throat. Later, the brothers dug up the body and hid it in the barn that had burned. After the barn was burned down, defendants ground the bones into dust and threw them into the river. The remainder of the body was in a hollow stump. At trial, Stephen confessed and substantiated the informant's story. Although both men were given the death penalty, Jesse's sentence was commuted to life, and Stephen was not executed because "victim" was found in New Jersey. Victim was allegedly found because of an advertisement Stephen had placed in a Vermont newspaper that led to victim being found in New Jersey and lured back to Vermont to prove the brothers' innocence. However, the book *The Counterfeit Man* by Gerald W. McFarland posits that the "victim" was actually an imposter.

Source: http://www.trivia-library.com/b/guilty-or-innocent-the-boorn-brothers-of-vermont-part-2.htm

Keywords: **Life, Informant**

Case 42

Defendant: **Nicholas Paul Brasic**

Victim: Christine Marie Honson

Trial: July 1986 Jurisdiction: Kent County, Michigan

Murder: 1974

Evidence: Defendant was convicted of first-degree murder for the murder of Christine Marie Honson in 1974. At trial, a friend of defendant's testified that he saw defendant beat and sexually assault a woman named Chris and that the next day defendant confessed he had "taken care" of the woman. Two other friends of defendant testified that he admitted killing a woman and burying her body near South Bend, Indiana, eight years after the murder.

Source: "Life sentence is delivered," *The Argus-Press*, July 24, 1986

Keywords: **Confession to friends and family, Life**

Case 43

Defendant: **John Brinson**

Victim: Marilyn Brinson

Trial: October 2006 Jurisdiction: Clay County, Missouri

Murder: July 16, 2002

Evidence: Victim was married to defendant. The couple's adult children testified that defendant and victim had argued the night before her disappearance. Defendant stated that he had seen his wife go to bed the night before, and when he woke up she was gone. He assumed she went to work, but her boss called to ask why she was not at work. Victim's wedding ring was found at the house, and her car was found abandoned in the middle of the street. The car had a partially burned paper towel in the gas pipe as if someone was trying to blow up the car. Defendant's bloody handprint was found in her car along with a large amount of victim's blood. The volume of blood in the car was so large that the medical examiner testified that someone could not survive losing that much blood. The victim's blood was also found in the parking lot of defendant and victim's home. Underneath defendant's fingernails was the same type of freshwater organisms that was on mud in the trunk of the car. Defendant maintained his innocence but admitted he had learned that his wife was having an affair.

Sources: North American Missing Person Network; Press release dated October 30, 2006, from Daniel L. White, Clay County Prosecutor; "Police accuse man of killing wife he reported missing last month," *Nevada Daily Mail*, August 14, 2002

Keywords: **Forensic evidence: DNA, Forensic evidence: Other**

Case 44

Defendant: **Cornelius Lemonza Brown**

Victim: Hope Anderson

Trial: October 1988 Jurisdiction: Multnomah County, Oregon

Murder: November 30, 1987

Evidence: Defendant and victim were romantically involved but had violent relationship. Defendant told friend he intended to have someone kill victim and throw her body in the river. Two months before her disappearance, police interviewed victim's daughter about allegations defendant had abused daughter. Defendant knew of investigation and threatened victim. She then provided police with evidence of defendant's drug dealing. Defendant was scheduled for probation revocation hearing, but victim disappeared and hearing never took place. In October 1987, defendant beat victim and was arrested. Trial was supposed to begin on December 4, but victim never appeared for trial. On evening of her disappearance, victim had relatives staying with her due to fear of defendant. Early the next morning, witnesses in house heard commotion and heard defendant in house, threatening victim. Victim's son saw defendant push victim into his car while holding her by the arm and hair. Defendant then drove off. Others in house and neighbors heard similar commotion. Defendant's car was located and two hairs consistent with the victim's were found inside. Defendant also confessed to a cellmate that victim "wasn't no trouble no more, you know, that, you know, (I) cut her loose." Defendant confessed to dumping her body where he had dumped bodies before. The defendant was convicted of aggravated murder and felony murder and sentenced to death. The aggravated murder conviction was reversed on appeal, but the felony murder conviction was upheld.

Source: *Oregon v. Brown*, 800 P.2d 259 (1990)

Keywords: **Eyewitness, Death penalty, Informant**

Case 45

Defendant: **Nettie Brown**
Victim: T.H. Brown
Trial: 1909 Jurisdiction: Oklahoma
Murder: April 1909
Evidence: Defendant was married to victim but sleeping with her stepson, Peter (A.P.) Brown, aged 20. Defendant was getting divorced from victim. Defendant and her stepson traveled to Wichita, Kansas, where they were arrested by police for sleeping together. Defendant was told by her lawyer that this arrest would defeat her petition for divorce. Defendant withdrew her divorce petition and tried to reconcile with victim. Victim sold all of his property and converted it to cash, about $2,500. Defendant, victim, stepson, and another child were camping when defendant disappeared. Defendant told others he had left them in the middle of the night. Witnesses testified that defendant made bank deposits under fictitious names totaling nearly $2,500. Four months after murder, evidence of a large fire and ashes, including teeth, bones and suspender buckles, were found near where group camped. Police were led to the site by stepson, who testified against defendant, which was controversial because he was also charged with murder. Defendant was found guilty.
Source: *Brown v. State*, 132 P. 359 (1913)
Keyword: **Codefendant testimony**

Case 46

Defendant: **Lindsey Bruce**
Victim: Emily Rimel
Trial: September 2005 Jurisdiction: Franklin County, Ohio
Murder: December 7, 2004
Evidence: Defendant was initially charged with kidnapping and rape of 5-year-old victim. He was convicted of kidnapping but not the rape. After trial, victim's skull was found near Big Walnut Creek, eight miles from her home, and he was tried for murder in 2007 and convicted. Victim's parents were friends with defendant, who sometimes stayed over at their house. Victim's mother left for work, and when the father woke up, victim was gone, as was defendant. The door was unlocked, which was unusual, because typically defendant would wake the parents when he left so one of them could lock the door behind him. Victim's DNA was found on defendant's genitals, and he had three small scratches on his arm. Defendant told police he had left the house at 3 a.m. but did not have an alibi until his appearance in an auto parts store at 9:30 a.m. Jailhouse informants testified at both trials that defendant confessed to murder, telling one he had raped victim and cut off her head. Defendant was sentenced to 10 years in the first trial and to life in the second trial, escaping the death penalty when the jury voted against it.
Sources: Cadwalladar, B., "Jury finds Bruce Lindsey guilty in girl's murder," *Columbus Dispatch*, March 23, 2007; http://vnnforum.com/archive/index.php/t-58121.html
Keywords: **Forensic evidence: DNA, Informant, Life**

Case 47

Defendant: **Whitey Bulger**
Victim: James Sousa
Trial: August 2013 Jurisdiction: Boston, Massachusetts
Murder: October 1974
Evidence: Bulger, leader of the Winter Hill Gang in Boston, feared that Sousa was going to snitch on the gang after he was arrested for a robbery gone wrong. Victim was shot in auto garage, and gunman, John Martorano, asked for a bucket to catch the blood. Body was buried off of Route 95. Martorano and mob hitman Steve Flemini testified against Bulger. Bulger was found not guilty of this murder, along with seven others, but convicted of 11 other murders.
Source: Boeri, D., "The victims," WBUR
Keywords: **Eyewitness, Informant**

Case 48

Defendant: **Thomas E. Burns**
Victim: Marie Coleman
Trial: April 1961 Jurisdiction: Philadelphia, Pennsylvania
Murder: January 10, 1959
Evidence: Defendant and victim were in a relationship. Victim's friend, Earthia Del Wooden, walked victim home early the morning of the 10th after a night of drinking. As Ms. Del Wooden was leaving the house, she heard a commotion inside the house. She returned to the house and defendant took her upstairs where she saw victim on the floor with blood on her forehead. Defendant said she had come at him with a knife and that she was not passed out drunk. At trial, witnesses testified that victim was very close to her family and regularly sent gifts and cards on vacations and telephoned family members. No one had heard from her after January 10. She had an excellent credit rating yet had failed to make any payments on a loan she had taken out in December 1958. Defendant never reported her missing to the police and got rid of her dog two weeks after she went missing. A witness testified that one week after she went missing, the witness asked defendant what had happened, and he replied that he had cut her up and put her in the trash. He told other witnesses he had fought with victim and hit her with a hammer and that he had cut her up and put her in the trash along with other stories, including one where he said he had buried her in the cellar. Defendant moved out of the house one month after she disappeared. He was convicted of first-degree murder and sentenced to life.
Source: *Pennsylvania v. Burns*, 409 Pa. 619 (1962)
Keywords: **Life, Confession to friends and family**

Case 49

Defendant: **David Bush**
Victim: Lynn Lynette Bush
Trial: March 2007 Jurisdiction: Natrona County, Wyoming
Murder: December 1990

Evidence: Victim and defendant were married. Defendant told police that he found his wife's truck on December 10 in a grocery store parking lot. He initially said he was home December 5 and 6, but it was later shown that he was using the family's credit card to get cash. Defendant said the family went camping on December 7, but defendant had actually spent the day with his girlfriend, who later testified that he spoke of killing his wife and threatened to kill her if she told anyone. The police were able to prove that he had not gone camping because the camping gear he said he had used was covered with dust. Witnesses and a gas receipt proved that defendant was not in Alcova as he said but instead in Kaycee. The police found victim's DNA (blood) in the trunk of the truck and on a vodka bottle. The prosecution also called a counselor, who testified that the defendant's daughter was suffering from post-traumatic stress disorder because she witnessed something her dad did to her mother. The daughter had told her therapist that "Daddy cut mommy" and that "Mommy got her head split open and she's dead." A trial, however, she testified that she did not remember anything. Other witnesses said defendant talked about burying bodies and committing the perfect murder. Defendant was found guilty of second-degree murder, and his conviction was upheld on appeal.

Source: Matteson, C., "Weeks of testimony ends in Bush conviction," *Star-Tribune*, March 21, 2007

Keywords: **Forensic evidence: DNA, Confession to friends and family**

Case 50

Defendant: **Miguel Bustamante, David Replogle**

Victim: Clifford Lambert

Trial: January 2011 Jurisdiction: Palm Springs, California

Murder: 2008

Evidence: The victim was a 74-year-old retiree, and the two defendants, along with others, swindled him of his money and stole his possessions. Bustamante was a bartender, while Replogle was an attorney. The victim was an art dealer, and the police caught Bustamante trying to clean out the victim's house after he went missing. Replogle had earlier arranged for a fraudulent power of attorney on behalf of Lambert but had used his thumbprint with a notary public and this had connected the scheme back to him. While the men originally planned to only kidnap victim, they feared their scams would come to light if they did not kill him. The men had also wired more than $200,000 from victim's account into their accounts. A Realtor grew suspicious when members of the gang tried to sell victim's house and called the police. The group's entire series of scams began to unravel. As part of their scams, they hired a hit man to kill victim. The group of men, including Bustamante, stabbed victim to death in his own home. They stuffed his body into the trunk of his Mercedes and buried him near a water tower in the desert. The evidence at trial included testimony from a jailhouse informant. Both men were convicted of first-degree murder and sentenced to life in prison without the possibility of parole.

Sources: http://www.trutv.com/library/crime/notorious_murders/classics/kaushal_niroula/1.html; Sandoval, E., "Pair sentenced to life in prison for murder of Palm Springs retiree," KESQ.com, September 27, 2011
Keywords: **Informant, Life, Codefendant testimony**

Case 51

Defendant: **Carl Campbell**
Victim: Robert Rose
Trial: 1984 Jurisdiction: Laurel, Indiana
Murder: July 1979
Evidence: Defendant, along with three others, beat and robbed victim, who supposedly had $700. The group put victim in the trunk and, after buying gasoline at a gas station, tried to burn victim. The fuel did not light, and the men tried to drown victim in a nearby river. Eventually, one of the men held victim under water and he was never seen again. One of the four men was charged with other crimes and confessed to the police. Eventually, defendant confessed to the police. Victim's brother and cousin testified at trial to victim's usual habits. Defendant was convicted of murder, robbery, and confinement, and sentenced to 30 years for murder.
Sources: *Campbell v. Clark*, 952 F.2d 1398 (7th Cir. 1992); *Campbell v. Indiana*, 500 N.E.2d 174 (Indiana S. Ct. 1986)
Keywords: **Confession to police, Codefendant testimony**

Case 52

Defendant: **John Campbell**
Victim: Baby daughter
Trial: May 1895 Jurisdiction: Hamilton County, Illinois
Murder: October 1893
Evidence: The defendant's conviction for murdering his newborn was reversed because the only testimony was from his mistress, who gave birth to the girl.
Source: 159 Ill. 9 (1895)
Keywords: **Eyewitness**

Case 53

Defendant: **Mario Bolestero Campos**
Victim: Fred Charles Moseley
Trial: July 2013 Jurisdiction: Amarillo, Texas
Murder: 1998
Evidence: Codefendant testified against defendant and told jury he saw defendant beating victim, and then helped defendant strangle victim with a cord in victim's backyard. Codefendant originally had an immunity agreement, but it was voided after inconsistencies in his story were found. Police were led to codefendant, as he was the last person seen with victim and he had expressed an interest in victim's shotgun. The shotgun was later recovered after codefendant told

the police where it was buried. Victim's body was allegedly put in a dumpster, which was emptied into a landfill.

Sources: Bryant, M., "Campos found guilty in Canyon teen's death, sentenced to life," *Amarillo Globe News*, July 18, 2013; Angli, R., "Murder trial heads to closing arguments," *Amarillo Globe News*, July 17, 2013

Keywords: **Life, Codefendant testimony**

Case 54

Defendant: **Thomas Capano**

Victim: Mary Ann Fahey

Trial: January 1999 Jurisdiction: Delaware

Murder: June 27, 1996

Evidence: Defendant was a prominent attorney active in Delaware politics, and victim was an aide to the governor who had an affair with defendant. The affair ended and victim began dating another man, which caused defendant to become jealous. Victim was last seen having dinner with defendant in Philadelphia on June 27. Defendant denied knowing anything about her disappearance. The police discovered victim's diary, which detailed her affair with "Tomas." When questioned by police, he lied about his whereabouts on the night of victim's disappearance, saying he had purchased cigarettes from a gas station at 10 at night when the station closed at 9:30. A search of defendant's house revealed blood-stain remover and blood stains in a great room in his house. A small sofa and rug were also missing. Police also discovered that defendant's brother, Gerry, had sold his fishing boat minus the anchor, and that another brother, Louis, who ran a construction company, had ordered a dumpster emptied before schedule. At trial, Gerry testified that defendant told him he had killed a man trying to extort him. He then helped defendant dispose of the victim's body at sea. They used Gerry's boat to toss a large cooler into the water. When the cooler would not sink despite being shot by a shotgun, the two men retrieved victim's body, wrapped anchor chains around it and tossed it back into the ocean. The two men also disposed of a bloody sofa and carpet in a dumpster owned by Capano's other brother, Louis. The cooler was later recovered at sea. At trial, defendant blamed another ex-lover of his for the murder. He was found guilty of murder and was originally sentenced to be executed. After a series of appeals, the sentence was changed to life in prison without parole.

Source: http://themoderatevoice.com/122781/breaking-news-murderer-thomas-capano-found-dead-in-his-prison-cell/; http://www.trutv.com/library/crime/notorious_murders/classics/capano/1.html

Keywords: **Codefendant testimony, Life**

Case 55

Defendants: **Frank Caracappa, Louis Eppolito**

Victim: James Hydell

Trial: April 2006 Jurisdiction: New York, New York

Murder: September 1986

Evidence: Defendants were former New York City Police Department detectives at the time of trial. They had retired from the force in the early 1990s. For years they had worked with the Mafia, providing information to the mob through an intermediary, Burton Kaplan. During their time on the force, defendants sold information to a Lucchese family underboss. This information included information on wiretaps, ongoing investigations, and who was acting as informants. At trial, Kaplan testified against defendants. Defendants not only passed information but participated in three murders, including victim's murder. In the fall of 1986, hit men tried to kill mobster Anthony Casso. The defendants provided the investigative file to Casso that pointed to victim as one of the hit men. They then helped track down victim at a coin laundry in Brooklyn and drove him to a Toys 'R Us parking lot. Casso beat victim and put him in the trunk of a car. Casso tortured and interrogated victim until he gave him the names of the other men involved in the hit. The mobster then killed him and hid the body. The mob informant also testified that the two detectives were put on a $4,000 a month retainer for the mob. Both men were sentenced to life for a variety of crimes, including conspiracy to commit murder.

Sources: Ackman, D., "Dispatches from a mob trial," *Slate*, March 17, 2006; Feuer, A., "In macbre detail, witness tells of murders for the mob by detectives," *New York Times*, March 16, 2006

Keywords: **Life, Informant**

Case 56

Defendant: **Robert Carlotto**

Victim: Blair Miller Carlotto

Trial: October 1991 Jurisdiction: Los Altos, California

Murder: December 7, 1990

Evidence: Victim was in a bitter divorce from defendant, and the two were scheduled to meet on December 7 to discuss the divorce. According to witnesses, defendant asked that victim wear a particular dress, and the victim refused, telling him "this is not a date." Although defendant said he dropped victim off at her home afterwards, she was never seen again. At trial, witnesses testified to the history of domestic violence between the two and defendant's violent temper. Police also found blood spatter in defendant's kitchen that matched a bloodstain recovered from victim's mattress pad through DNA. The defense argued that victim's diaries demonstrated she may have intentionally disappeared. Defendant was acquitted.

Sources: Domingue, J., "Investigators report dead-ends in cases of two Los Altos women," *Los Altos Town Crier*, July 18, 1995; https://www.facebook.com/Find.Sierra.LaMar/posts/108676155938319?comment_id=28521&offset = 9&total_comments = 84

Keyword: **Forensic evidence: DNA**

Case 57

Defendant: **Barbara Carrasco, Larry Carrasco**

Victim: Alexia Reale

Trial: 1999 Jurisdiction: Sacramento County, California
Murder: June 1997
Evidence: Victim was 6-year-old daughter of defendant. At trial, victim's 13-year-old sister testified that their family life was normal until her father lost his job and both parents began using meth. They began to say that demons and vampires were inside the girls. She testified about various abuse the girls suffered and said that both she and victim were forced to drink various beverages mixed with bleach for eight straight days. Eventually, victim died and the sister saw her lying on the floor as her mother tried to do CPR. The sister further testified that her parents cut up victim's body with a pruning saw and eventually burned the body in the family's fireplace. The remains were thrown into the Sacramento River along with the pruning saw. Defendants told police and family that victim had gone to live with her biological father in Illinois, a statement initially corroborated by the sister. Both defendants were convicted. Barbara was sentenced to 15 years to life and Larry was given 40 years to life.
Source: Charley Project
Keywords: **Eyewitness**

Case 58

Defendants: **Liz Carroll, David Carroll**
Victim: Marcus Fiesel
Trial: February 2007 Jurisdiction: Cincinnati, Ohio
Murder: August 6, 2006
Evidence: Victim was the developmentally disabled foster child of defendants. They wrapped him in a blanket with duct tape and placed him in a playpen inside a closet while they attended a family reunion in Kentucky. When they returned, he had died, probably from heat stroke. Defendants told the police that Liz had collapsed in a park and when she revived only three of the four children she had taken to the park were there. A huge search ensued, but suspicions quickly turned toward the foster parents. Eventually, defendants' live-in girlfriend, Amy Baker, told police what had happened. She told the police that victim had died days before the park hoax and that she had helped David burn the body and dispose of the remains in the Ohio River. Baker testified at the trial. Liz was sentenced to 54 years in prison, and David eventually pleaded guilty was sentenced to 16 years to life.
Source: Pittman, M., "Young boy's death at hands of foster parents led to change," *Oxford Press*, August 11, 2011
Keyword: **Codefendant testimony**

Case 59

Defendants: **David Cortez Carson, Leon Jones**
Victim: Darryl "Preach" Miller
Trial: March 2010 Jurisdiction: Spartanburg, South Carolina
Murder: July 2005
Evidence: Defendants and victim had been partying together. The three men went to victim's house where victim supposedly had a large

amount of cash. A witness at trial testified that when he saw Jones a few days later he said he killed "that guy." DNA and blood were recovered from the car where it was believed victim had been killed. That car was owned by Carson's ex-girlfriend and was recovered from a car refurbishing company. A witness from a meat processing plant testified that he saw a group of men furiously cleaning the car including removing its seats and carpet. Carson admitted helping dispose of the body in a remote area, but said victim had been killed during a robbery. Both defendants found guilty of murder and sentenced to 30 years in prison without the possibility of parole.

Source: Peters, C., "2 men found guilty of '05 murder," GoUpstate.com, March 18, 2010

Keywords: **Forensic evidence: DNA, Confession to friends and family**

Case 60

Defendant: **Mario Casciaro**
Victim: Brian Carrick
Trial: January 2012 Jurisdiction: McHenry County, Illinois
Murder: December 20, 2002
Evidence: Defendant and victim worked at a grocery store owned by defendant's family. Victim also dealt marijuana for defendant and allegedly owed defendant $500. Victim was last seen at the store, and a codefendant, Shane Lamb, testified that defendant confronted victim over the money he owed. Lamb hit victim inside a walk-in cooler and then defendant told him he would take care of victim. Victim's blood was found in and around the cooler. The defense attacked Lamb's credibility.

Sources: Marrazzo, A., "Man found guilty of Carrick's murder in retrial," *Chicago Tribune*, April 3, 2013; http://amandamarrazzo.com/2013/08/27/mario-casciaro-seeking-a-new-trial-3/

Keywords: **Codefendant testimony, Forensic evidence: DNA**

Case 61

Defendant: **Rodney Wayne Cearley**
Victim: Michael Wayne Grimes
Trial: December 2007 Jurisdiction: Nacogdoches, Texas
Murder: January 1999
Evidence: Defendant claimed he stabbed victim in self-defense during an argument at a house near a wrecking yard the defendant's parents owned. At trial, both sides agreed that defendant, his girlfriend, and victim had been partying at defendant's house. Victim asked defendant's girlfriend to take him to the drugstore so he could buy some ingredients to make meth. She refused to do so, and victim then threatened to kill her. The prosecution argued that the girlfriend left and defendant then stabbed victim. The defense argued that victim tried to stab the girlfriend and she left. Victim then threatened defendant who grabbed the knife and stabbed victim in self-defense. Three witnesses stated that defendant told them he had stabbed victim. One of those witnesses was defendant's mother, to whom he said

he had killed a man and had a tough time getting the blood off his hands. Defendant told police he did not want to talk about victim's disappearance when questioned. Victim's ex-wife testified on behalf of defendant and said her ex-husband was a violent man who had abused her in the past. Defendant was convicted and sentenced to 20 years in prison. It is believed that defendant buried victim's body in a wooded area.

Sources: http://www.tdcaa.com/node/1663; Charley Project

Keyword: **Confession to friends and family**

Case 62

Defendant: **David Christman**

Victim: Rena Christman

Trial: Fall 1996 Jurisdiction: Monroe County, Ohio

Murder: November 25, 1984

Evidence: Defendant and victim were married in 1978. The marriage faltered and victim moved into an apartment with their two children in 1983. Defendant told friends that he could dispose of body on farm owned by his parents or in poured concrete. One month before her disappearance, defendant asked his father for advice on how to dispose of a body. Shortly before her disappearance, victim bought a $2,000 certificate of deposit and placed personal items in a safe deposit box. Defendant removed these items after his wife's disappearance. The day of her disappearance, victim and defendant argued. Defendant reported her missing to mall security at 7:30 p.m. that evening about an hour away from where they were last seen together. He claimed he had last seen her at 3:30. A search was commenced. Within two weeks, defendant had removed all of victim's belongings from their apartment. He told various stories about his wife's disappearance, but witnesses did not come forward until nearly ten years later. In December 1985, defendant applied for Social Security survivor benefits and told a babysitter that he fed part of victim to the hogs and buried other part of her body in the basement. While discussing the investigation with his sister, defendant stated, "Don't they realize by now I would have moved the body?" Defendant was convicted and sentenced to 15 years to life.

Source: *Ohio v. Christman*, 1999 Ohio App. LEXIS 2486

Keyword: **Confession to friends and family**

Case 63

Defendants: **Greg Chrysler, Larry Weygandt**

Victim: Dominick Pendino

Trial: 2000 Jurisdiction: Orange County, New York

Murder: March 3, 1999

Evidence: Defendants murdered victim because they believed he had told police about Chrysler's marijuana operation, which led to Chrysler's arrest. Police found large quantities of blood outside victim's car in his driveway and demonstrated that no one could survive such a loss

of blood. Police also proved that Chrysler had taken victim's truck to a detail shop and forced the owner to clean the blood out of the truck.
Source: Doe Network
Keyword: **Forensic evidence: Other**

Case 64

Defendants: **Kenneth Clamp, Stewart Skuba**
Victim: Elias Sorokin
Trial: August 2011 Jurisdiction: Santa Cruz, California
Murder: July 2009
Evidence: Victim was at Skuba's house to sell 10 pounds of marijuana when he was beaten in Skuba's garage, loaded into his own truck, and dumped in a desolate area. His truck was burned and found one week later. Defendants used his check card and had a 19-year-old woman try to cash a check from victim's company. That same 19-year-old testified that she heard sounds of a scuffle the night of the murder and helped clean up the blood in the garage. She also saw the ten one-pound bags of marijuana and victim's possessions, including his laptop and wallet. Skuba later confessed that their plan to use chloroform on victim had not worked and that they had dumped victim's body off a cliff. Skuba and Clamp were found guilty of first-degree murder. In October of 2013, victim's skeletal remains were found by a utility worker.
Sources: http://www.contracostatimes.com/news/ci_24207227/remains-found-near-bonny-doon-linked-murder-victim; http://www.ksbw.com/Man-Sentenced-In-Sorokin-Santa-Cruz-Murder-Case/-/1824/4910316/-/110w689/-/index.html; http://www.dailycamera.com/ci_15016987
Keyword: **Eyewitness**

Case 65

Defendant: **Everett Drew Clark**
Victim: George B. Schick
Trial: 1924 Jurisdiction: San Diego, California
Murder: February 1923
Evidence: Victim was a wealthy San Diego investment broker. Defendant was a con man who claimed to be a psychic, a sheik, and a furniture salesman. He and victim met, and defendant convinced victim to purchase a house for him and his wife where they lived rent-free. In February 1923, defendant came to victim's home and told victim's wife that victim had fled to Mexico. He had several of victim's possessions, including his car, wallet, and keys. Later, he told victim's wife that victim had been killed by pirates on a lake in Mexico and his body fed to sharks. The police eventually uncovered evidence of a fight between defendant and victim in defendant's home the night before he disappeared, as well as evidence of a fire that burned for three days. There were reports that burning flesh could be smelled. Defendant also began seeing victim's wife and eventually had a baby

with her and controlled his estate. Defendant also confessed to a witness. He was convicted of murder and sentenced to life.

Sources: "Lie Detector Used in Schick Murder Probe," *The News* (San Diego), February 11, 1924; *Corpus Deliciti* by Diane Wagner; "Clark Conviction Upheld," *Los Angeles Times*, March 11, 1925

Keyword: **Confession to friends and family**

Case 66

Defendant: **Hadden Clark**

Victim: Michele Dorr

Trial: October 1999 Jurisdiction: Montgomery County, Maryland

Murder: May 31, 1986

Evidence: Victim was a 6-year-old girl who lived two doors away from defendant's brother, who had a child the same age as victim. Victim was playing in a backyard wading pool in the early afternoon when her father last saw her. He first believed she was at the neighbor's house playing with her friend, but he learned that they had not been home. Defendant became a suspect because he was at the neighbor's house (his brother's house) during the relevant time frame. He was questioned by police twice, and during the second interview, he became very upset, vomited when using the bathroom, and asked to see a psychiatrist. He told the police he may have done something when he blacked out. The police also spoke to a witness, who stated he had seen defendant leave his brother's house with a bag and a trunk.

Complicating the investigation was that victim's father was initially a suspect. Indeed, he confessed to suffocating his daughter and putting her in the sewer, and at other points saying he buried her near his father's gravesite. He had several nervous breakdowns and was hospitalized. At trial, he testified that he was not completely sure when he last saw his daughter, but it could have been as early at 12:30 or 1 p.m., which was crucial because the defendant was at his job as a bus boy at a country club by 2:45 p.m. (Interestingly, victim's father was allowed to testify about his memory of when he saw her after it had been aided by hypnosis.)

In 1992, another girl, 23-year-old Laura Houghteling, disappeared. Defendant, who had worked at the Houghteling's house as a handyman, immediately became a suspect in that disappearance. During their investigation of the Houghteling disappearance, the police discovered that the Clark family gravesite had been disturbed and tied it to the defendant through soil samples. The prosecution argued at trial that defendant had originally buried victim's body at his family's gravesite but later moved it. A witness at trial testified that he had seen defendant at the gravesite with a shovel and that two cadaver dogs had alerted on the site.

Defendant pleaded guilty to the Houghteling murder and was sentenced to 30 years in prison. While in prison, he confessed, in varying details, to five inmates about the death of Dorr. To one inmate, he admitted he found victim in his brother's house, slashed her with a knife, nearly decapitating her. He placed her body in a trash bag, cleaned up his niece's room where victim had been playing, and put the bags in his truck. He confessed to another inmate that he had killed victim, whom he knew as a friend of his niece's.

A subsequent search of the niece's room found blood in 85 different places. The defense put on a mitochondrial DNA expert, who testified that the blood in the room could not have come from either defendant or victim. The prosecution contended that there was not enough DNA to prove the source of the blood.

Defendant was interrogated by the police in both 1992 and 1998 and made incriminating statements but not a full confession. (The court noted that the police had violated defendant's rights during the 1992 interrogation, calling it, "the worst I have ever seen.")

Defendant was convicted of second-degree murder and given 30 more years. After his conviction, defendant led police to the location where he had buried victim's body.

Source: *Hadden Irving Clark v. Maryland*, 781 A2d. 918 (Md. App. 2001)

Keywords: **Forensic evidence: DNA, Informant, Confession to police**

Case 67

Defendant: **Kevin Clark, Helen Tibon**

Victim: Kristy Green

Trial: September 2002 Jurisdiction: Sacramento County, California

Murder: March 2000

Evidence: Defendants are brother and sister and allegedly murdered victim because they feared she was going to tell the police about a mail fraud scheme they were running. Victim was gone for three months before the police were notified, despite being the mother of a 3-year-old-child (Clark was the father.) Defendants tortured victim, and she suffocated while wrapped in plastic bubble wrap. Her body was then cut up, burned, and dumped into a river. Four accomplices testified about assisting defendants. Clark told a number of different stories about the murder, including that he did not know she was dead, that his sister had killed and dismembered her, and that his sister had killed her but admitted he had helped cut the body up. At trial, he testified that the whole thing was a ruse to frighten the accomplices from going to the police. Defendants were sentenced to 25 years to life. On appeal, defendants presented two witnesses who testified they had seen victim alive, but the appeal was rejected and the conviction upheld.

Sources: http://blogs.sacbee.com/crime/archives/2013/09/ask-sacto-911-crime-qa-what-happened-to-man-who-killed-woman-dumped-body-in-1.html; Charley Project

Keyword: **Codefendant testimony**

Case 68

Defendant: **Michael Lubahn Clark**

Victim: Carol Jeanne Lubahn

Trial: October 2012 Jurisdiction: Los Angeles, California

Murder: March 31, 1981

Evidence: Defendant and victim had been married for 10 years and had two children. Defendant was afraid his wife would divorce him, and she was pressuring him to sell their home. He told the police and others that she had left their home after an argument and never returned. Her car was found abandoned in a restaurant parking on April 6, and a witness testified it had been there for a week. The investigation showed she had never collected her last paycheck, used her credit cards, or collected Social Security. Defendant began dating a college classmate of his eight months after victim's disappearance and divorced victim in absentia in 1984. Over the 31 years before his arrest, he told the police several different stories about his wife's death, but after his trial he admitted that she had hit her head on a table, dying instantly. He later changed his story and admitted to punching her in the head and then dumping the body into the ocean. Defendant was an expert scuba diver, and he weighed the body down with a cinder block and dumped it 200 to 500 yards off shore. (He later changed his story again and said he buried her.) He was convicted and sentenced to 15 years to life. The case was based almost solely on defendant's inconsistent statements. There was no physical evidence or confession to anyone.

Sources: http://www.dailybreeze.com/general-news/20130107/michael-lubahn-clark-gets-15-years-to-life-for-1981-torrance-slaying-of-wife; Charley Project

Keywords: **N/A**

Case 69

Defendant: **Randy Cole (a.k.a. Randy Turpin) Bell**

Victim: Charles Mims

Trial: 1982 Jurisdiction: Chilton County, Alabama

Murder: 1981

Evidence: There was no physical evidence against defendant, and the evidence consisted of the testimony of two men, Michael Joe Hubbard and Joseph C. Austin, Jr. Hubbard testified that defendant asked him to call victim and tell him they had stolen property to sell to him. Defendant mentioned that victim often carried large amounts of cash. Victim was at a store when Hubbard called him, and victim told the storeowner that he was going to meet the two men. The storeowner said that victim had a large amount of cash. The three men then met at a campground. Defendant then pointed a gun at victim and told Hubbard to tie victim's hands together. At some point, an ex-girlfriend of defendant's drove by and saw defendant's Cadillac and victim's truck. When she drove by later she saw only victim's truck. When she later asked defendant about this, he told her to "shut up" and said she knew "too much." The men then put victim in the trunk of the Cadillac and drove to a remote location. Once there, they got victim out of the car and led him to a shallow grave in the woods. Defendant then shot victim twice at close range in the back of the head. Hubbard then ran back to the Cadillac and both men left. Hubbard said he looked back three times but victim never got up. They got two flat tires on the way back to town, and they drove on the tire after the second flat. Victim's wife and another witness saw the men driving on the flat back into town. Austin testified that defendant came by his house and told him that he and Hubbard had met victim to sell him stolen goods. They ended up robbing him instead, and defendant showed him some money. Defendant then left to fix his flat tire. Hubbard testified that defendant told him several times not to speak to the police. He also said he had moved victim's body and destroyed it with acid. Defendant applied for new license plates and his car was later found at a used car dealer. The trunk was wet and smelled of detergent. The police also found several cleaning agents and .25 caliber ammunition in the defendant's trunk. Defendant was convicted of capital murder and sentenced to die.

Source: *Bell v. Haley*, 437 F. Supp. 2d 1278 (M.D. Ala. 2005)

Keywords: **Codefendant testimony, Death penalty**

Case 70

Defendant: **Jamee Corean**

Victim: Troy Klug

Trial: August 2008 Jurisdiction: Rapid City, South Dakota

Murder: July 12, 2004

Evidence: Victim was purchasing meth from a man named Tony Teigen in order to sell it and repay a debt. Teigen kidnapped victim and bound and gagged him. He placed him in a large toolbox in a garage that defendant shared with her boyfriend. The boyfriend testified that he told defendant several times that the victim was in the toolbox, but she never called the police. Defendant was convicted of aiding and abetting the kidnapping and the murder and given life. Teigen was tried separately and was convicted of kidnapping. He later took the police to where the body was buried in Montana.

Sources: http://rapidcityjournal.com/news/belle-fourche-woman-serving-life-for-troy-klug-murder-seeks/article_ffd1fc80-b06a-11df-bf0c-001cc4c03286.html; http://rapidcityjournal.com/news/local/jamee-corean-found-guilty-could-face-life-imprisonment/article_8ed9a2d7-f1e3-5104-a1d5-f02020b487f9.html

Keywords: **Life, Codefendant testimony**

Case 71

Defendant: **Paul Kay Coronel**

Victim: Soledad Santa Cruz Coronel

Trial: 1989 Jurisdiction: Hawaii

Murder: July 1, 1986

Evidence: Defendant murdered his mother so he could take over her property. Defendant wrote letter he claimed was by mother, but letter was found to be forged.

Source: *Coronel v. Oku*, 29 F.3d 631 (9th Cir. 1994)

Keyword: **Life**

Case 72

Defendant: **Ronald Coulter**

Victim: Edwina Simms

Trial: February 2004 Jurisdiction: Charleston, South Carolina

Murder: April 2001

Evidence: Victim was defendant's ex-girlfriend. She had traveled from Virginia to visit defendant, who was the father of her child. She had told others she was afraid of defendant. She had an older child with another man that she had left behind during the visit. A witness testified that he saw defendant and his codefendant, Ivory Crocker, outside the hotel where victim was staying, wearing gloves and putting a large plastic trash bag into the trunk of a car. The witness wrote down a partial tag, which matched the last four digits of the car defendant had rented. There was also evidence that defendant and Crocker had had telephone conversations during the weekend victim was visiting. During the trial, Crocker pleaded guilty and agreed to testify against defendant in exchange for having the charges against him reduced. Crocker admitted he helped load victim's body into the car. Defendant then pleaded guilty during trial. Crocker led the police to victim's body.

Sources: Smith, G., "Missing woman was afraid, friends said," *The Post and Courier*, February 25, 2004; Smith, "Deal for 30-year term brings Sims case to end," *The Post and Courier*, February 26, 2004.

Keyword: **Codefendant testimony**

Case 73

Defendant: **Gustavo Covian**

Victim: Young Kim

Trial: February 2003 Jurisdiction: Santa Clara, California

Murder: November 13, 1998

Evidence: This was believed to be a murder for hire by defendant on behalf of victim's wife. The couple were having both marital and financial difficulties as well as affairs. The wife allegedly paid defendant $100,000 for the hit. Victim owned a diner where defendant and his wife had once worked, and he was killed after he entered his own garage after a night of drinking with a friend. Victim's wife found victim's car in their garage but did not report him as missing to the police until 16 days later. Defendant bragged to others and asked victim's wife to pay him for getting rid of her abusive husband. Defendant was convicted of first-degree murder. (The wife was later prosecuted but was acquitted.)

Sources: http://www.mercurynews.com/ci_20703042/sierra-lamar-alleged-killer-charged-murder-antolin-garcia-torres; http://groups.yahoo.com/neo/groups/botabolition/conversations/topics/67; http://blueribbonlaw.com/PDF/San%20Jose%20Mercury%20News%202-2-2003.pdf

Keyword: **Confession to friends and family**

Case 74

Defendants: **Lawrence Cowell, Donald Dimascio**

Victim: Scott Campbell

Trial: December 1989 Jurisdiction: Newport Beach, California

Murder: 1982

Evidence: Victim was lured onto a plane with defendants by Cowell telling him he could complete his inflight training. Cowell and victim had been friends since they were young. Defendants believed that victim was carrying a large amount of cash, but he only had a kilo of cocaine he was going to sell in North Dakota. Dimascio then beat and strangled victim, tossing his body into the ocean from the plane. Defendants hoped to mutilate victim enough to attract sharks and leave behind no evidence. After victim was reported missing by his parents, Cowell was caught with victim's car trying to sell it for parts. Cowell claimed he was acting in self-defense because Dimascio had a gun. Defendants were convicted in 1985 of first-degree murder, but that conviction was overturned on the ground that Cowell's confession to an undercover police officer had been improperly coerced. Cowell was retried in 1989 and convicted again. At his retrial, the defense presented an alibi witness that Cowell was buying marijuana from at the time of the murder.

Sources: http://sanjuancapistrano.patch.com/groups/police-and-fire/p/parole-denied-for-ex-mayor-sons-murderer; http://articles.latimes.com/1990-01-27/local/me-549_1_court-reform; http://blogs.ocweekly.com/navelgazing/2011/04/lawrence_rayburn_cowell_plane.php

Keywords: **Confession to police**

Case 75

Defendant: **Richard Crafts**

Victim: Helene Crafts

Trial: 1987, 1989 Jurisdiction: Newtown, Connecticut

Murder: November 19, 1986

Evidence: Defendant was an airline pilot and auxiliary police office, while victim was a flight attendant. They had a troubled marriage, and victim had confronted defendant over his womanizing. After victim disappeared, defendant told people that she had returned to Denmark, had gone to Germany, was in the Canary Islands with a friend, or had gone to her sister's house. Friends of victim told the police, however, that victim was upset with defendant and said that if anything happens to her do not assume it was an accident.

Police found a witness who told them that he had seen a man operating wood chipper near a lake in a bad snowstorm. It later came out that defendant had taken their three young children to his sister's house the day of the storm. Police searched the shore and found strands of blonde hair (the same color as the victim's), fingernails, and skin. The blood type from the parts found was "O," the same as victim's. (This was before DNA typing.) They also found pieces of mail with the Crafts' name on it among the chipped debris. Police also recovered a chain saw with the serial number scratched off, a receipt for a rental truck in defendant's possession, and evidence of the rental of a large freezer. Police believe the truck was used to temporarily store and transport the body. Pieces of carpet were missing from the master bedroom. Towels found in the house also had O-type blood on them.

The first trial hung 11–1 to convict, but defendant was convicted at a second trial. Defendant was sentenced to 50 years in prison.

Source: http://www.newstimes.com/local/article/23-years-ago-Richard-Crafts-was-more-willing-to-256633.php#; http://www.trutv.com/library/crime/notorious_murders/family/woodchipper_murder/index.html
Keywords: **Forensic evidence: Other, Eyewitness**

Case 76

Defendant: **Willie Crain, Jr.**
Victim: Amanda Brown
Trial: November 1999 Jurisdiction: Tampa, Florida
Murder: September 1998
Evidence: Victim was the 7-year-old daughter of Kathryn Hartman. Hartman met defendant at a bar and ended up hanging out with him over the course of a day and half. During that time, defendant met Hartman's daughter. At one point, defendant, Hartman, and her daughter were all sleeping in the same bed after Hartman had taken some pain medication. When Hartman awoke, both defendant and her daughter were gone. When she called defendant, he was at a boat launch (he was a fisherman and crabber) and said he had not seen victim. A witness testified that he saw defendant at the boat launch wearing a distinctive shirt that was never recovered and that he was carrying something wrapped in cloth. This same witness said that 18 months prior, defendant had boasted of his ability to get rid of a body. A police detective spoke to defendant two hours later and noticed a small scratch on his upper arm and that he had different clothes on than what the witness had described. Defendant had other scratches on his body that he told the police were from crabbing, but a forensic pathologist described them as consistent with being scratched by a 7 year old. Defendant told the police that he spent the early morning hours cleaning his entire house with bleach. A search of his bathroom turned up traces of blood and bleach, and the blood came back to a mixture of defendant and victim's blood on his toilet seat, a piece of tissue found in the toilet, and his boxer shorts. The odds of the blood being randomly the same as victim's and his were DNA was 1 in 388 million. Defendant also made some odd statements to other witnesses about whether he "did it" or not in relation to the disappearance of victim. Defendant testified that he did not kill victim, and when he left early in the morning from Hartman's house, victim was asleep. Defendant was found guilty of first-degree murder and kidnapping and sentenced to death.
Source: *Willie Seth Crain v. Florida*, No. SC00-661, October 28, 2004
Keywords: **Forensic evidence: DNA, Confession to friends and family**

Case 77

Defendant: **Mark Christopher Crew**
Victim: Nancy Crew
Trial: 1989 Jurisdiction: Santa Clara, California
Murder: August 1982
Evidence: The evidence at trial showed that defendant was hoping to bilk money from his bride of two months. He told one of his friends that he planned to kill her. Defendant also discussed with his stepfather

several ways to kill victim, including leaving her hanging from a tree in the wilderness so the bears would eat her. Victim was nervous about going on a cross-country trip with defendant and told a friend if she was not heard from in two weeks to call the police. Defendant and victim were supposed to drive from California to South Carolina, but they apparently never left California. Defendant was later seen with victim's possessions, including her Corvette and horse. He also had large amounts of cash consistent with the money victim had cashed from her bank accounts before they left on her trip. Defendant told another girlfriend a crazy story about a woman the mob had killed and that he had buried the body. At trial, a witness testified that defendant admitted he killed victim while they were hiking in the woods. Defendant admitted he shot her in the head and then left her in the mountains to die. He returned the next day and saw she was still alive. Along with an accomplice, he decapitated her, and put her body in a 55-gallon drum filled with cement and buried it in the accomplice's backyard. They put her head in a five-gallon drum, filled it with cement, and dumped her in the San Francisco Bay. Defendant admitted to another man that he had killed a woman and put her head and body into separate drums, burying one in a backyard and throwing another into the bay. Despite searches of the accomplice's backyard, victim's body was never found. Defendant was convicted and sentenced to death.

Sources: http://www.examiner.com/article/santa-clara-county-inmate-s-latest-appeal-denied-by-state-supreme-court; http://www.examiner.com/article/santa-clara-county-inmate-s-latest-appeal-denied-by-state-supreme-court; *People v. Crew*, 74 P.3d 820 (Cal. 2003)

Keywords: **Eyewitness, Confession to friends and family, Death penalty**

Case 78

Defendant: **Thomas Jessie Crews**

Victim: Sondra Denise Barrington

Trial: September 2006 Jurisdiction: Polk County, Florida

Murder: October 10, 2002

Evidence: Defendant and victim were boyfriend and girlfriend and had a young son together. They had had a violent relationship, and victim was scheduled to testify against defendant on October 11 for violating an injunction. Victim was last seen on October 10 with defendant on the highway, and her car was found three miles from the airport where she worked. Her purse and other belongings were found inside the car, but her pager and keys were missing. Victim's blood was found in defendant's gym bag, and defendant's wife testified that defendant arrived home late the night of the 10th and then went out again for an hour and a half. Defendant was convicted and sentenced to life.

Sources: Charley Project; Bowden, R., "Man sentenced to life in prison for abduction-murder," *DeSoto Sun*, October 24, 2006

Keywords: **Forensic evidence: DNA, Eyewitness**

Case 79

Defendant: **Felipe Cruz Hernandez**
Victim: Leticia Barrales Ramos
Trial: December 2009 Jurisdiction: Yolo County, California
Murder: April 2009
Evidence: On the day she disappeared, 28-year-old Leticia Barrales Ramos left behind her passport, purse, Mexican consulate card, Mexican voter registration card, $1,000 in cash, and her credit cards. Defendant was the last person to see her before she disappeared. Hernandez and Ramos were in the middle of a divorce and a custody battle for their young daughter. Defendant followed victim and her boyfriend in his car and then killed victim in his apartment. Defendant told people she had gone to Mexico, and her relatives were called by someone claiming to be her who said she was having trouble crossing the border. She was allegedly killed with a gun defendant borrowed from his brother. Traces of victim's blood were found on the carpet, under the carpet, and on furniture that had been rearranged to cover the stains. The police also found a receipt for a steam cleaner dated the day after victim disappeared. Hernandez was convicted and sentenced to 15 years in prison.
Sources: Charley Project; http://www.news10.net/news/local/story.aspx?storyid=73857
Keyword: **Forensic evidence: DNA**

Case 80

Defendant: **Raymond Cullen**
Victims: Mary Cullen, Daniel T. Boyer
Trial: August 1950 Jurisdiction: Riverside, California
Murder: January 3, 1949
Evidence: Defendant had been married to Mary Cullen for less than five months, and her father, Boyer, lived with them. Boyer was 81 years old at the time of his murder. The marriage between defendant and victim quickly soured, and by December victim was making plans to move out of defendant's home. The morning of January 4, defendant reported to a real estate broker that his wife and her father had fallen into the river while trying to retrieve a duck they had shot. Defendant then told the sheriff that their boat had gotten loose and was adrift down the river. The boat was later located empty down river from defendant's house with Boyer's hat inside. Defendant told various stories of their disappearance to their family. Defendant had also forged Boyer's name on his pension check and cashed it the day before he reported victims missing and then lied about who had cashed it. Victims' family noted that rugs in the house were wet and the police later learned defendant had recently washed the rugs. An extensive search of the river was made for the bodies, but they were never recovered, which is unusual for a drowning. About 150 yards from defendant's house a freshly dug hole was found. Two rings similar to those worn by Mary Cullen were found in the hole, even though defendant said she had been wearing them. Other jewelry was found in the house, but the $700 cash she had was never found. Blood was

found in the floorboards and in the rugs. Other spots of blood were found on defendant's clothes, his gloves, the doorjamb, Mary's raincoat, and Boyer's hat, along with other items in the house. Defendant made numerous incriminating statements to family members about the murder, including that they were both dead in the house and that he could not be convicted without a body. Defendant was convicted of both murders and sentenced to death.

Source: *People v. Cullen*, 37 Cal. 2d 614 (1951)

Keywords: **Forensic evidence: Other, Confession to friends and family**

Case 81

Defendant: **Benjamin Harry Crider**

Victim: Crystal Gayle Dittmeyer

Trial: 1998, 2004 Jurisdiction: Oklahoma City, Oklahoma

Murder: June 1996

Evidence: Victim, 12 years old, disappeared on Thursday, June 13. Defendant was her stepfather. Prosecution alleged defendant killed victim at their apartment, removed her body in a garment bag, transported it in his state-issued car, and then disposed of it at an unknown location. Prosecution presented evidence that there was victim's blood and a bloody towel in the master bedroom, that defendant could not account for his time or excess mileage on his car, and the presence of a bite mark on the defendant's forearm. In addition, the backseats reacted to luminol, and defendant's garment bag was missing and he purchased a new one after victim's disappearance.

Defendant was convicted of murder at his first trial and sentenced to life. Appellate court, however, reversed the conviction on three grounds: first, that the bite evidence should not have been admitted; second, that the luminol tests were irrelevant and should not have been admitted; and third, that a detective's testimony regarding ways in which a person might dispose of a body was irrelevant. The defendant was retried in 2004, but the jury was hung. Just before his third trial, he pleaded guilty to manslaughter and was sentenced to 10 years in prison, of which he had already served 9.

Sources: http://mylifeofcrime.wordpress.com/2013/09/05/parents-gone-wild-benjamin-crider-ii-killed-his-stepdaughter-12-year-old-crystal-gayle-dittmeyer-whose-body-has-never-been-recovered/; *Benjamin Harry Crider, II v. Oklahoma*, 29 P.2d 577 (2001)

Keyword: **Forensic evidence: DNA**

Case 82

Defendant: **Charles Cunningham**

Victim: John Scott

Trial: October 2007 Jurisdiction: Yolo County, California

Murder: June 3, 2006

Evidence: Defendant was a handyman for victim, a retired University of California at Davis professor. Victim caught defendant forging his names on checks. After victim disappeared, defendant was caught with a travel trailer that belonged to victim. Blood spatter belonging to victim was found in his house. Defendant admitted to police he had murdered victim. Defendant was convicted of first-degree murder and sentenced to 32 years to life. Victim's body was later found in a shallow grave on his property in April 2008.

Sources: http://www.trainorders.com/discussion/read.php?1,1519934; http://z13.invisionfree.com/PorchlightUSA/ar/t4769.htm

Keywords: **Confession to police**

Case 83

Defendant: **Andrew Curro**

Victim: April Ernst

Trial: January 1986 Jurisdiction: Brooklyn, New York

Murder: September 7–8, 1980

Evidence: The appeals court that upheld defendant's conviction summarized the evidence against defendant, a reputed member of the Gambino crime family, as follows: "(D)efendant was charged with the intentional murder of April Ernst, who disappeared sometime between September 7 and September 8, 1980. Her body has never been found. The only direct evidence implicating the defendant in her murder consisted of testimony by his brother, Gerard Curro, that the defendant had made certain admissions to him. According to Gerard, the defendant admitted that he had strangled Ernst because she was going to 'rat [him] out' [about an armored car robbery]. The defendant told his brother that he had cut her body into pieces in a bathtub, put the pieces in bags and then 'took them for a ride.' Another prosecution witness testified that the defendant told him in 1982 that he had shot his girlfriend because he believed that she was informing on him about his drug dealing, that he had disposed of her body in a garbage truck and that 'there wasn't enough left of her for them to identify the body.'"

The court also noted the following proof that the victim was dead: "Ernst was 19 years old when she disappeared in September 1980, and five of her close relatives testified that they had not heard from her since then. According to her mother, Ernst lived with her until she finished school at age 18. Although their arguments over Ernst's drug use caused her to leave home, the mother testified that Ernst thereafter always lived with close relatives and remained in contact [with] her. Ernst had been living with a paternal aunt at the time of her disappearance and her clothing and jewelry, including a diamond necklace she received on her sixteenth birthday, were left behind, Ernst's older sister testified that they had a very close relationship and that she would expect to hear from Ernst if she were still alive. Ernst's father, who lived in California, testified that, prior to her disappearance, he had been her main source of support, sending her money weekly, and that he had not heard from her since September 1980. Ernst's stepmother also testified that she had a close relationship with her and that, prior to Ernst's disappearance in September 1980, had heard from her at least once a week. The paternal aunt with whom Ernst lived in September 1980, testified that she believed she heard Ernst enter and leave the house around 6:00 A.M. on September 8, 1980 and had not seen or heard from her since then. She said that

Ernst and the defendant were dating at that time. Ernst did not take her clothing and jewelry with her when she left, and her car was found abandoned on Rockaway Parkway that same morning. The family contacted local hospitals without success. Finally, the People submitted evidence that there had been no activity on Ernst's social security account since September 1980."

The defendant was found guilty of second-degree murder in the second degree and sentenced to 25 years to life.

Sources: *New York v. Andrew Curro*, 556 N.Y.S.2d 364 (2nd Dept. 1990); http://officialcoldcaseinvestigations.com/showthread.php?p=65120

Keyword: **Confession to friends and family**

Case 84

Defendant: **Jeffrey Dahmer**

Victims: Richard Guerrero, Edward Smith, Anthony Sears, David Thomas

Trial: February 1992 Jurisdiction: Milwaukee, Wisconsin

Murders: May 24, 1988/June 1990/May 25, 1989/September 1990

Evidence: Defendant was a well-known serial killer who was alleged to have killed at least 17 young men over a period of 13 years. Defendant confessed to the police what he had done. During his trial, he pleaded not guilty by reason of insanity and did not contest that he had committed the four murders for which bodies were never found. It is believed he destroyed their bodies in vats of acid after they had been cut up. He was found sane, guilty, and sentenced to 957 years for the 15 murders for which he was tried.

Source: Murderpedia

Keyword: **Confession to police**

Case 85

Defendant: **James Edward Dailey**

Victim: Guadalupe Dailey

Trial: August 2001 Jurisdiction: Santee, California

Murder: July 1997

Evidence: Defendant and victim had been married but were in the process of getting divorced and had two young children. On Labor Day, victim made plans to go to Las Vegas with Alan Thompson, a man she worked with. The two spoke several times on the day they were to leave, and she seemed excited about the trip. Thompson never heard from her again, though. That same day, victim was also seen by two sailors, Eric Cameron and Tommy Tucker, who were roommates and either were having or had sexual relationships with victim. She borrowed an overnight bag from Cameron. Neither man ever saw her alive or spoke to her again. Both Thompson and victim's sister tried to page her but did not hear back. Victim's sister spoke to defendant, who said she had dropped off their children with him at 1:30 p.m. and had left at 6:30 p.m. He admitted they had had a fight about money. Defendant asked if the sister could babysit the children, and when she refused, defendant called another one of victim's sisters who agreed to babysit. Defendant admitted he took his boat out around

10:30 p.m., and although he had engine troubles, he was gone for three or four hours. Eventually Thompson reported victim missing. The police interviewed defendant and searched his apartment but did not find anything. The police cleared Thompson, Cameron, and Tucker as suspects. They learned, however, that defendant had threatened to kill victim many times, according to his coworkers. He specifically discussed killing her and dumping her body in the water near Catalina Island. He blamed victim for his problems and disapproved of what he saw as victim's permissive lifestyle. He told others he would kill her and bury her and that he would strangle her while he was making love to her. The police examined defendant's boat and discovered it had no spark plugs and appeared to have been out of the water for a long time. They also found victim's checkbook on board the boat with a check receipt written the day before she disappeared. There was evidence that victim was afraid of water and would have been unlikely to have gone on defendant's boat. Despite this evidence, the district attorney's office refused to prosecute the case until 2001. Soon after, the murder defendant fled to Indiana with his two children, and he was arrested there. At trial, defendant argued that victim's Social Security Number and cell phone had been used after her disappearance and that someone had seen victim alive after she disappeared. Defendant also sought to blame the other men she had been involved with and suggested she had fled to Mexico. The prosecution disproved these theories, and defendant was convicted of murder. He was sentenced to 25 years to life.

Sources: Charley Project; http://www.sandiegoreader.com/news/2002/jan/31/he-said-he-wanted-kill-her/

Keywords: **Confession to friends and family, Life**

Case 86

Defendant: **Kerry Dalton**

Victim: Irene May

Trial: 1995 Jurisdiction: San Diego, California

Murder: 1988

Evidence: Defendant, along with Sheryl Ann Baker and Mark Lee Tompkins, murdered victim by tying her to a chair, injecting her with battery acid, and then beating her with a skillet because defendant suspected victim of stealing her property. The three then stabbed her and disposed of body. Body was allegedly buried on an Indian reservation to make it harder to find. All three confessed their involvement to others, and Baker testified against defendant and statements of Tompkins were introduced. Defendant was convicted of murder and sentenced to death.

Sources: http://articles.latimes.com/1992-10-28/local/me-691_1_body-arrested-found; Murderpedia

Keywords: **Confession to friends and family, Codefendant testimony, Death penalty**

Case 87

Defendant: **Ralph Davis**
Victim: Susan Davis
Trial: March 1989 Jurisdiction: Boone County, Missouri
Murder: June 10, 1986
Evidence: Defendant and victim were married and had two children. They had a troubled marriage, and defendant suspected victim was having an affair. In May 1986, defendant and victim had a violent argument. Defendant was arrested, and victim also sought a protection order. Victim left marital home and drove to parents in Iowa. Defendant, in violation of court order, repeatedly came to home and once told a neighbor, "The only way to stop a whoring bitch like that is to shoot her." He told a friend that if victim did not quit "messing with him" he would "blow her away." On June 5, victim returned home. She learned that defendant had continuously violated the court's order by entering the home, and as she was talking to neighbor, defendant appeared and an argument ensued between all three people. The next day, victim filed new criminal charges against defendant, who was arrested again but released. On June 9, victim left her job and told coworker that she intended to drive straight home. That was the last time victim was ever seen or heard from. Around this same time, defendant rented a storage unit and stored victim's car in it with air fresheners. He retrieved his children, moved back into house, and filed for divorce from victim. Victim did not show for protective order hearing or divorce, so he was granted divorce and custody of children and all charges were dropped. In mid-June and late July, defendant apparently forged three checks on victim's personal account totaling nine hundred dollars. Defendant also forged victim's signature to a change of beneficiary form on defendant's policy of life insurance. In the 20 months following, defendant routinely lied about whereabouts of victim and victim's car. Police eventually found car in storage unit when defendant failed to pay rent. Car was heavily damaged and had blood and human bone fragments inside. Tissue recovered from the car had indications of a prescription drug the victim took. When confronted by police, defendant at first denied knowledge of where her car was. When told police had car and from where they got it, defendant changed his story, asserting that on the day victim disappeared, they got into an argument and victim pulled a gun on him. When asked about the blood in the car, defendant claimed that victim began to beat on the window with the gun as defendant drove away and in the process smashed the window running her hand through it and cutting her arm severely, and defendant drove away never to see victim again. Police found victim's diamond ring from prior marriage and shotgun at defendant's home and office. Tests revealed the shotgun had been fired. At trial, defendant admitted having lied to neighbors, friends, relatives, and the police concerning victim's disappearance but asserted on the stand that for the first time during this three-year period, he would "come clean" and tell what really happened, insisting that his current version

of the events was finally the truth. Jury found defendant guilty of first-degree murder, and defendant was executed in 1999.

Sources: *State of Missouri v. Ralph E. Davis*, 814 SW 2d 593 (Mo. 1991)(en banc); Murderpedia

Keywords: **Death penalty, Forensic evidence: DNA**

Case 88

Defendants: **Skylar Deleon, Jennifer Deleon, John Kennedy**

Victims: Thomas and Jackie Hawks

Trial: November 2006/October 2008 Jurisdiction: Orange County, California

Murder: November 15, 2004

Evidence: Victims were husband and wife who were selling their yacht for $440,000. The Deleons posed as husband and wife in order to lure victims out to sea. On a second visit to take the boat out to sea, Skylar Deleon was joined by Alonso Machain, a jail orderly that Syklar met while imprisoned, and John Kennedy, posing as Deleon's accountant. Once the ship was out to sea, the men overpowered victims and tied them up. They forced them to sign documents turning over the boat title to defendants. Both victims were then beaten and chained to the boat's anchor and tossed overboard. Deleon tried to backdate the documents to make it appear that the sale had occurred earlier than the date of the murder. Victim's brother became concerned when he did not hear from his brother and discovered the boat at the dock but in poor shape, which was uncharacteristic for his brother. He reported his brother missing, and the police soon discovered that the boat was now registered to Deleon. Deleon, when confronted by the police, "confessed" that he had purchased the boat with laundered drug money. He said that he had last seen victims when he had paid for the boat. Victims' car was found and Deleon was identified as being the person last seen in the car. Machain ended up cooperating with the police and testified at trial. He was sentenced to 20 years in prison. Skylar Deleon and John Kennedy were both convicted and sentenced to death. Jennifer Deleon was also convicted at a separate trial for assisting in the cleanup of the boat after the murders and her role in putting the victims' at ease. She was sentenced to two life terms.

Source: http://thedevilandthedeathpenalty.com/skylar-deleon-2/

Keywords: **Codefendant testimony, Death penalty, Life**

Case 89

Defendants: **Simona Denise Demery, Jeffrey Jones**

Victim: Alicia Verslais

Trial: July 2001 Jurisdiction: Pomona, California

Murder: May 7, 2000

Evidence: Victim, three years old, was one of defendants' twin daughters. Defendants reported her missing while they were with the twins in a park, which led to a large-scale search. The couple was eventually jailed on child endangerment charges. While jailed, police intercepted communications between the two, which led to murder charges. The letters revealed that Jones told Demery to keep her mouth shut and to stop referring to "the body." Another letter from Demery to Jones stated, "If they find her body, you have to do what you said you would do from the begging [sic], witch [sic] is say you did this, so that we both won't be in jail...." Demery also said that she told authorities her daughter died in her sleep and the couple buried her. Demery also told Jones: "I messed up one time and told my family the truth.... I can easily just say I was telling them what they wanted to hear." She also allegedly told Jones that her lawyer had said that if police could not recover a body, they would not be charged: "They can find her and then try to charge somebody with murder." Victim's twin told police that Demery "took Sissy and wrapped Sissy in a jacket and put her in a drain." Both defendants were convicted of second-degree murder and other charges and sentenced to 33 years to life. Their appeals were denied.

Sources: http://articles.latimes.com/2000/jul/15/local/me-53433; Charley Project

Keyword: **Confession to friends and family**

Case 90

Defendant: **Kenneth Lee Derring**

Victim: Everett Guy Travis

Trial: April 1980 Jurisdiction: Arkansas

Murder: June 1977

Evidence: The evidence was summarized by the Arkansas Supreme Court as follows: "On the last day he was seen, June 16, 1977, [the victim] had breakfast as usual with his friend and left about 7:30 a.m. for classes at a [vocational] tech school, driving his blue and white Dodge Dart. At about the same time the [defendant] was present at a nearby service station. [The defendant] left there afoot going toward Interstate 55, the highway the victim took to get to school. An instructor at the school testified he looked south from school and saw the victim on the viaduct standing beside his car talking with a black man about 7:50 a.m. The victim did not attend classes that day nor had the instructor seen him since. The victim would have completed his training in three months. A fellow student, on his way to school, saw the victim as the student crossed the interstate. A black man was in the passenger seat. [The defendant is black.] Sometime around the middle of June, 1977, the [defendant] attempted to sell a blue and white Dodge Dart in Sikeston, Missouri. The junk dealer testified that [defendant] was careful not to touch the car with his hand, pulling his sleeve down to cover his hand when he touched the car, even to open the door, and stated he wanted to 'destroy the car.' This dealer reported the incident to the police. When [defendant] was arrested in Sikeston, a .32 caliber revolver was taken from his person as well as an Arkansas safety inspection sticker from the victim's car. A search of the vehicle resulted in finding papers with the victim's name on them and a Bible with his name on the inside. School test papers, pictures, bank account records and his car license plate were found in the trash can behind the residence where the [defendant] was staying. [The defendant] told an acquaintance in Sikeston that he had shot and killed a man in Arkansas, had thrown him in the river, and was driving the 'guy's car he had killed.' Later, [the defendant] told a fellow inmate at the Mississippi County jail that he had shot a man with a .32 caliber revolver at the school in June of 1977 and had thrown his body off a bridge into a ditch about four miles from the school." In addition, defendant confessed to the police. Defendant was convicted of murder and sentenced to death. His appeal was rejected.

Sources: *Kenneth Lee Derring v. Arkansas*, 619 S.W. 2d 644 (1981)

Keywords: **Death penalty, Confession to police**

Case 91

Defendant: **Robert Dianovsky**

Victim: Peggy Dianovsky

Trial: 2003 Jurisdiction: Schaumberg, Illinois

Murder: September 1982

Evidence: Defendant and victim were married. They were in the midst of a bitter divorce and defendant admitted hitting victim once and knocking her down. The couple's sons were 7 and 9 at the time of victim's disappearance. Defendant did not report her missing until five days after she disappeared. There was also blood found on the top of the staircase, but it was not collected. In 2002, 20 years later, the sons came forward to the police. They testified that they saw defendant hold a knife to their mother and that they saw him beat her. They were impeached by their statements to the police at the time of victim's disappearance, however, which did not contain any of these statements. The trial was held before a judge, not a jury, and the court specifically noted that it seemed unlikely the children would not have told the police what they really saw when questioned at school in front of their principal. Years later, the boys taped their father in hopes of getting a confession, but he continued to deny, indeed denied it 112 times on tape, that he had any involvement in the victim's disappearance. At trial, a friend of the defendant's testified that defendant asked him for a gun so he could get rid of victim. The defendant was acquitted.

Sources: http://articles.chicagotribune.com/2004-11-05/news/0411050046_1_courtroom-gallery-police-officer-disappearance; Charley Project

Keyword: **Eyewitness**

Case 92

Defendant: **Shakara Dickens**

Victim: Lauryn Dickens

Trial: March 2012 Jurisdiction: Memphis, Tennessee

Murder: September 7, 2010

Evidence: Defendant was 19 years old and had victim, 8 months, and a son, 3 years old. She told the police that a friend of the father's came by to pick up victim, something the father, who was in jail at the time, denied. The father also denied knowing anyone matching the description of the woman who allegedly picked up victim and also told police that defendant had blocked his calls for a month. Victim was missing a week before she was reported missing, and then only at the insistence of defendant's mother did defendant report her missing. Defendant later gave inconsistent stories of the victim's whereabouts, saying she was with the father's parents and that she had put her up for adoption. Defendant was convicted. At her sentencing, she admitted putting her hand over victim's mouth until she went limp. She wrapped the body up in a trash bag and put it into an apartment building dumpster two buildings away from her own. She was sentenced to 19 years in prison.

Sources: Charley Project; http://www.wmctv.com/story/18857252/mother-admits-to-killing-her-own-daughter

Keyword: **N/A**

Case 93

Defendant: **Vincent Doan**

Victim: Clarissa Ann "Carrie" Culberson

Trial: July 1997 Jurisdiction: Wilmington, Ohio

Murder: August 1996

Evidence: Defendant and victim were in a tumultuous two-year dating relationship. Victim disappeared after a volleyball game. She was dropped off at her house but did not go home, instead getting in her car and driving away. When she was not home the next morning, her mother went looking for her and stopped by defendant's house. At first, he denied having seen her in three days, but he then changed his story. He said she came by that night but was drunk so he ignored her. (Victim's friends stated that she had had only one beer.) Next, he said he spoke to her, but she drove away after he said he did not love her anymore. One month before her disappearance, defendant beat victim with a space heater, sending her to the hospital to get stitches in her head. Defendant was charged with assault in the matter, but the charges were dropped when victim could no longer come forward because she had disappeared. After her disappearance, numerous witnesses came forward with stories of violence inflicted upon victim by defendant. It was clear that defendant was obsessed with victim and did not want her to leave him. Three days before her disappearance, victim told a friend that defendant had held a gun to her and threatened to kill her. The day of her disappearance, witnesses saw defendant at same bar as victim and saw them in a heated discussion with victim shaking her head no. There was also a witness who saw defendant assaulting victim at defendant's house early the morning of the disappearance. A relative of defendant's testified that he showed up at her house on that same morning covered in blood. Defendant asked for his brother, and then both men left with a gun and some trash bags. When they returned 90 minutes later, they both had blood on themselves. Defendant also made some incriminating statements to a cellmate in jail. Defendant was convicted and sentenced to life without the possibility of parole. The jury rejected the prosecution's call for the death penalty. To date, his appeals have been rejected.

Sources: http://cincinnati.com/blogs/ourhistory/2012/03/11/shocking-killing-still-haunts-blanchester/; http://news.findlaw.com/court_tv/s/20030319/19mar2003165458.html
Keywords: **Informant, Life**

Case 94

Defendant: **James Homer Docherty**
Victim: Sharon Martin
Trial: February 2008 Jurisdiction: Pensacola, Florida
Murder: March 21, 2006
Evidence: Defendant was a maintenance worker at an apartment building victim managed. Victim and defendant were close, and victim's husband suspected they were having an affair. A month after her disappearance, defendant used victim's credit card at a Walmart and tried to cash a forged check. A search of defendant's apartment turned up a bloodstained piece of carpet with victim's DNA. At trial, a witness testified that the night of victim's disappearance, he helped defendant lift a heavy trash can into the dumpster. The witness even asked defendant if it contained a body. Defendant paid the witness $450 for helping him. Another witness testified that he saw defendant looking through the dumpster with a flashlight later that night. Defendant was convicted of manslaughter but acquitted of murder. He was sentenced to 15 years in prison.
Source: Charley Project
Keywords: **Forensic evidence: DNA, Eyewitness**

Case 95

Defendant: **Ronnie O. Dorsey**
Victim: Vicky Dorsey
Trial: January 2000 Jurisdiction: Monroe, Louisiana
Murder: August 1999
Evidence: Defendant and victim were married and had children but had a tumultuous relationship. They separated in July 1999. On August 7, 1999, victim went to the Tropical Lounge, left the bar around 1 a.m., and was not seen again. A few minutes after victim's departure, two employees saw victim's car and her purses on the ground. One purse had blood on it. More blood and victim's shoes were found in a nearby alley. When police arrived, they found a nail in one of victim's tires and two large pools of blood in a gas station parking lot next to lounge. They also found a .380 caliber magazine lying in one of the pools of blood with six live rounds. Police followed a blood trail to alley and found drag marks and victim's shoes. Defendant's truck was searched, and victim's blood was found inside on driver's armrest, passenger side door and window, rear window, and on a pair of blue shorts. At his house, her blood was also found on a comforter, a wall near a light switch, a wristwatch, a tube of toothpaste, a soap dish, a Northwest Territory shirt, a black pair of tuxedo pants, and a towel in a box that had been thrown on top of the roof of a shed in the backyard. Also found were a .380 caliber bullet in the black tuxedo

pants and a box of .380-caliber ammunition on top of a television set. The amount of blood lost, as evidenced by the pools of blood, was inconsistent with life. The prosecution also produced a witness that testified that defendant asked her for a nail, the same type of nail found in victim's tire. There was a history of violence by defendant against victim, and police had to use pepper spray to subdue defendant during one response to an incident between defendant and victim. In addition, several witnesses had previously seen defendant with a .380. Defendant was found guilty of second-degree murder and sentenced to life. His appeal was rejected.

Source: *Louisiana v. Dorsey*, 796 So.2d 135 (2001)

Keywords: **Life, Forensic evidence: DNA**

Case 96

Defendant: **Thomas Dudley**

Victim: Roger Breckenridge

Trial: 1968 Jurisdiction: Columbus, Ohio

Murder: September 17, 1967

Evidence: Victim was a night watchman at iron plant. On night he went missing, he failed to make required reports to alarm company. An officer sent to check on him could find neither him nor his car, but did find a bloody cap on the floor. The car was later located and had blood the same type as victim's inside out. In addition, a crowbar with victim's blood on it was located in the car. Defendant spoke to police and told them he was at the plant at the time victim went missing, saw blood at the scene, and admitted he had blood on his pants. He stated that he had burned his pants and shoes because he was afraid of being accused of the crime, since he had been accused of assaulting another plant employee. Defendant's father said that defendant said he had spilled ketchup on his pants at a bar. A witness testified that defendant had a crowbar in his pants when he saw him that night. Both the crowbar and the cap had hairs that matched victim's hair. A witness identified defendant as the man he saw hitting victim with a crowbar. Defendant was not charged with murder but assault with intent to kill. He was found guilty. His appeal was rejected.

Source: *Ohio v. Dudley*, 19 Ohio App. 2d 14 (1969)

Keywords: **Forensic evidence: Other, Eyewitness**

Case 97

Defendant: **Roger Dale Dunford**

Victim: Barbara Jean Pauley Hunt

Trial: 1995 Jurisdiction: Marion, Virginia

Murder: January 1985

Evidence: Victim was last seen in a bar in Marion. She appeared to be intoxicated on either drugs or alcohol. Victim had earlier told her sister she was supposed to report to jail that day and that the police wanted her to inform on her friends. She was seen leaving the bar with four other women. The women borrowed a car, which subsequently had a flat tire. They were also seen loading something into the trunk. When the women returned to the bar, victim was not with them. Defendant, her boyfriend at the time, was charged with her murder 10 years later, but the jury could not reach a verdict.

Sources: Charley Project; "Lacking body, murder case will be tough sell," *The Free Lance Star*, June 19, 1995

Keyword: **N/A**

Case 98

Defendants: **Raymond and Donald Duvall**

Victims: Brian Ognjan, David Tyll

Trial: October 2003 Jurisdiction: Arenac County, Michigan

Murder: November 1985

Evidence: Victims were on a hunting trip together when they disappeared. Victims encountered defendants, who beat victims to death after an argument. One witness testified to seeing the murder, and other witnesses stated that defendants boasted about killing victims, cutting them up, and feeding them to pigs. Eyewitness changed her story multiple times, revealing details of the crime but denying that she witnessed it firsthand until late in the investigation. Defendants convicted of two counts of first-degree murder and sentenced to life imprisonment.

Sources: *People v. Duvall*, Court of Appeals of Michigan, No. 252487, 252720, May 26, 2005 (2005 WL 1249238); https://www.michigandaily.com/content/two-sentenced-murder-detroit-hunters

Keywords: **Eyewitness, Confession to friends and family, Life**

Case 99

Defendant: **Mark Eby**

Victim: Theresa Suarez Eby

Trial: 1993 Jurisdiction: Island County, Washington

Murder: May 16, 1993

Evidence: Victim was defendant's wife. Defendant was arrested at a motel in Everett shortly after victim's disappearance. Defendant was a sailor and confessed to NCIS agent that he put victim's body in a suitcase and threw it off the Deception Pass Bridge. Prosecutors had a petite woman curl up into a suitcase to prove that a body would fit. Defendant court-martialed and convicted by a military court jury and sentenced to life imprisonment.

Sources: http://www.seattlepi.com/local/article/Guilty-verdicts-without-a-body-rare-1148209.php; http://community.seattletimes.nwsource.com/archive/?date=19931101&slug=1729365

Keywords: **Life, Confession to police**

Case 100

Defendant: **Christopher A. Edwards**

Victim: Jessica O'Grady

Trial: March 2007 Jurisdiction: Douglas County, Nebraska

Murder: May 2006

Evidence: Victim and defendant were coworkers and friends who had begun a sexual relationship. Victim disappeared on her way to meet defendant at his home after texting him all day. Victim's last phone call was to defendant. When victim disappeared, defendant claimed she never arrived at his house. When police began investigating defendant, he admitted to his girlfriend and other witnesses that he had sex with victim and that she may have been pregnant. Victim's car was found parked near her place of employment. Victim's blood was found in defendant's bedroom, spatters on the mattress and walls, on a short sword found in his closet, on the handle of garden shears, and in the trunk of his car. Blood spatter demonstrated at least seven swings of an object wet with blood. There was also evidence of cleanup, including a trash bag with bloodstained towels and a receipt for cleaning supplies and poster paint that had been applied to the bedroom ceiling. Search history on defendant's computer showed Google searches on the human arterial system. Defendant convicted of second-degree murder and use of a deadly weapon and sentenced to 100 years to life imprisonment. Judgment affirmed in 2009. In 2012, the state granted defendant an evidentiary hearing, scheduled for March 2014, to establish whether state officers planted forensic evidence. The lead crime scene investigator had been convicted of tampering with evidence collected in another homicide investigation.

Sources: *State v. Edwards*, 767 N.W.2d 784 (Neb. 2009); *State v. Edwards*, 821 N.W.2d 680 (Neb. 2012); http://netnebraska.org/article/news/more-fake-evidence-convicted-omaha-murderer-claims-csi-planted-evidence

Keywords: **Forensic evidence: DNA, Forensic evidence: Other**

Case 101

Defendant: **Darrin Elliott**

Victim: Brian Vaughn

Trial: June 2001 Jurisdiction: Lincoln County, Oklahoma

Murder: August 15, 2000

Evidence: Benjamin Martin, who lived with defendant in a house south of Wellston, told authorities that he heard an argument between defendant and victim while they were shooting guns in the backyard. Martin saw victim with his ear bleeding, and victim complained that defendant had fired near his head, perhaps bursting his eardrum. Defendant tried to apologize, but victim did not accept apology. Martin then saw defendant shoot Vaughan five or six times in the face with a .22-caliber semi-automatic rifle. Defendant dragged victim off the porch, and Martin washed the blood off the porch. Defendant later wrapped the body in plastic garbage bags and a tent and discussed possible locations in which to dispose of the body, including weighing the body down and throwing it into water. Government sought the death penalty, but defendant given life without parole.

Sources: Chris Ross; http://newsok.com/murder-victims-family-wont-rest-until-his-body-is-found-woman-accomplice-sentenced-in-killing/article/2810441

Keywords: **Eyewitness, Life**

Case 102

Defendant: **Charles W. Elmore**
Victim: Bella Elmore
Trial: July 1988 Jurisdiction: Military
Murder: March 17, 1988
Evidence: Victim was defendant's wife. Witnesses claimed that the couple was mutually abusive and argued frequently. Defendant had joked to his friends that he wanted to cut victim up and use her as shark bait. Defendant was stationed in Exmouth, Australia, when victim disappeared. Defendant gave four different accounts of what happened the night of victim's disappearance, one of which stated that she fell from a pier into the Gulf of Exmouth. Defendant waited until the next morning to search for victim. Defendant's car was seen heading off base toward the pier after 3:30 a.m. Victim's shorts and bedspread were later found at a beach near the pier, and a diver testified that no one could have swum in the currents that night. Defendant's vehicle and house were cleaned thoroughly after victim's disappearance, though witnesses testified both were usually messy. Blood matching victim's blood type was found on the sheets at their house, in a position inconsistent with menstrual bleeding, and on defendant's knife. Prosecution believed that defendant threw his wife into the shark-infested waters of the Gulf of Exmouth. Defendant convicted of premeditated murder by general court martial and sentenced to life imprisonment.
Source: *United States v. Elmore*, 31 M.J. 678 (A.C.M.R. 1990)
Keywords: **Life, Forensic evidence: Other**

Case 103

Defendant: **Stephen Epperly**
Victim: Gina Hall
Trial: December 1980 Jurisdiction: Pulaski County, Virginia
Murder: June 28, 1980
Evidence: Gina Hall, 18, was a freshman at Radford University. On Saturday, June 28, 1980, at about 10 p.m., she went to a dance at the Blacksburg Marriott Hotel. At the dance, she met up with some of her friends and was introduced to the defendant. Defendant's friend, Bill King, was caring for a cabin on Claytor Lake, and she was invited to go to the lake with him, to which she agreed. She called her sister to check in at around 1 a.m. from the cabin. King and his friend, Robin Robinson, arrived at the cabin at around 4 a.m. They saw defendant, but not victim, and talked briefly. While King and Robinson were at the lake, defendant left. Prior to 7 a.m. the next day, victim's car was seen parked, trunk open, on the side of the road. The car was still there on Monday, June 30, when her friends began to search for her. By the next day, there were broadcasts made on local radio stations that victim was missing and requesting information regarding her whereabouts. The same day, the defendant asked to speak to a friend's brother, who was an attorney, and asked him "if there was anything that they could do to him if they didn't find a body." On July 2, defendant spoke to police and allowed them access to the cabin to be searched. This search returned

numerous partially cleaned bloodstains, a few items belonging to victim, and traces of hair, which included pubic hair. It was obvious a violent struggle took place. A search of the Radford area led to the discovery of victim's clothes tied in a bundle and stained with blood. On July 10, a tracking dog was taken to the location where victim's car had been abandoned, and the dog was scented with items from defendant. The dog led them on a long track from the car and across town, passing the locations where the clothing had been found, and led investigators to defendant's home. When defendant was presented with the information of the dog's pursuit, he put his head on his hands and stated "That's a damn good dog" numerous times. Based on the circumstantial evidence gathered, the dog tracking evidence, and the unlikelihood that victim would take her own life, flee, or fall victim to an accident, defendant was charged and convicted of first-degree murder. He was sentenced to life imprisonment and appealed. The court affirmed the verdict.

Sources: *Epperly v. Virginia*, 294 S.E. 2nd 882 (1982); Murderpedia

Keywords: **Forensic evidence: Other, Life**

Case 104

Defendant: **Miguel Estrella**

Victim: Juan Disla

Trial: October 2003 Jurisdiction: New Haven, Connecticut

Murder: July 21, 2000

Evidence: Victim and defendant were rival drug dealers. Codefendant testified that defendant ordered him and another associate to meet victim at a Dairy Queen to purchase cocaine that defendant had ordered the day before. Defendant instructed them to hijack victim's van to rob him of his cocaine. Victim's van was hijacked at gunpoint, and victim was bound with duct tape and shot in the leg. Defendant drove in a separate car and met them in a wooded area, where victim was robbed of the cocaine in his van. Codefendant did not see the murder but saw victim's motionless body under a tree when he left. Defendant and others abandoned the van, and codefendant saw defendant burning something in his backyard. FBI recorded defendant talking to jailhouse snitch about the murder. On the recordings, defendant claimed to have suffocated victim, dismembered with a chain saw, and then dissolved the remains in acid. Defendant convicted of murder, felony murder, and conspiracy to commit murder. Judgment affirmed in 2006.

Source: *State v. Estrella*, 893 A.2d 348 (Conn. 2006)

Keywords: **Codefendant testimony, Informant**

Case 105

Defendant: **Lee Anthony Evans**

Victims: Michael McDowell, Randy Johnson, Alvin Turner, Melvin Pittman, Ernest Taylor

Trial: November 2011 Jurisdiction: Essex County, New Jersey

Murder: August 20, 1978

Evidence: The five victims were all 16 or 17 years old and were suspected of stealing defendant's marijuana. Victims were last seen on their way to defendant's house or riding in defendant's pick-up. Case went cold until 2008, when codefendant, defendant's cousin, Philander Hampton, confessed to his role in helping defendant lure the boys into an abandoned house, shut them in a closet and nailed the door, and set the house on fire. No physical evidence was found to corroborate codefendant's confession, and the case relied entirely on codefendant's testimony. Defendant represented himself at trial. Defendant acquitted of all charges. Codefendant pleaded guilty and was sentenced to 10 years imprisonment.
Source: http://www.nytimes.com/2011/11/24/nyregion/jury-acquits-man-in-1978-murder-of-5-newark-boys.html?_r=0; http://usatoday30.usatoday.com/news/nation/2010-03-23-NJ-5-teens-killing_N.htm
Keyword: **Codefendant testimony**

Case 106

Defendant: **Randy Evans**
Victim: Danny Wolf
Trial: September 2013 Jurisdiction: Gentry County, Missouri
Murder: May 2011
Evidence: Defendant found guilty of first-degree murder. Defendant's former girlfriend testified that she saw defendant kill victim in defendant's kitchen. Two friends of defendant said that he confessed the murder to them. Bloodstains on the floor were tied to victim, and a bullet recovered from a repaired part of the ceiling was traced to defendant's .45. The defense tried to argue that victim was not dead by putting on testimony about a text message sent by victim the day after the murder, and testimony from a girlfriend of victim's who said he threatened to leave or kill himself if she broke up with him.
Sources: "Mo. man guilty of murder in case with no body," *San Francisco Gate*, September 28, 2013; http://www.newspressnow.com/news/local_news/article_eccef140-5bcf-567f-af8e-0e0bff05653f.html
Keywords: **Eyewitness, Confession to friends and family, Forensic evidence: DNA**

Case 107

Defendant: **Kenneth Dwayne Ezell**
Victim: Daniel Sites
Trial: 1998 Jurisdiction: Hillsborough County, Florida
Murder: August 5, 1996
Evidence: Victim was a confidential police informant and a drug dealer who sold cocaine, marijuana, LSD, and ecstasy. Defendant owed a debt to several other dealers. Investigators believe defendant was hired by one of these dealers to kill victim. A witness testified that defendant confessed to beating victim, shooting him, and burying him. Most of the witnesses against defendant were criminals. Defendant acquitted of first-degree murder but convicted of conspiracy to murder and sentenced to nine years imprisonment. He was paroled in 2005.

Source: Charley Project
Keyword: **Confession to friends and family**

Case 108

Defendant: **James Arthur Fannings, Jr.**
Victim: Stacey Hazelton
Trial: December 2006 Jurisdiction: Bolivar County, Mississippi
Murder: May 2004
Evidence: Victim was defendant's girlfriend. Victim moved from Pennsylvania to Mississippi with defendant and a friend. A month later, victim told her parents she wanted to come home and said she would drive back to Pennsylvania once her car was repaired. Victim stopped communicating with her parents thereafter, so they contacted the police, who found victim during a welfare check. Victim's car was found in an impound lot. Witnesses saw defendant driving victim's car in June, contradicting defendant's testimony that he hadn't seen victim or her car since April. Defendant provided other inconsistent statements as well. A year later, investigators spoke with a witness, who said he and victim left Mississippi for Pennsylvania in May 2004 and provided investigators with enough information to arrest defendant. Witness later added to his testimony, testifying that defendant was abusive, shot victim in the head in their apartment, and forced witness at gunpoint to help in the disposal of the body. Defendant cleaned the blood from the apartment and burned victim's body in a metal barrel for seven hours before burying it. Defendant threatened to kill witness if he told anyone. Defendant also confessed to two fellow inmates that he had killed victim by shooting her in the head and burying her. Defendant convicted and sentenced to life imprisonment. Conviction upheld in 2008.
Source: *Fannings v. State*, 997 So.2d 953 (Miss. App. 2008)
Keywords: **Life, Eyewitness, Confession to friends and family**

Case 109

Defendant: **Lawrence Allen Fassler (a.k.a. John Prescott)**
Victim: Warren Hudson
Trial: February 1971 Jurisdiction: Riverside County, California
Murder: October 13, 1968
Evidence: Defendant was a member of a narcotics smuggling ring based in Mexico that included several codefendants. Victim was a pilot responsible for flying contraband into the United States. Victim enlisted two accomplices to steal the money from one of his marijuana deliveries. One of victim's accomplices rejoined defendant's ring and then helped defendant arrange to recover the money and kill victim. This accomplice became the chief witness against defendant and was granted immunity for his testimony. Defendant paid codefendant to kill victim and provided him with hundreds of dollars of guns and tear gas. Codefendant was seen digging with a pick and shovel the night before the murder. The next day, they called victim's girlfriend and told her to leave because something bad had happened to victim.

Codefendants lured victim from his hotel, killed him, and destroyed the body with sulfuric acid. Codefendant was later arrested for a separate charge and was wearing victim's jewelry. While under questioning for the smuggling operations, one codefendant told investigators victim was dead. On codefendant's rented property, investigators dug up containers of sulfuric acid, gas masks, coiled rope, and rolls of plastic. Defendant convicted.
Source: *People v. Lawrence*, 25 Cal.App.3d 498 (Cal. Ct. App. 1972)
Keywords: **Codefendant testimony, Forensic evidence: Other**

Case 110

Defendant: **James V. Faulkner**
Victim: William B. Rose
Trial: September 1987 Jurisdiction: Williamson County, Illinois
Murder: July 4, 1984
Evidence: Victim was defendant's friend and was having an affair with defendant's wife. The night of the murder, defendant and his wife went out to a tavern with victim and then brought him back to their house. Defendant's teenaged son was a chief witness against him. Defendant's son heard defendant and victim talking about having sex with defendant's wife. Defendant brought his son into the bedroom where defendant's wife was having sex with victim. Defendant then pushed his wife off of the victim and stabbed him in the chest with his knife and dragged him, still alive, into the bathtub. Defendant instructed his son to bring him a baseball bat. Defendant shut the door and beat victim for several minutes. Defendant, his wife, and his son dropped the body down an embankment then piled trash and tires on top of it. They scrubbed the bedroom floor and soaked the carpet in coconut oil. The knife was thrown into a reservoir where it was later recovered. Defendant's son reported the incident three years later. Victim's two daughters also testified to overhearing the murder, but defendant's wife claimed that she and her son had fabricated murder to authorities in an attempt to escape defendant. Defendant made incriminating statements to investigators and was overheard making incriminatory and threatening statements to his wife. Defendant convicted of murder and sentenced to life imprisonment.
Sources: *People v. Faulkner*, 542 N.E.2d 1190 (Ill. App. Ct. 1989); http://books.google.com/books?id=hyJ9YrgALK4C&pg=PA171&lpg=PA171&dq=james+faulkner+murder+illinois+1984&source=bl&ots=cRHtykOHaU&sig=b4ygtaabDQM-i0PCMeW5gbDRsN4&hl=en&sa=X&ei=qEjZUpLgG_fJsQSYlYDIBQ&ved=0CDMQ6AEwAQ#v=onepage&q=james%20faulkner%20murder%20illinois%201984&f=false
Keywords: **Codefendant testimony, Eyewitness, Life**

Case 111

Defendants: **Samar Fawaz, Bashar Farraj**
Victim: Raed Nayef al-Farah
Trial: June 2005 Jurisdiction: Macomb County, Michigan
Murder: October 17, 2003

Evidence: Defendants were coworkers and close friends who drove to work together every day. Victim was a student who had previously been involved in real estate deals with defendants and was close friends with Farraj. A coworker found defendants at work early in the morning when they were not usually present. Defendants attempted to make excuses for the smell of vomit and the bloodstains, and the coworker found an empty box for a kitchen knife that defendant claimed was his. Defendants admitted to cleaning the scene and replacing bloodstained mats with new ones. Blood was found in the hallway and spattered on the walls, and blood in the carpet and inside a vacuum cleaner matched victim's DNA. Blood was found in the cargo area of one defendant's truck that both were seen riding in on a daily basis, and part of the carpet in the back of the truck had been cut out. Defendants convicted of second-degree murder.

Sources: *People v. Farraj*, Court of Appeals of Michigan, Docket No. 264235, March 22, 2007; *People v. Fawaz*, Court of Appeals of Michigan, Docket No. 264703, March 22, 2007; http://mortgagefraud.squarespace.com/display/ShowJournal?moduleId=78225&categoryId=7135¤tPage=2

Keywords: **Eyewitness, Forensic evidence: DNA**

Case 112

Defendant: **Paul William Ferrell**

Victim: Catherine Denise Ford

Trial: 1989 Jurisdiction: Grant County, West Virginia

Murder: February 17, 1988

Evidence: Defendant made 206 phone calls to bookstores and libraries across the country posing as a doctor and requesting that female employees read excerpts to him from a book on anal sex. This was used at trial to show that defendant used fraud to entice victim. Victim, a Maryland resident, received a call from someone posing as a magistrate in Grant County and asked her to come to his office, and then another call from someone posing as an undercover officer investigating her family's restaurant. Victim left work to meet with the alleged officer, and was last seen on her way to Grant County. Two other women received phone calls from a man posing as a magistrate, though both the county's magistrates were female at the time. Defendant had recently begun working as a deputy sheriff and was seen using a payphone outside the magistrate's office the morning of the murder. Defendant's family store was within view of victim's restaurant. Defendant's neighbor heard banging and screaming from defendant's trailer the day of the murder, followed by the sound of a gunshot. Afterward, the neighbor saw defendant leave and return several times before burning something behind the trailer. The next day, defendant replaced carpeting in his bedroom, saying there had been stains and a smell, a fact that witnesses contradicted. Blood spatters were later found throughout the home. Defendant was obsessed with stories about victim's disappearance, claiming to have had an affair with her once. Defendant became involved in a search party, trying to call it off and then asking them not to search two roads where he claimed police had found evidence. Victim's car was burned on these roads. Defendant wrote an anonymous letter to victim's family that included $200 and alleged that victim had run away. His handwriting was later identified, and he had withdrawn $200 from his account. Victim's wristwatch was found behind defendant's trailer. Defendant convicted of second-degree murder and kidnapping, sentenced to life imprisonment. Sentence later commuted and defendant paroled in 2005.

Sources: *State v. Ferrell*, 399 S.E.2d 834 (W.Va. 1990); http://charleston-daily-mail.vlex.com/vid/ex-deputy-granted-parole-murder-case-64438225

Keywords: **Eyewitness, Life**

Case 113

Defendant: **Albert Fish**
Victim: Grace Budd
Trial: March 1935 Jurisdiction: Westchester County, New York
Murder: June 1928

Evidence: Defendant was a serial killer, child rapist, and cannibal who killed three known victims and indicated that the number could be as high as 100. Defendant was a self-proclaimed child rapist obsessed with torture, sexual mutilation, and sadomasochism. Defendant had tortured and raped several victims before abducting 10-year old victim. Defendant found victim when he answered a classified advertisement for victim's older brother, who was looking for work. Defendant planned to mutilate and kill victim's brother, but decided to abduct victim instead when he met her. Defendant claimed he was going to a niece's birthday party and asked for permission to bring victim with him. Victim disappeared, but another suspect was arrested after being accused by his estranged wife. In 1934, victim's parents received an anonymous letter detailing her abduction, death by strangulation, dismemberment, and subsequent cannibalism. Defendant convicted of murder and sentenced to death. Investigators tracked defendant based on a unique emblem on the letter's envelope. Defendant confessed to murder, and confessed that his plan was initially to kill victim's brother. He purchased several tools, including a cleaver, a saw, and a butcher knife. Defendant murdered victim at a remote country house, where investigators uncovered some small bones and a skull. More than fifty fingers, legs, and other bones were collected around the house. Bone fragments were dug up from the cellar. Defendant also confessed to two other child homicides and was suspected of six other child homicides. Executed by electric chair in 1936.

Source: http://www.trutv.com/library/crime/serial_killers/notorious/fish/capture_3.html?sect=2; http://www.nydailynews.com/new-york/1928-murder-grace-budd-albert-fish-gallery-1.1277430?pmSlide=1.1277419

Keywords: **Death penalty, Confession to police**

Case 114

Defendant: **Jerry Wayne Fisher**
Victim: Joyce Alice Fisher

Trial: May 1988 Jurisdiction: Van Buren County, Michigan
Murder: April 15, 1978
Evidence: Victim was defendant's soon-to-be-ex-wife. Victim told witnesses that defendant was abusive and testified during divorce proceedings that he had threatened to kill her. On the morning of her disappearance, victim had breakfast with defendant and left with defendant in his car to have a vehicle title transfer notarized and was never seen or heard from again. Witnesses testified to victim's routine and reliability as evidence that she would not have voluntarily disappeared. Several years later, defendant remarried and lied to his second wife about his prior marriage but made no incriminating statements. Defendant convicted of involuntary manslaughter but reversed on appeal due to insufficient evidence. Prosecutor failed to challenge the appeal, and court issued a directed verdict so defendant could not be tried again.
Source: *People v. Fisher*, 483 N.W.2d 452 (Mich. Ct. App. 1992)
Keyword: **N/A**

Case 115

Defendant: **Thomas James Fisher**
Victim: Barbara Baughman
Trial: 1990 Jurisdiction: Bexar County, Texas
Murder: November 6, 1988
Evidence: Victim was defendant's girlfriend. Defendant told a witness that victim was angry with him for taking too long to come home and pulled a gun on him. He grabbed victim, strangled her with an electrical cord, and then drowned her in the bathtub. Defendant then decapitated victim, cut off her fingers, and cut off one of her arms and tried to put it down the garbage disposal. Defendant also burned her fingertips on the stove so she could not be identified. The same witness and others saw defendant scattering ashes and bones in an alleyway. Defendant gave witness a trash bag and asked him to put it with his own trash. Defendant also put a suitcase with victim's name and Social Security Number in the trash. Blood was later found on the garbage disposal and plumbing trap. Defendant convicted of murder. This case changed Texas law, which had previously required a body for a murder conviction.
Sources: *Fisher v. State*, 827 S.W.2d 597 (Tex. App. 1992); *Fisher v. State*, 851 S.W.2d 298 (Tex.App. 1993)
Keyword: **Confession to friends and family**

Case 116

Defendant: **Brandon Lee Flagner**
Victim: Tiffany Jennifer Papesh
Trial: July 1985 Jurisdiction: Cuyahoga County, Ohio
Murder: June 13, 1980
Evidence: Victim was an 8-year-old girl and a stranger to defendant. Defendant had previously told a woman he was in love with her 10-year-old daughter. He was later arrested for intruding in their

house. Defendant also became sexually intimate with a 13-year-old girl after his release from prison. Victim disappeared in the early afternoon while running an errand to a nearby convenience store. Defendant participated in searches for victim, appeared fixated by her disappearance, and tried to convince victim's father to sell T-shirts with her picture. Defendant drove to victim's house with witnesses and insisted on searching for victim's body, even though she was only missing. Defendant told his brother that his safe deposit box contained evidence about victim's death, materials that were destroyed by defendant's minor girlfriend and her mother after defendant was arrested for assaulting young girls. While in prison for those charges, defendant wrote an anonymous letter to the FBI in 1983 and then confessed to kidnapping and murdering victim, describing a scar on victim's knee that was not generally known. Defendant had also confessed to his mother, two ministers, and his girlfriend's mother. Defendant also admitted to faking an alibi by using his work timesheet. Defendant convicted of murder and kidnapping and sentenced to life imprisonment.

Source: *State v. Flagner*, Court of Appeals of Ohio, Eighth District, Cuyahoga County, No. 50815, October 16, 1986 (WestLaw Citation: 1986 WL 11653)

Keywords: **Confession to police, Confession to friends and family, Life**

Case 117

Defendants: **Chad Floyd, Shannon Floyd**

Victim: Michael Eugene Golub

Trial: July 2007/April 2008 Jurisdiction: Stanton County, Kansas

Murder: May 20, 2005

Evidence: Defendants were married. Victim was Shannon's ex-boyfriend and father of her child. The couple argued frequently with victim, primarily over child custody issues. Victim disappeared when he went to defendants' house to pick up his child. Defendants said he never arrived, and victim's vehicle was later found abandoned on a county road. Defendants purchased a gun the day of victim's disappearance and victim's blood was found beneath their front porch, where it had dripped down from between the planks. Chad Floyd told witnesses he would pay victim to drop the case and wished he would disappear. Defense argued that neighbors would have heard a gunshot and that victim's disappearance could be related to his role as an informant in a local drug case. The first and second trial resulted in hung juries. Charges were dropped in November 2008.

Sources: http://www.monnat.com/2008/11/22/murder-case-dismissed-against-southwest-kansas-pair/; Charley Project

Keyword: **Forensic evidence: DNA**

Case 118

Defendant: **Carlton Foley**

Victim: Tim Sizemore

Trial: November 1997 Jurisdiction: Knox County, Kentucky

Murder: July 1996

Evidence: Victim and defendant were neighbors who had been involved in a property dispute. A judge ruled in victim's favor shortly before his disappearance, and witnesses heard defendant threaten victim. Victim disappeared after going out for a ride on his ATV. The vehicle was later recovered 40 yards from defendant's home, with solid masses of victim's blood and blood spatters consistent with extreme trauma. Bloody clothing was found in defendant's home as well. Defendant convicted of murder and sentenced to 20 years imprisonment but was released in 2009. Body found in 2003 in Harmon Creek. First no-body murder conviction in Kentucky.

Sources: http://www.wkyt.com/news/headlines/44196867.html; http://news.google.com/newspapers?nid=1696&dat=19971115&id=SvIaAAAAIBAJ&sjid=2UcEAAAAIBAJ&pg=6580,2139663

Keyword: **Forensic evidence: DNA**

Case 119

Defendants: **Karl Allen Fontenot, Thomas Jesse Ward**
Victim: Donna Denice Haraway
Trial: 1985/June 1989 Jurisdiction: Pontotoc County, Oklahoma
Murder: April 28, 1984

Evidence: Victim worked at a convenience store and was abducted by defendants when they came to rob the store. Defendants both made statements to police inculpating themselves and each other, alleging that they robbed victim, abducted her, and took her to a power plant where they raped her. Defendants claimed a third suspect was responsible for stabbing victim to death and burning her body in an abandoned house, but the third suspect was eliminated as a suspect because of clear proof he had not been an accomplice. When victim's remains were later recovered, they showed no evidence of burning or stabbing but had a bullet wound to the skull. Witnesses saw victim leaving work with Ward and another man, who may or may not have been Fontenot. Both men were convicted, but convictions were reversed on appeal. Both men were convicted at second trials with Fontenot resentenced to death. His sentence was later commuted to life imprisonment without the possibility of parole, and Ward was sentenced to life. Victim's remains were recovered during second trial. As of August 2013, the Innocence Project is planning to file a brief to overturn Fontenot's conviction, alleging that he had an alibi and that investigators mishandled forensic evidence.

Sources: http://newsok.com/report-sparks-debate-over-innocence-of-karl-fontenot/article/3868927; *Fontenot v. State*, 881 P.2d 69 (Okla. Crim. App. 1994); *Ward v. State*, 755 P.2d 123 (Okla. Crim. App. 1988); *Fontenot v. State*, 742 P.2d 31 (Okla. Crim. App. 1987)

Keywords: **Codefendant testimony, Life**

Case 120

Defendants: **Richard Herman Ford, Robert Anthony Von Villas**
Victim: Thomas Weed
Trial: 1988 Jurisdiction: Los Angeles County, California
Murder: February 1983

Evidence: Defendants were LAPD detectives hired by victim's estranged wife to kill victim. Victim's car was recovered a month later at the Los Angeles Airport, where it had been parked since February 23 or 24. Investigators also recovered forged credit card invoices from victim's account. Victim's sister found a note in victim's apartment saying his estranged wife, with whom he had had several problems, threatened to kill him. Investigators discovered that victim's estranged wife had hired defendants to kill victim for $20,000 at the suggestion of a friend. Victim's wife and two others pleaded guilty to their roles in the murder and testified against defendants. She stated that her friend contacted defendants, who approached her in disguise and offered to kill victim. A professional makeup artist testified to providing defendants with the wigs and makeup, which investigators later uncovered. Investigators recovered a note in Von Villas' car, in his handwriting, that contained victim's wife's name and telephone number. They also found a shotgun and shells in Ford's home and recorded an incriminating conversation between Ford and his wife while Ford was in jail. Defendants convicted of first-degree murder and conspiracy to murder and sentenced to life imprisonment without parole.

Source: *People v. Von Villas*, 43 Cal.Rpter.2d 233 (Cal. Dist. Ct. App. 1995)

Keywords: **Codefendant testimony, Life**

Case 121

Defendant: **Richard Gustave Forsberg**

Victim: Marcia Ann Forsberg

Trial: December 2012 Jurisdiction: Orange County, California

Murder: February 9, 2010

Evidence: Victim was defendant's wife of 39 years. Defendant confessed to beating victim with a Hindu figurine and dismembering and decapitating her. Defendant burned the limbs in various campsites throughout Ventura County. Surveillance photos captured defendant purchasing two freezers and renting an RV for this purpose. Defendant covered up victim's death for six months before victim's best friend filed a missing persons report. Defendant fled to the desert after being interviewed by police and tried to kill himself before the arrest. Defendant convicted of second-degree murder and sentenced to 15 years to life imprisonment.

Sources: http://www.ocregister.com/news/forsberg-414183-marcia-friends.html; http://articles.latimes.com/2010/sep/01/local/la-me-0901-missing-wife-20100901; http://abclocal.go.com/kabc/story?id=8910363

Keyword: **Confession to police**

Case 122

Defendant: **Ralph Forsythe**

Victim: Charles Conner

Trial: December 1957 Jurisdiction: Allen County, Ohio

Murder: August 10, 1957

Evidence: Victim and defendant were acquaintances. Victim was celebrating his birthday and went to defendant's house with three witnesses. Defendant then accused victim of stealing a gun. When victim did not respond, defendant shot him in the head in front of the witnesses. One of the witnesses, drunk, went to a nearby bar and told the bartender what he had seen. The caretaker at a roadside park 200 miles away saw defendant and his wife washing out defendant's vehicle with water from a park well. Caretaker burned bloodstained rags, clothes, and newspapers. Human blood was found in defendant's kitchen, in his vehicle, and on one of his gloves. Defendant convicted of manslaughter and sentenced to 1 to 20 years imprisonment.

Sources: http://limaohio.com/apps/pbcs.dll/article?avis=LI&date=20131023&category=news&lopenr=310239994&Ref=AR; http://news.google.com/newspapers?nid=888&dat=19571118&id=UJlSAAAAIBAJ&sjid=P3YDAAAAIBAJ&pg=4372,1466360

Keyword: **Eyewitness**

Case 123

Defendant: **Roderick Fountain**
Victim: Kendrick Jackson
Trial: October 2011 Jurisdiction: Harris County, Texas
Murder: April 7, 2006

Evidence: Victim was defendant's 3-year-old son. Witnesses testified that defendant was abusive toward victim and had hit, punched, and dunked victim in a bathtub. Defendant confessed to two fellow inmates that victim was dead, that he hit victim hard enough to kill him, and that he threw victim's body off a boat ramp. Victim's mother testified that defendant was abusive and that she frequently saw injuries on victim. Evidence was introduced that defendant was previously suspected in the murder of a 16-year old boy, and an ex-wife testified that defendant confessed that murder to her. Defendant convicted of felony murder and sentenced to life imprisonment.

Sources: http://www.chron.com/news/houston-texas/article/Dad-convicted-in-death-of-son-whose-body-wasn-t-2238045.php; http://www.khou.com/news/Punishment-phase-testimony-under-way-in-trial-of-Houston-dad-who-killed-3-year-old-son-132713493.html

Keywords: **Life, Informant**

Case 124

Defendant: **Ernest Freeby**
Victim: Edwina Atieno Onyango
Trial: January 2012 Jurisdiction: Carbon County, Pennsylvania
Murder: December 2007

Evidence: Victim was defendant's estranged wife. Investigators found large quantities of victim's blood and some of her hair in the coal bin in the basement of defendant's home. Defendant's girlfriend at the time testified that he had threatened to kill victim to get out of his marriage. Defendant made contradictory statements to investigators. Defendant lied about receiving communications from victim and used her credit

card, although he told investigators that he had not seen it. Defendant convicted of first-degree murder and sentenced to life imprisonment.
Sources: http://www.tnonline.com/2012/jan/31/freeby-convicted; http://www.contracostatimes.com/ci_20620065/pa-man-formally-sentenced-death-wife
Keywords: **Forensic evidence: DNA, Life**

Case 125

Defendant: **Thomas Freeman**
Victim: Tawnya Fay Parker
Trial: November 2003 Jurisdiction: California
Murder: December 1999
Evidence: Victim was defendant's live-in girlfriend. Victim had a drug addiction, had been arrested several times for prostitution, and was known to live a high-risk and transient lifestyle. Couple had a history of problems. Defendant called police when victim slashed his tires and scratched his car, and then victim accused defendant of raping her. Blood from the victim, who was terminally ill, was found on defendant's mattress and under the carpet in his room. Defendant convicted of second-degree murder.
Sources: Doe Network; http://www.nampn.org/cases/parker_tawnya.html
Keyword: **Forensic evidence: DNA**

Case 126

Defendant: **Duane Lee Frey**
Victim: Hopethan Johnson
Trial: February 2003 Jurisdiction: York County, Pennsylvania
Murder: May 26, 2002
Evidence: Victim and defendant were connected through drug activity. Victim bought a motorcycle shortly before his disappearance and left it in a friend's garage. The next morning, the friend's neighbor heard gunshots in the woods behind the home. A truck registered to defendant was in the driveway. Police received an anonymous tip that a murder happened behind the same residence, and investigators found shotgun wads in the woods and shells in defendant's house and car. They also found a garbage bag containing victim's cell phone. Victim's motorcycle, embedded with shotgun pellets, was found hidden near defendant's place of employment. Defendant later confessed, saying he had owed victim money and was afraid of him. Defendant convicted of murder and sentenced to life imprisonment. In 2008, victim's skeletal remains were found near the Susquehanna River. Defendant successfully filed a motion for discovery, claiming that the new timeline for victim's death rules him out.
Source: *Pennsylvania v. Frey*, 41 A.3d 605 (Pa.Super.Ct. 2012)
Keywords: **Confession to police, Life**

Case 127

Defendant: **John Wayne Gacy**
Victim: Robert J. Piest

Trial: February 1980 Jurisdiction: Chicago, Illinois
Murder: December 1978
Evidence: Victim worked at a Des Plaines, Illinois, pharmacy and was last seen at work at 9 p.m. on December 11, 1978. Gacy was in the pharmacy earlier that day checking on a job that his construction company was involved in. Just prior to his disappearance the victim told coworkers that he was "going to see the contractor." With this information, the police were able to obtain a search warrant for the Gacy home. Police found a receipt that the victim had recently obtained for a roll of film that he had purchased at the pharmacy just prior to his disappearance. A second search warrant was obtained following interviews with a Gacy employee, where the employee stated that the crawl space in Gacy's home may contain some bodies. Subsequent to the second search warrant, Gacy confessed to police to luring boys to his home where he would sexually assault them, torture, and then kill them. Gacy on occasion would identify himself to victims as a police officer to gain trust. Gacy told police that he dumped his last four victims in the Des Plaines River because he ran out of room in his crawl space. Gacy was known to keep personal items from some of his victims. Gacy admitted to a total of 33 homicides, including this victim. The trial focused on whether he was sane. The jury found him sane, guilty, and he was sentenced to death. He was executed on May 10, 1994.
Sources: http://law.jrank.org/pages/3314/John-Wayne-Gacy-Trial-1980.html; Sullivan, T., Maiken, P., *Killer Clown: The John Wayne Gacy Murders*, Pinnacle Books, Windsor Publishing, 2000; http://www.clarkprosecutor.org/html/death/US/gacy237.htm
Keywords: **Confession to Police, Death penalty**

Case 128

Defendant: **Johnny Ray Gambrell**
Victim: Lois Bridges Gambrell
Trial: November 2005/February 2006 Jurisdiction: Anderson County, South Carolina
Murder: July 2004
Evidence: Defendant and victim were husband and wife. Prior to her homicide, victim had been hospitalized following a beating that she received from defendant. Defendant told his landlord that he had severely beaten victim because she was "running around" on him. Victim and defendant had separated at least once, prompting victim to ask the landlord to change the locks on the home because defendant was moving out. Victim was last seen by neighbors at her home on or about July 15, 2004. The landlord testified that defendant was at the house on the 16th, and he appeared sweaty and nervous. On the night of the 16th, several neighbors later reported that they saw defendant build a large fire in Gambrell's backyard, and the landlord saw him tending the fire at 4 a.m. Defendant vacated the home the following day. During the cleanup at the home, the landlord found what appeared to be a large bloodstain and evidence of a fight or struggle in the house. The birth certificate, Social Security card, and numerous personal items belonging to the victim were also found in the home. Most of the debris from the fire pit was bagged and disposed of by

the landlord; the remaining was placed in garbage bins and left at the house. Victim was reported missing by family on or about August 23, 2004. Police then received permission from the landlord to search this home and property. Found in and around the fire pit area were buttons and zippers from clothing, a pair of eyeglasses that belonged to victim, and some car keys. Bone fragments from the fire pit were found and compared to a DNA sample taken from victim's biological mother, and there was a familial match. Victim's three siblings (all from the same mother) were all alive and accounted for. The crime lab was not able to determine if the bloodstain found in the home was of human origin. The bone fragments were also identified by a forensic anthropologist as belonging to a woman approximately 40 years old and 5 feet, 4 inches tall, matching victim. An arson investigator testified that when he visited the site, he smelled burned flesh. After the jury hung in the first trial, defendant was convicted of first-degree murder at a second trial and sentenced to life.

Sources: *South Carolina vs. Johnny Ray Gambrell*, No. 2008-UP-063 (January 22, 2008); "Anderson murder trial ends in hung jury" *Spartanburg Herald-Journal*, November 20, 2005; http://www.websleuths.com/forums/archive/index.php/t-32437.html

Keywords: **Forensic evidence: DNA, Forensic evidence: Other, Life**

Case 129

Defendant: **Mario Flavio Garcia**

Victim: Christie Wilson

Trial: November 2006 Jurisdiction: Sacramento County, California (Moved from Placer County due to pretrial publicity)

Murder: October 5, 2005

Evidence: Victim disappeared after leaving a Lincoln casino in the early morning hours of October 5, 2005. Earlier, victim had been playing cards in the casino at the same table as defendant. Police believe this was the first time that victim and defendant had met. Victim reported missing the following day by her boyfriend, who informed police that victim was at the Lincoln casino the night that she was last seen by family or friends. (The boyfriend was initially a suspect in the disappearance, since he and victim had a history of domestic violence, but he was alibied for the night of the disappearance.) Police obtained casino security video of victim and defendant sitting next to each other at the card table, and this same video later showed victim and defendant leaving the casino together and walking toward defendant's car. The casino provided player club card information identifying the parties as victim and defendant. Others at the same table were identified and later interviewed by the police. Police learned that the day after the murder, defendant went to work, where several coworkers noticed cuts and bruises on his face. When confronted with this information, defendant told police that the injuries occurred when he fell while pruning a tree. (Defendant later sought treatment for a series of infections potentially caused by scratches and human saliva.) Witnesses at the card table stated that defendant had no visible injuries to his face when he was in the casino with victim. These same witnesses stated that at one point victim borrowed some money from defendant, and that victim and defendant appeared to be "a couple." The suspect's car was seen leaving the casino on the surveillance video and was later searched by police. Hairs belonging to the victim (DNA) were found on the passenger side door handle, the passenger side floor, and in the trunk. Blood stains on the rear seat were matched to victim, and others were mixtures of the victim and defendant's blood. Approximately 10 days after victim went missing, the police searched defendant's work computer and found that he had accessed websites dealing with forensic evidence, the *FBI Handbook*, general information about search warrants, and information on the rave rape drug. On the date that victim was reported missing, the police found her car at the casino. This car was searched, but nothing of evidentiary value was found. Defendant's whereabouts were also tracked through cell tower records. Defendant was convicted of first-degree murder and sentenced to 59 years to life. To date, victim's remains have not been located.

Sources: *California vs. Mario Garcia*, 171 Cal. App. 4th 1649 (2009); http://www.crimeshots.com/forums/showthread.php?t=4428&page=4; Charley Project

Keywords: **Forensic evidence: DNA, Forensic evidence: Other**

Case 130

Defendant: **J. Ted Garner**
Victim: Fred Iwert
Trial: March 1984 Jurisdiction: Washington County, Kansas
Murder: April 20, 1983
Evidence: Victim was a farmer in Washington County, Kansas. Defendant was a semi-retired chiropractor who dabbled in real estate and buying and selling antiques. Victim and defendant met in 1981. In 1982, defendant began helping with chores at the victim's farm. According to defendant, he approached victim in September 1982 about leasing with the option of buying victim's farm. Defendant stated that victim agreed to this arrangement and signed a contract drafted by defendant for the lease-buy agreement. Defendant stated that this contract was signed by both parties that same month, and that he gave victim $30,600 in cash at the time of signing. In early 1983, defendant approached a local cattle consignment firm and told them that he had purchased victim's farm and cattle and stated that he wanted to sell the cattle on consignment. On the morning of April 20, 1983 (the date victim was last seen), defendant went to an area veterinary clinic and purchased 50 cc of euthanasia solution, telling the veterinarian that he had an old horse that needed to be euthanized. On the afternoon of April 20, 1983, victim's brother stopped at victim's house after hearing that victim's cattle had been placed for sale on consignment. The brother stated that he spoke with victim at that time and was told by victim that he had sold nothing to defendant and that the cattle were not defendant's to sell. At trial, evidence was introduced indicating that victim had purchased large quantities of feed and veterinary supplies for his cattle just prior to his disappearance, indicating that he had no intentions of selling the livestock. Bank records for victim were also introduced, showing no record of a $30,600 transaction between defendant and victim, as

reported. A handwriting expert also testified that victim's signature, as it appeared on the lease to buy agreement, was a forgery. Police investigators testified that during an interview with defendant, he denied the purchase of the euthanasia solution and stated that he had never visited any of the local area veterinarians. After victim disappeared, and prior to the arrest of defendant, defendant was telling area residents that victim had abruptly traveled to Mississippi to visit a girlfriend. No one in the area, including victim's brother, was aware of any female acquaintances that victim may have had. It is also noted that during the late afternoon of April 20, 1983, victim's brother drove by victim's house and noted that victim's truck was gone and that defendant's car was parked in the driveway. A while later, on another drive by victim's house, the brother noted that victim's truck was now parked in the drive and defendant's car was gone. Defendant was convicted of first-degree murder and sentenced to life.

Sources: "Man receives life sentence in murder of Kansas farmer," *Lawrence Journal World*, March 7, 1984; *Kansas vs. Garner*, 699 P.2d 468 (1985)

Keywords: **Forensic evidence: Other, Life**

Case 131

Defendant: **Lawrence Gaudenzi**

Victim: Lisa Kathy Gaudenzi

Trial Date: May 2009 Jurisdiction: Caroline County, Virginia

Murder Date: January 1995

Evidence: Defendant reported victim as missing to police in January 1995. Defendant told the police that he last saw victim when he dropped her off at a bus station in Richmond, Virginia, on January 26, 1995, stating that victim had a bus trip planned to Petersburg that day. Victim was active duty military at the time, and the defendant told police that she was going to Petersburg for military training. Police found that no buses were going from Richmond to Petersburg on that date. In 1997, defendant and his young daughter vanished from the area. In 2002, police found defendant and his daughter in Harrisonburg, Virginia, following a televised update on victim's disappearance. Defendant was working at a discount retailer under the name Randy Evans, a Richmond homeless man who was last seen in 1998. Defendant had also established a new identity for his young daughter. In 2008 witnesses who were fearful of defendant finally came forward; defendant was arrested in May 2008 and charged with the first-degree murder. In May 2009, three days into his trial, defendant agreed to plead to a charge of second-degree murder. In June 2009, following his conviction, defendant told police that victim's death was the result of an accident when she fell and broke her neck. Defendant led police to victim's remains that he had placed in a drum of acid and buried in a remote field. The only evidence found at the burial site was shreds of a sleeping bag that victim had been wrapped in and a porcelain dental bridge that was identified as belonging to victim. The investigation revealed that on the date prior to victim's disappearance, she had asked the babysitter to keep their infant daughter overnight, as she (victim) had planned to ask defendant for a divorce that night. Defendant was sentenced to 25 years.

Sources: http://www.nbc12.com/Global/story.asp?S=12645346; http://fredericksburg.com/News/FLS/2008/052008/05172008/380268
Keywords: **Confession to friends and family, Confession to police (postconviction)**

Case 132

Defendant: **Henry Gibson**
Victim: Lafeyette Miller
Trial Date: 1945 Jurisdiction: Lee County, Kentucky
Murder: November 1, 1944
Evidence: Defendant and victim were acquaintances. Victim was an elderly farmer who lived alone in a rural area; he was reputed to have a large sum of money hidden in a metal trunk and several guns in his home. During the afternoon of his death, a neighbor overheard gunshots coming from the direction of victim's house. Neighbors went to check on victim at about 8:30 that night and found his home on fire. One neighbor was able to look in a window and reported seeing what appeared to be a human skeleton/remains in the home. The fire had progressed to the point where the neighbors were not able to enter the home. Not knowing if it was victim that they saw in the home, the neighbors first went to the home of defendant's mother, a person that victim was known to socialize with, and then to defendant's home looking for victim. Victim was not located at either home. During the fire scene investigation, a metal trunk was found in the home. It had been forced open, and its contents were missing. None of the firearms were found, either. The human remains found in the fire scene had what appeared to be bullet fragments in the skull. During the fire scene investigation, defendant went to victim's home and met with members of victim's family. Defendant then offered the family $10, stating that he had owed this money to victim for a handgun that he had pawned with victim several weeks back. Victim's family told police that victim had in his possession, nine days before the fire, the same handgun that defendant now possessed. Although the human remains found in the fire scene were never positively identified, victim was never seen or heard from after the fire. Defendant was arrested and tried for the murder of victim. Defendant was convicted, but that conviction was later overturned due to faulty jury instructions by the court.
Source: *Commonwealth v. Gibson*, 192 S.W.2d 187 (1946)
Keyword: **Forensic evidence: Other**

Case 133

Defendant: **Larry Gibson**
Victim: Thomas Gibson
Trial: 1995 Jurisdiction: Glendale, Oregon
Murder: 1991
Evidence: Defendant was a deputy with the Douglas County, Oregon, sheriff's department. He was off duty and at home at the time of victim's disappearance. Victim, who was 2½ years old, was last seen playing in the front yard of the family's rural home located in a heavily

wooded area. Defendant's wife and daughters were in the home at the time of the disappearance. Defendant told police that he decided to go for a jog and that he left victim to play in the front yard alone until he returned home. Defendant indicated that he always carried a handgun to shoot some of the numerous stray cats on his property. Defendant told police that he shot at a cat that was near victim's location just before he went on his jog. Defendant stated that victim was gone when he returned from his 45 minute run. After reporting the disappearance to the police, the community organized and began searching for victim. During the early part of the search, defendant remained in his home drinking coffee. Several hours into the search defendant approached several members of the search party and told them to go home because it was snowing heavily. Defendant's 4-year-old daughter initially told police that she saw an unidentified couple pull into the family driveway and take victim. Several years later, this same witness changed her statement and told police that on the morning of victim's disappearance, she saw her father beat and then drive off in his squad car with victim. Following the second statement from defendant's daughter, defendant was arrested. Defendant had a history of abusing his children. Defendant made a veiled admission to police that he could have accidentally shot the victim. Defendant was convicted of second-degree manslaughter and sentenced to three years in prison.

Sources: Charley Project; *Gibson v. Georgia*, 505 S.E.2d 63 (Ga. App. 1998)

Keyword: **Eyewitness**

Case 134

Defendant: **Daniel Gilbert**

Victim: Chimene Ellena

Trial: November 1999 Jurisdiction: Springfield, Illinois

Murder: Memorial Day Weekend 1999

Evidence: Defendant admitted to police his involvement in the murder of victim, his girlfriend. Defendant stated that he was under the influence of drugs at the time of the murder and disposed of the remains. Defendant told police that he dumped the remains in southern Wisconsin County and even gave police a detailed description of the dump site. Not knowing a specific area, and with the rural setting described, police were not able to locate victim's remains until after the trial and conviction of defendant. In November 1999, defendant was convicted of first-degree murder and sentenced to 45 years in prison. Victim's remains were discovered in October 2000. Victim was identified from medical and dental records and from clothing items found at the scene.

Source: Daniel Gilbert-Chimene Ellena ("Body found near road may be that of Illinois woman"—Google News), *Wisconsin State Journal*, October 25, 2000

Keywords: **Confession to police, Forensic evidence: Other**

Case 135

Defendant: **Robert S. Gilchrist**

Victim: Christina Zane

Trial: September, 1982 Jurisdiction: Mobile County, Alabama
Murder: April 28, 1982
Evidence: In early 1982, defendant and victim had several brief sexual encounters. Defendant was in a long-term relationship with another woman at the time. On April 28, 1982, while defendant and victim were driving in a remote area, they experienced car trouble during a heated argument. During this argument, victim threatened to "make trouble" for defendant over the sexual encounters. Defendant and victim got out of the car, at which time defendant began to beat victim. He then tied her up and beat her to death with a log. Defendant hid remains in some nearby dense undergrowth. When the police located victim's car, they also found defendant's phone number in victim's personal belongings. When defendant found out he was focus of the missing person's investigation, he returned twice to the dump site, first to move remains further off road, and the second time to bury victim. Defendant's girlfriend testified at trial that defendant had confessed to her his involvement in murder. Defendant was tried for the murder and found guilty. The conviction was appealed based on the fact that the prosecutor had also testified as a witness at the trial. Retrial was ordered, and defendant was again convicted and sentenced to life. Following the second trial, defendant tried to assist law enforcement in locating remains, but to date victim is still missing.
Sources: *Gilchrist v. Alabama*, 585 So. 2d 165 (Ala. 1991); "Officer testifies he overheard accused confess killings," *Gasden Times*, September 16, 1982; "Killer tries to find body," *The Tuscaloosa News*, January 30, 1989
Keywords: **Confession to friends and family, Life**

Case 136

Defendants: **James Gilliland, Oliver Lee**
Victims: Albert Jennings Fountain, Henry Fountain
Trial: After 1896 Jurisdiction: Tularosa, New Mexico
Murder: February 1, 1896
Evidence: Victim Albert Jennings Fountain was the chief investigator and prosecutor for the Southeastern New Mexico Stock Growers Association. This association was formed by cattle ranchers to stop cattle rustling gangs, including a gang that included the two defendants. In January 1896, victim secured 32 indictments against known rustlers, including defendants. Victim by this time already had 20 convictions for rustling to his credit. During the hearings to secure the indictments, victim received a threatening letter telling him to stand down or he would never see the rest of his family again. Following the indictments, victim and his 8-year-old son began the 140-mile horse and buggy trip back home. When victim and son didn't arrive home, a posse was sent to search. Along the designated route, the posse found blood evidence, spent rifle casings, and a bloody handkerchief with a dime rolled up in one corner. This matched a handkerchief and dime that the 8-year-old victim was known to carry. In a nearby town, victim's buggy was found stripped and abandoned. The remains of neither victim have ever been found. Several years after their disappearance, defendants were indicted and tried for the murders. Both were acquitted.

Source: http://www.desertusa.com/mag06/mar/murder.html
Keyword: **Forensic evidence: Other**

Case 137

Defendant: **Kim Williams Gonzales**
Victim: Andrea Gonzales
Trial: 1997 Jurisdiction: Russellville, Alabama
Murder: November 1993
Evidence: At the time of her disappearance, victim, who was 5 years old, was living with her father, Paul Gonzales, and her stepmother, while defendant lived in a mobile home in Russellville, Alabama. On November 20, 1993, Paul Gonzales and defendant reported victim missing, telling police that she vanished sometime during the night. There were no signs of forced entry to victim's home, and tracking dogs brought to the scene tracked only as far as the front porch of victim's home. During the investigation, both Paul and defendant submitted to polygraph exams. Paul passed, but defendant failed. A massive search for victim was unsuccessful. Victim had severe emotional and behavioral problems at the time of her disappearance. During interviews with defendant, she kept referring to victim in the past tense. In February 1995, defendant went to the police and confessed, stating that on the night of the disappearance, she had accidentally scalded victim while bathing her. Defendant stated that she provided medical attention and some pain medication to victim before putting her to bed. Defendant stated that she checked on victim several hours later and found her dead. Defendant stated that she panicked and wrapped victim in a garbage bag and tied it to a cement block. Defendant then threw remains from a bridge into a river. The river was searched, the garbage bag and cement block were found, but victim's remains are still unaccounted for. During subsequent interviews, Paul admitted to helping dispose of the body. Police believe victim was abused and then murdered. Both Paul and defendant were charged with capital murder in a death penalty case. Defendant was found guilty of child abuse and received a 10-year sentence. Paul had earlier pleaded to manslaughter and also received a 10-year sentence.
Sources: Charley Project; http://littlegirllostag.angelfire.com/
Keywords: **Confession to police, Codefendant testimony**

Case 138

Defendant: **Fred Grabbe**
Victim: Charlotte Grabbe
Trial Date: June 1985 Jurisdiction: Clark County, Illinois
Murder: July 1981
Evidence: Victim and defendant had a turbulent marriage. Early on they got divorced and later married again. At the time of victim's disappearance, defendant had a girlfriend. The girlfriend was at defendant's farm in a tool shed with defendant when victim entered. There was a heated argument between defendant and victim, and defendant strangled victim to death. Defendant then injected victim's remains

with grease and loaded her into a barrel on the back of his truck. Defendant and girlfriend took remains to a nearby river bank, where defendant filled the barrel with diesel fuel and then burned the victim's remains. The burning took place very near a large maple tree. During the investigation, the police found a lock box that belonged to victim. In that box was a letter from victim that was to be read only in the event of her death or disappearance. In the letter, victim stated that she feared defendant was going to kill her. Several years after the murder, defendant and his girlfriend split up, the girlfriend then went to the police and told them of the murder. The girlfriend was granted immunity from prosecution and testified at the trial. The defendant's adult son and daughter also testified for the prosecution. The defendant was found guilty of murder, but that conviction was overturned and the defendant was retried in 1988. One month prior to the second trial, defendant's adult son vanished. Defendant was found guilty and sentenced to life. The prosecution had scientists from the University of Illinois testify at both trials about the presence of petroleum in the tree roots of the maple tree where victim was burned. The scientists were able to determine that the petroleum entered the root system in 1981.

Sources: http://www.wthitv.com/news/look-back-grabbe-trial; http://articles.chicagotribune.com/1988-10-07/features/8802050780_1_jennie-charlotte-conviction

Keywords: **Eyewitness, Life, Forensic evidence: Other**

Case 139

Defendant: **Geralyn Graham**

Victim: Rilya Wilson

Trial date: January 2013 Jurisdiction: Miami, Florida

Murder: 2000

Evidence: Victim, four at the time of her murder, entered the foster care system at the age of five weeks after being removed from her mother's custody. In 2000, victim was in foster care with defendant. At the time, defendant also had a domestic partner in the household. When the Florida Department of Children and Families (DCF) went to conduct a check on the victim, they discovered that she was no longer with defendant. Defendant told DCF that "some mystery worker" from DCF had picked the child up for a mental health assessment. DCF denied this and indicated that no record exists of any DCF worker taking custody of the child. In 2005, defendant was in jail on fraud charges when she confessed to a cellmate her involvement in the death and disappearance of victim. Defendant told cellmate that she smothered victim with a pillow because victim was evil and needed to be put out of her misery. Defendant also told cellmate she buried victim somewhere near the water in South Miami-Dade. During the investigation, defendant's domestic partner came forward and told police that she witnessed defendant often bind victim to the bed rails with flex-cuffs for the night to prevent her from getting out of bed. This same witness also told police defendant would often lock victim in the laundry room for extended periods of time as punishment. There was a 15-month interval between visits to defendant's home by DCF, and victim vanished sometime during this 15-month period. Defendant was also charged with fraud, as she continued to collect monetary benefits in victim's name after victim disappeared. Defendant was convicted of kidnapping and child abuse and sentenced to 55 years in prison. The jury was hung on the murder charge. Victim's remains have never been found.

Sources: http://topics.nytimes.com/top/reference/timestopics/people/w/rilya_wilson/; Anderson, C., "Geralyn Graham sentenced to 55 years in the Rilya Wilson case," *The Huffington Post*, February 12, 2013

Keywords: **Confession to friend, Informant testimony, Eyewitness**

Case 140

Defendant: **Curtis Grayer**

Victim: Baby Kevin

Trial Date: November 2005 Jurisdiction: Dekalb, Georgia

Murder: 2002

Evidence: Defendant was married to the mother of an 11-year-old girl. Defendant first raped his stepdaughter when she was 7 years old, oftentimes when the mother was in the same room. Prosecution described mother as borderline retarded and very easily led. At the time of the stepdaughter's 11th birthday she learned that she was pregnant. The stepdaughter reported during the investigation that defendant would often stomp on her stomach or make her wear tight belts around her stomach in an attempt to force the girl to miscarry. Defendant also removed the stepdaughter from school, fearing someone would recognize that she was pregnant. The stepdaughter home delivered a baby boy on October 18, 2002, while using the toilet; the gestational age was estimated at 24 weeks. The stepdaughter named the baby Kevin. Defendant refused to take the stepdaughter or victim in for medical attention, fearing that his involvement in the sexual assaults would be discovered. Victim died within hours of birth. The stepdaughter stated that victim was dressed in baby clothes and placed in a small box; this was the last time that she saw victim. A month after the birth and death of victim, the stepdaughter and her mother moved away from defendant to an area in Virginia near family. It was then that the stepdaughter confided in her family what had happened. Defendant was arrested in September 2003. Police searched defendant's home and a nearby lake for remains and found none. Police found the windows of the home nailed shut and all exit doors could be opened only with a key from both sides, just as the mother and stepdaughter had told police. Defendant admitted to police that the stepdaughter had indeed given birth, but denied fathering that child and denied any involvement in the death or disappearance of victim. Defendant blamed his wife for the disappearance of victim. Research information indicates "medical testing could not prove or disprove that the victim was raped or had given birth." To date, victim has not been located. Defendant was convicted of the murder and sentenced to life.

Sources: "Girl tells horrific tale of rape, murder," *Atlanta Journal Constitution*, June 12, 2005; *Grayer v. State*, 647 S.E.2d 264 (2007)

Keywords: **Life, Eyewitness**

Case 141

Defendant: **Michael Green**
Victim: Kim Williams
Trial: 1999 Jurisdiction: San Diego County, California
Murder: June 1995
Evidence: Victim was defendant's girlfriend. Witness overheard a violent fight between victim and defendant and called the police, but before the police got there, defendant drove away from the home in his van with the victim "sitting motionless" upright in the front passenger seat. Defendant never returned to live at the apartment, but was seen sneaking in during the night to move out his property. Defendant was also seen with blood on his pants just before driving away on the day of victim's disappearance. Victim had made prior comments to a friend that showed fear for her life. Defendant would often beat her and tie her up while he was away at work. Defendant had a violent past, and just prior to arrest had attacked a woman and nearly killed her. Defendant convicted of murder despite no DNA, physical evidence, or a confession and sentenced to 131 years to life.
Source: Tad DiBiase
Keywords: **N/A**

Case 142

Defendant: **James Robert Griffin**
Victim: Diana Deloise Goldston
Trial: December 1996 Jurisdiction: Denton, Texas
Murder: Kidnapped July 1, 1996
Evidence: Victim was kidnapped from a nightclub parking lot on July 1, 1996. Witnesses to the kidnapping told police that they observed a man force a woman into a pickup truck. Witnesses then heard a gunshot inside of the truck as it was exiting the parking lot. Two suspects connected to victim were identified as being involved in the kidnapping; one was defendant. Police learned that victim's remains had been buried by a nearby lake. By the time this information became known and a search effort launched, police learned that one of the kidnappers had apparently returned to the burial site, removed remains, and reburied body in a different location. During a search of the kidnap vehicle, bloodstains were found inside. Kidnappers believed that victim owed them money, and kidnapping took place because victim had failed to pay that money back. Victim's remains have never been found. Defendant was convicted of the kidnapping, as was his female accomplice.
Sources: Charley Project: Diane Deloise Goldston; NamUs—Diane Goldston; Diane Deloise Goldston, July 1, 1996: Porchlight International
Keywords: **Eyewitness**

Case 143

Defendant: **Richard Grissom**
Victims: Joan Butler, Christine Rusch, Theresa Brown
Trial: 1990 Jurisdiction: Johnson County, Kansas

Murder: June 1989
Evidence: Defendant was a maintenance man who had key access to apartment complexes where he worked as a painter. After victims went missing, defendant was found using a car that had been rented to victim Joan Butler. When the police approached, defendant fled on foot. When police later found Butler's car they recovered the defendant's fingerprints, wallet, and checkbook from the car. During a search of defendant's car, police found bank cards belonging to victims Rusch and Brown, as well as keys belonging to the apartment that they had been renting. Defendant had done some painting at their apartment complex prior to their disappearance. Police tracked defendant to the Dallas-Fort Worth Airport, where he had planned to meet another female acquaintance. Defendant never told the police where the three victims' remains were but stated, "You'll dig them up." Defendant was suspected in the murder of a fourth female victim whose remains were found in Johnson County a week before the Butler, Rusch, and Brown disappearances; he was never charged in that murder. To date, the remains of these three victims have not been found. At trial, the prosecution called more than 100 witnesses, and the combination of the circumstantial evidence found and what defendant said during his interrogation convinced the jury. Defendant was convicted of murder and sentenced to life.
Sources: Murderpedia; http://www2.ljworld.com/news/2009/jul/04/victims/
Keywords: **Life, Forensic evidence: Other**

Case 144

Defendant: **Jason Gross**
Victim: Rochelle Battle
Trial: October 2011 Jurisdiction: Baltimore County, Maryland
Murder: March 6, 2009
Evidence: Victim, 16 years old, was highly dependent on her cell phone, placing as many as 1,900 calls and texts in a one-month period leading up to her disappearance. On March 6, 2009, at about 10 p.m. victim answered a call on her cell; after that, all incoming and outgoing activity on the victim's cell phone stopped. Cell phone tower and cell GPS information placed victim and defendant together at a Baltimore bus stop, and later as they were traveling in a vehicle. This same information also placed victim and the defendant together at defendant's home late that night. Police also had surveillance video that disproved defendant's alibi. Police believe defendant sexually assaulted victim and then killed her. Police also believe defendant disposed of victim by incinerating her remains at a landfill site where he worked. Victim's remains have never been found. Defendant was convicted of second-degree murder and sentenced to 30 years for the murder and an additional 10 years for the sexual assault.
Sources: http://weblogs.baltimoresun.com/news/crime/blog/2010/04/cops_make_murder_arrest_despit.html; http://baltimore.cbslocal.com/2011/10/13/trial-begins-for-man-charged-with-missing-girls-murder/
Keyword: **Forensic evidence: Other**

Case 145

Defendant: **Robert Guevara**
Victim: Corrine Erstad
Trial: 1993 Jurisdiction: Minnesota
Murder: June 1, 1992
Evidence: Victim, 5 years old, was last seen walking alone to a park near her home at about 7:30 p.m. Victim's older brothers were sent to get her about five minutes after she left the home, but they were unable to locate her. Victim's mother and stepfather reported her as missing about two hours after she disappeared. A child witness at the park saw a young girl matching victim's description at the park talking with a man who was walking a dog, and the girl was petting the dog. The police viewed defendant as a suspect from the onset after learning that defendant was a friend of victims parent's and that he often stayed at victim's home when he was too intoxicated to get back to his own house. Police learned that when defendant stayed at victim's home, he oftentimes slept in the same bed as victim. Defendant was reportedly at victim's home early on the day that she disappeared. After his departure, victim confided in her mother that defendant had just molested her. Victim's mother did not share this information with the police until two days after victim's disappearance, stating that she "forgot." A police K-9 tracked the victim's scent to defendant's home after her disappearance. Defendant arrested four days after disappearance and charged with kidnapping, rape, and murder. The police found a dress identical to dress victim was wearing at the time of her disappearance and a pair of girl's underwear. These items were found in a storage locker being rented by defendant. These clothing items had blood and semen stains that were "consistent" with defendant's DNA. Blood evidence was also found on the shower curtain in defendant's home. At the time of trial, much of the DNA evidence was not allowed because defendant's attorney argued that the storage locker where the clothing items were found had never been locked and evidence could have been planted. To date, the victim's remains have not been found. Defendant was acquitted.
Sources: Charley Project; http://www.twincities.com/ci_22699816/dead-missing-victims-families-cope-different-ways
Keyword: **Forensic evidence: DNA**

Case 146

Defendant: **James Guilford**
Victim: Sharon Nugent
Trial: May 2008 Jurisdiction: Syracuse, New York
Murder: On/about February 6, 2007
Evidence: Victim and defendant lived together and had three children together. Victim was last seen at about 2 a.m. on February 6, 2007, when she left a house party. Defendant reported victim missing to police two days later, telling police that victim arrived home around 3 a.m. on February 6 and left for work at about 5 a.m. On the day that defendant reported victim missing, he fled to Atlanta with the three children. Defendant arrested seven weeks after victim's

disappearance, when he made an appearance in the Syracuse Family Court on another matter. During the investigation, police found a substantial amount of blood on the mattress in victim's bedroom. Blood evidence that had been painted over was also found on the walls and ceiling of victim's bedroom. A hammer that defendant took with him to Atlanta was recovered, and a DNA match to victim was found on hammer. Defendant told police that he disposed of victim's remains in a dumpster near their home. Defendant testified at his trial and maintained his innocence. A total of five witnesses also testified at trial that defendant admitted his involvement in the murder and disposal of victim's remains. Defendant was convicted of murder and sentenced to life. Defendant appealed his conviction based on a 49-hour interrogation by police, where defendant was provided little food and no sleep. The Court of Appeals granted defendant a new trial and threw out his confession.

Sources: Charley Project; Patterson, S., "State's highest court gives convicted killer new trial due to Syracuse Police interrogation," *Syracuse.com*, June 4, 2013

Keywords: **Life, Confession to friends and family, Confession to police, Forensic evidence: DNA**

Case 147

Defendant: **Steven Dodson Halcomb**

Victim: Karen Jo Smith

Trial date: December 2004 Jurisdiction: Marion County, Indiana

Murder: December 27, 2000

Evidence: Victim was last seen by her son, who said she was sitting in her living room with defendant late in the evening. Defendant was victim's former husband. The son told police that victim appeared to be experiencing drug-induced sleepiness at the time. Victim's children heard nothing unusual in the home that night. The following morning, victim was gone, but her car and personal belongings were still at her home. Victim's children reported her missing to the police. Defendant also vanished that day and failed to show up for work in the days that followed. Defendant turned himself in to the police on January 11, 2001, for parole violation. Defendant was returned to prison for the parole violation and remained incarcerated until 2003. Upon release, defendant vanished again. Defendant was indicted in absentia for victim's murder in August 2003. He was later located and arrested. At trial, a cellmate of defendant testified that defendant had confessed to him his involvement in the strangulation death of victim. The prosecution also presented evidence that defendant had been abusive toward victim during their marriage, that he had stalked her, and that he once tried to hire an undercover police officer to kill victim prior to her disappearance. Prior to her disappearance, victim had confided in family members that she felt threatened by defendant. The defendant was convicted and sentenced to 95 years.

Source: Charley Project

Keywords: **Confession to friends and family, Informant**

Case 148

Defendant: **Freddie Lee Hall**
Victim: James K. Britt
Trial: January 2013 Jurisdiction: Portsmouth, Virginia
Murder: April 2011
Evidence: Victim was in used car business in Portsmouth, Virginia, and defendant was in used car business in Florida. Victim and defendant were business acquaintances who had bought and sold cars from each other. Prior to his disappearance, victim told several friends that he had been visited numerous times late at night by defendant, and that he did not like or trust him. After victim disappeared, his family reported him missing to police. At victim's home, police found what appeared to be a very violent crime scene. Blood spatter linked by DNA to victim was found throughout the home. Portions of the carpets had been bleached or completely removed from the home. Some blood spatter evidence had been painted over. In garage police found a bag with teeth from victim and a spent 9 mm casing. A paint can with defendant's latent prints was also seized. Additional latent prints from defendant were found in numerous locations throughout victim's home. A large section of carpet with blood evidence from victim's home was found at defendant's home. The police also discovered that defendant had two of the victim's prized cars, an anniversary-edition Corvette and a Jaguar. Friends of victim testified that victim would never have parted with these two cars. Defendant also had in his possession several other car titles belonging to victim. Defendant was interviewed several times by police and was cooperative throughout; however, he never confessed or admitted any part in the murder and disappearance of victim. Defendant was described by police as being a con man, one who often paraded around in the full dress uniform of a U.S. Air Force colonel, even though there was no record of him ever serving in the military. Defendant found guilty of murder. Victim's remains have not been located.
Sources: Bryant, J., "Jury says life for murder of Portsmouth businessman," *The Virginian-Pilot*, February 1, 2013; Bryant, J., "Body still lost, but Portsmouth jury finds it to be murder," *The Virginian-Pilot*, January 31, 2013
Keywords: **Life, Forensic evidence: DNA, Forensic evidence: Other**

Case 149

Defendant: **Henry William Hall, Lee Philip Mileham**
Victim: Ted Lindberry
Trial: September 1999 Jurisdiction: Phoenix, Arizona
Murder: April 25, 1997
Evidence: On April 25, 1997, victim was last seen leaving a bar with defendant Mileham. Several days later Mileham began a spending spree using a credit card belonging to victim. One charge to victim's credit card was for a hotel room and replacement sheets for a bed in that room. In May 1997 police conducted a traffic stop on victim's new Chrysler Sebring, which was being driven by Mileham at the time. Mileham was taken into custody on some outstanding warrants. The

arresting officer left victim's car at the scene of the traffic stop, intending to return an hour later after booking Mileham into the jail. When the officer did return, the car was gone. Several hours later, victim's car was again involved in a traffic stop by police. During this incident Hall was driving. After attempting to flee and nearly striking an officer with the car, Hall was arrested and jailed. In July 1997, a cellmate of Hall's contacted police and provided information indicating that Hall had confided in him his involvement in the kidnapping, robbery, and beating death of victim. Hall also told his cellmate that he and Mileham disposed of victim's remains by wrapping him in a bed sheet and dumping victim in the desert somewhere between Phoenix and New Mexico. During the investigation, police found blood and urine evidence in the trunk of victim's car, and there was a familial match with one of the victim's biological brothers. At trial, the cellmate and four other earwitnesses all testified that Hall had confessed to them his involvement in the kidnap, robbery, and beating death of victim. All of these witnesses came into question because of their own extensive criminal histories or because of their levels of intoxication at the time of the admissions by Hall. Hall was found guilty and sentenced to death. An automatic appeal to the Arizona Supreme Court affirmed the conviction for auto theft but reversed the convictions for murder, armed robbery, and kidnapping. To date, victim's remains have not been located.

Source: *Arizona v. Hall*, 65 P.3d 90 (Az. 2003)

Keywords: **Informant, Confession to friends and family, Forensic evidence: DNA**

Case 150

Defendants: **Junious Hall, Jeffrey Holmes, Michael Monford**

Victim: Larry Nelson

Trial: February 2001 Jurisdiction: Detroit, Michigan

Murder: 2001

Evidence: Victim hired three defendants to renovate a home that he bought. During a visit to the property to check on the progress, defendants beat victim and forced him to make a taped message to his wife directing her to give the defendants $150,000 in cash. Defendants then beat victim with a shovel and shot him to death with a rifle. Victim's remains were then disposed of in a dumpster. During the investigation, all three defendants told police that they were present when victim was attacked but offered different accounts of their personal involvement in the attack. Monford and Holmes also discussed the killing with others not involved in the murder. Holmes told police that Hall used a potato to muffle the fatal gunshot and that Hall had also purchased a knife prior to the murder that he intended to use in the assault. Holmes also told police that Hall had planned to shoot victim in his penis. Police identified witnesses who heard Holmes bragging about the fact that Hall had shot the victim twice. Holmes bragged to these same witnesses that he beat the victim with a shovel and that he had struck him in the ribs with a two-by-four after he had been shot. Defendants were tried together before separate

juries. Holmes and Hall were convicted of first-degree murder, and Monford was convicted of second-degree murder.
Source: *Michigan v. Jeffrey Holmes* #244123
Keywords: **Confession to friends and family, Codefendant testimony**

Case 151

Defendants: **Leisha Hamilton, Timothy Smith**
Victim: Roger Scott Dunn
Trial: 1997 Jurisdiction: Lubbock, Texas
Murder: May 16, 1991
Evidence: Hamilton and victim were dating and living together when Hamilton began having an affair with Smith. Hamilton called victim's parents (who lived several hundred miles away) two weeks after victim's disappearance to tell them that she had not seen victim in weeks. Victim's parents filed a missing persons report. During the investigation, Hamilton told police that she went to work on or about May 16, 1991, and that when she returned home on that date, victim was gone. Police found a large section of the living room carpet missing from the apartment that Hamilton and victim shared, and large red stains were seen in the flooring where the carpet had been. Blood spatter evidence was found in victim's bedroom after a luminol application, and blood evidence was linked to victim by DNA. Police and the medical examiner determined that based on the amount of blood found in the apartment that it was not possible for victim to have survived the attack. Defendants were arrested and tried in 1997. At trial, a witness testified that he was told by Hamilton that there was no way she would be convicted without a body and without a weapon. Hamilton was found guilty of murder and sentenced to 20 years. Smith was found guilty of a lesser charge and sentenced to 10 years. In 2012, the victim's remains were found four doors away from the murder scene by maintenance men at an apartment complex. Victim had been buried in a grave only 1.5 feet deep, wrapped in a heavy blue vinyl material that police believed was the mattress cover from a waterbed. Victim's remains were mummified and well preserved. Victim identified with dental records.
Sources: https://www.google.com/search?q=Blood+evidence-the+disappearance+of+Roger+Scott+Dunn&ie=utf-8&oe=utf-8&aq=t&rls=org.mozilla:en-US:official&client=firefox-a; *Texas v. Leisha Hamilton*, NO. 07-97-0167-CR, Court of Appeals of Texas, Seventh District, Amarillo
Keywords: **Forensic evidence: DNA, Confession to friends and family**

Case 152

Defendant: **Sam Harmon**
Victim: Shakeima Ann Cabbagestalk
Trial: October 2008 Jurisdiction: Dillon, South Carolina
Murder: July 22, 1993
Evidence: Defendant told police that he took victim, his 10-year-old stepdaughter, to a nearby grocery store where he left her. She has

not been seen since. Police learned that on the day that defendant reported victim missing, he went partying at several nightclubs with friends, showing no concern over the fact that his stepdaughter was unaccounted for. Police also learned that in 1992, victim reported that she had been victim of a sexual assault by defendant. This matter was investigated, but no charges were brought. Police believe this may have been the motive in victim's disappearance. Two weeks prior to victim's disappearance, defendant told victim's uncle ways he could dispose of a body where it would never be found. Defendant was arrested 12 years after the victim disappeared after witnesses came forward and told police that they saw victim leave grocery store with defendant on the day that she disappeared. Police also learned that defendant had told a friend of his that "they don't have a body, and they weren't going to find one." At trial, defendant was found not guilty of the murder, but guilty of kidnapping. He was sentenced to 12 years in prison.

Sources: Charley Project; "Harmon acquitted on murder charges," *WMBF News*, October 23, 2008; Shakeima Ann Cabbagestalk-Endangered Missing

Keyword: **Eyewitness**

Case 153

Defendant: **Calvin Harris**

Victim: Michelle Harris

Trial: 2007/2009 Jurisdiction: Ithaca, New York

Murder: September 11, 2001

Evidence: Defendant owned several large car dealerships in the Ithaca area and lived on 252-acre estate with his wife (victim) and four young children. At the time of victim's disappearance, she was in the process of seeking a divorce from defendant. Both defendant and victim were having affairs at the time of her disappearance. Just prior to her disappearance, victim told defendant that she was going to New York City on September 13, 2001, to visit with an old college friend. She told close friends that the purpose of her planned trip to New York City was to pawn her Rolex watch and her two-karat diamond engagement ring. Victim worked her usual shift on September 11 and left work at 9:30 that evening. Victim never made it home. On September 12 a groundskeeper at victim's home found her abandoned vehicle on an approach road to the family estate, the keys were in the ignition, and there was no sign of foul play. During the investigation, defendant allowed open access to his home by police. Police found trace blood evidence linked to victim in the kitchen and doorway area leading to the attached garage. Defendant was unusually calm and nonchalant about victim's disappearance. One week after victim disappeared, defendant was preparing to sell her personal belongings at a garage sale and was openly involved with another woman. Police believed that an expensive divorce was the motive behind the victim's disappearance. Defendant was tried and convicted of the murder in 2007 and sentenced to 34 years in prison. That conviction was thrown out by a judge, and the defendant was retried and again convicted. Second conviction was reversed in May 2013.

Sources: Charley Project; Smith, R., "Did the millionaire murder his wife?" *CBS News*, July 14, 2009
Keyword: **Forensic evidence: DNA**

Case 154

Defendant: **Raphello Harris, Sr.**
Victim: Judith Harris
Trial: July 1990 Jurisdiction: Virgin Islands
Murder: August 14, 1989
Evidence: Victim was defendant's former wife. Defendant had history of abuse against victim and had previously threatened her. Victim disappeared after flying from St. Kitts to the Virgin Islands. Victim frequently traveled back and forth between the islands but had recently divorced defendant, who lived in the Virgin Islands. Defendant drove a friend to the airport the same day, and was witnessed waiting at the airport terminal for several hours waiting for the plane from St. Kitts. When victim deplaned, she asked witnesses if they had seen defendant. Several days later, defendant asked one of the witnesses whether she had seen him leave the airport with victim and then stated that he did not care whether they found her because she had caused him a lot of problems. The day of the murder, defendant's son saw him mopping his bedroom floor and the front door and had stains on his pant leg. A few days later, defendant's son smelled a strong scent of blood in his father's apartment and saw blood spots on the wall and shower curtain and around the bed. A storage chest under the bed was filled with blood, and the bed sheets were missing. Items victim had packed were found in the apartment. Defendant's son later photographed stains on the bed and gave it to police. Defendant convicted of first-degree murder and sentenced to life imprisonment without parole.
Source: *Government of Virgin Islands v. Harris*, 938 F.2d 401 (3rd Cir. 1991)
Keyword: **Life**

Case 155

Defendant: **Ronald Harshman**
Victim: Melvin Elwood Snyder
Trial: 2001 Jurisdiction: Franklin County, Pennsylvania
Murder: May 1985
Evidence: Victim was having an affair with defendant's wife. Victim and defendant's wife fled Pennsylvania the day she revealed the affair, afraid that defendant would kill them. Defendant caught them and rammed his car into victim's pickup before firing several shots at him. Defendant's wife and victim returned to the state several weeks later. Defendant became angry and went looking for victim, who then disappeared. His truck was found abandoned days later. Fifteen years later, investigators found a spent shell casing from a .25-caliber gun where defendant once lived, and it matched a shell casing found in victim's barn after his disappearance. Two jail inmates testified against defendant, claiming he had confessed to them. Defendant

convicted of first-degree murder. Informants later admitted to perjuring themselves in exchange for special consideration from the Franklin County district attorney's office, but defendant was not granted a new trial.

Sources: http://news.google.com/newspapers?nid=2004&dat=20010712&id=ysAiAAAAIBAJ&sjid=aLYFAAAAIBAJ&pg=6090,2875990; http://www.publicopiniononline.com/ci_12986921; http://articles.herald-mail.com/2013-03-28/news/38107968_1_melvin-elwood-snyder-ronald-harshman-harshman-trial

Keywords: **Forensic evidence: Other, Informant**

Case 156

Defendant: **Gary Head**
Victim: Daisy Belle Marshall
Trial: 1999 Jurisdiction: Vandeburgh County, Indiana
Murder: June 15, 1993
Evidence: Victim was defendant's ex-wife, but the couple was still living together. Witnesses stated that defendant was very upset by the divorce. Victim left behind all her personal belongings, but had quit her job the day before her disappearance. A few weeks later, defendant abruptly left for Florida. A coworker testified that defendant had offered him $30,000 to kill victim, and four other witnesses testified that he had talked about killing her. Defendant acquitted of murder because of a lack of physical evidence.
Sources: Charley Project; http://www.nampn.org/cases/marshall_daisy.html; http://www.seacoastonline.com/articles/20130103-NEWS-301030416
Keyword: **N/A**

Case 157

Defendant: **Johnny Joseph Head**
Victim: Dianne Thomas Gabriel
Trial: March 1985 Jurisdiction: Iredell County, North Carolina
Murder: July 1983
Evidence: Victim was a real estate agent who disappeared after going to meet someone for a 7:30 p.m. appointment. When victim went missing, her husband searched their home and found a handwritten note in the garbage can with directions to defendant's house. Victim's car was found parked at a restaurant where she had told witnesses she was going to meet her appointment. A volunteer searcher found a plastic trash bag near a road that contained sexually oriented magazines, duct tape, nylon rope, towels, plastic eating utensils, and a pen. Seven latent fingerprints were lifted from the bag and magazines, all matching defendant. Victim's hair was found on the rope as well as dog hairs matching those recovered from defendant's house. Several months later, several items of victim's clothing and personal belongings were recovered from the same area, including victim's keys and her notepad, containing directions to defendant's house. Victim's hair was found on her clothing with tissue adhering at the root, along

with the same dog hair recovered from defendant's house. The clothing fibers matched those recovered from the duct tape found earlier. Fibers recovered from defendant's bedroom door matched victim's clothing. Defendant represented himself to victim as "McCorkle" and represented himself by the same name to another witness. The tape and magazines recovered in the woods matched tape and magazines found in defendant's home. Defendant convicted of second-degree murder.

Source: *State v. Head*, 338 S.E.2d 908 (N.C. Ct. App. 1986)

Keyword: **Forensic evidence: Other**

Case 158

Defendant: **Steve Heflin**

Victim: Hilda Victoria Brown

Trial: September 1976 Jurisdiction: Columbia County, Oregon

Murder: February 9, 1976

Evidence: Defendant was a bus mechanic for a school at the same garage where victim was a driver. Suspected blood was found on garage wall, but defendant, who had arrived at work early that day, denied it was blood. During subsequent search for victim, defendant claimed to have found her purse in a small pond. A witness stated she had heard a scream, a scuffle, and a single gunshot the evening before. A student reported seeing a man matching defendant's description driving away in pickup shortly after this. Blood was found in defendant's pickup and on .22 Ruger recovered from his home. Also found inside his truck were hairs consistent with the color of victim's hair. The .22 had blood inside of barrel, and forensic expert testified that gun was no more than three feet away from target when fired. Defendant was convicted and sentenced to death, but sentence was commuted to life.

Sources: http://news.google.com/newspapers?nid=1310&dat=19760924&id=hmdYAAAAIBAJ&sjid=COgDAAAAIBAJ&pg=5220,5836139; *Murder Two: The Second Casebook of Forensic Detection* Evans, Colin, John Wiley & Sons, Inc., 2004

Keywords: **Forensic evidence: Other, Life**

Case 159

Defendant: **Samantha Anne Heiges**

Victim: Sydney Heiges

Trial: 2008 Jurisdiction: Dakota County, Minnesota

Murder: May 6, 2005

Evidence: Victim was defendant's newborn daughter. Defendant drowned victim in a bathtub immediately after giving birth. The body was placed in a shoebox for several days before it was dropped down the garbage chute. Defendant then attempted suicide. Defendant and her boyfriend gave conflicting stories about their relationship, their feelings about defendant's pregnancy, and what happened at the birth and murder of the child, with defendant claiming her abusive boyfriend made her do it. Defendant confessed the murder to her new boyfriend a year later. Neighbors testified that they suspected defendant was pregnant when she wore baggy clothes for several months and then suddenly lost weight and wore tight clothing after May. Another witness stated that defendant confessed her pregnancy and said she was ingesting large amount of drugs and alcohol in an attempt to induce miscarriage. The witness reported this conversation to the police. The same witness said defendant later confessed to killing the baby. Defendant also confessed to a detective. Defendant convicted of second-degree murder and sentenced to 25 years imprisonment.

Source: *State v. Heiges*, 806 N.W.2d 1 (Minn. 2011)

Keywords: **Confession to police, Confession to friends and family**

Case 160

Defendant: **Linda Henning**

Victim: Girly Chew Hossencofft

Trial: October 2002 Jurisdiction: New Mexico

Murder: September 10, 1999

Evidence: Victim's husband was having an affair with defendant. Victim's husband was an abusive con artist who doctored his transcripts, posed as a doctor, and was engaged to three different women, including defendant, while married to victim. Victim filed for divorce in January 1999 and moved out. Victim was reported missing when she failed to show up for work. Victim's apartment smelled strongly of bleach, and Luminol revealed extensive blood evidence. Police questioned defendant, who claimed to never have met victim. However, victim had worked at defendant's bank and had been her teller. Defendant purchased a ninja sword the morning of the murder, and defendant's blood was found in victim's apartment. Police later recovered victim's clothing and found a piece of duct tape with defendant's hair. Defendant told witnesses she ate victim so her remains would never be found. Victim's husband pleaded guilty and was sentenced to life imprisonment. He later testified in defendant's defense, claiming he had masterminded the murder and planted evidence. Defendant convicted of first-degree murder and sentenced to life imprisonment.

Sources: *Arbogast v. Miller*, 445 Fed.Appx. 116 (10th Cir. 2011); http://www.cnn.com/2003/LAW/01/07/ctv.henning.trial/index.html?_s=PM:LAW; http://www.vanceholmes.com/court/trial_hossencofft.html

Keywords: **Life, Forensic evidence: DNA**

Case 161

Defendant: **Lyle Herring**

Victim: Lesley Herring

Trial: April 2013 Jurisdiction: Los Angeles County, California

Murder: February 2009

Evidence: Victim was defendant's wife. Victim discovered missing when she failed to show up for work. Witnesses testified that victim was meticulous. Victim's purse, identification, bank cards, and other personal items were all found stuffed into a larger purse on the floor of her bedroom closet. A week later, customs officers stopped defendant when reentering California from Mexico. A cadaver dog was alerted to human decomposition in the trunk of defendant's two cars. Defendant was caught on surveillance tape purchasing coffee from Starbucks two days after victim's disappearance, the receipt for which he planted in victim's purse in an effort to cover his tracks. Defendant also left voicemails with victim's mother, inquiring about victim's whereabouts. The search history on his computer revealed keywords that included "which country do I flee to?" One witness testified to seeing defendant on the night of victim's disappearance pushing a dolly with a large roll of carpet wrapped around something. Defendant had also made incriminating statements to his cousin, saying he could not come back from what he did and he would burn in hell. Defendant's cousin also testified to seeing a gun holster around defendant's ankle and to seeing him place a large plastic bag in his car containing a woman's sweater, shoes, and jeans. Defendant convicted of second-degree murder and sentenced to 15 years to life imprisonment.

Source: http://www.thedailybeast.com/articles/2013/03/28/lesley-herring-the-hollywood-murder-case-with-no-body.html;http://hollywood.patch.com/groups/editors-picks/p/former-hollywood-resident-sentenced-in-wifes-murder

Keyword: **Forensic evidence: Other**

Case 162

Defendant: **Albert W. Hicks**
Victims: George Burr, Smith Watts, Oliver Watts
Trial: May 1860 Jurisdiction: New York, New York
Murder: March 1860

Evidence: Defendant was a crew member on the *E.A. Johnson*, a fishing sloop. Defendant killed the Watts brothers and then the captain, seizing $230 and the clothes of all three men. Defendant, piloting the sloop by himself, crashed into a schooner and abandoned the ship. He landed in Staten Island and eventually made his way into Manhattan, where he attracted attention for his odd behavior and lavish spending. The *E.A. Johnson* was found abandoned and showed evidence of a struggle with blood "wide and thick on its deck" and human hair found in clumps. He was convicted after a six-day trial and sentenced to death by hanging.

Sources: http://www.nytimes.com/1860/07/14/news/execution-hicks-pirate-twelve-thousand-people-bedloe-s-island-scenes-tombs-bay.html?pagewanted=2; Wikipedia

Keywords: **Death penalty, Forensic evidence: Other**

Case 163

Defendant: **Gary Hicks**
Victim: Ron Simpson
Trial: 1983 Jurisdiction: Monterey County, California
Murder: Unknown

Evidence: Victim was a parolee, killed by defendant during a drug- and alcohol-influenced argument in his mobile home. Primary evidence against defendant was blood evidence. Defendant convicted of murder and sentenced to life imprisonment.

Source: http://www.montereyherald.com/ci_14503681

Keywords: **Life, Forensic evidence: Other**

Case 164

Defendant: **James Hicks**

Victim: Jennie Lynn Hicks

Trial: March 1984 Jurisdiction: Penobscot County, Maine

Murder: July 19, 1977

Evidence: Victim was defendant's wife. Defendant made sexual advances toward their 15-year-old live-in nanny. The nanny informed victim the following day, after which victim told her sister that either defendant would be moving out the next weekend or she would leave with her children. At dinner that night, defendant became angry when victim would not let him kiss her and smashed his dishes in the sink. The nanny left that night and returned at 4 a.m. At some point during the night, a neighbor heard victim screaming, "Stop, Jimmy, please stop" or "Stop, you're killing me." Defendant's trailer then became silent, though a light was still on, and witness then heard the sound of wood being chopped or sawed. When the nanny returned, she saw victim lying awkwardly on a love seat with her hair over her face. Defendant claimed victim was asleep, but the nanny was suspicious. Defendant's story contradicted nanny's story. Victim was gone the next morning, leaving behind her glasses, purse, and vehicle. When the nanny pointed out that victim had not taken her glasses, defendant dropped the nanny off at his mother's house. When she returned to defendant's trailer, the glasses were gone and defendant suggested victim had come back for them. Defendant continued to tell witnesses about seeing and talking to victim long after her disappearance, and told witnesses that victim had been cashing checks. Bank records show victim did not cash any checks after her disappearance. When victim's mother accused defendant of killing victim, defendant said, "You'll never prove that." Defendant convicted of fourth-degree murder and sentenced to 10 years imprisonment, of which he only served 6 years. Defendant was arrested for assaulting and robbing a woman in Texas in 2000, after which he led police to victim's body and to two other bodies of women he had killed. He was sentenced to two life sentences for the other murders.

Source: *State v. Hicks*, 495 A.2d 765 (Me. 1985); http://bangordailynews.com/2014/01/05/news/state/no-body-no-conviction-3-maine-murder-cases-had-guilty-verdicts-without-recovered-remains/

Keyword: **Eyewitness**

Case 165

Defendant: **Colvin "Butch" Hinton**

Victim: Shannon Melendi

Trial: August 2005 Jurisdiction: Fulton County, Georgia

Murder: March 26, 1994

Evidence: Victim was a 19-year-old college student kidnapped from a softball game, which defendant was umpiring and victim was scorekeeping. Defendant's wife was out of town that day, and he made excuses to try and get out of his umpire duties, telling some that he had a "hot date." Witnesses stated that defendant neglected his duties to look at or converse with victim. Victim and defendant were seen leaving within several minutes of each other. Victim's car was found crookedly parked at a gas station, unlocked with the keys in the ignition. The vehicle, along with other evidence, was compromised early in the investigation because police believed victim had run away. Both victim and defendant were seen at the gas station that afternoon. Defendant asked one witness to lie to the FBI because their stories wouldn't be consistent. Defendant made phone calls to police and victim's university, indicating victim was alive and that he would make demands. As proof, he left victim's ring in a cloth bag at a payphone for investigators, who identified the bag as the type used in the facility where defendant worked. Defendant had previously assaulted two other women, tying or attempting to tie them up and sexually assaulting one of them. Defendant made incriminating statements to several witnesses, including jailhouse informants. Defendant convicted of malice murder and felony murder and sentenced to life imprisonment. After his conviction, defendant confessed to raping and strangling victim with a necktie while she was handcuffed to a bedpost. He then burned and buried victim's body in his backyard.

Sources: *Hinton v. State*, 631 S.E.2d 365 (Ga. 2006); http://abcnews.go.com/TheLaw/LegalCenter/story?id=2201120; http://www.gpo.gov/fdsys/pkg/CREC-2009-10-27/html/CREC-2009-10-27-pt1-PgH11793-4.htm

Keyword: **Life**

Case 166

Defendant: **Stobert "Toby" Lindell Holt**

Victim: Robert Arthur Wiles

Trial: February 2012 Jurisdiction: Polk County, Florida

Murder: April 1, 2008

Evidence: Victim and defendant were coworkers at victim's father's business. Tension was reported between victim and defendant, particularly about leadership in the company. Victim disappeared from work. Two days later, victim's family received a ransom text note from victim's cell phone demanding $750,000 for victim's safe return. No one picked up the ransom and no further demands were made. Cell phone records later showed that defendant's and victim's cell signals followed an identical path following the disappearance, suggesting defendant was the one to use victim's phone to send the message. Victim's car was left at his father's business, and victim missed a scheduled flight to Dallas. A gun was found in defendant's car. Defendant convicted of manslaughter and extortion and sentenced to 30 years imprisonment.

Sources: http://www.theledger.com/article/20120131/NEWS/120139881?p=1&tc=pg#gsc.tab=0; http://www.theledger.com/article/20120509/NEWS/

120509308; http://www.abcactionnews.com/dpp/news/region_polk/stobert-toby-holt-sentenced-to-30-years-for-manslaughter-extortion

Keyword: **Forensic evidence: Other**

Case 167

Defendant: **Gary W. Homberg**

Victim: Ruth Ann Homberg

Trial: 1989 Jurisdiction: Dane County, Wisconsin

Murder: November 5, 1983

Evidence: Victim was defendant's wife. Defendant was having an affair with victim's daughter-in-law, to whom he confessed the murder. Defendant had previously told her that victim was a "pain in the ass" and he did not love her but was reluctant to divorce her. He told witness that he would find another way for them to be together, and he wanted to make it look like victim committed suicide by drugging her with sleeping pills and then poisoning her in the garage with carbon monoxide. The day defendant reported victim missing, defendant's girlfriend saw him driving victim's car to the airport parking lot. Defendant told her that victim was gone and not coming back, but that there was no body. He said that victim had found out about the affair and threatened to tell defendant's boss that defendant was embezzling, and then said that "that is when it happened." No physical evidence was found, likely because investigators did not search defendant's house until three years after he reported victim missing. Defendant convicted of first-degree murder.

Sources: *State v. Homberg*, 473 N.W.2d 610 (Wis. Ct. App. 1991); http://news.google.com/newspapers?nid=1499&dat=19880406&id=KlcaAAAAIBAJ&sjid=ECsEAAAAIBAJ&pg=7045,4097202

Keyword: **Confession to friends and family**

Case 168

Defendant: **Andrew Hudspeth (a.k.a. Charles Hudspeth)**

Victim: George Watkins

Trial: 1891 Jurisdiction: Marion County, Arkansas

Murder: 1886

Evidence: Victim's wife was having an affair with defendant. Victim and defendant's families were living together on the same farm. Victim and defendant left the farm one day in a wagon to go to Yellville, and defendant returned home that night alone. Victim's wife and defendant were both arrested, and after a lengthy interrogation, victim's wife accused defendant and later testified against him. She stated that she and defendant had plotted the murder before, but that she was not involved in the actual killing. Defendant tried and convicted twice and sentenced to death. Defendant executed by hanging on December 30, 1892. Victim was reportedly found alive later, but this is still disputed.

Sources: *Hudspeth v. State*, 9 S.W. 1 (Ark. 1888); http://www.law.northwestern.edu/legalclinic/wrongfulconvictions/exonerations/ar/charles-hudspeth.html; http://files.usgwarchives.net/ar/marion/newspapers/188802.txt; http://forejustice.org/db/Hudspeth—Andrew-J.html

Keyword: **Codefendant testimony**

Case 169

Defendant: **Caleb Daniel Hughes**
Victim: Melissa Lee Brannen
Trial: 1991 Jurisdiction: Fairfax County, Virginia
Murder: December 1989
Evidence: Defendant abducted 5-year-old victim from a Christmas party in victim's apartment complex club room that more than 100 people attended. Defendant also attended the party and had worked at the apartment complex as a groundskeeper. Other partygoers testified that defendant seemed very interested in victim, and victim's mother testified that defendant stayed with them for a long time and asked several questions about victim. When victim and her mother were preparing to leave the party, defendant made attempts to speak to victim but victim ignored him. Victim disappeared around 10 p.m. when her mother went to get her coat. Victim's mother found the utility room unlocked and a full-length window was open. In the next few hours, apartment employees tried to contact party guests to see if they had seen child. Defendant never responded. Defendant's wife testified that he came home about 12:20 a.m. and immediately put his clothes and shoes in the dryer before taking a shower. When questioned by police, defendant claimed he had never seen victim at the party. Clothing fibers and hair found in defendant's car were similar to fibers in child's clothing and her mother's clothing, and fibers in the carpet of defendant's car were similar to fibers in child's home. Defendant convicted of abduction with intent to defile and sentenced to 50 years imprisonment.
Source: *Hughes v. Com.*, 446 S.E.2d 451 (Va. Ct. App. 1994)
Keyword: **Forensic evidence: Other**

Case 170

Defendant: **Bruce Allen Hummel**
Victim: Alice Hummel
Trial: August 2009 Jurisdiction: Whatcom County, Washington
Murder: October 1990
Evidence: Victim was defendant's wife. Defendant molested their 12-year-old daughter for nine years, and victim was growing suspicious of the molestation and began asking their daughter questions. Victim disappeared a few days after her daughter told her about the abuse. Victim left behind personal belongings, including medication, personal identification, and bank cards. Defendant later sold victim's belongings, telling his children that he was sending them to their mother in California. Evidence indicated that defendant forged several letters to his children, purportedly from victim. Defendant was collecting victim's disability payments. Under investigation several years later, defendant claimed that victim died and he began collecting her disability payments. He indicated that the victim committed suicide, left a note that she did not want the kids to know, and he accordingly dumped her body in Bellingham Bay. Defendant's description of the water conditions was inconsistent with records. Defendant told a jailhouse inmate that he had ground up pills in victim's apple cider.

Defendant convicted of first-degree murder. Conviction reversed in 2012 based on jury selection errors. Defendant currently awaiting second trial.

Source: *State v. Hummel*, 266 P.3d 269 (Wash. Ct. App. 2012)

Keyword: **Informant**

Case 171

Defendant: **Joseph Gamsky (a.k.a "Joe Hunt")**

Victim: Ron Levin

Trial: April 1987 Jurisdiction: Los Angeles County, California

Murder: June 1984

Evidence: Defendant led a group called the "BBC" or "Billionaire Boys Club," which generated income through various Ponzi schemes and sanctioned lying, cheating, and stealing as necessary to achieve personal and professional goals. Victim was significant investor in BBC who promised to advance several million dollars but later admitted that his dealings were fraudulent and he had swindled BBC. Defendant planned to retaliate through extortion and murder. Defendant and another BBC member killed victim and disposed of the body in a remote area, and a third BBC member provided their alibi but later testified against them. Defendant convicted and sentenced to life imprisonment without parole. Reported sightings of victim almost led to a new trial, but defendant's motion was ultimately denied.

Sources: *Eslaminia v. White*, 136 F.3d 1234 (9th Cir. 1998); http://pqasb.pqarchiver.com/latimes/doc/293338918.html?FMT=ABS&FMTS=ABS:FT&type=current&date=Jul%2013,%201996&author=ALAN%20ABRAHAMSON&pub=Los%20Angeles%20Times%20(pre-1997%20Fulltext)&edition=&startpage=&desc=Billionaire%20Boys%20Club%20Leader%20Denied%20New%20Trial; http://articles.chicagotribune.com/1986-11-10/news/8603240974_1_joe-hunt-ron-levin-arthur-barens; http://articles.latimes.com/1993-05-21/local/me-37803_1_billionaire-boys-club

Keywords: **Life, Codefendant testimony**

Case 172

Defendant: **William Francis Hurley**

Victim: Catherine Patricia Hurley

Trial: 1984 Jurisdiction: Montgomery County, Maryland

Murder: August 11, 1983

Evidence: Victim was defendant's estranged wife. Victim and defendant had been living separately since 1981, and defendant was paying child support, alimony, and mortgage. Victim left work and drove to defendant's office. Victim's 5-year-old daughter was waiting in the car when she heard a scream. Defendant later left alone, and later said victim had stayed behind to make a phone call. She was never seen again. Defendant brought his daughter to his home then left again, variously telling investigators that he had returned to the office or checked on jobs or went to victim's home to get clothes for the children. He was witnessed putting victim's car in voluntary repossession with a local car dealer, though he later denied doing so. He told an employee there not to say anything about seeing him and said that victim was "raping" him financially. A witness said that defendant's truck had a flat tire, and defendant took it to get washed the next day because it was caked with mud. Witnesses' statements regarding the replacement of defendant's flat tire and the washing of his truck contradicted defendant's version of events. Victim was last seen with defendant. Defendant convicted of manslaughter and sentenced to 10 years imprisonment. Two and a half years later, defendant's former girlfriend led investigators to victim's body, and defendant confessed to strangling her.

Sources: *Hurley v. State*, 483 A.2d 1298 (Md. Ct. Spec. App. 1984); http://articles.baltimoresun.com/2000-10-01/news/0010010079_1_body-montgomery-county-riggins/2

Keyword: **Eyewitness**

Case 173

Defendant: **John Kennard Ingersoll**

Victim: Robert Lynn Manley, Jr.

Trial: 1992 Jurisdiction: Maricopa County, Arizona

Murder: October 9, 1990

Evidence: Defendant believed his wife was having an affair with victim. Defendant was scheduled to install cabinets for a work client but missed the appointment. His vehicle was still at his apartment complex with his luggage and tools, and his keys and wallet were inside his locked apartment. Witness testimony suggested that defendant confronted victim at his apartment and fatally shot him and then buried his body in the desert. Blood was found in the back of defendant's pickup. Defendant convicted.

Sources: http://news.google.com/newspapers?nid=886&dat=19911008&id=mFdLAAAAIBAJ&sjid=u30DAAAAIBAJ&pg=4313,1315982; http://phoenix.gov/webcms/groups/internet/@inter/@dept/@police/@coldcase/documents/web_content/087993.pdf

Keyword: **Forensic evidence: Other**

Case 174

Defendant: **Stephen A. Jackson**

Victim: Julie Ann Church

Trial: 1985 Jurisdiction: Los Angeles County, California

Murder: October 17, 1982

Evidence: Victim was last seen with defendant at local nightspots. One witness overheard victim rejecting defendant's advances. Victim's car was found abandoned a week after her disappearance. More than 200 witnesses testified at trial. Defense witnesses testified that victim was likely to disappear because she had just broken up with her boyfriend, lost her job, and withdrawn all the money from her bank account. She also owed money to a drug dealer, who testified that defendant confessed to killing victim. Other witnesses testified to seeing victim after her alleged date of death. Defendant acquitted of first- and second-degree murder after a 22-month trial, but the jury was deadlocked on the charge of manslaughter. Body found in 1992 near defendant's home, but defendant cannot be retried.

Sources: http://articles.latimes.com/1985-01-17/local/me-7776_1_murder-charge; http://articles.latimes.com/1992-01-18/local/me-240_1_antelope-valley

Keyword: **Confession to family and friends**

Case 175

Defendant: **Dennis James Jaggers**

Victim: Barbara Lynn Stewart

Trial: July 2002 Jurisdiction: Harris County, Texas

Murder: April 26, 1999

Evidence: Defendant was victim's ex-boyfriend, but the two were staying together at an inn at the time of her disappearance. When a friend came to pick victim up for work on April 26, 1999, defendant claimed that victim had already left and that she "got what she deserved." Victim was not at work and was not seen again. Witnesses testified that defendant had assaulted victim on several occasions and had threatened her with death before. Defendant's former roommate testified that he (defendant) was constantly suspicious that victim was having an affair and talked about killing her. After victim's disappearance, one witness stated that defendant sought her help in disposing of a wicker basket large enough to contain a corpse. She stated that the inn room where defendant was staying smelled strange, and defendant wanted to dispose of the basket away from the inn. He later told the witness that he had killed victim and her body was in the basket, but later retracted the statement. Defendant also told his mother she had spawned a murderer. While under arrest for a separate charge, defendant told police that he and victim had had a suicide pact to overdose on cocaine and that he injected her with enough cocaine to kill her then dumped her body in the wicker basket. Defendant convicted and sentenced to 99 years imprisonment. Conviction upheld in 2003.

Source: *Jaggers v. State*, Court of Appeals of Texas, Houston (1st Dist.), No. 01-02-00725-CR, December 4, 2003

Keywords: **Confession to police, Eyewitness, Confession to family and friends**

Case 176

Defendant: **George Jaime, Sr.**

Victim: Starlette Vinning

Trial: November 2013 Jurisdiction: Houlton, Maine

Murder: October 1998

Evidence: Victim was defendant's girlfriend. While drunk, he beat and stabbed victim. At trial, his son and son's friend testified against him. They testified defendant admitted killing victim and incinerating the body in a commercial furnace in the basement of a pawn shop defendant owned. The son also admitted that he and his friend helped defendant clean up the scene.

Source: http://www.sunjournal.com/news/maine/2014/01/05/maine-prosecutors-get-guilty-verdicts-without-reco/1474063

Keywords: **Eyewitness, Confession to friends and family**

Case 177

Defendant: **Elijah James**

Victim: Danielle Brown

Trial: April 2013 Jurisdiction: Leon County, Florida

Murder: February 2010

Evidence: Victim was defendant's girlfriend. Victim's family last saw her leaving home with defendant in her car, and the two were having a heated argument. Defendant told several cellmates that he and victim were arguing in her car. He pulled over to beat her, have sex with her, then beat her to death. He then took money out of her pocket and later burned her car and his clothes. Victim's burned car was later found in a city dump with traces of blood inside. Defendant also told witnesses that he had chopped victim up and fed her to the hogs. Defendant's sister testified that he had purchased a chainsaw, shovel, and pair of gloves the day after victim disappeared. Defendant convicted of second-degree murder and sentenced to life imprisonment.

Sources: http://tallahasseeo.com/2013/03/28/murder-trial-inmates-say-james-confessed-body-was-fed-to-hogs/; http://www.timesenterprise.com/x663516068/Relative-describes-James-demeanor; http://www.wtxl.com/news/local/update-guilty-verdict-in-elijah-james-trial/article_319b5aae-9ace-11e2-ad70-0019bb30f31a.html

Keywords: **Life, Confession to family and friends**

Case 178

Defendant: **Reggie Carnell James**

Victim: Raymond "Popeye" Thomas

Trial: January 2007 Jurisdiction: Madison County, Tennessee

Murder: May 2005

Evidence: On the night of the murder, defendant and victim were using cocaine together in defendant's house with two witnesses. Defendant had a gun in hand throughout the encounter. One witness heard and another saw defendant shoot victim in the upper body and saw victim slump over on the couch. Witnesses asked defendant why he shot victim, but defendant did not respond and did not allow witnesses to take victim to the hospital. The next evening, witness asked defendant about victim, and defendant claimed he was still on the couch. One of the witnesses testified that they went outside, but defendant went back in the house and witness heard another gunshot. Then one witness and defendant left in victim's pickup, and witness abandoned it in a remote area. Both witnesses were heavy cocaine users and could not remember the exact date or week of the murder. Victim's wife had reported him missing and told police he had been to defendant's house. Police received an anonymous call claiming there was blood in defendant's home. When police searched defendant's house, they found a large stain in the carpet where defendant had been cleaning with Resolve. In an interview with police, defendant admitted killing victim and blamed drug-induced paranoia. Exposure to the elements and cleaning products degraded DNA present in the blood stains. Defendant led police to where he had dumped the couch victim died on. Defendant convicted of first-degree murder and sentenced to life imprisonment.

Source: *State v. James*, Court of Criminal Appeals of Tennessee, at Jackson, No. W2007-00775-CCA-R3-CD, March 10, 2009

Keywords: **Life, Confession to police, Eyewitness**

Case 179

Defendant: **Frank Janto**

Victim: Bongak "Jackie" Koja

Trial: July 1998 Jurisdiction: Honolulu County, Hawaii

Murder: June 9, 1997

Evidence: Victim disappeared while jogging at 3 a.m. on June 9, 1997. A few hours later, a witness found a deep pool of blood on the grounds of a nearby high school that she hosed off. Witness did not report the blood until she found out victim was missing. Investigators found remaining traces of the blood on the grounds, and drops that led down a hallway and on the outside of a dumpster, the contents of which had already been incinerated. A mace canister and headphones were found in a trashcan. Investigators also found eyeglasses and dental bridgework matching victim's. Defendant approached investigators first, claiming he wanted to talk about a missing person but then denying knowledge of victim's disappearance. Defendant came back a second time and admitted he killed victim. He stated that when he approached her, she maced him and so he smashed her head against the cement and then dragged her body into the dumpster. Defendant convicted of second-degree murder and sentenced to life imprisonment. Conviction upheld in 1999.

Sources: *State v. Janto*, Supreme Court of Hawaii, No. 21576, October 21, 1999; http://archives.starbulletin.com/98/04/27/news/story1.html

Keywords: **Forensic evidence: Other, Confession to police, Life**

Case 180

Defendant: **Brandon L. Johnson**

Victim: Diane Fosse

Trial: February 2001 Jurisdiction: Burlington County, New Jersey

Murder: April 14, 1999

Evidence: Victim was defendant's live-in girlfriend. In the months before the murder, victim obtained and then dropped a restraining order against defendant after he choked and robbed her. Defendant reported victim missing and, in the subsequent police interview, confessed to accidentally strangling victim. He later recanted his confession, but investigators were permitted to play back defendant's taped confessions. Investigators found a towel with bloodstains that matched victim's DNA. Defendant convicted of second-degree manslaughter and sentenced to eight years' imprisonment.

Sources: http://articles.philly.com/2001-02-21/news/25317028_1_manslaughter-body-verdict; http://articles.philly.com/2001-01-10/news/25309561_1_dna-evidence-dna-findings-brandon-johnson

Keywords: **Confession to police, Forensic evidence: DNA**

Case 181

Defendant: **Gary Johnson**

Victim: Adrianne Gilliam

Trial: 1988 Jurisdiction: San Diego County, California

Murder: June 22, 1979

Evidence: Victim was defendant's live-in girlfriend. Victim's sister testified at trial that she had seen defendant strike victim multiple times. Victim was 16 years old when she moved in with defendant and lived with him for three years until she disappeared on June 22, 1979. Defendant reported victim missing and participated heavily in the search for her, contacting several of her family members and checking frequently with police for updates. Defendant told several witnesses conflicting stories about how victim had disappeared. The case went cold until it resumed in 1985, and police contacted defendant again, which made him upset. Defendant had married, and his wife testified that he once beat her and threatened to kill her, saying that what happened to victim would happen to her too. In county jail, defendant confessed to a fellow inmate. Defendant convicted of second-degree murder. Defendant was also found guilty of the first-degree murder of another man whom he killed during the course of a failed drug transaction. Defendant sentenced to life imprisonment without parole.

Source: *People v. Johnson*, Court of Appeal, Sixth District, California, No. H005433, August 14, 1991

Keywords: **Confession to friends and family, Life, Informant**

Case 182

Defendant: **Earl Jones**

Victim: Nellie Adams Jones

Trial: 1929 Jurisdiction: Butler County, Pennsylvania

Murder: October 19, 1928

Evidence: Victim was defendant's wife and was last seen at his place of business the night of her disappearance. A few hours later, a vacant farmhouse three miles away was set on fire. Afterward, human blood and pieces of human bone were found in the ashes, in addition to women's accessories that matched those belonging to victim. At defendant's house, investigators found victim's clothing and some of her belongings burned in the fireplace. After extensive police questioning, defendant admitted that he and victim argued, that she drew a revolver, and that during the struggle the gun exploded and killed her. He admitted to placing her body in the vacant farmhouse and setting it on fire. Defendant later recanted his confession on the witness stand. Defendant convicted of voluntary manslaughter.

Sources: *Com v. Jones*, Supreme Court of Pennsylvania, 297 Pa. 326, July 1, 1929; http://news.google.com/newspapers?nid=1144&dat=19281218&id=q0sbAAAAIBAJ&sjid=J0sEAAAAIBAJ&pg=4120,1515705

Keywords: **Confession to police, Forensic evidence: Other**

Case 183

Defendant: **Michelle Jones**

Victim: Brandon Jones

Trial: 1997 Jurisdiction: Marion County, Indiana

Murder: July 1992

Evidence: Victim was defendant's 5-year-old son. Defendant was 15 years old when she gave birth to victim and did not assume custody of him until two years before his murder. Defendant's friends noticed victim missing in July 1992, and defendant told conflicting stories about his whereabouts. Defendant's neighbor witnessed her frequently washing the inside and outside of her car after victim's disappearance. Defendant's apartment manager noticed hundreds of flies covering the inside front bedroom window of defendant's apartment and went inside to find very strong urine smell in victim's bedroom. When defendant vacated her apartment in January 1993, the apartment manager found a large brown stain on the floor of victim's bedroom. Victim's father reported him missing in December 1993. Defendant confessed to her new roommate that she had left victim home alone for a weekend and returned to find him dead, so she dumped the body in a wooded area. Defendant also confessed to several other witnesses after checking into a mental health center. Defendant attempted to lead police to the body but was unsuccessful. In September 1994, defendant removed victim as beneficiary from her life insurance policy. In November 1995, defendant confessed to another friend that she had beaten victim before leaving him home alone for several days, that she "guessed" she had beaten victim to death, and that she intentionally lied to police about the body's location. Defendant convicted of murder and neglect of a dependent. Defendant sentenced to 50 years imprisonment for the murder and 3 years for neglect.

Source: *Jones v. State*, Court of Appeals of Indiana, No. 49A02-9706-CR-391, November 13, 1998

Keywords: **Confession to family and friends, Confession to police**

Case 184

Defendants: **Richard Kemp, Randy Duey, James Dye, David Tate**

Victim: Walter West

Trial: October 1985 Jurisdiction: Spokane, Washington

Murder: May 1984

Evidence: Defendants, ex-gang members, murdered West, who was bludgeoned with a sledgehammer and shot to death with his own gun. An eyewitness to the murder, Dye, testified in exchange for a plea agreement. West was reportedly buried in a shallow grave two hours by car from Hayden Lake but never found. After the killing, Dye testified that the men washed their shovels in a stream.

Source: http://news.google.com/newspapers?id=l1lWAAAAIBAJ&sjid=Me8DAAAAIBAJ&pg=6999%2C8762357
Keyword: **Codefendant testimony**

Case 185

Defendants: **Michael Kent, Prentice Kent, Donna Pulsifer Kent**
Victim: Michelle Pulsifer
Trial: August 2004/November 2006 Jurisdiction: Huntington Beach, California
Murder: July 1969
Evidence: Murder happened in July 1969 but was prosecuted 35 years later. Michael Kent was going to testify against wife but died before trial and trial ended in hung jury (10–2 for conviction), as Donna Kent blamed Michael Kent for murder. The case was dismissed after the second mistrial. Michael Kent claimed that Michelle Pulsifer was discovered dead in the home and he helped bury the child in a remote canyon.
Sources: http://www.charleyproject.org/cases/p/pulsifer_michelle.html; https://mylifeofcrime.wordpress.com/2010/05/25/michelle-kelly-pulsifer-murder-july-1969-silverado-canyon-ca/
Keyword: **Codefendant testimony**

Case 186

Defendant: **Patrick Kiffe**
Victims: Aubrey Bowen, Prince Horne, Trenton Scipio
Trial: March 1995 Jurisdiction: New Orleans, Louisiana
Murder: May 5, 1993
Evidence: Stowaways Bowen, Horne and Scipio, all of Guyana, were discovered hiding aboard a 350-foot barge being towed by a tug captained by Kiffe on May 5, 1993. Kiffe said he had given the men life jackets and bottles of water and had forced them overboard. Various witnesses said the shore was four to five miles away. Prosecution witnesses said the current would have pushed the men in a line parallel to the coast in shark-infested waters, and relatives said they never returned home.
Source: http://www.nytimes.com/1995/03/27/us/man-who-put-stowaways-overboard-goes-free.html
Keyword: **Eyewitness**

Case 187

Defendants: **Martin Kilbane, Owen Kilbane**
Victim: Andrew Prunella
Trial: 1983 and August 2004 Jurisdiction: Cuyahoga County, Ohio
Murder: 1983
Evidence: There was a mistrial in first trial when codefendant Phillip Christopher refused to testify. Defendants beat and shot victim, an alleged pimp, gambler, and FBI informant, on a boat off Euclid Beach and then dumped body in Lake Erie. The body was tied with chicken wire and weighed down with a manhole cover. At the second trial, defendants pleaded guilty before the same judge and were sentenced

to three to five years' imprisonment. Defendants were already serving time for killing a judge's wife in 1968 after they were hired by the judge to do so.

Source: http://www.vindy.com/news/2004/aug/17/murder-trial-convicted-brothers-admit-killing-man/?print

Keyword: **Codefendant testimony**

Case 188

Defendant: **Alvie Copeland Kiles**

Victim: Shemaeah Nicole Gunnell

Trial: 2000 Jurisdiction: Yuma, Arizona

Murder: February 10, 1989

Evidence: Triple murder of a mother and her two daughters by her boyfriend, Alvie Kiles, but the only body never found was that of the 5-year-old daughter, Shemaeah. Police found a tire iron and large amounts of blood in children's bedroom. Defendant bragged about murder and was sentenced to death for the murder of his girlfriend after two trials.

Source: http://www.charleyproject.org/cases/g/gunnell_shemaeah.html

Keywords: **Confession to friends and family, Forensic evidence: DNA, death penalty**

Case 189

Defendants: **Kenneth and Sante Kimes**

Victim: Irene Silverman

Trial: May 2000 Jurisdiction: New York, New York

Murder: July 5, 1998

Evidence: Defendant Kenneth Kimes rented a room from the victim and planned to swindle her out of her house. She became suspicious, so defendant and his mother decided to murder her. On July 5, 1998, Kenneth Kimes grabbed victim and dragged the struggling 4-foot-10-inch woman into her bedroom. "I walked up to the bed with Irene Silverman, and my Mom turned the TV on,'" he said. "And my Mom had a stun gun and hit her in the head with the stun gun and then said, 'Do it.'" Kenneth Kimes said he then strangled victim, wrapped her body in several garbage bags, and loaded the body in a duffel bag. He then placed it in the trunk of a car he had left parked nearby and drove to New Jersey in search of an isolated spot with a trash bin. Defendants were convicted and sentenced to life.

Source: http://www.nytimes.com/2004/06/24/nyregion/murderer-reveals-new-details-in-slaying-of-socialite-in-1998.html

Keywords: **Confession, Life**

Case 190

Defendant: **Ervin King**

Victim: Arthur Thompson

Trial: November 1964 Jurisdiction: Lee County, Mississippi

Murder: April 19, 1963

Evidence: Defendant ran a bootlegger's joint, and victim was a patron. On April 19, 1963, witnesses testified that the two men got into a dispute over the cost of whiskey. Defendant knocked victim down and then stomped on victim and victim's head was mashed in. Defendant's employee testified that he assisted defendant in loading the body of victim into a pickup truck. Defendant and another man drove the truck around and, after having obtained shovels at the home of defendant, attempted to bury the body in one place but were unable to do so. The body was then transported to another place where a pit was dug, and the body was put into the grave, face up. Defendant found guilty of manslaughter.
Source: http://www.leagle.com/decision/1964412251Miss161_1396
Keyword: **Eyewitness**

Case 191

Defendant: **Jack Lee King**
Victim: Johnny Perez
Trial: November 2009 Jurisdiction: Bexar County, Texas
Murder: July 1993
Evidence: Defendant and victim attended a party together. Victim was acting drunk, obnoxious, intimidating, and insulting. At one point, defendant left the party on foot, but returned 15 minutes later. Witnesses stated that after defendant returned, he shot victim in the head and then drove away with victim in the car with him. Some witnesses stated that defendant later told them he had shot victim and buried the body. Defendant, who testified on his own behalf, said that he was with victim that night, but that when they stopped for gas, victim left with a lady in a brown or maroon Cutlass. Victim's body was never found. Defendant made incriminating statements on recorded jailhouse calls. Defendant convicted of murder and sentenced to 60 years.
Source: http://www.leagle.com/decision/In%20TXCO%2020110202800
Keywords: **Eyewitness, Forensic evidence: Other**

Case 192

Defendant: **Charles Michael Kirby**
Victim: David Franklin Reid
Trial: July 15, 1977 Jurisdiction: Los Angeles, California
Murder: December 16, 1976
Evidence: Victim lived with his girlfriend and disappeared from his home after an argument with her. Defendant was involved with the same woman, and he confessed to assaulting victim after he learned victim had beaten woman. Worried that he would be sent back to prison since he was on probation, he kidnapped victim, drove him to a canyon, and disposed of body. He told woman to clean up scene, and she did. He confessed murder to her the next day. She notified police three days later. Police searched canyon and found hair, blood, skull fragments, and shotgun pellets. Blood matched stains found in house. Defendant was arrested, and blood caked on his knife and boot spur was too small to be typed but was determined to have been human. Defendant was convicted of first-degree murder.

Source: http://www.newspapers.com/newspage/30381148/
Keywords: **Forensic evidence: Other, Eyewitness**

Case 193

Defendant: **Michael Koblan**
Victims: Christopher J. Benedetto, Janette Piro
Trial: 2005 Jurisdiction: Singer Island, Florida
Murder: November 11, 1998
Evidence: In June 2003, defendant was arrested and charged with murder. Prosecutors stated that defendant killed Benedetto while on a fishing trip at sea and after Benedetto pressed defendant for a payback on a loan. They believe defendant weighed Benedetto's body down with the missing anchor and chain and dumped it in the ocean, then went back to shore and killed Piro, as she was the only person who knew defendant and Benedetto were together. Defendant was convicted of all charges in 2005 and sentenced to life in prison. Benedetto's body has never been found.
Source: http://www.charleyproject.org/cases/b/benedetto_christopher.html
Keyword: **Life**

Case 194

Defendant: **Bruce Koklich**
Victim: Jana Carpenter-Koklich
Trial: October 2003 Jurisdiction: Lakewood, California
Murder: August 20, 2001
Evidence: Prosecutors allege defendant killed his wife sometime after midnight the morning of August 18, 2001, after she returned to their Lakewood home from a concert. Defendant was the only other person in the house when she was killed that night. On the following Monday, defendant planted her white Pathfinder in a crime-ridden Long Beach area with the windows rolled down and a gun and his wife's purse in full view. Prosecutors believe defendant wanted someone to steal the vehicle and be blamed for the murder. The investigators' focus turned to the couple's bedroom when their housekeeper told investigators that bed sheets, among other items, were missing. Investigators subsequently found bloodstains in the bedroom and in victim's vehicle. Victim had $1 million life insurance policy on her. Victim's body has never been found. Defendant was sentenced to 15 years to life after initial trial hung 7–5 to convict.
Sources: http://articles.latimes.com/2003/oct/08/local/me-koklich8; http://www.charleyproject.org/cases/c/carpenter-koklich_jana.html
Keyword: **Forensic evidence: Other**

Case 195

Defendants: **Harold Konigsberg, Anthony Provenzano, Salvatore Briguglio**
Victim: Anthony Castellitto

Trial: 1978/1980 Jurisdiction: Ulster County, New York
Murder: June 6, 1961
Evidence: In 1961, Provenzano recruited Konigsberg and Briguglio to kill Castellitto, who was a popular member of Local 560 and who posed a threat to Provenzano's control of the union. On June 6, 1961, Konigsberg, Briguglio, Salvatore Sinno, and others committed the murder by hitting victim on the head and strangling him. Briguglio was killed while under indictment for the Castellitto murder, and on June 21, 1978, Provenzano was sentenced to life imprisonment for his part in the murder of Castellitto.
Sources: http://hudsoncountyfacts.getnj.com/hudsoncounty/?tag=anthony-provenzano; http://law.justia.com/cases/federal/appellate-courts/F2/334/678/108861/
Keyword: **Life**

Case 196

Defendant: **Paul Kovacich**
Victim: Janet Kovacich
Trial: January 2009 Jurisdiction: Placer County, California
Murder: 1982
Evidence: In 1982, defendant was a sergeant with the Placer County Sheriff's Department and assigned to the jail. His wife, Janet, was a homemaker, and the couple had two young children. The last person to see victim was the driver of a car pool who took victim's children to school at 8 a.m., and the last person to talk to victim was Marion Entz in a phone call at 10 a.m. Since then, victim was never seen or heard from again. There were no cars missing from the house, and victim, who had recently undergone surgery, was in no physical condition to drive or walk away from the home. There was no evidence of a break-in at the home, and defendant's police dog was home that morning. In October 1995, two people walking on the dry lake bottom of Rollins Lake noticed a weathered, partial human skull buried in the silt with what was later proved to be a bullet hole in its right side. DNA tests performed on the skull showed that the skull was likely that of victim. Defendant was convicted of first-degree murder with use of a firearm and sentenced to 27 years to life.
Source: http://www.placer.ca.gov/departments/da/news/2009/april/news item,-d-,kovacich4_24
Keyword: **Forensic evidence: DNA**

Case 197

Defendant: **Frank Phillip Kretz, Jr.**
Victims: Jesse Work, Joyce Ramsey
Trial: 1972 Jurisdiction: Riverside, California
Murder: February 1959
Evidence: Work was last seen in Hemet, California, late at night on February 6, 1959, when he disappeared with his 15-year-old girlfriend, Joyce Ramsey. The next day, Work's convertible was found abandoned on a dirt road near Hemet. Defendant later confessed to

murdering the couple. The killings had been part of an eight-hour crime spree where defendant shot at his ex-wife and missed, assaulted her roommates and stole their car, carjacked another man's vehicle, and raped a woman after tying up her husband. Defendant was sentenced to life in prison, but he was paroled in 1964, then jailed again for parole violation in January 1970. Kretz confessed to the murders and led police to Ramsey's body in February 1971. Work's body was never found. Kretz was convicted of first-degree murder in 1972 and died in prison in August 1996.

Sources: http://www.charleyproject.org/cases/w/work_jesse.html; http://www.newspapers.com/newspage/31030226/

Keyword: **Confession to police**

Case 198

Defendant: **Daniel Kutz**
Victim: Elizabeth Kutz
Trial: January 2001 Jurisdiction: Dane County, Wisconsin
Murder: July 2000

Evidence: At the time of her disappearance, defendant and victim were married, had been together approximately 12 years, and had two children. They were having marital problems, and about a week before her disappearance victim had moved out of the house she shared with defendant near Poynette, Wisconsin, and taken the two children to live with her mother in Poynette. On July 27, 2000, victim went to work in the morning and left at 3:15 p.m., but she did not return to her mother's house. Her family reported her missing later that day, and police began to search for her, defendant and the vehicles each had been driving. The car defendant had been driving that day was found about 11 p.m. parked behind a closed business down the street from victim's job. Also at about 11 p.m., police picked up defendant walking north along Highway CV, near the airport, without shoes or a shirt. They dropped defendant off at his brother's house in DeForest, where DeForest police located him. They questioned defendant and, approximately two hours later, placed defendant under arrest. One of the items taken from him in the search incident to the arrest was a wristwatch, which was later tested and revealed traces of victim's blood. Her blood was also found in her Jeep. Her body was never located. Defendant is serving a life sentence.

Sources: http://www.wicourts.gov/html/ca/02/02-1670.htm; http://www.charleyproject.org/cases/k/kutz_elizabeth.html

Keywords: **Life, Forensic evidence: Other**

Case 199

Defendant: **Damien James Lamb**
Victim: Brandon LaBonte
Trial: October 2006 Jurisdiction: Berkshire County, Massachusetts
Murder: February 16, 2005

Evidence: Victim was renting a room from a friend of defendant. Defendant drove victim and a witness to defendant's father's house on the night of the disappearance, telling victim he could work off a $150 debt. After arriving at his father's house, defendant showed the witness victim's body lying in front of a pickup truck with a shovel over his face. Defendant told witness that he had handcuffed victim, strangled him with a rope, then beat him to death with a shovel. He then stomped on the body, saying he was doing his "river dance." Defendant then buried the body inside a beaver lodge on his stepfather's property with the help of two witnesses. Defendant's mother was a part-time police officer who worked at a waste management facility, sometimes disposing of large animal carcasses, and had the means to incinerate the body. Defendant convicted of second-degree murder and sentenced to life imprisonment.

Sources: http://www.berkshireeagle.com/ci_5575628; http://www.masslive.com/news/index.ssf/2013/08/appeal_filed_in_2006_becket_mu.html

Keywords: **Life, Eyewitness, Confession to friends and family**

Case 200

Defendant: **George H. Lamb**
Victim: Sarah S. Lamb
Trial: 1858 Jurisdiction: St. Louis County, Missouri
Murder: December 1857
Evidence: Victim was defendant's wife. Defendant confessed to a justice of the peace that he had drowned victim in the Mississippi River. In a written statement, defendant explained in detail his plans to murder his wife. He admitted to attempting to murder victim twice with strychnine poison before holding her head under water in the river. He then disposed of the body by sinking it with stones. He stated that he was dissatisfied with his marriage and believed he had married someone who was not his equal. Two witnesses knew of defendant's plans to murder victim. Defendant convicted of first-degree murder.
Source: *State v. Lamb*, Supreme Court of Missouri, 28 Mo. 218, March Term, 1859
Keyword: **Confession to police**

Case 201

Defendant: **Kirk Matthew Lankford**
Victim: Masumi Watanabe
Trial: April 2008 Jurisdiction: Honolulu, Hawaii
Murder: April 12, 2007
Evidence: Victim was a Japanese national and a tourist in Hawaii. Victim was last seen getting into defendant's work truck on April 12, 2007. Defendant was on a service call for work when he met victim. Several witnesses saw her getting into his truck, and some testified that she looked as if she were being coerced. One witness testified to seeing defendant digging a hole at the Kahana Fishpond that evening, and when witness approached him defendant hurried to his work truck and drove away. Defendant had scratches on the backs of his hands, consistent with fingernail marks, and blood matching victim's DNA

was found in his truck. A pair of glasses matching victim's prescription were also found in defendant's truck. Defendant claims victim became hysterical, and, because she could not speak English, he could not calm her down before she jumped out of the truck. After hiding the body in his work truck all day, defendant attempted to bury it where he was seen by a witness, so he instead dumped the body in the ocean. Defendant convicted of second-degree murder and sentenced to life imprisonment with the possibility of parole. Conviction upheld in 2011.

Source: *State v. Lankford*, Intermediate Court of Appeals of Hawai'i, No. 19187, May 13, 2011

Keywords: **Life, Forensic evidence: DNA, Forensic evidence: Other, Eyewitness, Confession to police**

Case 202

Defendant: **Michael Robert Lawrence**

Victim: Melchor Tabag

Trial: October 2000 Jurisdiction: Honolulu County, Hawaii

Murder: March 27, 1999

Evidence: Victim was a Filipino immigrant and vacuum salesman, last seen alive at defendant's home, where he was demonstrating a Kirby vacuum cleaner. Prosecution contended that defendant struck victim with a hammer and then dismembered and disposed of the body. Defendant's mother came home the day of the murder and found defendant standing over victim's body. Defendant said he had tripped and fallen, then raised a hammer, causing his mother to flee to her bedroom and lock the door. When she came out of her room again, defendant told her to "mop it up," referring to a large pool of blood on the patio floor. Defendant was arrested driving victim's car. In a nonjury trial, defense pleaded insanity, citing evidence that defendant had suffered brain injuries from two car accidents, drug use, and a prior blow to the head. In the months prior to the murder, defendant's family testified that his behavior had changed drastically, and he had become very withdrawn. Defendant claimed to hear voices telling him to kill victim and chop him up, that the murder was part of a mission. Defendant acquitted of second-degree murder on the basis of insanity, and he was committed to the Hawai'i State Hospital in Kane'ohe.

Sources: http://archives.starbulletin.com/2001/03/29/news/story9.html; http://the.honoluluadvertiser.com/article/2002/Apr/04/ln/ln03a.html

Keywords: **Eyewitness, Confession to police**

Case 203

Defendant: **Henry Leftridge**

Victims: Joshua Crowder, James Johnson

Trial: September 15, 1900 Jurisdiction: Atoka County, Oklahoma

Murder: December 8, 1896

Evidence: Defendant confessed to shooting two trappers in 1896 along with one Lemon Butler. The main evidence was defendant's confession, where he stated he had helped to kill victims and threw the bodies into the river. The confession described several different personal items belonging to victims, including $17 from older victim and a gold watch from younger victim, and stated where they could be found. This property was recovered and identified by one victim's relatives. Defendant also admitted taking a .38 carbine Winchester and one No. 10 breech-loading shotgun along with numerous items belonging to the victims. There was also witness testimony that placed the decedents at the camp of the accused on the evening that he was last seen. The witness left the camp, with the decedents and the accused still present, and returned to his home. Shortly thereafter, he heard shots coming from the direction of the camp. The witness also testified that shortly thereafter, he witnessed the accused with a shotgun that had belonged to the decedents. The defendant was found guilty.

Source: *Oklahoma v. Leftridge*, 97 SW 1018 (1906)

Keyword: **Confession to police**

Case 204

Defendant: **Marvin Cecil Lemons**

Victim: Debbie Kelly

Trial: June 1980 Jurisdiction: Baltimore County, Maryland

Murder: December 14, 1969

Evidence: Defendant and victim were both employed by White Coffee Pot. The alleged date of murder was amended twice during the course of the indictment and trial from October 1968 to November 4, 1971, to December 14, 1969. Defendant confessed to the murder of a girl named "Debbie" to his live-in girlfriend in 1974, stating that he struck victim with a baseball bat, scalped her and took her hair out, then cut all the flesh from her bones with a knife on the kitchen table. He then claimed to have flushed the flesh down the commode until it was plugged. Defendant also told his girlfriend that he sawed off victim's hands and pulled out her teeth and eyes so she couldn't be identified, then put her head, hands, bone fragments, feet, and hair into dog food bags and put them in a garbage truck. The witness relayed information to police when defendant was under arrest on a separate charge in 1979. Defendant also confessed a murder to his girlfriend's daughter. Defendant confessed to police, saying he had brought victim to his house to have sex, beat her to death, then had sex with her corpse. Witness testimony established defendant took hallucinogenic drugs for several years, damaging the credibility of his confession. Defendant convicted of first-degree murder and sentenced to life imprisonment. Conviction reversed on appeal in 1981 because there was insufficient evidence to prove victim was dead, independent of defendant's statements. The only other evidence presented was that victim had not returned to her place of employment, but her manager testified she was a liar and that he was not surprised when she did not return to work.

Sources: *Lemons v. State*, Court of Special Appeals of Maryland, No. 1591, Sept. 1, 1981; http://articles.baltimoresun.com/2000-10-01/news/0010010079_1_body-montgomery-county-riggins/2

Keywords: **Confession to police, Confession to friends and family**

Case 204

Defendant: **George Leniart**
Victim: April Dawn Pennington
Trial: February 2010 Jurisdiction: New London, Connecticut
Murder: May 29, 1996
Evidence: Victim, 15 years old, snuck out of her parents' house on May 29, 1996, and then disappeared. One witness, a friend of victim, testified that he and defendant picked victim up that night and raped her. Defendant dropped witness off at home, and told him the next day that he had strangled victim and disposed of the body. One witness testified to being sexually assaulted by defendant six months' prior to victim's murder, and another testified that defendant had raped and choked her when she was 13 years old. Defendant was out on bail, awaiting trial for that rape, when victim disappeared. Defendant bragged to fellow inmates that police would never find victim's body, so he would never be charged with murder. Defendant told inmates that he dismembered victim's body and put it in lobster pots, then disposed of it with his fishing boat. He told other witnesses that victim's body was in the mud of the Thames River, in Long Island Sound, or in a well. Jailhouse snitches were the primary witnesses against defendant. Defendant convicted of murder and sentenced to life imprisonment.
Sources: http://www.theday.com/article/20100303/nws02/303039930/1017; http://www.norwichbulletin.com/x655500157/Leniart-found-guilty-of-murdering-teen?photo=0
Keywords: **Life, Confession to friends and family, Codefendant testimony, Informant**

Case 206

Defendant: **Lewis Lent, Jr.**
Victim: Sara Anne Wood
Trial: March 1997 Jurisdiction: Herkimer County, New York
Murder: August 18, 1993
Evidence: Defendant is a suspected child serial killer. Victim, 12 years old, disappeared while riding her bike in a rural area on August 18, 1993. Defendant was arrested in January 1994 after a failed attempt to abduct another 12-year-old girl. Defendant pleaded guilty to killing a 12-year-old boy in Massachusetts in 1990 and was sentenced to life imprisonment. In 1997, defendant pleaded guilty to victim's abduction and murder and was sentenced to 25 years to life. Prosecution presented evidence that defendant was building a space where he planned to kidnap, torture, and kill children. In July 2013, defendant admitted to killing a 16-year-old boy in 1992. Victim's disappearance led to the establishment of the Center for Missing and Exploited Children in Utica.
Sources: http://www.cnycentral.com/news/story.aspx?id=922099#.Us8FK6X0BcQ; http://www.berkshireeagle.com/ci_23662976/berkshire-da-joins-news-conference-1992-disappearance-westfield; http://www.berkshireeagle.com/ci_23663858
Keyword: **Confession to police**

Case 207

Defendant: **Jay E. Lentz**
Victim: Doris Faye Lentz
Trial: 2006 Jurisdiction: Alexandria, Virginia
Murder: April 23, 1996
Evidence: Victim was defendant's ex-wife. The couple separated in 1993, and victim moved to an apartment in Arlington, Virginia, where she requested that the manager lock the passkey to her apartment in a safe to keep it away from defendant. She also paid extra to be able to park underground. After the divorce in 1995, the couple continued to argue over marital assets and custody of their daughter. Victim testified that defendant had been abusive and had threatened her, and also told friends that she feared defendant would kill her because he had become increasingly threatening. Witnesses had seen bruises on victim, and police had previously responded to a domestic assault call in August 1991. In 1996, Family Court ordered defendant's wages garnished for child support, and defendant told coworkers he would kill victim before he let her have custody of their daughter. Defendant left victim a voicemail asking victim to pick up their daughter at his Maryland home on April 23, the day before their custody hearing. On that day, defendant's real estate agent removed a lockbox key from his house at his request, and saw a blue tarp in the foyer. Defendant claimed he was painting the interior, but she saw no painting supplies and never saw the interior repainted. Victim left to pick up her daughter that night, but was never seen again. Defendant placed several calls to his mother in Indiana that night, where their daughter was staying, and left a voicemail with victim saying the flight had been rescheduled. Records show that the victim's daughter was never scheduled to return from Indiana by April 23, as defendant had represented to victim. Victim's car was found abandoned on the route to defendant's house, and all her personal identification, money, and keys were inside in plain view, an apparent attempt to lure a car thief. The driver's seat had been adjusted for a taller driver, and the interior was stained with mud and victim's blood. Neighbors testified to seeing victim's car parked in defendant's driveway the week of the murder, though she normally waited in the car because she was afraid of defendant. Defendant first arrested in 2001 and convicted for interstate kidnapping resulting in death. Defendant's motion for judgment of acquittal was granted, and then the Fourth Circuit reversed the judgment of acquittal, affirmed grant of new trial, and remanded. After a retrial, defendant convicted again and sentenced to life imprisonment.
Sources: *United States v. Lentz*, United States Court of Appeals, Fourth Circuit, No. 06-4691, May 12, 2008; http://www.washingtonpost.com/wp-dyn/content/article/2006/06/23/AR2006062301483.html
Keywords: **Life, Forensic evidence: DNA, Forensic evidence: Other**

Case 208

Defendant: **Larry Lee Lerch**
Victim: Michael Hanset

Trial: April 1982 Jurisdiction: Multnomah County, Oregon
Murder: April 1982
Evidence: Victim and defendant both lived near Colonel Summers Park in Portland, and defendant had a prior conviction for sexually abusing a 5-year old boy. Victim was 7 years old and was last seen at the park with defendant, who asked a witness for change so he could buy victim lemonade. Another witness saw defendant give victim money and saw defendant play wrestling with victim. Defendant and a friend were drinking at the park and met again later at defendant's apartment, where an unidentified man told him defendant was talking to someone and would meet him later at the park. Victim was reported missing that night. Two days later, defendant told one of his sisters he wanted to talk to her about the missing boy and said victim was in his apartment on Monday and that he had later seen his white canvas bag in a drop box with a body in it. Another witness testified to smelling a dead body in a garbage drop box that week. Defendant told another sister he had seen his duffle bag in a drop box with a body inside, and police were contacted. Defendant was arrested on a separate charge. In defendant's apartment, investigators found stains on the floor that may have been fecal matter. Hairs found in the apartment matched samples taken from victim's coat. Defendant confessed to bringing victim to his apartment and strangling him, but claimed he was under the influence of drugs. Defendant convicted of murder and sentenced to life imprisonment with the possibility of parole. Conviction upheld in 1984, and defendant denied parole in 2013.
Sources: *State v. Lerch*, Supreme Court of Oregon, En Banc, No. C 81-09-34281; CA A24731; SC 29862, February 8, 1984; http://www.oregonlive.com/portland/index.ssf/2013/03/notorious_child_killer_larry_l.html
Keywords: **Confession to police, Confession to family and friends, Forensic evidence: Other, Life**

Case 209

Defendant: **Albert Lesko**
Victim: Cindy Marie Lesko
Trial: 2001 Jurisdiction: Macomb County, Michigan
Murder: October 23, 1994
Evidence: Victim was defendant's soon-to-be-ex-wife. Defendant was returning home with the couple's children after a weekend visit with defendant's parents. When they arrived at the house, victim and defendant interacted. One witness stated that she saw the couple arguing. Afterward, defendant drove the children back to his parents' house four hours away. Victim was never seen again. Defendant claims that she had been irate because he had returned late with the children and told him to go back and get them ready for school himself. The children claimed to have been asleep for most of the car ride, and the whole time they were parked in the driveway. Victim's car was found abandoned with her purse inside, and defendant admitted he was responsible and that he did it out of spite because of the divorce. Victim's handgun was missing, and the couple had a history of domestic abuse. Victim ceased all contact with friends and family and failed to take a nursing exam

she was preparing for. Investigators found uncashed checks and jewelry in victim's home. Defendant's children testified that they believe victim left of her own free will. Defendant acquitted because evidence was insufficient to show victim was dead.

Sources: Doe Network; http://www.delayedjustice.com/?p=3351

Keyword: **N/A**

Case 210

Defendant: **Wilma Lettrich**

Victim: Niece

Trial: Jurisdiction: Allegheny County, Pennsylvania

Murder: November 8, 1941

Evidence: Victim was defendant's 8-day-old niece. Victim and victim's mother were discharged from the hospital the day of the murder. Victim's mother was defendant's unmarried younger sister. Both sisters lived at home with their parents. Defendant admitted that after leaving the hospital, she put her sister on a bus and then suffocated victim by stuffing pieces of tissue into her mouth then concealing the body under papers at home. A few days later, she burned the body in a furnace. Defendant recanted her confession at trial and claimed to have given victim to her putative father. A witness testified to driving defendant to the hospital, then picking her up. Defendant placed a bundle in the back seat, saying it was soiled clothes and that her sister had taken victim to be adopted. A few days after her sister's discharge, defendant told the doctor that her sister and victim were doing well. Victim's father testified that defendant never gave him the infant. Defendant convicted of first-degree murder and sentenced to life imprisonment. Conviction upheld in 1943.

Source: *Pennsylvania v. Lettrich*, 31 A.2d 155 (1943)

Keywords: **Life, Confession to police**

Case 211

Defendant: **Matthew James Levine**

Victim: Dorothy Vivian Autrey

Trial: April 2009 Jurisdiction: San Luis Obispo County, California

Murder: February 20, 2008

Evidence: Victim was defendant's 84-year-old grandmother. Defendant and his girlfriend were living with victim at the time of the murder, and defendant told his girlfriend that when victim died, he would inherit the house and some bank accounts. Victim demanded that defendant and his girlfriend move out after they were arrested for driving under the influence. Victim also told defendant he was permanently out of her will. Defendant moved back in a few years later, and victim amended her estate plan so defendant would inherit her house and would share her bank accounts with his siblings. Defendant told his girlfriend that he was back in the will and that victim did not have much longer to go. Defendant told a dental assistant that if a body were thrown in the ocean, there would be no evidence. In January 2008, victim told witnesses she was upset because defendant was taking her stuff to a thrift store and tearing up her house, and she wanted defendant to move out. Investigators found blood in victim's vehicle, house, and garage. Defendant later came to police department and stated that he and victim had an argument and that he accidentally struck victim in the chest with his elbow when he turned around. Victim fell and looked as though her back was broken. Defendant panicked and put the body in a suitcase that he threw over an embankment into the ocean. Defendant claimed to be grieving victim's death. An expert witness testified that it was unlikely defendant could visually determine victim's back was broken and it was also unlikely that such a fracture would result in rapid death. Another expert testified that the amount of blood was consistent with a stabbing. Defendant reported victim missing. Defendant convicted of first-degree murder and sentenced to 25 years to life.

Sources: *People v. Levine*, Court of Appeal, Second District, Division 6, California, 2d Crim. No. B217691, July 21, 2010; http://www.sanluisobispo.com/2010/04/29/1121983/dorothy-autrey-killed-in-cayucos.html

Keywords: **Life, Confession to police, Forensic evidence: Other**

Case 212

Defendant: **Clifford E. Lewin**

Victim: Louis Boggs

Trial: 1981 Jurisdiction: Washington County, Louisiana

Murder: January 1979

Evidence: Victim was defendant's stepfather. Victim's biological son reported him missing in January 1979, stating that victim disappeared from the lounge he owned after receiving a phone call and leaving to run an errand. After victim went missing, defendant was found asleep in victim's car in a wooded area of Washington County. Inside the trunk, investigators found a new shovel caked with dirt and a bloody knife. Defendant acquitted in a nonjury trial but later sentenced to 50 years for a pipe bomb that crippled a police officer. This was the first no-body murder trial in Louisiana.

Sources: http://news.google.com/newspapers?nid=1755&dat=19920318&id=T_ccAAAAIBAJ&sjid=D3wEAAAAIBAJ&pg=6751,2558818; Doe Network

Keyword: **Forensic evidence: Other**

Case 213

Defendant: **Carson Lewis, Jerry York**

Victim: Christopher C. Coffee

Trial: April 1929 Jurisdiction: Clarke County, Alabama

Murder: November 11, 1928

Evidence: Victim left his hunting camp and was walking alone through the woods when he was attacked and killed by defendant and three others. Victim was robbed and his body burned. One witness to the murder led searchers to a place in the woods where, under a fire heap, they discovered bone fragments and pieces of clothing and trinkets that were worn by victim. Defendant was taken into custody and led police to the fire heap. Investigators uncovered a long-handled axe with blood splotches and hair resembling victim's at defendant's house. The witness to the murder claimed it looked as if defendant was wielding the same axe. Defendant convicted of first-degree murder and sentenced to life imprisonment. Conviction upheld in 1930.

Sources: *Lewis et al. v. Alabama*, 125 So. 802 (Ala. 1930); http://www.algw.org/clarke/articles/coffee.htm

Keywords: **Life, Confession to police, Eyewitness**

Case 214

Defendant: **Martin Lewis**

Victim: David Barnes

Trial: January 2004 Jurisdiction: New York County, New York

Murder: 1997

Evidence: Victim was defendant's grandfather. Defendant was a convicted drug dealer who had been raised by victim and was living with victim at the time of the murder. After victim first went missing, defendant told family members he was in Brooklyn with a girlfriend. Defendant received victim's Social Security checks for months and forged several checks payable to himself and to his friend, who had no connection with victim. Defendant admitted to stealing $27,000 from victim's bank account, but denied the murder. Defendant had previously told several witnesses that he would get victim's apartment if anything happened to him. Defendant convicted of second-degree murder and sentenced to 37½ years imprisonment. Investigators suspect defendant may have also killed his grandmother as well.

Sources: *New York v. Lewis*, 44 NY A.D.3d 422 (2d Dept. 2007); http://www.nydailynews.com/archives/news/grandson-double-killer-article-1.630264; *New York v. Lewis*, Brief for Defendant-Appellant, No. 2007-01700, September 25, 2007

Keywords: **Forensic evidence: Other**

Case 215

Defendant: **Gerald "Jerry" Casimer Libertowski**

Victim: Janeice Langs

Trial: 1976 Jurisdiction: Elkhart County, Indiana

Murder: November 1973

Evidence: Victim had formerly dated defendant. Victim disappeared after leaving work. Defendant was also charged in the death of another ex-girlfriend whose body was never recovered, but those charges were dropped. Investigators found victim's pill bottle and the wallet of defendant's other girlfriend in the foundation of his house after their disappearance. Defendant claimed he witnessed another person bury victim alive. Defendant acquitted of murder.

Sources: Doe Network; http://articles.southbendtribune.com/2012-09-03/news/33567394_1_murder-cases-murder-trials-venus-stewart; Charley Project

Keyword: **N/A**

Case 216

Defendant: **Joyce Wade Lindsey**
Victim: Ashley Lashay Jones
Trial: 1999 Jurisdiction: Shelby County, Tennessee
Murder: September 16, 1996
Evidence: Victim was defendant's 4-year-old niece. Defendant moved back to Tennessee and contacted her sister, victim's mother. Defendant's sister visited her at a motel and found defendant drunk and pregnant. Defendant's sister brought her home, where she lived with her husband and two daughters, aged 12 and 4. Defendant had never met her nieces before and asked to spend time with them the next day. The next day, victim and defendant were home alone. When victim's sister returned home from school, victim was gone. Defendant abducted victim's sister under the pretense that they were shopping, and took her to several banks to try and cash checks and withdraw money from her sister's account. Defendant befriended a tow truck driver after her car got a flat tire and persuaded him to check into a motel for her and seemed anxious whenever he was near her vehicle. Victim's sister saw the trunk was full of bags of clothing. The next day, defendant purchased laundry soap, rubbing alcohol, and bleach and then instructed victim's sister to wash all the clothing from the backseat while defendant washed the car. Victim's sister later saw that the carpeting had been removed from the trunk and it smelled like bleach. Defendant then dropped victim's sister back at home, then drove away. Victim's father chased her down, and authorities found a .45 pistol in defendant's purse. In her trunk, they found blood spatters that matched victim's DNA. Defendant attributed the blood to victim cutting her hand on glass. Victim's mother believed that victim's murder was revenge because defendant believed that victim's mother helped defendant lose custody of her own daughter. Defendant convicted of second-degree murder and aggravated kidnapping, and sentenced to 33 years imprisonment. Conviction upheld in 1999.
Source: *Tennessee v. Lindsey*, 1999 Tenn. Crim. App. LEXIS 1107
Keywords: **Forensic evidence: DNA, Eyewitness**

Case 217

Defendant: **Werner Lippe**
Victim: Faith Nanette Lippe
Trial: February 2010/September 2010 Jurisdiction: Westchester County, New York
Murder: October 2008
Evidence: Victim was defendant's soon-to-be-ex-wife. The couple was in the midst of a divorce, and defendant stood to lose $1.5 million. Defendant confessed the details of the crime to a friend who was wearing a wire, stating he struck victim with a plank of wood then burned her in a barrel outside his home and possibly used acid to destroy the bones and teeth. Defendant disavowed the content of the confession, saying that he was afraid of the friend in question and told a story he thought he could easily disprove because he thought he was being framed. Defendant disposed of the barrel and admitted to

asking a mortician how to burn people. Defendant's first trial ended in a hung jury. At the second trial, defendant convicted of murder and sentenced to 25 years to life in prison.

Sources: http://www.huffingtonpost.com/2010/02/15/werner-lippe-now-claims-h_n_462938.html; http://www.nydailynews.com/news/crime/werne-lippe-jeweler-stars-burned-wife-body-barrel-charge-prosecutors-retrial-article-1.441259; http://nypost.com/2011/03/29/white-plains-jeweler-werner-lippe-sentenced-to-25-to-life-for-killing-wife/

Keyword: **Confession to friends and family**

Case 218

Defendant: **Leonard Lipsky**

Victim: Mary C. Robinson

Trial: December 1981 Jurisdiction: Monroe County, New York

Murder: June 14, 1976

Evidence: Victim was working as a prostitute in Rochester, and defendant was an accounting student at a local community college. Days after the alleged murder, defendant decided to move to Arizona. Helping him pack, defendant's fiancée found the assorted personal belongings of a woman, including a police identification card with victim's name and some family pictures. In February 1979, defendant confessed to a probation officer and a psychiatric social worker that he strangled victim when she tried to leave after he paid her for sex. The state found no additional proof of the murder. Defendant convicted of second-degree murder. After defendant's post-verdict motion, the verdict was set aside and the indictment dismissed. Prosecution appealed, and the court of appeals reversed and reinstated verdict. Defendant was sentenced; however, the judgment reversed and the indictment dismissed on appeal because the defendant's confession was not sufficiently corroborated, and his statement was taken in violation of his Miranda rights.

Sources: *New York v. Lipsky*, 443 N.E.2d 925 (N.Y. App. 1982); *New York v. Lipsky*, 478 N.Y.S.2d 441 (N.Y. App. 1984)

Keyword: **Confession to police**

Case 219

Defendant: **Henry Lisowski**

Victim: Rosa Lisowski

Trial: February 2010 Jurisdiction: San Diego County, California

Murder: March 24, 2008

Evidence: Victim was defendant's estranged wife. Victim had initiated child support proceedings against defendant, who threatened to kill her if she didn't drop the case. Defendant had made several threats on victim's life before. Defendant's search history on his computer showed he had researched information about poison and had once given his son green powder to put in his mother's drink, which his son poured into the carpet. Investigators found victim's blood on defendant's kitchen counter, in the trunk of his car, and inside the passenger door. Defendant went to Mexico after victim's disappearance and returned several months later with a letter stating victim had likely died from injuries she received falling down a staircase and that he placed her body in a dumpster out of fear he would be blamed for her death. Experts testified that the trauma was not consistent with a fall, but was the result of a violent attack with a hammer or having her head slammed into something. Defendant convicted of first-degree murder with a special circumstance allegation of murder for financial gain. Defendant committed suicide before sentencing.

Sources: http://www.10news.com/news/officials-wife-killer-henry-lisowski-found-dead-at-vista-jail; http://www.sdnews.com/view/full_story/1996331/article-OB-man-eyes-trial-in-alleged-murder-of-estranged-wife

Keywords: **Forensic evidence: Other, Forensic evidence: DNA**

Case 220

Defendant: **Kelley Jean Lodmell**
Victim: Acacia Patience Bishop
Trial: January 2005 Jurisdiction: Bonneville County, Utah
Murder: May 26, 2003

Evidence: Victim was defendant's 19-month-old granddaughter. Victim was abducted from her great-grandmother's home. Defendant had been diagnosed with bipolar disorder and paranoid schizophrenia, and was not taking medication when she abducted victim. Defendant told victim's parents that she killed her by jumping into Snake River in Idaho Falls with her in an apparent murder-suicide attempt. That same day, defendant told employees at a nearby hydroelectric plant that she had accidentally dropped victim in the river. Baby shoes and a doll were recovered from the riverbank, as well as defendant's shoes. Victim's parents believe victim is still alive and may have been given to one of defendant's acquaintances. Defendant acquitted of murder based on insanity, and committed indefinitely to a mental hospital.

Sources: http://publicsafety.utah.gov/bci/UTAHmissingpersons.html; Charley Project

Keywords: **Confession to police, Confession to friends and family**

Case 221

Defendant: **Adolph Louis Luetgert**
Victim: Louise Luetgert (nee Bicknese)
Trial: 1897/1898 Jurisdiction: Cook County, Illinois
Murder: May 1, 1897

Evidence: Victim was defendant's wife. The couple had a history of domestic abuse, and defendant allegedly had a violent temper. Defendant was having multiple affairs and was facing financial difficulties with his sausage plant. Defendant dissolved victim's body in a sausage vat filled with lye at his sausage plant, and then burned the remains in a furnace. A witness who was a night guard at the company saw victim and defendant entering the night of her disappearance, and testified that defendant paid him to leave and take the night off. The witness testified that defendant had barricaded the office door and had fired up the broiler. The day before the murder, defendant accepted a delivery of 378 pounds of crude potash and 50 pounds of arsenic, although the factory had been closed for 10 weeks. Defendant told conflicting stories about victim's disappearance, alternately stating that she had gone to visit family or that she had run off with another man. Investigators drained a vat next to the factory furnaces and recovered victim's ring and the fragment of a human skull. First trial resulted in a hung jury. At second trial, defendant convicted and sentenced to life imprisonment, but only served two years before he died in prison. Defendant was believed to have killed at least one other person.

Sources: http://articles.chicagotribune.com/1986-08-03/features/8602250600_1_file-grinder-testimony; http://www.examiner.com/article/the-sausage-king-kills-the-strange-story-of-adolph-luetgert; http://www.murderbygaslight.com/2009/11/luise-luetgert-sausage-vat-murder.html

Keywords: **Eyewitness, Life**

Case 222

Defendant: **Joel Lung**
Victim: Celina Lung
Trial: May 1965 Jurisdiction: Snohomish County, Washington
Murder: October 24, 1964

Evidence: Victim was defendant's estranged wife. Victim was discovered missing when her vehicle was left parked outside her place of employment overnight. Inside the vehicle, investigators and witnesses found, alongside other personal effects, victim's bloodstained coat with a .30-caliber bullet hole through it. Defendant signed a statement admitting to shooting his wife. Defendant claimed victim was accidentally shot when a rifle discharged in the house. Defendant panicked and put the body in his panel delivery truck, drove to a log dump, and disposed of the body in the Snohomish River. At defendant's shop, investigators found a rifle with a live cartridge in its chamber. Defendant confessed again to accidentally shooting victim, but altered the circumstances of the accidental shooting. Defendant convicted of second-degree murder. This was the first no-body murder conviction in Washington State.

Sources: *Washington v. Lung*, 423 P.2d 72 (Wa. 1967); http://community.seattletimes.nwsource.com/archive/?date=20000609&slug=4025628

Keyword: **Confession to police**

Case 223

Defendant: **Kenneth Andrew Lynch**
Victims: Portia Sumter Washington, Angelica Livingston
Trial: May 2012 Jurisdiction: Lexington County, South Carolina
Murder: June 2006

Evidence: Victims were defendant's girlfriend and her 7-year-old granddaughter. Defendant was living with victims at the time of their disappearance. Defendant was allegedly abusive, and Portia was unhappy with him. Eight days after victims disappeared, Portia's car was found at a bus depot in Seattle, Washington. Defendant was found two hours north of Seattle on a Greyhound bus, apparently on his way to Canada, and was arrested for grand larceny. On his way to Seattle, he had withdrawn all the cash from his bank account. Charges against defendant were amended to include two counts of murder after investigators found bloodstains belonging to Angelica in victims' house. Defendant convicted of murder in a nonjury trial and sentenced to life imprisonment.

Sources: http://www.wtoc.com/story/5049223/no-new-leads-in-west-columbia-missing-persons-case; http://www.wistv.com/story/18182652/kenneth-lynch-to-serve-life-in-prison; Charley Project

Keywords: **Life, Forensic evidence: Other**

Case 224

Defendant: **Edward Lyng**
Victim: Stephanie Anne Lyng
Trial: 1994 Jurisdiction: Cook County, Illinois
Murder: October 25, 1977

Evidence: Victim was defendant's soon-to-be-ex-wife. Defendant faced the loss of his company in their divorce, and victim expressed to witnesses that she feared for her life. She drew up a will because she was afraid she would be killed and wanted guardians other than defendant to take care of her daughters. When victim disappeared, defendant suggested she had run off with someone else. The case went cold until a witness with whom defendant had been having an affair came forward in 1992 and testified that defendant confessed to murdering victim but threatened to kill her if she ever told anyone. According to the witness, defendant ambushed victim in the garage when their daughters were in school and bludgeoned her with a pistol before stabbing her to death. Defendant convicted of murder and sentenced to 15 to 50 years. After his imprisonment, defendant was convicted of soliciting hit men from prison to kill witness and one other man.

Sources: *People v. Lyng*, Brief and Argument for the Plaintiff-Appellee, Appellate Court of Illinois, First District, Second Division, No. 1-94-1098, 1994; http://articles.chicagotribune.com/1996-09-04/news/9609040195_1_murder-for-hire-bitter-divorce-battle-jury

Keyword: **Confession to friends and family**

Case 225

Defendant: **Alan MacKerley**
Victim: Frank Lee Black, Jr.
Trial: March 2003 Jurisdiction: Martin County, Florida
Murder: February 24, 1996

Evidence: Victim and defendant were business competitors in the charter-bus industry. Defendant's girlfriend lured victim to West Palm Beach for a fake business deal and then brought him to defendant's home, where defendant shot him. Victim reported missing when he did not return from the business trip. Defendant's girlfriend was seen using victim's credit card the day after the murder and rented a car with cash, driving 423 miles in less than three days. Shortly after the murder, defendant recarpeted the house and disposed of the two vacuum cleaners he used to clean up. Defendant asked a friend to fly him over the ocean, admitting that he killed victim and dumped the body from his boat, and he wanted to see if the body was floating. Defendant later claimed that he lured victim, but that his girlfriend killed him in self-defense. Defendant's girlfriend convicted of third-degree murder and false imprisonment and was released in 2004. Defendant tried three times before convicted of first-degree murder and sentenced to life imprisonment.

Sources: *Mackerley v. State*, 754 So.2d 132 (Fla.Dist.Ct.App. 2000); http://www.tcpalm.com/news/2009/jun/12/snapped-tv-program-prompts-recollections-murder-ca/?feedback=1; http://jacksonville.com/apnews/stories/051603/D7R2P83G0.html

Keywords: **Life, Confession to friends and family**

Case 226

Defendant: **Thomas J. MacPhee**
Victim: Lori Ann Keaton
Trial: April 2005 Jurisdiction: McDowell County, West Virginia
Murder: January 30, 2003

Evidence: Lori Ann Keaton and her husband, James Keaton, sold one of their homes to MacPhee and his wife, Deborah, who paid for their new home in cash. Sometime after the sale, the Keatons became social with the MacPhees and Danny Wade England. Tension arose when James Keaton started to become offended by the affections England was displaying toward his wife. Victim gave a large amount of money to England, either as a loan or for him to hold. Defendant stated these funds may have, in part, been the money for the sale of their home. Victim repeatedly attempted to retrieve these funds, although England said he had already returned the money. Victim disappeared on January 30, 2003 after a visit to her children from a previous marriage in Michigan. She had a son and a daughter. Her daughter testified in the trial that her mother usually traveled with lots of money and never traveled without her dog, Tonka. After her disappearance, Tonka was found in Salem, Virginia. When questioned by police in February 2003, defendant claimed to have no information regarding victim's location. In April 2003, police got information from a hunter in woods approximately 8–10 miles away from defendant's residence. They found a shallow grave, which contained no remains, but did contain personal items belonging to victim, including her jacket, belt buckle, and some jeans fabric stained with blood. The jeans had victim's DNA, matched to a sample given by her relatives. The police recovered her Mercury Grand Marquis in May 2003 under a tarp, missing its license plate, at the home of Kenneth Jerry Wood. Wood testified that in January 2003 around 4 a.m., defendant arrived at his home and requested to leave the vehicle, stating it belonged to his wife, Debora, and they needed a place for safe keeping during their move to New Jersey. Wood agreed, and defendant gave him their local phone number, which he wrote on a wall next to his couch, and a shotgun that had been contained in the vehicle's trunk. The police questioned defendant again at his home, bringing Wood along to positively identify defendant as the person who left the vehicle at his residence. While being questioned, defendant explained to the police that England shot and killed victim in his home. Defendant claimed that he did not witness the murder or know it was going to occur but that he had helped to hide the body. There were several key components to this statement and several different versions. In one version, defendant stated that England and victim were arguing within his home, about the monetary issue, and that he was on the porch during the argument. He claimed to be startled by a gunshot, ran indoors, and found England holding a shotgun and victim on the ground suffering from a gunshot to the chest. He claimed that he then helped England with the body due to his fear that England would shoot him next. Defendant then helped with the cleaning of the blood and in wrapping victim's body in plastic and blankets, and said that they proceeded to destroy these materials and victim's purse in a fire in defendant's backyard. The body was then placed into defendant's Jeep, and they drove to the gravesite. Defendant said that England suggested they submerge the car in a mine shaft, but instead they drove the Grand Marquis to Wood's residence. Defendant said he drove Tonka to the area of Salem, Virginia, and let him go; the dog was later recovered there. In another version, defendant stated that he came home and victim's body was already wrapped and lying in his yard, that England was present, but that he was not informed of how she died. In a third version, defendant stated that he was in fact present for the argument but stepped to his porch, where he was startled by the shot, and that although he believed her to already be deceased that he attempted to contact 911 and was stopped by England. In this same version, he claimed the shotgun belonged to England but that England had left it in his home for a matter of days prior to the murder. In yet a fourth and final version, he again admitted to his involvement placing the vehicle at Wood's residence versus England's mine shaft suggestion. (England died before he could be charged with murder.) Defendant consented to a search of his residence and property. Police retrieved flooring from the home that contained victim's blood. Also recovered was the victim's car's missing license plate, which was buried in the backyard. At trial, statements given to the police were admitted. Along with the admissions, a jailhouse informant who was housed with defendant testified that defendant confessed to beating a woman to death with an accomplice, stealing her drug money, and disposing of the body in a mine shaft. Massey said defendant believed he would get away with this crime due to lack of evidence. Defendant was found guilty of first-degree murder and sentenced to life. His convictions were upheld on appeal.

Source: *West Virginia v. MacPhee*, 656 S.E.2d 444 (WV 2007)

Keywords: **Confession to police, Forensic evidence: DNA, Informant, Life**

Case 227

Defendant: **Clifton L. Mahaney**

Victims: Nancy Joan Webster, Betty Coulter Dinkle

Trial: December 1974 Jurisdiction: El Dorado County, California
Murder: March 23, 1974
Evidence: Webster disappeared on or about March 23, 1974. Her daughter from another marriage, Betty Coulter Dinkle, who was 19 years old at the time, also disappeared, and neither woman has been seen since. Both women left behind all of their personal belongings. Defendant was extradited from Colorado to face a grand jury on the charges of murdering his common law wife and was convicted of manslaughter.
Source: http://www.officialcoldcaseinvestigations.com/showthread.php?p=62280
Keyword: **N/A**

Case 228

Defendant: **David Malinski**
Victim: Lorraine Kirkley
Trial: February 2000 Jurisdiction: Tippecanoe County, Indiana
Murder: July 21, 1999
Evidence: Kirkley vanished with her 1994 Green Ford Explorer on the evening of July 21, 1999. The car was set on fire in a cornfield located within Laporte County and discovered four days later. Numerous bullets were recovered from the floor boards. Victim was a nurse at Cardiac Rehabilitation Center of Porter Memorial Hospital, and investigators believed she was taken from her home after her shift but prior to her husband's return at around 10 p.m. On July 20, one of victim's neighbors witnessed a person on a bicycle approach the victim's home, enter through the garage door, and leave within 15 minutes. The neighbor was unable to identify the gender of this person. The day of victim's disappearance, this occurred again, except this time the person did not leave. Subsequently, victim arrived home and also entered through the garage and closed it behind her. Within 20 minutes, the garage opened again and the neighbor witnessed victim's vehicle leave with the garage door still open. When victim's husband arrived home, the garage was still open, all of the lights were on in the house, and there was a note left on the kitchen wall stating "there is a gun pointed at your head." State investigators conducted a full-scale search of victim's home and surrounding areas looking for victim or any evidence as to her whereabouts. The search of victim's home revealed victim's blood on a butter knife as well as the kitchen floor, one of her earrings under the refrigerator, and a lens from victim's eyeglasses under the oven. They also found that victim's underwear drawer was emptied. Victim's entire luggage set was accounted for. According to police records, victim's house had been burglarized on February 2, 1999, and again on July 21, the night of her disappearance. Following the burglary, two days later, a plastic bag was located in Valparaiso and was turned in to the police. The bag contained the keys to victim's vehicle as well as a handwritten letter addressed to victim's husband stating, "Please give this letter to Mr. Kirkley; His wife is missing." Within this letter the author claimed he had killed victim due to her recognizing him during the commission of him robbing her home on July 21. The author went on to say she had bitten his right middle finger during

the confrontation. The letter stated, "I had no plans to kill her, but unfortunately I had to.... You will never find the body." A search of where the plastic bag had been found uncovered one of victim's biking shoes in a dumpster. Malinski was placed under arrest four days later due to his wife contacting police and acknowledging him as a suspect. She informed the police that her husband worked with victim at Porter Memorial Hospital. When the police took the defendant into custody, they realized he had what appeared to be a bite wound on his right hand. The police also observed other injuries on defendant's body, and all were photographed. Coworkers of defendant told the police they had witnessed bruises and scratches on defendant in the days following victim's disappearance. Defendant told one witness that these injuries had taken place while he helped his brother to move some cabinets, but his brother later testified that this was not true. During questioning, defendant acknowledged that he was the author of the letter, despite the fact that the police had never mentioned the existence of the plastic bag, its contents, or the letter. Defendant went on to state that the bloodstain found in victim's home belonged to victim, as well as another stain in his home, and that he was responsible for both. Defendant changed his story during the investigation, and even though he admitted authoring the letter, he maintained that he had not kidnapped or harmed victim. Defendant claimed victim had vanished due to her unhappy life, although victim had serious medical conditions that required medications. Her medication for these conditions was never removed from her home, and FBI search found that her medications were not filled anywhere in the United States. According to victim's pharmacist, she had been extremely reliable about her medication refills and maintaining a regimented daily pill schedule. Defendant was initially held on charges related to the February 2 and July 21 burglaries of victim's home and for the theft and destruction of victim's vehicle. The charges were later amended to include a charge for murder. Even after the murder charge was brought against defendant, the police continued to search for the victim's body, but the body was never located. Subsequent to his arrest, police learned that defendant had told a fellow inmate, who was expected to be released, that he had taken photographs of victim and hidden them on a country road. He asked the inmate to find and destroy these images. The photographs were discovered on August 26, 1999, along a country road as described, and were said to be extremely graphic in nature. They depicted victim handcuffed and gagged in defendant's master bedroom while being sexually assaulted. Defendant was found guilty on all seven of the alleged crimes. The court ordered that the burglary, murder, and criminal deviate conduct sentences run consecutively for a total of 125 years, and consecutive to a 30-year sentence on the remaining counts, for a total sentence of 155 years in prison. Defendant appealed his sentence, but it was affirmed. In 2005 defendant experienced a religious conversion and finally confessed that he had killed victim and offered to lead the police to her remains. He told police he had buried her on a property once owned by his father, now by his brother, near Rensselaer in Jasper County. After 6½ hours of searching, the police discovered victim's grave, and a coffee can was also recovered. Inside of the coffee can was a copy of the July 23, 1999, edition of the *Post-Tribune*. Shortly after this discovery, a tarp containing victim's remains were found about 5 feet deep.

Sources: *Indiana v. Malinski*, 794 N.E.2d 1071 (Ind. 2003); Nevers, K., "Lorraine Kirley is found: Mystery ends with grim discovery," *Chesterton Tribune*, October 3, 2005; Porter County Sherriff's Office.

Keywords: **Forensic evidence: DNA, Forensic evidence: Other, Confession to police, Informant**

Case 229

Defendant: **Derek Maner**
Victim: Erica Bradley
Trial: February 2009 Jurisdiction: Allendale County, South Carolina
Murder: November 6, 2006

Evidence: Bradley was last seen in Allendale, South Carolina, on November 6, 2006, after her shift at Hardee's restaurant. She was supposed to get a ride from her boyfriend, Derek Maner, but when he did not show up, her cousin arrived. Along the way, they spotted defendant and pulled off in front of the county courthouse. Witnesses say the couple began to argue, victim got into defendant's car, and the two drove away. This was the last time victim was ever seen. Defendant later stated victim had made accusations of infidelity. Defendant said that he offered to introduce victim to the woman he was accused of having an affair with, in attempt to prove its inaccuracy, but that on the way to do so, victim leapt from the vehicle and headed to the nearby woods. He claimed to have stopped and searched for her, but when he did not find her, he assumed she had walked the four miles to their home. Defendant informed her family of her disappearance two days later. With the assistance of cadaver dogs, the police conducted a search of the area where defendant claimed victim entered the woods, but no trace of her body was found. Later, the police enlisted the use of a scuba team from the Beaufort County Sherriff's Department to help in the search. The search of the woods did lead to the recovery of victim's shoes, clothing, and pieces of her hair extensions. The police also conducted a search of defendant's vehicle and discovered forensic evidence, which included victim's hair, blood, and tissue, all removed from the bottom of the vehicle. There was also evidence someone had attempted to clean the vehicle. The police suspected defendant had hit victim with this vehicle. Due to victim's personal relationships, job history of good attendance, and the fact that she left her then-5-month-old child behind, defendant's claims that she had run away was not credited. Defendant was arrested in April 2008 and charged with murder. Defendant maintained his innocence throughout the entire time of his February 2009 trial, stating the forensic recoveries from his vehicle were from an animal he had hit and that he did not know what happened to victim. He was convicted of murder and sentenced to life in prison without the possibility of parole. Defendant appealed his conviction, and the appellate court affirmed it.

Sources: Appellate Case No. 2009-117006; Charley Project
Keywords: **Forensic evidence: DNA, Forensic evidence: Other, Life**

Case 230

Defendants: **Charles Manson, Steve "Clem" Grogan, Bruce Davis, Charles "Tex" Watson**
Victim: Donald Jerome "Shorty" Shea
Trial: November 1971 Jurisdiction: Sacramento, California
Murder: August 26, 1969
Evidence: At the time of his death, Shea worked as a ranch hand at the Spahn Ranch, where the Manson family took up residence. Victim initially got along with the group fine, but following his marriage to an African-American woman, Manson began to act differently toward him. The defendant's family had multiple run-ins with law enforcement, so victim offered to help George Spahn evict them from the ranch. Defendant ordered the murder of victim due to his belief victim had a part in a police raid of the ranch that occurred on August 16, 1969. This raid resulted in the arrest of several Manson family members on the suspicion of theft. Manson told Davis, Watson, Grogan, "Little" Larry Bailey, and Bill Vance that victim "needed to be taken out" because victim was a "snitch." They were to request a ride from victim to a parts store down the road from the ranch and then kill him on the way. The men, accompanied by Manson, requested the ride as ordered. According to Davis, victim sat in the back seat with Grogan, and Davis stated that Grogan then hit the victim with a pipe and Watson began stabbing him repeatedly. Afterward, the men removed victim from his vehicle and descended a hill behind the ranch where they stabbed, tortured, and killed him. Davis claimed he was not a participant in the burial and was not aware of its location. On December 9, 1969, victim's 1962 Mercury was found parked on a side street. Inside police recovered a bloody pair of victim's cowboy boots and his footlocker that contained personal belongings. Davis's palm print was located on the outside of this footlocker, which indicated he was the one responsible for the vehicle and possessions being discarded. Barbra Hoyt also resided on the Spahn Ranch in summer 1969 and was a witness during defendants' trial. She had not been a part of any crimes committed, but she had known victim and she had given him dinner the night prior to the Manson families' move to the desert. While preparing to sleep, Hoyt heard a loud cry of pain, it subsided, and then returned. She testified that she believed these were the sounds of victim's murder. Ruby Pearl, who was a fellow employee at the ranch, also testified at the trial that she had a brief encounter with victim late one evening and he had stated his anxiety over staying at the ranch. He had requested to stay in her home but changed his mind and slept in his vehicle on the ranch. As she was departing the ranch, she witnessed Manson, Watson, Grogan, and Davis approach victim, but they were quickly no longer visible. This was the last time she saw victim. When she returned to the ranch the following day, victim was no longer there nor was his vehicle. In November 1971 Manson was convicted on charges of murdering two individuals,

including victim, and he was sentenced to life in prison. Davis was also sentenced to life, but Grogan was convicted and sentenced to death. The judge later commuted that sentence to life, based on the fact that Grogan was mildly retarded and acted only on Manson's orders to kill victim. In 1977, Grogan drew a map that led police to victim's remains that had been buried on the ranch. Grogan was released on parole in 1985. He is the only Manson family member to ever be freed from prison.

Sources: Bugliosi, V., and Gentry, C., *Helter Skelter*, W.W. Norton & Co., 1974; Murderpedia

Keywords: **Codefendant testimony, Forensic evidence: Other, Life**

Case 231

Defendant: **Perry March**

Victim: Janet March

Trial: August 2006 Jurisdiction: Davidson County, Tennessee

Murder: August 15, 1996

Evidence: Perry March was a successful attorney, and he shared a home with his wife, Janet March, who was an up-and-coming painter just starting to become well-known. Together they had a son and a daughter. The defendant worked at a local law firm after some ethical issues at his prior law firm caused him to leave that firm. While his life seemed ideal, this existence began to crumble when victim disappeared on August 15, 1996. Defendant told her family that his wife had decided to take a 12-day vacation following a bitter argument. He claimed she had left a to-do list of chores for him to take care of while she was away, and defendant claimed she made him sign it as if it were a contract. She allegedly loaded her bags into the 1996 gray Volvo 850 they owned. The victim's family found this difficult to believe, since she had sent out invitations for their son's birthday party, which was meant to take place only 10 days later. Victim never arrived at the party or to her son's first day of school and never was seen again. Defendant claimed he did not initially contact the police because his wife's parents did not want to get them involved, as it would embarrass their daughter if their marital issues became public. Victim's family said it was in fact defendant that did not want police involvement. Either way, it was not until August 29, two full weeks after victim's disappearance, that the police were finally notified. Victim's car was located and recovered 10 days later outside an apartment complex in Nashville. Her purse and her luggage were found, but she was not. The police went through all of the personal effects with victim's family, and it struck victim's mother as odd that certain things essential to such a long trip were not present among the items. She testified at trial that "this looked like a bag that a man had packed." Since her disappearance, there had been no financial activity on victim's accounts or credit, and on September 12, the police announced they were now treating this case as a homicide rather than a missing persons case. Police conducted a search of the March home, defendant's office, and an apartment he had rented. They took several items as evidence, including a stained shirt, the bathmat, and several computer disks. They also found, upon further investigation, that the hard drive was missing from the personal computer. Investigators also found that defendant had replaced the tires on his vehicle six days after his wife went missing. When the police questioned the shop employees, they stated that the tires were not even worn and that they informed defendant of this but he insisted anyway. More than a month after the disappearance, defendant announced he would be moving with and his children to just outside Chicago. This enraged victim's family, who began court proceedings to remain in contact with their grandchildren. Police were notified that when defendant packed his office, the only thing left behind was his wedding photograph. Victim's family won their court battle, earning visitation rights, but when it came time for defendant to bring the children to their first visit, he did not arrive. They later found out that he had fled with the children to Mexico, where his father, Arthur March, lived. Once there, defendant began a new life, starting his own business and opening a restaurant. A year later, defendant remarried. Victim was declared legally dead by a Tennessee court only two months prior to defendant's wedding. Following this, victim's family filed several legal proceedings against defendant The first froze their daughter's assets, which were valued at $200,000; the second was a wrongful death suit; and the third was for full legal custody of their grandchildren. Eventually, the family traveled to Mexico to retrieve the children, and, after some tense confrontation, they returned home with the children. Defendant hired two attorneys and fought the custody ruling, and after another court battle, the victim's parents were required to return the children to their father, which they did. On August 15, 2006, defendant was placed under arrest in Mexico for second-degree murder and extradited back to Tennessee. While in custody, defendant befriended a fellow inmate named Russell Farris, and eventually the two agreed that defendant would pay Farris's bond and get him set up with a new life in Mexico, with the help of his father, in exchange for the double homicide of victim's family. Arthur March was involved in this arrangement through telephone conversations with his son while he was in jail and when he received a phone call from Farris that "the job was done." He agreed to pick him up at the airport, where he was subsequently arrested. Farris had been cooperating with the police and prosecutors the entire time. On October 28, 2005, both March men were charged with conspiracy to commit first-degree murder and solicitation to commit first-degree murder. This case went to trial on June 1, 2006. Farris was the state's star witness, and a jury found the defendant guilty on all counts. Two months later, in August 2006, he was tried for the murder of his wife in Chattanooga, Tennessee. The state had testimony that there was a "rolled-up rug" in the March home following victim's disappearance and that fibers were recovered from defendant's vehicle that were consistent with that type of rug. The main witness in the victim's trial was defendant's father, Arthur March, who was too sick to appear in court but gave a video deposition in which he admitted helping his son clean up bloodstains in the house and disposing of the computer's hard drive before the house was searched.

He also admitted to helping his son move victim's body from where it was initially buried due to the fact that the site would soon be under construction. After his deposition, Arthur March tried to lead the police back to the location but was unable to do so. On August 17, 2006, a jury found him guilty on all counts. Arthur March received an 18-month sentence and 3 years of parole, versus a possible 20-year sentence, in exchange for his cooperation. This deal was rejected, however, and he was given 5 years in prison for his participation. Defendant was sentenced to 56 years in prison.

Sources: "Where is Mrs. March?" *48 Hours Investigates*, January 1, 2005; Crime Library

Keywords: **Informant, Confession to friends and family, Forensic evidence: Other**

Case 232

Defendants: **Irwin Margolies, Donald Nash**

Victims: Lena Margaret Barbera, Jenny Soo Chin

Trial: May 1983/May 1984 Jurisdiction: New York County, New York

Murder: January 5, 1982/April 12, 1982

Evidence: Margolies was the head of the Candor Diamond Co. His controller was a woman named Lena Margaret Barbera, and her assistant and the companies' bookkeeper was a woman named Jenny Soo Chin. Barbera claimed that Margolies was making false invoices in order to make the company look like it was making a generous profit and in turn get advanced funds from the financing company. Documentation showed these fraudulent proceeds were laundered through foreign companies, and estimates of this embezzlement were $6 million. Barbera had already pleaded guilty to this fraud and was going to testify in an inquiry involving the diamond company. Chin was also aware of this illegal activity, and Margolies was told that the two coworkers and close friends were cooperating with the government. Margolies then hatched the scheme to get rid of these women in an attempt to undermine the fraud investigation. Margolies' attorney, Henry Oestericher, helped him to facilitate a "hit man" named Donald Nash, whom Margolies then paid $200,000 to murder the women. Soon after Margolies found out about the women's cooperation, Chin disappeared on January 5, 1982, after visiting with Barbera. Chin was seen being pushed into her car by a man in a ski mask, and her car was found six days later. It was abandoned and bloodstained with a .22 caliber casing inside. At trial, there was testimony that Nash provided a photo of her body to Margolies as proof she was dead. Prior to the murder of Barbera, Nash stalked her for four months. Barbera had requested police protection twice and was denied both times. Nash then abducted her, and during her abduction, three bystanders were also murdered due to their attempt to come to her aid. These three people were all employees of CBS and had been nearby when Barbera was shot. Barbera was found dead in an alley in lower Manhattan with bullet wounds to the back of her head. Police found evidence from this scene, which included DNA, shell casings, tire tracks, and license plate information given from witness accounts. The police tracked Nash through his 1980 Chevrolet van and arrested him. After arresting Nash, the police ran a DNA test to determine a match as well as ballistics tests, and they reviewed his telephone records. There was a record of a call from a relative of Nash's to the home of Barbera. This number was unlisted, and the prosecutor claimed he could have only gotten this number from Margolies. The police conducted a search of Nash's home and found a .22 caliber bullet casing that matched those found inside Chin's car and the site of Barbera's murder. During Nash's trial, 127 witnesses were called to testify, and the prosecutor presented 380 items as evidence. Nash was convicted of conspiracy to commit murder and four counts of second-degree murder, and he was sentenced to 100 years in prison. Margolies pleaded guilty to 51 counts of fraud in a federal indictment in 1982 and was sentenced to 28 years in prison. When he was tried for his part in these two murders, the key witness against him was his attorney, who was granted immunity for his testimony. He testified that he met with Margolies in the back room of a midtown delicatessen on December 1, 1981, and the two conspired to commit these murders. The attorney also admitted that he located the gunman on Margolies' behalf. Margolies was convicted of two counts of murder and was sentenced to 50 years in prison for a combined total of 78 years in prison.

Source: *The CBS Murders: A True Story of Greed and Violence In New York's Diamond District* Hammer, Richard, William Morrow & Co.

Keywords: **Forensic evidence: DNA, Forensic evidence: Other, Codefendant testimony**

Case 233

Defendants: **Jordan Martell, Jittawee Curley Bear Cub**

Victim: Richard Red Dog

Trial: October 16, 2007/December 2007 Jurisdiction: Cascade County, Montana

Murder: December 12, 2003

Evidence: On the night of December 12, 2003, a group of people was gathered on the Fort Peck Indian Reservation. Richard Red Dog was driving around with Jordan Martell, Trisha Martell, and Jittawee Curley Bear Cub. The three survivors admitted partying together and using prescription medications, alcohol, and marijuana. That night, victim disappeared, and no one has heard or seen him since. Jordan Martell instigated a fight in which victim was hit with a baseball bat by Trisha Martell and knocked to the ground. Jordan Martell gave a statement that he instructed Bear Cub, the victim's cousin who beat him with a chain connected to a padlock, that they "could not let him go alive" and handed him a knife. Victim was repeatedly stabbed by Bear Cub and was disposed of in the Missouri River. Police and volunteers performed a search of the riverbanks in March 2004. Another search was conducted in August 2004, surveying the river for about eight miles south east of Poplar for numerous days after the Fort Peck's Criminal Investigation Department received an anonymous tip. Although these efforts turned up no remains, a ripped jacket and sweatshirt were located. A hunter also came across a bloodstain and was later a witness for the prosecution. Jordan Martell admitted that all of the weapons used in this murder belonged to him but claimed he was not "directly involved" in victim's death. Trisha Martell testified that she hit victim with a bat and witnessed Bear Cub stab victim. She was not charged with a crime in this case. Bear Cub was charged with first-degree murder but pleaded guilty to a lesser crime of second-degree murder and was sentenced to 15 years, 8 months in prison and nearly $8,000 in restitution. Despite Jordan Martell's claims, he was charged with and later found guilty of first-degree murder. He was sentenced to life in prison with no possibility of parole.

Source: Montana Memory Project

Keywords: **Codefendant, Forensic evidence: Other, Life**

Case 234

Defendant: **Robert Anthony Marquez**

Victim: Bryan Cole Thorne

Trial: February, 14 2005 Jurisdiction: Los Angeles, California

Murder: January 12, 1998

Evidence: Bryan Thorne, 16, went out with a group of friends to see the taping of the TV show *Third Rock From the Sun*. The group of teens, mostly students from Brea Canyon High School, then went to the home of Robert Anthony Marquez, 26. After arriving at defendant's home, the group was socializing when defendant asked victim and one of his friends if they would like to go out to the backyard to smoke marijuana. While in the yard, the witness stated defendant suddenly and without reason stabbed victim in the throat with a military-style knife. News of the murder quickly traveled through defendant's home to the other teens. Defendant threatened them all with death if anyone said what he had done, and he came up with a story he told them all to stick to. The teens told victim's parents that he had been dropped off at a liquor store near his home and they assumed he walked home from there. The missing persons report was filed the next day, January 13, 1998, and the group kept this deadly secret for years to come.

Shortly after victim disappeared, defendant was convicted of an unrelated extortion case and was incarcerated for six years. Upon hearing of his release nearing, Cynthia Perez, defendant's past girlfriend and now mother of his child, feared for her safety and the safety of her child, so she finally decided to come forward with the truth. Perez, along with Chris Soto and Christopher Horn, spoke to the authorities, and the information they gave police led to a murder charge against defendant.

Detectives found that defendant went by nicknames such as "Satan" and "Evil," calling himself a fallen angel. His prison cell was plastered with photos of headless animals, and he had tattoos of satanic verses on his body. Police believed his satanic practices could be his motive for victim's murder and dismemberment. The police never recovered victim's remains. According to the group of teens, defendant was a manipulative person, very charismatic, and that at times he even used a gun to get what he wanted when his charm failed. When confronted by police in prison, defendant confessed to the murder. Perez testified that she was terrified of defendant—"we saw what he was capable of doing"—and she also told the story of a time she had angered him and he hung her over a balcony. She testified that he repeatedly bragged about killing victim. Christopher Horn also testified against defendant. He said that, "Robert told me if I told anyone, he'd kill me, he said he's seen my mother and knows where I live." He also testified that defendant bragged about killing the victim: "He said it was his 25th time doing it, you could hear chopping and sawing." He also testified that defendant carried trash bags wrapped in blankets to the car and ordered him to drive to Lucky's store where he supposedly put the dismembered parts of victim's body in a trash bin. None of the informants faced charges for keeping their secret because police said "their years of fear were punishment enough." Defendant was found guilty of first-degree murder and sentenced to 51 years to life in prison.

Sources: Legaleagle; Charley Project; "Ex-High School Football Star Faces Trial for '98 Murder," Associated Press, November 11, 2004; Brea Police Department

Keywords: **Eyewitness, Confession to police, Life**

Case 235

Defendant: **Adolfo Romo Martinez**

Victim: Lilia Edith Anguiano

Trial: July 2000 Jurisdiction: Merced County, California

Murder: August 21, 1999

Evidence: Victim was defendant's former girlfriend and mother of his two children. Defendant had been abusive and threatening to victim. Defendant was recently ordered to pay child support but had told friends he would not pay and then threatened victim. Neighbors witnessed defendant and victim talking shortly before her disappearance. When confronted by police, defendant faked an alibi and then gave friends and family inconsistent alibis. Defendant convicted of second-degree murder and sentenced to 15 years to life imprisonment.

Sources: *People v. Martinez*, Court of Appeal, Fifth District, California, No. F036712, April 29, 2002 (2002 WL 749398); Doe Network

Keyword: **N/A**

Case 236

Defendant: **Vartasha Heichel Mason**

Victim: Harantoa Teugh Santoro

Trial: March, 2003 Jurisdiction: King County, Washington

Murder: February 19, 2001

Evidence: Santoro was a 31-year-old immigrant from Indonesia who regularly sent money back home to his family. He lived in Kirkland, Washington, and worked as a nursing assistant at a retirement home. On February 19, 2001, he vanished and was never seen or heard from again. His former lover was Kim Heichel Mason, a 24-year-old kick boxer from Redmond, Washington, who had previously worked with victim. On January 23, 2001, prior to victim's disappearance, he went to the police to file a complaint against the defendant, informing them that he had been attacked by the defendant. During this attack defendant knocked victim unconscious; when he awoke, he was bound and gagged with duct tape. Victim stated that defendant pointed a 9 mm gun at him and extorted $700 from him. He had choked him and threatened to kill him, saying that he threatened to inject him with drain cleaner, and although defendant denied the allegations, police found a bottle of drain cleaner, syringes, and a detailed letter in defendant's condo. A few days later, defendant was arrested and charged with first-degree robbery and first-degree kidnapping, but his father, who was retired city assistant police chief John Mason, convinced a judge to allow defendant to be released into his custody until trial. Victim was so terrified of defendant that he begged police for protection, asking them to even incarcerate him or allow him to sleep on the station floor, but his requests were denied. Police believe defendant attempted to extort more money from victim, and when he refused, he was murdered. The investigation led to the discovery of blood all over victim's apartment. None of this blood was defendant's, and no fingerprints were found. It was believed defendant broke into victim's apartment, slit his throat, and stabbed him to death. Police later recovered a knife they believed was the murder weapon. Defendant then hid the body and drove victim's Mustang to the Seattle International Airport to make it appear victim had fled the country. There was a large trail of blood leading from victim's apartment to victim's car, and blood from both defendant and victim were found in the car. Defendant called his girlfriend to come pick him up and bring him a change of clothes. When she arrived, his clothing and hands were covered in blood. Upon his arrest, she gave him an alibi for the time of the murder, but she later recanted that alibi. In exchange for immunity from prosecution, she testified against defendant at his trial.

When the police investigated further they found blood in her car belonging to both victim and defendant. She told police she gave defendant a ride home, helped him to dispose of his bloody clothing, and stitched a large wound on his thigh with a sewing needle. She went on to explain defendant then left for three days and told her he had gone to "decapitate" victim to make identification more difficult and that he "would no longer be a problem." Defendant was charged with first-degree murder. Along with the blood, DNA evidence, and witness testimony from defendant's girlfriend, there were 70 witnesses and 400 pieces of evidence used against defendant at trial. After a 10-week trial, he was found guilty of aggravated first-degree murder and sentenced to life in prison without the possibility of parole. The prosecutor did not seek the death penalty. His conviction was affirmed.

Sources: *State v. Mason*, 126 P. 3d (Wa. 2005); *State v. Mason*, 129 P. 3d 346 (Wa. 2006); *State v. Mason*, No. 77507-9, argued October 26, 2006–July 19, 2007.

Keywords: **Eyewitness, Forensic evidence: DNA, Forensic evidence: Other, Life**

Case 237

Defendant: **David Mays**
Victim: Shannon Rayanne Turner
Trial: March 19, 2004 Jurisdiction: Marion County, Indiana
Murder: December 4, 1997

Evidence: Turner was an exotic dancer working at Babe's Showgirls West. She was seeing Mays, who worked as an enforcer for the Outlaws motorcycle gang. On December 4, 1997, she left work in the early hours of the morning and disappeared. Coworkers told police later that her car had been being repaired for several days prior to her going missing and she had been receiving rides from defendant. Victim's landlord saw victim and defendant in her apartment on December 3 the night before she disappeared, and neighbors witnessed her chain up her dog in the backyard, which was her routine, before she went to work. They contacted the Humane Society when she never returned home. The investigation uncovered that victim and defendant had plans to apply for their marriage license in early December, but for unknown reasons, victim canceled their appointment. According to family and friends, victim called her mother collect on December 1 and explained that she had intended to end the relationship. Her family began to worry when she did not arrive for Christmas as planned, and her landlord called them on January 1, 1998, to inform them that victim had not returned to her home since early December. They traveled to pick up her stuff and saw that there were no signs of a struggle in her home. They filed a missing person's report six weeks after she disappeared. Searches were conducted for victim or any sign of her whereabouts in October 2003 in Perry Township, as a property there had ties to the Outlaws motorcycle gang, but were unsuccessful. Defendant was incarcerated on unrelated for three years following victim's disappearance. He was questioned repeatedly but always denied any involvement. In early 2002, he was charged, along with several other members of the gang, with multiple racketeering charges that included victim's murder. However, after a two-month trial, he was acquitted of all of these charges in 2004. Authorities were hoping to refile state charges for the murder.

Sources: Indiana Police Department Case # 685348GA; Doe Network Case File 1910 DFIN; MJA Case File I.D. SRT 043

Keyword: **N/A**

Case 238

Defendant: **Latasha Charmay "Tasha" McCoullough**

Victim: Kynanda Kalehje Bennett

Trial: February 10, 2006 Jurisdiction: Horry County, South Carolina

Murder: September 27, 2002

Evidence: Kynanda Kalehje Bennett was 4 years old when her mother, Vartasha Charmay "Tasha" McCoullough, called 911 reporting her missing from a Kmart in Whiteville, North Carolina, on September 29, 2002, at 5 p.m. The area and store were searched extensively, but no sign was ever found, and the surveillance cameras inside the store never spotted victim. The next day, volunteers searched a wide area for her but still she was not located. Defendant and victim's father, Kevin Bennett, were questioned, and the investigators that did these interviews included police and a behaviorist from South Carolina. On October 1, the parents' vehicle was taken and searched. When the searches in Whiteville for victim failed, the Center for Missing Persons extended the search to South Carolina. A lie detector test was conducted on defendant on October 8. She failed, and Mr. Bennett refused to take one at all. A DNA warrant was issued on both parents. The authorities at this time began to doubt if victim was ever in North Carolina, as there was no evidence proving this. Victim's grandparents called the police the day before she went missing to report the possibility of abuse. On October 9, the police revealed the existence of a videotape showing victim in South Carolina, and while they did not say where it was taken it was believed to be the last time anyone saw her alive. It was filmed two days before the missing persons report was filed in North Carolina. Volunteers distributed fliers, performed campaigns through e-mail and offered rewards for any information leading to the recovery of victim or her remains. As with the initial searches, many people volunteered in the search for victim, includng volunteers on foot, horses, off-road vehicles, boats, planes, and with the use of dogs. Case was featured on *America's Most Wanted Searchlight* and *Crime Stoppers*. Police searched the defendant's house and determined the house had been previously sanitized with bleach, but they were able to find biological evidence in several of the rooms. This indicated that a crime had indeed taken place there, and the DNA evidence matched victim. While interviewing possible witnesses, more people admitted the parents seemed very disinterested in finding any information regarding victim. Both of victim's parents were arrested in February 2003, but Mr. Bennett was released and charges were dropped in December 2005. Defendant was tried and found guilty of homicide by child abuse on February 10, 2006. She was also found guilty of bodily injury of a child, and was sentenced to 20 years in prison.

Sources: http://www.ncmissingpersons.org/kynande-bennett/; Charley Project

Keywords: **Forensic evidence: DNA, Forensic evidence: Other**

Case 239

Defendants: **Donald "Mac'"McDonald, Jack Anton Ibach, James Kerwin**

Victim: Laura Henderson Ibach

Trial: November 1986/April 1987 Jurisdiction: Kodiak, Alaska

Murder: March 28, 1986

Evidence: Laura Henderson Ibach was married to Jack Anton Ibach but sued for divorce on November 12, 1984. She was employed at Kodiak Women's Resource Center and residing in a separate home. The two had joint custody of their daughters, but the victim was attempting to get full custody at the time of her disappearance. Coworkers Cathy Wilson and Janet Carter testified that the victim was seeking full custody in order to make a move to Oregon with the girls. Mr. Ibach was suspected of inappropriate behavior toward his children and a child from another relationship, but none of these incidents resulted in charges until after the victim vanished. In May 1986, he was arrested for molestation of his 4-year-old daughter. Victim was contacted by a man claiming to have evidence that could help in her custody disagreement. Wilson also testified that victim spoke of this evidence as being a recorded conversation regarding illicit drugs and Mr. Ibach, and that the man arrived in a white van. Wilson and Carter both testified victim was supposed to obtain this evidence on the day of her disappearance. Prior to her disappearance, victim also contacted her attorney and confided in him the same information. During the course of the initial investigation, police discovered that victim had a prior relationship with Donald "Mac" McDonald, and the two had known one another for years. McDonald was residing in a recovery home for his alcohol dependency and was the owner of a white Dodge van. Carter also testified, among other witnesses, that a man matching McDonald's description came to call upon victim at her work. Another witness testified that they saw victim with McDonald later in the evening along with another man on the night of her disappearance. At trial, the state's theory was that Mr. Ibach hired McDonald to murder victim and that he had lured victim into his van with the possibility of giving her the evidence she had been contacted about. On March 29, 1986, a warrant was executed on Mr. McDonald, and the van belonging to him was seized and searched. While making the arrest, it was discovered that Kerwin was the accompanying man in the van during this ordeal. Police recovered three knives from Kerwin and a passport recently issued to him. Police also recovered two weapons: a .30 caliber rifle and a .32 caliber revolver. After finding out that Kerwin was the other man, police questioned the recovery home's manager, Gladys Baldwin, who later testified that McDonald gave her a .357 caliber handgun in a paper bag to "hold for him," claiming it belonged to Kerwin. Baldwin further linked Kerwin to Mr. Ibach, stating that Kerwin had made introductions between them previously. The police arrested Kerwin and Mr. Ibach, and the FBI conducted hair and fiber analysis testing on the van and all clothing worn by the three defendants. The fiber and hair testing turned up no results linked to the victim, nor was there evidence showing a payment for the murder or evidence located in the van linking the victim to the van. The van was searched again, and still nothing was located. The molestation charges against Mr. Ibach were dropped subsequent to his arrest, and all three defendants were charged with kidnapping and murder in the first degree. McDonald and Mr. Ibach were tried jointly, while Kerwin had a separate trial. Nine days before the trial, a deputy working the case contacted a psychic hotline and was given the advice to search the van a third time. This time an earring resembling one worn by victim was located near the gas pedal. Due to the irregularity of this and its timing many, people of the community believed this earring was planted. Clothing resembling those worn by victim was located near Monashka Bay on the Pacific Ocean, and a handbag containing the victim's personal identification was located on the beach. The state theorized further that McDonald had disposed of victim's remains off a cliff located on the bay. In the first trial against, McDonald and Mr. Ibach, the jury deadlocked as to both charges regarding Mr. Ibach and on the murder charge against McDonald, but found McDonald guilty of the kidnapping charge. Subsequently, Kerwin was tried and found not guilty of all charges. Therefore, the state dropped the kidnapping charge and refilled the murder charge. In the second trial, both men were found guilty and sentenced to 99 years in prison.

Sources: *State v. McDonald* (April 12, 1994) Court of Appeals No. A-2211; *Donald McDonald v. State of Alaska* Trial Court No. 3AN-96-4824 CI; 3AN-86-8787 CR; the Free Mac Project; *Defrosting Cold Cases*
Keyword: **Life**

Case 240

Defendant: **Kenneth Allen McDuff**
Victim: Colleen Reed
Trial: February 1994 Jurisdiction: Travis County, Texas
Murder: December 29, 1991
Evidence: McDuff was a particularly vicious serial killer with perhaps 14 victims. On December 29, 1991, Reed vanished from a carwash in Austin, Texas. The defendant and an accomplice, Alva Hank Worley, kidnapped victim, a complete stranger that they saw at a carwash. She was a popular and well-liked accountant. Worley admitted in an April 1992 interview with the Bell County Sheriff's Department that he had raped Reed but stated that he did not participate in her murder. He further testified that defendant also savagely raped victim and beat her. After hearing defendant had hit victim, Worley said he put her in the trunk of defendant's car and never saw her again. He further testified that defendant asked him for a pocketknife and shovel and said he was "going to use her up." There were other witnesses against defendant who saw defendant and Worley kidnap victim, including one who identified defendant and actually called the police. In addition, five of Reed's hairs were found in defendant's car along with human blood. On October 3, 1998, shortly before his execution, defendant led police to Reed's remains and those of another victim. Defendant was convicted of Reed's murder and executed by lethal injection on November 17, 1998.
Sources: http://crimelife.com/killers/mcduff.html; *McDuff v. Texas*, No. 03-94-00307-CR, March 27, 1997
Keywords: **Forensic evidence: Other, Codefendant testimony, Death penalty**

Case 241

Defendant: **Wanda Joy Webb McIlwain**
Victim: George Fininis
Trial: July 14, 1992 Jurisdiction: Georgia
Murder: April 23, 1992
Evidence: Victim and the defendant were boyfriend and girlfriend. Defendant confessed to his murder, and a search warrant was executed at victim's house. The police found a large amount of blood in victim's home that, upon testimony of the medical examiner, demonstrated that victim almost certainly would have died as a result of such injuries. The medical examiner based this conclusion on his training, experience, and examination of the crime scene. At trial, the state produced a forged check from victim's account drawn after the murder occurred and questioned defendant's character. Despite the lack of remains, the forensic evidence and defendant's confession

were enough to prove to a jury the elements of murder beyond a reasonable doubt, and defendant was found guilty of felony murder with an underlying felony of aggravated assault. She was also convicted of theft by taking, and for these crimes was sentenced to life in prison plus a concurrent term of 10 years. Defendant was denied new trial and appealed on January 18, 1994. All judgments were affirmed.

Source: *McIlwain v. State*, 264 Ga. 382 (1994)

Keywords: **Confession to police, Forensic evidence: Other, Life**

Case 242

Defendant: **Thomas H. McMonigle**

Victim: Thora Chamberlin

Trial: February 18, 1947 Jurisdiction: Santa Cruz County, California

Murder: November 2, 1945

Evidence: On November 2, 1945, just after school hours on the grounds of the Campbell Union High School, Chamberlin was approached by a man, the defendant, who called out to her from his car. Victim called out to a fellow classmate stating that he was an "ex-service man" who needed a babysitter for his sister's children for a while that afternoon. The classmate declined and said she was going to "the game." Victim told the classmate to hold her a seat and that she would be along shortly. Victim was described as wearing school colors for this occasion, which included a red skirt, blue sweater, and two pairs of socks, one red and one blue on each foot. She was also described as carrying her schoolbooks, a binder, and a cowbell. Defendant was described as wearing Navy issue trousers, a Navy-type white T-shirt with a blue insignia bearing the words "Londonderry, Ireland" on its front, along with several service medals that included a Purple Heart emblem, and a garrison hat with a slip cover on the top to protect it from water. A while later, another student witnessed the victim getting into the car with defendant and leaving. The student stated there was no one else in the car with them, and victim never returned from this trip. After victim did not return home, her family contacted the police, and shortly thereafter the FBI became involved. Agents tracked down defendant while he was on the run. He had registered at numerous hotels and was using a fake name. At one of these hotels, which he stayed in during November 1945, defendant left behind a set of luggage that the hotel manager later testified belonged to the defendant, and inside was a .32 caliber revolver. He was taken into custody on the morning of December 6, 1945. He had taken a large amount of sleeping pills and was taken to the hospital for examination. Defendant volunteered to give a number of written statements to the authorities with varying explanations of what happened to victim. All were signed by defendant, and there were several things that remained consistent, one of which being that victim was shot with a .32 caliber revolver while in the front seat of defendant's car. Defendant stated that he dropped victim's body off of a 300-foot cliff called Devils Slide. The FBI conducted extensive searches of this area and along the base of the cliff. Although no remains were located, pairs of red and blue socks were recovered about two-thirds of the way down the face of the cliff, and these were later identified as victim's by her parents. Defendant claimed in his statements that the bullet that killed victim ended up in the doorframe of his car. He removed it and buried it under a tree at his house. The bullet was located and recovered by the FBI, and the hole in the car was examined. Both were used as evidence in his trial. An in-depth investigation into defendant's life, including his work, revealed that defendant was given the task of building a ramp on a property by filling in a small ditch with concrete. This area was exhumed, and uncovered were multiple items belonging to victim—her brown shoes, schoolbooks, binder, and cowbell she had with her when she disappeared. They also recovered a pair of trousers and a T-shirt that defendant admitted were the same ones he wore the night of the murder. Defendant's employer later testified to this project and defendant's participation in it. Upon a search of defendant's home, a footlocker was recovered inside the garage. When questioned about this item, defendant admitted he had stolen it from inside the car of a serviceman. When this serviceman was questioned during trial, he testified that on September 21, 1945, his footlocker bearing his name and rank was stolen from his car. It contained a Navy T-shirt with the "Londonderry, Ireland" insignia and a pair of slate gray Navy issue trousers. These were identified by victim's classmate as the ones defendant wore on the day of the murder. At trial, defendant was charged with first-degree murder, and he entered a dual plea of not guilty and not guilty due to insanity. He was found guilty of murder in the first degree and judgment imposed the death sentence. He was granted appeal in which the judgment was affirmed.

Source: *California v. McMonigle*, 177 P.2d 745 (1947), In re McMonigle 31 Cal. 2d 246 (1947)

Keywords: **Confession to police, Eyewitness, Forensic evidence: Other, Death penalty**

Case 243

Defendant: **Jerry Dale Meeks**

Victim: Hope Meeks

Trial: October 2013 Jurisdiction: McCurtain County, Oklahoma

Murder: February 21, 2002

Evidence: Defendant and victim were married and had three children. Defendant told police that he took the children on a camping trip, and when they returned at midnight on February 21 because it was too cold, victim was gone. Her truck, car keys, eyeglasses, and cell phone were left behind. He admitted they were in the process of getting separated and said he had given her $500 before he left. He failed to report her missing until five days later. Victim worked for the McCurtain County Sheriff's Department, and it was unlike her to be missing. Fifteen days after she disappeared, defendant filed for divorce. One of the children told police that her parents had been fighting and that the fight ended when her mother got very quiet. The same child told police that she and her brother had helped defendant cut up the carpet in her parent's bedroom. There was also evidence that defendant had purchased two 50-gallon totes from Walmart and withdrew $1,000 from his bank account. Victim had accused defendant of having an affair with a coworker and had called his office the day before she disappeared. Defendant was convicted of first-degree murder and sentenced to life without the possibility of parole.

Sources: Charley Project; Belser, A., "Jury convicts Valliant man of killing wife 11 years ago," KTEN, October 30, 2013

Keywords: **Eyewitness, Life**

Case 244

Defendant: **Andrew Merola, Nicholas " Nicky" Pari**

Victim: Joseph "Onions" Scanlon

Trial: 1979 Jurisdiction: Providence County, Rhode Island

Murder: April 3, 1978

Evidence: Pari and Merola were mob associates who believed that Scanlon was a police informant. The two defendants decided that they would "take care of" him and in doing so make themselves a name within their criminal syndicate. They abducted victim and his girlfriend, who was holding their infant child at the time, and took them into a building. Pari hit victim in the face, and Merola shot victim in the head. The bullet passed through victim's skull and removed the top of one of Pari's fingertips. Victim's girlfriend was ordered to leave the room and was later described as a "stand-up girl," which meant defendants believed she would not speak to the police or anyone else. When she returned, defendants had wrapped victim in plastic from head to toe. They had removed all of his jewelry and his shoes. Defendants were wrong about victim's girlfriend, and she did speak to the police and eventually testified against them at trial. However, for years following this event, the police got different "tips" about the remains' location, but none of them turned out to be accurate. Both defendants admitted the crime and were convicted for this murder in 1979, but in 1982 the state Supreme Court overturned their convictions. Defendants pleaded no contest to lesser charges and agreed to a deal that would lead the police to victim's remains after four years of searching. When the deal was struck, two defendants told the police that they had dumped victim's body in Narragansett Bay. Years later, after defendants were released and Merola had died, Pari was arrested for a multitude of small crimes. The 78-year-old man, who was also dying of cancer, finally admitted to the police that the two had lied about what they had done with the victim's remains and told police the remains of the victim were located at the Lisboa Apartments at 378 Bullocks Point Ave. in East Providence. Parsi admitted the two men had buried victim behind the apartments. Police used a backhoe to excavate the area and found a boot, jacket, and bones. The medical examiner took DNA from victim's siblings and was able to accurately match these specimens to the located remains, and the remains were positively identified as the victim's.

Sources: "Remains of Joe Onions identified," *Boston Globe*, July 16, 2009; http://www.nytimes.com/2008/12/22/us/22land.html?pagewanted=all&_r=0

Keywords: **Confession to police, Eyewitness, Forensic evidence: DNA, Forensic evidence: Other**

Case 245

Defendant: **Charles "Chuck" Merriman**
Victim: William Merriman
Trial: December 15, 2009 Jurisdiction: Charlevoix County, Michigan
Murder: June 15, 2006
Evidence: Charles Merriman lived at his parent's home, and his brother, William, had attempted to get him to get a job and move out. Charles Merriman was charged with the murder of his brother. William's body was never discovered, and there were no witnesses to the murder or the disposal of his body. The prosecution proceeded with charges based upon the inconsistent stories Charles told them throughout the investigation, his incriminating statements made to third parties, and the physical evidence found at the scene of their parents' home. There was a large amount of blood found inside the residence, and Charles claimed this was due to an injury his brother sustained to his hand. However, several expert witnesses testified that the amount of blood found was far too substantial to have been the result of such an injury. In fact, the amount of blood loss could only be from a serious and life threatening injury. There was an extensive search of a nearby landfill that yielded a couch cushion belonging to the Merriman household that had a very large bloodstain on it matching defendant's brother's DNA. Since William's disappearance he had no bank activity and he had no contact with his family, friends, or other associates. Charles Merriman was convicted of second-degree murder and was sentenced to serve 20 to 40 years in prison.
Sources: Zucker, S., "Charles Merriman charged in brother's murder," Petoskey News.com, October 24, 2007; *Michigan v. Merriman*, No. 285959, Court of Appeals of Michigan, 2009 Mich. App. LEXIS 2562, December 15, 2009
Keyword: **Forensic evidence: DNA**

Case 246

Defendant: **Leon A. Merrow**
Victim: Vedah Merrow
Trial: September 1946 Jurisdiction: Baxter County, Arkansas
Murder: June 9, 1946
Evidence: Leon A. Merrow was a farmer in Mountain Home, Arkansas, with his wife, Vedah Merrow. Defendant went to visit relatives on June 14, 1946, without victim and made excuses for her not attending, saying she was ill and would arrive in a day or two. It was later found that he had filed for divorce the following day. After victim still did not arrive to visit as planned, her family began to worry and contacted the police. Police investigation led to the discovery that victim had made a bus reservation for the trip, leaving on June 10, but she had never gone to collect the ticket or cancel it. Police conducted a search of defendant's home that led to the discovery of a log fire located on defendant's land. Inside the fire, police located human bones. The bones were identified as those of a human by Dr. T. B. Stewart of the Smithsonian Institute, and other state's witnesses said a dental bridge found in the ashes was Mrs. Morrow's. The police also

found buttons, which were identified as being from a dress that victim wore. Witnesses reported that they had heard a woman's scream coming from the farm the day of victim's disappearance. (Sheriff later hired a woman to reenact the scream from the brush while he was escorting defendant around the farm in order to trigger a confession. It did not work.) Defendant was arrested. At trial, defendant testified that all he knew about victim's disappearance was that she had gone to their former home in Decatur, the same place defendant was arrested, and that he had no knowledge of her whereabouts. He also denied that the bone found in the fire belonged to victim. Victim at this time had been missing for three months. The jury deliberated for less the two hours before returning a guilty verdict. Defendant was sentenced to life in prison.

Sources: *Daily Journal-Gazette*, June 25, 1946: Newspaper Archive; *Tipton Tribune*, June 25, 1946, Newspaper Archive; http://archiver.rootsweb.ancestry.com/th/read/ARBAXTER/2005-05/1117381073; http://www.baxtercountysheriff.com/history_view.php?id = 11

Keywords: **Forensic evidence: Other, Life**

Case 247

Defendant: **Michael Messick**
Victim: Anne Suazo
Trial: May 2003 Jurisdiction: Clark County, Nevada
Murder: April 3, 2001

Evidence: Suazo worked at See's Candy at Meadows Mall. She had been separated from her husband since 2000 and lived with her daughter, Bethany Rodriguez. Shortly after her separation, she began to see Michael Messick, who was a pizza deliveryman. Bethany did not like defendant or the way he treated her mother. She told police that he only arrived after her mother got paid and between paychecks was nowhere to be found. She said he constantly apologized for this and made excuses but never changed the behavior. Bethany asked her mother not to see defendant anymore, but she did not listen. Bethany found out that defendant had stayed at their house on the morning of April 3, 2001, and the two had a disagreement about this. Victim left with defendant in her vehicle at approximately 6 a.m. Bethany told police that defendant appeared as though he had not slept in a long time, and he was reportedly a heavy amphetamine addict at the time. Victim's family reported her missing on April 6 after she had no contact with them in days. Her minivan was located three days later with the floor mats, steering wheel cover, and a towel all taken from the inside. Defendant claimed, when questioned, that he had not seen victim since April 3. Tests were run on the minivan for blood, but the results were negative. Defendant lived in a condo with his mother. Police attempted to question him at his home on more than one occasion, but no one ever answered the door. Investigators executed a search warrant and found the remains of defendant's mother wrapped in plastic in the bathtub. She had been beaten and stabbed. Defendant was arrested and charged with the murder. Upon this arrest, the police took possession of his vehicle and searched it thoroughly. They found blood matching victim in the cargo area.

Defendant was convicted of first-degree murder for his mother and second-degree murder of victim in May 2003 and sentenced to two life sentences without possibility of parole. Defendant appealed and lost in February 2005.

Sources: Charley Project; "Man loses appeal in killing of his mother, girlfriend," *Carson City Reporter*, February 4, 2005.

Keywords: **Forensic evidence: DNA, Life**

Case 248

Defendant: **Anton D. Meyers**

Victim: Kathy Engles

Trial: June 17, 1994 Jurisdiction: Seminole County, Florida

Murder: May 25, 1987

Evidence: On the evening of May 24, 1987, Engles's grandparents left her at a convenience store with her friends, Lorna Brown and Autumn Pemberton. With them was Anton D. Meyers. They were seen by adults at each of the three girls' homes. By the next day, victim's grandparents attempted to contact her at the Brown home and found out she had not stayed the night there as they had believed. They began to search for her and then contacted the police. When questioned, defendant told Lorna and later the investigating officer that he and victim had headed toward her home when they stopped by a convenience store. According to defendant, victim was using a pay phone last time he saw her and she disappeared. After his arrest, defendant confessed to a fellow inmate that he had attempted to rape victim, and when she fought back he slit her throat. The photographs taken of bruising on defendant's body at his arrest corroborated the inmate's story of defendant's confession. Jury convicted defendant of first-degree murder, and even though victim's remains were not located, the jury recommended death for defendant by unanimous vote. Trial court sentenced defendant to the death penalty. Defendant appealed this sentence and the court affirmed judgment. On September 14, 2001, defendant made a deal to escape execution, agreeing to finally lead authorities to victim's remains, reducing his sentence from death to life in prison. The remains were located where defendant stated, but as part of his deal he was also supposed to admit to the murder and detail the account. He has not held up this end of the deal and was sent back to death row.

Sources: "Authorities Find Human Remains," *Star Banner*, September 23, 2001; Supreme Court of Florida Case No. 85617

Keywords: **Forensic evidence: Other, Informant, Death penalty**

Case 249

Defendant: **Sean Mihajson**

Victim: Shalonda Monique Morris

Trial: December 2012 Jurisdiction: Riverside County, California

Murder: October 12, 2007

Evidence: Morris was last seen on October 12, 2007, leaving her residence between 12:30 and 1:30 in the afternoon. She went to meet a friend, the defendant, at a local store. Victim was reported missing the next day. Defendant disappeared at the same time; however, no missing persons report was filed. Police recovered victim's vehicle along with evidence that indicated a crime had taken place. Defendant, along with his twin sister, Vanesa Michelle Mihajson, his brother, Victor Mihajson, and a Katie Leigh Weddle were all sought for questioning. It was discovered that Weddle helped the Mihajson family leave the state. Defendant was located in North Carolina, thanks to the social networking site MySpace, and was arrested in October 2008 and charged with first-degree murder. On April 27, 2009, Vanessa Michelle Mihajson was also arrested in North Carolina. Victim was murdered during a drug deal gone bad and was believed to be buried on a five-acre area in Sky Valley, California. Sean Mihajson was arrested for harboring a fugitive, Vanessa Michelle Mihajson was charged as an accessory after the fact, and Victor Mihajson was arrested for being a felon in possession of a firearm. Vanessa Michelle Mihajson was originally charged with murder, but this was pleaded down due to her cooperation, and she was ultimately convicted of being an accessory to a felony and was sentenced to three years' probation and 120 hours of community service. She testified at her brother's trial that she knew of defendant's plot to kill victim. She had purchased plastic sheeting and duct tape to aid in this act, letting him borrow her van, and she delivered the items to her brother but was not there when he committed the crime. Defendant was tried in December 2012 and found guilty of first-degree murder. The jury also found a special circumstance, since this murder took place during the commission of a robbery, and defendant was sentenced to life in prison.

Sources: http://palmdesert.patch.com/groups/police-and-fire/p/jury-deliberations-resume-in-mihajson-trial; Charley Project

Keywords: **Confession to friends and family, Forensic evidence: Other, Codefendant testimony, Life**

Case 250

Defendant: **Gerald Wesley Miller**

Victims: Carol Miller and Crystal Miller

Trial: March 17, 1993 Jurisdiction: Marion County, Oregon

Murder: 1984/1989

Evidence: Defendant was arrested on May 15, convicted, and sentenced to two life sentences on March 17 1993, one for each victim. This case was the rare double no-body murder and had no physical evidence directly tying the defendant to the crime. Defendant suggested at one point that one of the victim's may have been taken by a UFO. This case resulted in conviction based entirely on circumstantial evidence. There was no DNA evidence, no witnesses, and no confession.

Sources: "Murder suspect won't get bail," *The Bend Bulletin*, July 1, 1992; Murderpedia; *Erased: Missing Women, Murdered Wives*, Strong, Marilee, Powelson, Mark, John Wiley & Sons Publishing, 2010, p. 44; "Oregon Man Guilty of Murdering Wives," *Seattle Times*, March 18, 1993

Keyword: **Life**

Case 251

Defendant: **Adam Jan Modelski**
Victim: Jeanne Modelski
Trial: 1984 Jurisdiction: Kalamazoo County, Michigan
Murder: April 26, 1980
Evidence: Defendant and victim were married and frequently had loud arguments that included violence and allegations of infidelity by defendant. Defendant started calling around "looking for his wife" after April 26, and the next day, defendant told a coworker, while out together seeing a movie, about a man who murdered his wife, and that the man had shot victim in the head. Victim was reported missing by her mother on May 1, 1980. Police discovered defendant had given away to a coworker all of victim's personal belongings, including her purse, which contained her identification and marriage license. In February 1981, defendant confessed to his lover that he had shot his wife. In 1982, defendant joined the Army and gave a full confession to his supervisor. In 1983, in a drunken fit of rage, he told two friends he had killed his wife and dumped her body in a swamp in northern Indiana, saying he crossed state lines in the hopes it would be more difficult for the police to find her remains. Defendant was arrested on October 11, 1983, after which he gave another confession to police. He stated that victim was emotionally unstable, unpredictable, and that she had given him venereal disease. After confession, defendant accompanied police to attempt to locate the remains; however, no body was found. Defendant was charged with first-degree murder. Victim's parents testified that there was a history of the two fighting and that victim would leave but that she usually returned after one day and had never been gone longer than three days. Defendant's lover testified to defendant's confession. Defendant was convicted of manslaughter and sentenced to 10 to 15 years in prison. Defendant appealed his judgment in November 1987, and the judgment was affirmed. Victim's remains were located in 1987 in Indiana.
Sources: Flint Michigan's News Channel 3, "Daughter finally tracks down her mother's grave," August 3, 2003; *People v. Modelski*, 416 NW2d 708 (1987)
Keywords: **Confession to friends and family, Confession to police**

Case 252

Defendant: **Mohammed Monie**
Victim: Robert Perruquet
Trial: November 2007/January 2009 Jurisdiction: San Mateo County, California
Murder: April 29, 1989
Evidence: Defendant plotted to kill victim for the parts to victim's prized baby blue Monte Carlo. Victim's mother last saw him prior to going out with defendant, Jesse Rodriguez, and a female companion. At the time of the murder, defendant had a 1979 Monte Carlo and wanted the costly parts victim had installed on his Monte Carlo. Defendant supplied drugs to and instructed Rodriquez to commit the murder. The

disappearance did not go unnoticed among victim's friends and family, as victim was supposed to meet up with his girlfriend and never showed up, and he also had planned to move to southern California to begin a new job. Victim's car was found four days later, abandoned at a train station near San Francisco and covered in primer paint. The investigation went cold until 2005, when Rodriquez told police defendant made him kill victim and that he shot him multiple times with a gun stolen from his father. The two then drove the body in the trunk to Half Moon Bay, where they dumped him down a ravine. The remains were not located. Rodriquez confessed to all aspects of this murder in 2004. He could not be tried for his part in the crime, however, because when the crime took place in 1989 he was 14 years old. At the time he confessed, he was over the age limit (25 years old) to be incarceration for a juvenile offense, but he did testify against the defendant. Defendant was charged with first-degree murder, with special circumstances, since the murder occurred during the commission of a robbery. First trial ended in a mistrial. The case began to be tried again in 2009, when defendant pleaded guilty to voluntary manslaughter and other charges. He was given 30 years in prison with a minimum requirement of 15 years.

Sources: Manekin, M., "Muscle-car killing heads to retrial in Redwood City," *San Mateo County Times*, November 11, 2008; *Leagle.com*

Keywords: **Confession to police, Forensic evidence: Other, Codefendant testimony**

Case 253

Defendant: **Aurelio Montano**

Victim: Maria Guadalupe Montano

Trial: October 2013 Jurisdiction: St. Charles, Illinois

Murder: July 1990

Evidence: At trial, defendant's daughter, who was 10 at the time of her mother's disappearance, testified that she last saw her mother on a day that victim and defendant had argued about the victim's choice of clothes. He dropped daughter off at a relative's house, saying he would be back later that afternoon, but he did not return until the next day. There was also testimony that defendant had asked several family members to assist him in burying victim's body on a horse farm owned by his family. Defendant's sister testified that she saw victim's body wrapped up in a rug with a rope around her neck. (A rug was later found buried at the farm, and three cadaver dogs had positive hits for human remains in 2007.) Defendant told her, "I sent the snake to hell." Defendant told two nephews that his wife had "badmouthed" the family and had been unfaithful, so he had killed her. One nephew testified that a year after victim disappeared, defendant showed him a plastic bag that he said contained victim's head and hands and that he needed to get a wood chipper so he could dispose of the body and not get convicted. There was also testimony that the victim left many items behind, including jewelry she rarely took off and her purse and wallet. Defendant was convicted and was already serving a life sentence for two other murders.

Source: http://beaconnews.suntimes.com/23439837-417/montano-found-guilty-of-murder.html
Keywords: **Forensic evidence: Other Eyewitness, Life**

Case 254

Defendant: **Antonio Moore**
Victim: Michael Jay Francis
Trial: March, 2008 Jurisdiction: Anne Arundel County, Maryland
Murder: April 14, 2007
Evidence: Moore went to the house where he had been staying off Brookwood Road with a friend of his and his girlfriend, Sierra Monet Anderson. When he arrived, he had a large bag containing a rifle. Sometime during the night, another person Teiko Tyronne Jhonson, arrived at the house. Defendant attacked Jhonson, hitting him with the rifle and demanding marijuana from him. Anderson joined in and helped in the attack. Victim arrived early in the morning on April 14, 2007, and attempted to deter defendant from his attack. Jhonson was able to escape. Victim was not so lucky, and he was never seen again. According to witness accounts, while pleading for his life, victim was shot by defendant at close range with a 9mm handgun and was stuffed into the trunk of a car. Police recovered the weapon in a forested area near the crime scene. The vehicle was found not far from the crime scene, with victim's clothing and puddles of blood found inside. Anderson told investigators that defendant had forced her to drive him with the body in the trunk. She was not charged with any crimes and was placed in witness protection. Defendant was arrested and charged with attempted murder and other charges. Later, these charges were amended to first-degree murder. Defendant's first trial was in March 2008 and resulted in a mistrial. He was tried a second time in May 2008. Defendant was not convicted of the murder charge but convicted of the first-degree assaults along with the two lesser charges in the Johnson beating. He was sentenced to 25 years in prison. On April 20, 2008, the skeletal remains of a person were found in Baltimore near defendant's aunt's home. The remains were missing its hands. A year later, it was positively identified as the victim. In May defendant was tried a third time for murder. He was found guilty of first-degree murder and was sentenced to life in prison.
Sources: http://articles.baltimoresun.com/2008-02-28/news/0802280335_1_arundel-county; Charley Project; Daugherty, S., "Man shot, thrown in trunk," *Capital Gazette*, April 16, 2007
Keywords: **Eyewitness, Forensic evidence: Other, Life**

Case 255

Defendant: **Larry Moore**
Victim: Brad Brisbin
Trial: November 1992 Jurisdiction: Gallatin County, Montana
Murder: November 9, 1990
Evidence: Deputy Brad Brisbin of the Gallatin County Sherriff's Department in Montana made national news with his disappearance

on November 9, 1990. The victim was having an affair with a married woman, the wife of Larry Thurman Moore, during their separation. Defendant found out about the affair, and his friends later testified that the defendant said if this was true that he would kill victim. Michelle Moore was issued a protection order against her husband due to his attempting to strangle her about a month prior to victim's disappearance. On the day victim vanished, he met defendant at a truck stop. Defendant had lured him there under the false pretense that he needed a ride. Victim agreed and told his wife, Rene Brisbin, where he was going. The following day when victim did not return home, his wife feared the worst. Police searched the West Yellowstone gravel pit for possible remains, but the search was unsuccessful. Defendant admitted to police he had a struggle with victim, but said victim pulled gun on him, and during the struggle the gun went off, hitting victim. Defendant claimed victim was not hurt and drove away in his car. Defendant was arrested on December 1, 1990, and charged with deliberate homicide. A search of defendant's trailer revealed a piece of human flesh. The flesh was examined and determined to be brain tissue that matched victim's brain tissue. Defense tried to get this evidence dismissed due to the fact that the use of DNA in a trial had never been done before. On November 19, 1990, the defendant was found guilty and sentenced to 60 years in prison. The Montana Supreme Court ruled on appeal that the DNA evidence was admissible and judgment was affirmed. In 1995, defendant was charged in connection with another crime and made a plea agreement confessing to victim's murder. He led the police to victim's remains and the murder weapon. He has been denied parole twice.

Source: http://mylifeofcrime.wordpress.com/2007/03/03/brad-brisbin-murder-110990-west-yellowstone-mt/

Keywords: **Forensic evidence: DNA, Confession to police**

Case 256

Defendant: **Eric Mora**

Victim: Cynthia Alonzo

Trial: February 2012 Jurisdiction: Almeda County, California

Murder: November 2004

Evidence: Mora and Alonzo lived together under an agreement that involved trading sex for illegal drugs. When victim did not arrive as planned at a family gathering in San Francisco on Thanksgiving Day, November 25, 2004, she was reported missing. During the course of the investigation in January 2005, a search of both victim's and defendant's home revealed an amount of blood located in victim's room, and the home looked as though someone had attempted to clean up, including sanding the bedroom floors. Defendant had multiple lacerations on his hands and soon left town. Defendant was not arrested until 2007, even though authorities viewed him as a suspect in 2005. He was subsequently arrested, and while incarcerated, defendant attempted to buy a false alibi from another inmate. This backfired, and the inmate became a key witness in the case against him. The inmate stated that defendant had confessed to him that he had cut up victim's remains and dumped them off a bridge into a body of water located in Sonora. He told the informant that he was going to sell his home and did not want victim to get any part of the proceeds. He went on to say that he had hit victim in the head with a hammer and she had fallen down the stairs. The defendant was convicted of second-degree murder and was sentenced to 15 years to life in prison with the possibility of parole if he leads the authorities to the victim's remains and admits his own guilt.

Sources: http://www.fugitive.com/2012/01/17/eric-mora-stands-trial-in-alleged-murder-of-missing-girlfriend-cynthia-linda-alonzo/; http://www.fugitive.com/2010/05/12/eric-mora-is-said-to-have-told-informant-that-he-murdered-cynthia-alonzo-at-6201-brookside-ave-in-oakland-2004/

Keywords: **Forensic evidence: DNA, Forensic evidence: Other, Informant, Life**

Case 257

Defendant: **Marcos Morales, Beatriz Morales**

Victim: Lisa Morales

Trial: October 1992 Jurisdiction: Orange County, California

Murder: 1977

Evidence: Charges against the defendants, parents of the 5-year-old victim, were brought in 1991 when an older sister of the victim recalled through psychotherapy that her parents had killed her sister and wrapped her in plastic at a Mexican beach. Victim had drowned in the bathtub and was subjected to abuse throughout her life. Defendants claimed they had given up victim for adoption in Mexico.

Source: http://articles.latimes.com/1992-10-20/local/me-585_1_beatriz-morales

Keyword: **Eyewitness**

Case 258

Defendant: **Robert Thomas "Bobby" Nauss, Jr.**

Victim: Elizabeth Ann Lande

Trial: December 1977 Jurisdiction: Philadelphia County, Pennsylvania

Murder: December 1971

Evidence: Victim was defendant's girlfriend. Defendant was a member of the Warlock motorcycle gang. Victim was with two friends on December 11, 1971, when she received a call from defendant asking her to spend the weekend with him. Later that night, a neighbor witnessed victim getting into a vehicle. On December 13, defendant's friend witnessed victim hanging from the rafters in a garage behind his apartment house. Defendant told the witness he had killed her and that she wouldn't bother him anymore. The witness then helped defendant to dispose of the body in the Pine Barrens of New Jersey. Defendant had apparently choked victim to death after an argument. Defendant chopped off victim's hands and feet to hide her identity. In 1977, the witness tried to lead investigators to victim's body, but housing subdivisions had been built up. Defendant convicted and sentenced to life imprisonment.

Sources: http://pennsylvaniamissing.com/lizlande.html; http://articles.philly.com/1990-11-02/news/25925615_1_graterford-prison-rapone-second-convict; http://articles.mcall.com/1990-11-01/news/2773288_1_marshal-escaped-three-children

Keywords: **Eyewitness, Life**

Case 259

Defendant: **Thomas James Negri**

Victim: Shirley Dean Cowan

Trial: July 2007 Jurisdiction: Llano County, Texas

Murder: January 2001

Evidence: Victim was defendant's mother-in-law. Defendant and victim had fought in the past, but victim had recently hired defendant as a general contractor for a house she wanted to build. The project was near completion when victim disappeared, but victim expressed dissatisfaction with the work and planned to replace defendant. Defendant had a safe deposit box with $300,000,and gave the only extra key to her daughter, defendant's wife. Victim disappeared shortly after asking defendant's wife to return the extra key. Defendant began telling family that victim had taken a trip and had left her dogs in his car, though victim had always taken her dogs on her vacations in the past. Defendant also claimed that victim told him to sell her trailer because she was out of money. When victim's granddaughter entered victim's trailer, she found unwashed dishes and rotting meat in the fridge, though victim had been very clean. After victim's disappearance, defendant's wife opened victim's safe deposit box three times, though victim had been the only one to access it before. The last outgoing call on victim's phone was to defendant. A witness working on the house project testified that defendant asked him not to come into work one day because he had a private meeting with victim. The next day, witness noticed speckles and dents on the cabinets, and the unfinished concrete floor had been painted white in a trail that led from the kitchen to the master bedroom closet. There were red and brown spots in the paint. Defendant claimed victim had swung at him with a pipe and cut her hand on a cabinet and then went into the closet to cry. Based on testimony from several other witnesses, investigators removed tiles and carpeting from the house and found the paint trail, which tested positive for victim's blood. In the closet, the imprint of the blood showed a body in the fetal position. Another worker at the site was seen driving victim's car and made incriminating statements but denied the statements at trial. Defendant convicted of first-degree murder and sentenced to 20 years imprisonment. Conviction upheld in 2009, and defendant's petition for writ of habeas corpus denied in 2012.

Sources: *Negri v. State*, Court of Appeals of Texas, Austin, No. 03-07-00588-CR, May 6, 2009; *Negri v. Thaler*, United States District Court, W.D. Texas, Austin Division, No. A-11-CV-106-SS, May 29, 2012

Keyword: **Forensic evidence: DNA**

Case 260

Defendant: **Jimmie Allen Nelson**
Victim: Cherita Janice Thomas
Trial: October 2010 Jurisdiction: Iosco County, Michigan
Murder: August 3, 1980
Evidence: Victim was last seen with defendant at a bar on the night of her disappearance. Defendant first testified that he did not see victim after leaving the bar. Twenty-four years later, defendant was arrested for lying to police and obstructing the investigation. Defendant changed his testimony and stated that he saw her a second time that night when she told him she was having car trouble. Witnesses saw victim having car trouble on the road and saw victim getting into a blue pickup with a bearded Caucasian male. He stated that he drove her to a friend's apartment and then to a restaurant. The friend in question contradicted this testimony, and the restaurant owner testified that his establishment had long been closed when defendant would have arrived. A cadaver dog handler was convicted of planting evidence while searching for victim's remains in 2003. Case thrown out in 2005 but reversed by Michigan Court of Appeals. Defendant convicted of second-degree murder in October 2010 and sentenced to 25 to 50 years imprisonment. Conviction overturned in 2012 by the Michigan appeals court because mere evidence that defendant was covering his tracks was not enough to sustain a murder conviction. Iosco County authorities were barred from pursuing defendant again on the same charge.
Sources: *People v. Nelson*, Court of Appeals of Michigan, Docket No. 271768, December 23, 2008; http://abclocal.go.com/kgo/story?section=news/local&id=7771114
Keyword: **N/A**

Case 261

Defendant: **Ruth Neslund**
Victim: Rolf Neslund
Trial: 1985 Jurisdiction: San Juan County, Washington
Murder: August 1980
Evidence: Victim was defendant's husband. On August 8, 1980, defendant called her niece and told her she had fought with victim and victim had hurt her, so defendant's brother held him down while defendant shot him. Defendant also told her that victim was outside burning in a barrel. Defendant's other brother testified that defendant told him that she shot victim twice in the head and killed him. He also testified that he overheard conversations between defendant and their brother detailing the murder and the body's subsequent dismemberment and burning. Defendant also confessed to a friend and to her son. Defendant and victim had apparently been fighting because defendant withdrew $75,000 of victim's pension money and put it in her own account. Eighteen months after the murder, investigators recovered a .38 caliber Smith & Wesson handgun from defendant's master bedroom that tested positive for blood. The spatters on the gun were consisted with high velocity back spatter of a gunshot wound to an uncovered area of a human being or animal from a distance of three

feet or less. Defendant convicted of first-degree murder while armed with a deadly weapon and sentenced to life imprisonment. Defendant died in prison in 1993.

Sources: *State v. Neslund*, 749 P.2d 725 (Wash. App. 1988); http://community.seattletimes.nwsource.com/archive/?date=19930218&slug=1686192

Keywords: **Confession to family and friends, Forensic evidence: Other, Life**

Case 262

Defendant: **Charles Chi-Tat Ng**

Victims: Deborah Harvey, Sean Dubs, Jeffrey Gerald, Paul Cosner, Clifford Peranteau, Brenda O'Connor, Lonnie Bonds, Lonnie Bonds, Jr., Kathy Allen, Mike Carrol, Scott Stapley

Trial: October 1998–February 1999 Jurisdiction: Orange County, California

Murder: Various times

Evidence: Defendant was a serial killer believed to have killed between 11 and 25 victims. Defendant immigrated from Hong Kong and joined the U.S. Marine Corps, where he met his future accomplice, Leonard Lake. Defendant was dishonorably discharged for theft and served two years in a military prison. After his release in 1982, defendant went to live with accomplice in a remote cabin, beside which accomplice had constructed a custom-built dungeon. Defendant and accomplice began murdering in 1983, and victims included neighbors, workmates, and relatives of prior victims. Defendant and accomplice killed men and children quickly and then filmed themselves raping and torturing the women before murdering them. In 1985, defendant and accomplice were arrested after defendant shoplifted and police found a gun with a silencer in accomplice's trunk. Accomplice committed suicide while in custody after swallowing cyanide pills sewn into his clothes, revealing his and defendant's identities prior to death. Defendant fled to Canada while investigators uncovered the dungeon. Investigators unearthed 40 pounds of human bone fragments from at least 12 bodies that had been smashed and burned. They also found two buckets. One contained envelopes and IDs, suggesting up to 25 victims. The other bucket contained accomplice's journals and two videotapes depicting the torture of two victims. Defendant was serving a prison sentence in Canada for separate charges. Defendant extradited from Canada after a six-year legal battle centered on the death penalty. Prosecution against defendant was the most expensive in California history. Defendant convicted on 11 counts of first-degree murder and sentenced to death by lethal injection. Defendant is currently on death row at San Quentin State Prison.

Sources: http://newspaperarchive.com/lethbridge-herald/1998-11-12/page-9; http://news.bbc.co.uk/2/hi/americas/382498.stm; http://www1.umn.edu/humanrts/undocs/html/dec469.htm

Keywords: **Death penalty, Codefendant testimony, Forensic evidence: Other**

Case 263

Defendant: **Donald Nicely**
Victim: Delores "Jeannie" Nicely
Trial: 1986 Jurisdiction: Tuscarawas County, Ohio
Murder: April 23, 1985
Evidence: Victim was defendant's wife. Victim and defendant had a bad relationship, and victim's daughter was holding $130 from each of victim's paychecks so she could save enough money to leave defendant. On April 23, 1985, victim left work to change her blouse, leaving her purse and other personal effects, but never returned. That night, defendant drove to his son's house in victim's car with a mattress and slept there for a few hours before driving to victim's daughter's trailer at 4:30 a.m. to tell her that victim had left and would never contact her again. He also instructed victim's daughter to call victim's place of employment to tell them victim had quit. Defendant admitted to investigators that he and his father abandoned victim's car on a back road near a creek the next day, but lied about its location and told conflicting stories about its location to victim's daughters. Investigators found the car with the license removed and found blood on the pavement. The car trunk was wet and had spots of blood, pine needles, and grass. Blood matching victim's blood type was found in several places inside the vehicle. A spot of blood matching victim's blood type was found on defendant's trousers. In the creek near where the vehicle was abandoned, investigators found a sunken bag filled with victim's belongings. Investigators also found substantial blood throughout victim's trailer that matched her blood type. In a phone call from jail, defendant expressed concern about victim's body being found and requested that his father change the tires on his truck. Defendant convicted of aggravated murder and sentenced to 15 years to life, but judgment vacated on appeal because evidence did not establish corpus delicti, or the elements of murder. New judgment found defendant guilty of felonious assault. The Ohio Supreme Court reversed the lower court's judgment and reinstated the murder conviction.
Source: *State v. Nicely*, 529 N.E.2d 1236 (Ohio 1988)
Keywords: **Forensic evidence: Other, Confession to friends and family**

Case 264

Defendant: **Rebeca Nivarez**
Victim: Mario Hernandez
Trial: February 2011 Jurisdiction: Orange County, California
Murder: March 18, 2005
Evidence: Victim was an elderly jewelry salesman and defendant was a regular customer. Victim disappeared after packing a substantial amount of jewelry and leaving for an appointment with defendant. The last numbers dialed from victim's phone were to defendant, but defendant claimed victim never showed up. Defendant told her 19-year-old son she killed victim because of information defendant had received from a psychic that killing victim would break a curse. Defendant's son later testified at his own trial that he walked in on a struggle between victim and defendant, and he intervened by striking

victim with a golf club, stabbing him with his own knife, then strangling him with a light cable. Defendant and her son put the body in victim's vehicle and moved it twice before dumping the body in an apartment dumpster. The next day, defendant asked her daughter to hold a bag containing $4,000 worth of jewelry and not to tell anyone about it. Beginning the day victim was killed, defendant also pawned $2,500 worth of jewelry at several different pawnshops. Shortly after the murder, both defendant and her son left California. Eight months later, defendant told her daughter that her son killed victim after victim pulled a knife on him. In February 2006, defendant's daughter agreed to record a phone conversation with defendant's son, who confessed to the murder and disposal of the body. Defendant's son's DNA was found on a glove inside victim's abandoned car. Defendant convicted of first-degree murder and sentenced to 25 years to life. Defendant's son also convicted after being extradited from Mexico. At his trial, defendant's son testified that defendant was using witchcraft as a pretext for the murder and that he himself had no intention of robbing victim.

Sources: http://oc-da.com/home/index.asp?page=8&recordid=2922&returnurl=index.asp%3Fpage%3D8; http://www.ocregister.com/news/hernandez-285542-nivarez-yellin.html; *People v. Diaz-Nivarez*, Court of Appeal, Fourth District, Division 3, California, GO46945, May 22, 2013

Keywords: **Forensic evidence: DNA, Forensic evidence: Other, Confession to friends and family**

Case 265

Defendant: **John Thomas Noser**

Victim: Brenda Lee Borowski

Trial: April 2000 Jurisdiction: Lucas County, Ohio

Murder: August 1995

Evidence: Victim was defendant's ex-girlfriend. Defendant was upset about the breakup and told witnesses that if he could not have victim, no one could. Witnesses said defendant was desperate to be with victim and called her incessantly. Defendant admitted to calling victim 18 times from different payphones the morning of her disappearance. Victim was last seen on an ATM video in her vehicle with defendant on August 15, 1995. Two days later, police found defendant camping nearby with victim's car and possessions with him. Some of victim's clothing, makeup, and jewelry were found burned in the same woods. Defendant claimed victim was killed in a shoot-out over a drug deal in Toledo but could not lead police to a location that matched his description, and the Drug Enforcement Administration denied knowledge of a shoot-out. Defendant convicted of first-degree murder and sentenced to 15 years to life imprisonment.

Sources: *State v. Noser*, Court of Appeals of Ohio, Sixth District, Lucas County, No. L-00-1154, December 7, 2001; http://www.ohioattorneygeneral.gov/Files/Law-Enforcement/Investigator/Ohio-Missing-Persons/Cold-Case-Missing-Adults/Borowski

Keyword: **Forensic evidence: Other**

Case 266

Defendant: **Casey Nowicki**
Victim: Marcy Jo Andrews
Trial: July 2005 Jurisdiction: Cook County, Illinois
Murder: February 1984
Evidence: Victim was drinking liquor with two friends when they decided to seek out defendant, a convicted drug dealer, to purchase marijuana. Defendant drank and smoked weed with the three women at his apartment. Afterward, defendant agreed to drive the women home, but crashed into a concrete viaduct. Victim's ankle was swollen after the accident, but defendant did not want to bring her to the hospital because he had been driving without insurance. Defendant took victim back to his house by taxi, leaving victim's friends behind. Victim called a friend and said defendant would not take her to the hospital until the next morning, but that she did not want to stay the night at his apartment. When her friend came to pick her up, no one answered. Defendant told victim's friends that she left and threatened to throw battery acid at victim's friend when she came to his apartment looking for victim. Witnesses saw a girl lying on a bed, handcuffed to a radiator, apparently drugged, with headphones in her ears. One witness testified that on February 18, 1984, defendant called him and said victim had died of an overdose and he needed help moving the body. Defendant loaded the body in his mother's vehicle. Defendant told investigators that victim left on her own. Defendant was convicted of counterfeiting in 1988, and evidence of victim's disappearance was presented at his sentencing hearing. Defendant was sentenced to nine years, and was charged with victim's murder in 2000. Defendant convicted of first-degree murder and rape and sentenced to life imprisonment. Judgment affirmed in 2008.
Sources: *People v. Nowicki*, 894 N.E.2d 896 (Ill.App.Ct. 2008); http://articles.chicagotribune.com/1989-04-30/features/8904080834_1_smell-humboldt-park-drug
Keywords: **Life, Eyewitness**

Case 267

Defendant: **Aaron W. Null**
Victim: Brynn M. Null
Trial: December 2010 Jurisdiction: Boone County, Illinois
Murder: November 16, 2002
Evidence: Victim was defendant's wife. The couple had a history of domestic violence. Defendant had been arrested for domestic battery, and victim had sought shelter on multiple occasions when defendant attacked her. Victim was last seen with defendant, and after family reported her missing, defendant stated she had disappeared and left behind her keys, wedding ring, and vehicle. Defendant beat victim to death with an object. A large bloodstain was found on couple's bed, and blood spatter was found on the walls and ceiling of the bedroom, and a bloody towel was found in defendant's vehicle. All the blood matched victim's DNA, and blood spatter indicated that they were the result of at least two

impacts. Defendant convicted of first-degree murder and sentenced to 50 years imprisonment. Conviction upheld in 2013.

Sources: *People v. Null*, 991 N.E.2d 875 (Ill. App. Ct. 2013); http://www.wifr.com/news/headlines/Boone-County-Murderers-Conviction-Upheld-212486581.html

Keyword: **Forensic evidence: DNA**

Case 268

Defendant: **Michael O'Shields**

Victim: Ruby Oliver

Trial: May 1995 Jurisdiction: Dallas County, Alabama

Murder: March 1990

Evidence: Victim was defendant's ex-wife. Victim was last seen with defendant after he picked her up so she could collect her belongings from his trailer. Witnesses testified that defendant was angry that victim was dating a black man. After the murder, defendant confessed to several witnesses who notified investigators. Defendant confessed to police in a video-recorded interview that he choked victim to death and that he and a friend dumped her body in the Alabama River. Defendant's friend also testified against him. Defendant convicted of murder and sentenced to life imprisonment. Defendant appealed because his confession was taken after he had requested counsel. The court found that the confession should not have been admitted into evidence but that it was a harmless error.

Sources: *O'Shields v. State*, 689 So.2d 227 (Ala. Crim. App. 1996); http://news.google.com/newspapers?nid=1817&dat=19950526&id=JYMfAAAAIBAJ&sjid=DqYEAAAAIBAJ&pg=4672,7637986

Keywords: **Confession to police, Life, Confession to friends and family**

Case 269

Defendant: **Michiel Oakes**

Victim: T. Mark Stover

Trial: October 2010 Jurisdiction: Skagit County, Washington

Murder: October 28, 2009

Evidence: Defendant was dating victim's ex-wife. Defendant was a security expert and met victim's ex-wife when she sought help protecting herself from victim, who was harassing and stalking her. Defendant and victim had several confrontations for months prior to the murder. Defendant admitted to killing victim during a meeting at victim's house but says he was lured to the meeting when victim threatened his children. Defendant claimed he shot victim in self-defense after victim pointed a handgun at him and the two wrestled over the weapon. Defendant said he dumped the body in the Swinomish Channel. Defendant also shot victim's guard dog three times. Witnesses saw defendant trespassing on victim's property the day of his disappearance. One witness saw defendant moving something that looked like a body wrapped in tarp. On the day of the murder, defendant told victim's ex-wife that he had been hired for a dangerous mission that had gone bad. Evidence showed defendant purchased camouflaged clothing, rope, and weights prior to the meeting. Defendant claimed to have purchased the items for his own protection, and presented a dented armored vest to show where victim's bullet had hit him. As a security expert, the prosecution argued that defendant would have reported threats to the police and would not have gone to defendant's home. The prosecution also suggested that defendant may have been hired to kill victim. Defendant convicted of first-degree murder and sentenced to 26 years imprisonment. Defendant appealed when it was discovered that a juror sent out several tweets throughout the trial. Conviction upheld in 2012.

Sources: http://seattletimes.com/html/localnews/2013234720_dogtrainer23m.html; http://www.seattleweekly.com/home/873430-129/story.html

Keywords: **Confession to police, Eyewitness**

Case 270

Defendant: **Gerald Oelerich**

Victim: Darlene Oelerich

Trial: May 1995 Jurisdiction: Ozaukee County, Wisconsin

Murder: October 1994

Evidence: Victim was defendant's estranged wife. Victim wanted a divorce, but defendant was strongly against it. In an earlier petition for divorce, victim claimed defendant had threatened to kill her. Victim was packing her car to leave when defendant attacked. Defendant bludgeoned victim to death with a sledgehammer and then dumped her body in Lake Winnebago. During the seven hours it took victim to die from her injuries, defendant watched her die and wrote 15 pages of notes detailing her suffering and his actions. Defendant then called his brother, confessing to the murder and threatening to kill himself. Police went to defendant's home and found the garage covered in blood. Defendant was in his fishing boat on the lake, several hundred yards offshore. Defendant shot at police and led them on an all-night boat chase. Defendant convicted of first-degree intentional homicide. Victim's torso was recovered from the lake in 1998.

Sources: http://news.google.com/newspapers?nid=1499&dat=19941019&id=XxAuAAAAIBAJ&sjid=MH8EAAAAIBAJ&pg=6721,5883516; http://news.google.com/newspapers?nid=1683&dat=19950505&id=3UocAAAAIBAJ&sjid=8CwEAAAAIBAJ&pg=1695,5087753

Keywords: **Confession to friends and family, Confession to police, Forensic evidence: Other**

Case 271

Defendants: **Alejandro Orona, Kelly Munn**

Victim: Scott Anthony Sartain

Trial: May 2009 Jurisdiction: Tarrant County, Texas

Murder: September 6, 2007

Evidence: Victim was a homeless man addicted to methamphetamine and an insulin-dependent diabetic. Victim convinced a friend to cash a forged check for which she was arrested. The arrested friend's husband confronted victim at defendants' house, striking him.

Defendants attacked victim when he tried to leave, brutally beating him. Several witnesses saw the beating and fled. The next day, one of the witnesses heard moans coming from defendants' garage and saw blood on defendants' shoes. The defendants' told several witnesses over the next few days that victim was in the garage and referred to him as the "dog." Munn told a witness they had beaten victim because he owed them money. A few days after the fight, Munn asked a witness to bring floor cleaner. The witness stated that the house smelled like garbage and dryer sheets had been stuffed into air vents. The witness saw a hacksaw and knives on a table, and saw Munn hold up victim's severed head. Munn told another witness that they had cut up victim's body and asked for help loading trash bags into a trailer. More witnesses helped abandon the trailer, cut up victim's car for scraps, and burn the trash bags. Investigators were tipped off several months later and found possible traces of blood in defendants' house. Defendants convicted of murder and sentenced to life imprisonment. Orona's writ of habeas corpus denied in 2013.

Sources: *Orona v. State*, 341 S.W.3d 452 (Tex. App. 2011); *Orona v. Stephens*, United States District Court, N.D. Texas, Fort Worth Division, No. 4:12-CV-662-A, July 17, 2013; http://www.star-telegram.com/news/story/1642274.html

Keywords: **Eyewitness, Forensic evidence: Other, Life**

Case 272

Defendants: **Raogo Ouedraogo, Rami Saba**

Victim: Donald Leo Dietz

Trial: March 2011/May 2011 Jurisdiction: Ionia County, Michigan

Murder: September 2007

Evidence: Victim was a reclusive retiree with few social contacts living in a secluded area of Michigan. Victim had $450,000 in retirement savings. Victim last contacted his bank on September 11, 2007. A few days later, someone with a Middle Eastern accent impersonating victim called his credit union to request a complete transfer of his money to a Lebanese bank account controlled by Saba's father. Victim's signature was forged on two checks. Defendants were close friends. Saba lived near victim, and Ouedraogo visited him frequently from Philadelphia. Both defendants were near victim at the time of his disappearance, as evidenced by phone records. Saba was a sales representative and reviewed victim's savings in order to persuade him to buy life insurance. Saba was having financial difficulties and was failing to meet his sales quota at work. Defendants were visiting and calling each other with increasing frequency in the months before the murder, funded in part by Saba, despite his financial difficulties. Defendants were deceptive during police interviews when questioned about the frequency of their visits. Two months before the murder, defendants procured pepper spray and a stun gun. Ouedraogo changed hotels inexplicably the day victim disappeared. Defendants kept a SIM card that their wives were unaware of so they could communicate in secret, and Saba used a Tracfone ostensibly to cover his call history. The Tracfone was used to call victim's bank to transfer money. When defendants had difficulty transferring the money, they forged a notary letter and impersonated victim to seek the help of victim's brother. Defendant confessed to a fellow inmate. Saba convicted and sentenced to 32 years. Ouedraogo was convicted of kidnapping resulting in death, but a judge later acquitted him because the evidence did not support the charges and only implicated Saba. Ouedraogo was released in 2011, but in September 2013, the Sixth Circuit affirmed only the ruling on the kidnapping-resulting-in-death charge and reinstated defendant's convictions for conspiracy and disallowed a new trial.

Source: *United States v. Ouedraogo*, 531 Fed.Appx. 731 (6th Cir. 2013)

Keywords: **Forensic evidence: Other, Informant**

Case 273

Defendant: **Alvin Owens**

Victim: Ernest Vereen

Trial: January 1985 Jurisdiction: Horry County, South Carolina

Murder: October 10, 1984

Evidence: On the night of October 10, 1984, Vereen, a 72-year-old man, was kidnapped, and murdered during the commission of this kidnapping. His body was never found, although there was evidence of a struggle at his home and his medication was left behind. The victim had a reputation for being dependable and had pending business plans at the time of his disappearance. The victim had a substantial amount of available income and credit that he never made an attempt to use. His son received a ransom demand and a threat that his father, who was allegedly "under sedation," would be murdered if he did not respond. Several drafts of this note, along with marked ransom money, were found in defendant's possession. Defendant made several incriminating statements both to investigators and other inmates, and although he raised several allegations of mistakes made, all of these were found to be without merit. In affirming, the court held that given the unlikelihood of victim's voluntary absence and in light of the circumstantial evidence, there was sufficient cause to establish the corpus delicti of his death by the criminal act of another. Defendant was convicted of kidnapping and sentenced to life imprisonment. Based upon the same facts, he was also convicted of murder in 1986 and was sentenced to death. The court affirmed his conviction and sentence, but his death sentence was later vacated and defendant was granted a new trial on the murder charge. In February 1991, Owens was retried for murder, convicted again, and sentenced to life in prison. This conviction and sentence were affirmed.

Source: *South Carolina v. Owens*, 424 S.E.2d 473 (1992)

Keywords: **Life, Informant, Confession to police**

Case 274

Defendant: **Rodney E. Owens**

Victim: Glenda Gail Furch

Trial: October 2008 Jurisdiction: Tarrant County, Texas

Murder: September 2007

Evidence: Victim was defendant's neighbor. Victim had very predictable habits and routines, and disappeared after leaving work in September 2007. Victim's daughter went to victim's apartment and found a large bleach stain on the bedroom carpet, and saw that victim's comforter and top sheet were missing. The carpet had been vacuumed, but the vacuum cleaner and all the trash cans were removed. In the apartment dumpster, investigators found used rolls of duct tape and electrical wires cut and tied into ligatures. Witnesses saw defendant driving victim's car shortly before it was abandoned and set on fire. Defendant had recently broken up with his long-term girlfriend and was very upset. Shortly after victim's car was burned, defendant carjacked a woman at gunpoint and then fired shots at his girlfriend's new boyfriend. When defendant was apprehended, investigators found duct tape, surgical gloves, and phone cords tied into ligatures. DNA analysis linked both victim and defendant to each of five trash bags found in the dumpster that were determined to have come from victim's apartment. Specifically, defendant's DNA and fingerprints were found on items in the trash bag that had belonged to victim. Defendant convicted and sentenced to life imprisonment.

Sources: http://www.tdcaa.com/node/3890; http://www.star-telegram.com/2008/10/09/963141/owens-gets-life-in-prison-for.html; http://www.wfaa.com/news/local/64591437.html

Keywords: **Life, Forensic evidence: DNA**

Case 275

Defendant: **Robert William Pann**

Victim: Bernice Gray

Trial: January 2001 Jurisdiction: Macomb County, Michigan

Murder: December 26, 1991

Evidence: Victim was defendant's estranged girlfriend. Victim had recently moved out of defendant's home, and defendant was angry because victim rejected his marriage proposal and wanted to date other men. Victim told witnesses that defendant had threatened to kill her after she rejected his marriage proposal. A witness heard a gunshot near the daycare of victim's daughter. The prosecution contended that defendant shot victim in her car after taking their daughter to daycare, and then buried her body. Witnesses testified about victim's routine and the unlikelihood of her abandoning her daughter to prove that victim would not have voluntarily disappeared. When victim went missing, defendant was unwilling to look for her. Victim's car was found four days later with victim's blood inside. Investigators also recovered two shell casings and a spent bullet. Medical examiner testified that victim was shot in the driver's seat and then pushed onto the passenger seat. Defendant returned the engagement ring he had bought that day and tracked mud into the store. He also told victim's mother he had been digging all day. One witness had seen two pistols in defendant's home prior to the murder. Defendant convicted of first-degree murder and sentenced to life imprisonment without the possibility of parole.

Sources: *People v. Pann*, Court of Appeals of Michigan, Docket No. 27103, September 13, 2007; *Pann v. Warren*, United States District Court,

E.D. Michigan, Southern Division, No. 5:08-CV-13806, September 29, 2011

Keywords: **Life, Forensic evidence: DNA, Eyewitness**

Case 276

Defendant: **Sam Parker**

Victim: Theresa Parker

Trial: August 2009 Jurisdiction: Walker County, Georgia

Murder: March 21, 2007

Evidence: Victim was defendant's wife. Defendant had a history of alcohol and domestic abuse, and he and victim were in the process of a divorce. Victim had found her own apartment and was in the process of moving when she disappeared. Witnesses testified that defendant frequently bragged that he knew the local woods well enough to ensure that he could successfully hide a body if need be. Prosecutor's relied heavily on the timeline, showing how defendant had opportunity to kill victim and put her body in his trunk, meet a friend to establish an alibi, and then bury victim. Defendant's former wife testified that defendant once put a gun to her head, choked her, dragged her through broken glass by her hair, and handcuffed her to a bed. Defendant made several inconsistent statements to police regarding victim's disappearance and did not participate in searches for her. Blood matching both victim and defendant was recovered from defendant's car. Defendant was fired a few months later for keeping explosives in his locker at work. Defendant convicted of first-degree murder and sentenced to life imprisonment. Body found in September 2010, 12 miles from defendant's house.

Sources: http://www.daltondailycitizen.com/local/x124774099/Theresa-Parker-s-body-found-more-than-three-years-after-disappearing; http://www.chattanoogan.com/2009/9/3/158127/Sam-Parker-Found-Guilty-Of-Murder.aspx; http://www.wrcbtv.com/story/10938561/parker-files-appeal

Keywords: **Life, Forensic evidence: DNA**

Case 277

Defendant: **Christopher Matthew Payne**

Victim: Tyler Christopher Payne

Trial: February 2009 Jurisdiction: Pima County, Arizona

Murder: March–September 2006

Evidence: Victim was defendant's 4-year-old son. Defendant and his girlfriend starved and abused victim to death along with his 3-year-old sister, whose remains were found in a trash bin. Defendant's girlfriend complained about the children misbehaving, so defendant started locking the children in a closet while he was away. By June 2006, they were permanently locked in the closet. Defendant stopped feeding them, bathing them, or allowing them out to use the bathroom. Victim's sister died in August 2006, and her corpse was left with victim until he died one week later. In September, defendant put the bodies in a tote box, which stayed at a rented storage unit until defendant failed to pay the rental fee. Staff opened the unit and threw the tote box away because of the smell. One staff member contacted police, who found victim's sister's remains in the dumpster. Defendant confessed to allowing the children to die. In the closet, investigators found blood and patches of body fluids. A hole in the wall was stuffed with human hair and feces. Defendant's girlfriend agreed to testify against defendant as part of her plea bargain. Defendant convicted on two counts of first-degree murder and sentenced to death. Conviction and death sentence upheld in November 2013.

Sources: *State v. Payne*, 674 Ariz. Adv. Rep. 5, (Ariz. 2013); *State v. Payne*, 306 P.3d 17 (Ariz. 2013)

Keywords: **Death penalty, Confession to police, Codefendant testimony, Forensic evidence: Other, Forensic evidence: DNA**

Case 278

Defendant: **Joseph A. Peel, Jr.**
Victims: Judge Curtis and Marjorie M. Chillingworth
Trial: 1961 Jurisdiction: Palm Beach County, Florida
Murder: June 14, 1955

Evidence: Victims were a state judge and his wife, and defendant was a municipal court judge. Defendant had been committing several ethical violations and believed victim, his superior, was going to expose him and thereby end his career. Defendant hired Floyd "Lucky" Holtzapfel to kill victims. Holtzapfel and an accomplice forced victims into a boat at gunpoint after waking them up in the middle of the night, drifted out to sea, then threw victims overboard with weights strapped to their legs. The next day, investigators found a shattered porch light, drops of blood, and two used spools of adhesive tape in victims' home. Case was highly publicized, and Holtzapfel began bragging about his knowledge of the murder to a witness. The witness cooperated with law enforcement in getting Holtzapfel drunk in a hotel room and asking him details about the murder. Investigators in the adjacent room recorded the conversation. Holtzapfel and accomplice testified against defendant, alleging that defendant also had other targets. Defendant pleaded *nolo contendere* to being accessory before the fact to first-degree murder and was sentenced to life imprisonment.

Sources: *Peel v. State*, 210 So.2d 14 (Fla. Dist. Ct. App. 1968); http://www.historicpalmbeach.com/tag/chillingworth-murders/; http://thetallahasseenews.com/index.php/site/article/trial_of_the_century_happened_in_florida_a_glimpse_of_prison_life_of_the_ki

Keywords: **Life, Codefendant testimony**

Case 279

Defendant: **John Christopher Peeler**
Victim: Chris Cummings
Trial: 1995 Jurisdiction: Arkansas
Murder: December 19, 1992

Evidence: Victim allegedly raped defendant's 15-year-old girlfriend, later his wife. Victim, a high school sophomore, disappeared after telling his parents he was going to watch a movie with "Amy," the name of defendant's girlfriend. Two years later, defendant's wife told a witness that defendant killed victim for raping her. Defendant's wife was arrested and testified about her role in kidnapping victim, implicating defendant in his murder. She stated that she picked victim up her in car, with defendant hiding in the rear floorboard. Defendant tied victim up and put him in the trunk, then took his girlfriend home. He told her the next day he had killed victim and dumped the body in water. Defendant confessed to his mother and his uncle and at least one other witness. Defendant convicted of murder and sentenced to life imprisonment without parole.

Source: *Peeler v. State*, 932 S.W.2d 312 (Ark. 1996)

Keywords: **Life, Codefendant testimony, Confession to friends and family**

Case 280

Defendants: **Alphonse "The Kid" "Allie Boy" Persico, John "Jackie" DeRoss**

Victim: William "Wild Boy" Cutolo, Sr.

Trial: 2006/November 2007 Jurisdiction: Brooklyn, New York

Murder: May 26, 1999

Evidence: Persico was a member of the Colombo crime family that was competing with other members for leadership, leading to an intra-family war that resulted in about a dozen killings. Victim supported defendant's rival during this war. After the factions reconciled, defendant became acting boss and victim became his underboss, but most of the family believed victim aspired to be boss himself. Witnesses within the family indicate that victim's death was planned well in advance. The day before victim's disappearance, defendant and victim contacted each other several times, and victim told his girlfriend that an appointment had been moved to the next day. He told his wife that he had to meet defendant. A witness dropped victim off near an overpass where he frequently met with defendant, after which victim disappeared. Codefendant DeRoss, the new underboss, went to victim's house eight hours later and demanded records from victim's wife, and threatened victim's family about making statements about victim's death or disappearance. Victim's wife stated that if victim had gone on the run, he would have taken the $1.65 million he had hidden in their house. Members of other crime families testified that it was protocol for the crime family to investigate the disappearance of a member, but no such investigation was conducted for victim. Codefendant DeRoss made statements that victim "had to go" because he was too powerful and cancelled the debts that other members owed victim. Victim's son, also a Colombo member, made undercover recordings of defendant threatening victim's family. First trial resulted in a hung jury. Victim's wife did not testify at first trial because of defendant's threats against her family. At second trial, victim's wife testified, and defendant and codefendant were convicted of murder in aid of racketeering. FBI recovered victim's buried body on October 6, 2008.

Sources: *United States v. Persico*, 645 F.3d 85 (2nd Cir. 2011); http://www.justice.gov/usao/nye/pr/2007/2007dec28.html

Keywords: **Confession to family and friends, Informant**

Case 281

Defendant: **Christopher Michael Phillips**

Victim: Trinity Nicole Robinson

Trial: August 2010 Jurisdiction: Miami-Dade County

Murder: May 1993

Evidence: Victim was defendant's 18-year-old girlfriend. Witness testified that defendant was jealous and abusive. At the time of her disappearance, victim's coworkers were collecting money so victim could flee back to her home in North Carolina. Defendant told 13 conflicting stories about victim's disappearance and tried to claim her last paycheck. Defendant admitted to several witnesses that he had choked victim to death. Case was reopened in 2000 after defendant's new wife told police that defendant abused her and had threatened to make her go missing like victim. Investigators believe that defendant's roommates at the time, convicted for a separate murder, helped him dispose of the body. Defendant convicted of second-degree murder and sentenced to life imprisonment.

Sources: http://articles.sun-sentinel.com/2010-09-02/news/fl-miami-phillips-trial-20100902_1_robinson-case-lon-martin-south-miami-dade; http://www.digtriad.com/news/story.aspx?storyid=149337

Keywords: **Life, Confession to friends and family**

Case 282

Defendant: **Dominick "Skinny Dom" Pizzonia, Alfre DiCongilio**

Victim: Frank "Geeky" Boccia

Trial: May 2007 Jurisdiction: Brooklyn, New York

Murder: June 1988

Evidence: Defendants and victim were associates of the Gambino crime family. Victim punched his mother-in-law, who was married to an imprisoned member of the Gambino family. In retaliation, defendants allegedly lured victim to a club, shot him to death, took the body out on a boat, punctured the lungs to let out the air, then sank the body. Six months later, Pizzonia became a made member of the Gambino family, allegedly as a reward for the murder. Victim's brother-in-law, who defected from Gambino family, testified about his role in the murder and stated that he witnessed Pizzonia shoot victim to death. Defendants acquitted of murder because jury felt there was insufficient evidence without a body. Pizzonia was later indicted for two other murders.

Sources: http://www.nytimes.com/2007/04/11/nyregion/11mob.html?scp=6&sq=%22Dominick%20Pizzonia%22&st=cse; http://www.nydailynews.com/new-york/contract-old-queens-gang-lair-article-1.1037328

Keyword: **Eyewitness**

Case 283

Defendant: **Farid "John" Popal**
Victim: Samiya Haqiqi
Trial: April 2006 Jurisdiction: Queens, New York
Murder: November 12, 1999
Evidence: Victim was defendant's girlfriend, an Afghan immigrant and a student at Quinnipiac College. Defendant allegedly killed victim when she rejected his marriage proposal. Victim was on her way home from school when she disappeared. Her abandoned car was found in a parking lot one block away from defendant's home in Queens. Phone calls from defendant's cell phone place him in the area at the time of disappearance. Defendant's brother was charged with helping dispose of the body and personal effects by burning them in an auto repair garage where investigators later found a singed lock of victim's hair and maggots in the catch basin. A witness saw a man carrying a rolled up carpet into the garage. Defendant's brother told a witness that defendant had beaten up his girlfriend and dumped her body upstate. Defendant asked other witnesses for help cleaning up evidence of a fire in the garage and replacing the front passenger seat of his car. He then filed a false police report saying his car was stolen. After the murder, defendant and his brother went to Canada and then California. At his arrest, defendant stated that victim was a whore and he had to be a hero in Afghanistan. Defendant convicted of second-degree murder and sentenced to 26 years to life imprisonment.
Sources: *People v. Popal*, 62 A.D.3d 912 (N.Y. App. Div. 2009); http://queensda.org/Press%20Releases/2002%20Press%20Releases/08-August/08-06-2002a.htm; http://www.qchron.com/editions/north/two-arrested-in-disappearance-of-law-student-from-flushing/article_bdf0bc48-8e46-5866-aada-3034f77deaf3.html
Keywords: **Forensic evidence: DNA, Forensic evidence: Other, Confession to friends and family**

Case 284

Defendant: **John "Nazi John" Franklin Price**
Victim: Donald Jessup
Trial: November 2008 Jurisdiction: King County, Washington
Murder: December 2004
Evidence: Defendant and victim were members of rival motorcycle gangs. Defendant believed victim stole his Harley-Davidson and was trying to sell it back to him for $800. Defendant allegedly beat victim with an axe handle then shot him in the face. Two witnesses in defendant's house at the time testified to hearing a gunshot, and one testified to seeing victim's body and hearing defendant call someone to say the "garbage had to be disposed of." Defendant wrote one of the witnesses letters from jail, asking her to lie about what she knew. Witnesses stated that defendant admitted to rolling victim's body in a rug and burying him. Defendant convicted of murder and sentenced to 35 years imprisonment. Conviction and sentence reversed because defendant was not allowed to watch part of the jury selection.

Defendant pleaded guilty to murder in 2012 and admitted to shooting victim in the mouth.

Sources: *State v. Price*, 162 Wash.App. 1054 (Wash. Ct. App. 2011); http://seattletimes.com/html/localnews/2008263501_price14m.html; http://www.kirotv.com/news/news/prison-intercepts-photos-human-skeleton-another-bo/nXj8q/

Keywords: **Eyewitness, Confession to family and friends**

Case 285

Defendant: **Lemuel Prion**
Victim: Diane Vicari
Trial: January 1999 Jurisdiction: Pima County, Arizona
Murder: October 22, 1992

Evidence: Victim was last seen leaving a bar with defendant; however, the witness was initially unable to identify defendant until his picture was published in the newspaper 17 months later. Victim's severed arms were recovered from a downtown dumpster. Defendant convicted of murder and sentenced to death. Conviction overturned on appeal because trial court committed reversible error by excluding evidence of another suspect who had also been seen with victim on the night of her disappearance and had been fired from work the next day for being disheveled and disoriented. Defendant was also charged at the same trial with sexually assaulting another woman, and the Arizona Supreme Court ruled that the cases should not have been heard at the same time. On March 14, 2003, Pima County Attorney's Office dismissed all charges against defendant.

Sources: http://www.deathpenaltyinfo.org/arizona-1; http://tucsoncitizen.com/morgue2/2000/10/04/143743-victim-s-mom-finally-with-diana/; http://www.law.umich.edu/special/exoneration/Pages/casedetail.aspx?caseid=3551

Keyword: **Eyewitness**

Case 286

Defendant: **Michael Duane Pyle**
Victim: Golda Millar
Trial: 1972 Jurisdiction: Kiowa County, Kansas
Murder: April 1971

Evidence: Victim was defendant's grandmother. Defendant lived with victim for several years, but tension developed when defendant married and his new wife moved in as well. Defendant began abusing victim and eventually moved out. Victim revoked her will, which had left defendant as primary beneficiary, but defendant was unaware of this revocation at the time of the murder. Defendant also tried to have victim declared incompetent so he could take control of her ranch, after which she revoked his power of attorney and then tried to sell her ranch. Victim was last heard from on April 5, 1971, and three days later, her ranch home burned to the ground. In the interim, defendant told sheriff that victim had been drunk for three weeks and was vomiting blood. Defendant and his wife told witnesses about a fire at the ranch days before the actual fire. Defendant called his wife, in front of a witness, to report victim's death by fire two hours before he was informed about it. Victim's dog's body was found in the house with a .22 caliber shell casing lodged in one eye socket. When defendant's alibi began to fall apart, he attempted suicide. In the hospital, he told police that victim had threatened to kill his wife, so when she was passed out drunk, he burned down the house. He later stated that he burned the house down because he was angry victim was trying to sell the ranch. Defendant convicted of first-degree murder and arson and sentenced to life imprisonment.

Sources: *State v. Pyle*, 532 P.2d 1309 (Kan. 1975); http://hutchnews.com/news/dead-town-Belvidere-Kansas—1

Keywords: **Life, Confession to police**

Case 287

Defendant: **Eric Cornelius Quick**

Victim: Linda Darlene Holder Watts

Trial: December 2008 Jurisdiction: Lee County, North Carolina

Murder: May 11, 2004

Evidence: A witness saw two men forcing victim into a vehicle as she walked home from work. The witness was later unsure whether the woman being forced was actually victim. Investigators later found her belongings and a pool of her blood nearby. Charges against defendant were dismissed at his trial because there was no physical evidence linking him to the crime and one of the state's witnesses failed to appear to testify.

Sources: Charley Project; http://www.wral.com/news/local/story/4101684/; http://www.seacoastonline.com/apps/pbcs.dll/article?AID=/20130103/NEWS/301030416

Keywords: **Forensic evidence: DNA, Eyewitness**

Case 288

Defendant: **Eugene Quillin**

Victim: Chris Duffy

Trial: 1985 Jurisdiction: Pierce County, Washington

Murder: Unknown

Evidence: Victim was an acquaintance of defendant and defendant's half-brother. Victim's mother's car was stolen at the same time victim disappeared, and defendant was seen driving it for several days before it was abandoned and burned. The clothing victim was last seen wearing was found in the vehicle. Defendant admitted to witnesses that he had killed victim. Another witness testified that victim was going to meet defendant the night of his disappearance. Defendant ultimately made a taped statement confessing to cutting victim's throat with a box cutter during a fight. Defendant told police that the fight started when defendant paid $2,000 for victim's car and victim would not give him the title. Defendant told another witness that the fight started when victim did not want defendant to drive his mother's car. Defendant and his half-brother then dumped the body over a bridge, and defendant tried to lead investigators to the spot. Defendant's half-brother pleaded guilty to second-degree murder. Defendant convicted of first-degree felony murder.

Sources: *State v. Quillin*, 741 P.2d 589 (Wash. Ct. App. 1987); http://community.seattletimes.nwsource.com/archive/?date=20000609&slug=4025628

Keywords: **Confession to friends and family, Confession to police**

Case 289

Defendant: **John Racz**

Victim: Ann Mineko Racz

Trial: August 2007 Jurisdiction: San Fernando, California

Murder: March-April 1991

Evidence: Victim was last seen dropping her three children off at the residence of her husband, the defendant, on March 22, 1991. Victim and defendant had separated four days prior. After victim's disappearance, defendant claimed that she had left on an extended vacation. Investigators found cold pizza in victim's condominium, contrary to her reputation as a meticulous housekeeper. Victim had very methodical habits, strong ties to the community, and was unlikely to vanish on her own. Victim had expressed to friends that she was afraid of defendant and thought he might kill her. Nearly 30 witnesses testified at trial, including the couple's children and a pastor who saw scratches on defendant's face. Defendant was convicted of first-degree murder.

Sources: *People v. Racz*, Second District Court of Appeals No. B203267; Charley Project; http://www.laweekly.com/2007-09-20/news/former-deputy-gets-life-in-prison/; http://www.dailynews.com/general-news/20070822/john-racz-convicted-of-murdering-his-wife

Keyword: **Eyewitness**

Case 290

Defendant: **Harvey Rader**

Victims: Michelle Houchman, Elaine Salomon, Sol Salomon, Mitchel Salomon

Trial: July 1992 Jurisdiction: Northridge, California

Murder: October 1982

Evidence: The four victims were an immigrant family from Israel. Defendant was a British citizen who owned a car dealership in Reseda, California. The father of the victims' family, Sol Salomon, invested $20,000 in Rader's dealership and was last seen with Rader on October 12, 1982, the day of the family's disappearance. Authorities discovered spatters of blood in the victims' family's residence and a piece of carpet had been removed. The victims' family's passports, wallets, and photos were scattered along the Antelope Valley Freeway. In 1983, defendant's cousin claimed that he witnessed defendant shoot Sol Salomon after he and defendant argued about Salomon's investment in the car dealership. Defendant's cousin claimed that the rest of the family was killed because they knew that Salomon had been with defendant. Defendant's cousin also claimed that he helped bury the family in the desert. Defendant's cousin offered testimony in exchange for immunity, but immunity was revoked after he failed a polygraph examination demonstrating that he was more involved in the murders than he claimed. Defense witnesses claimed to have seen another victim, Sol Salomon, in a pharmacy in Carpinteria after the date of the alleged murder. Defendant was acquitted of murder.

Sources: Charley Project; http://www.seacoastonline.com/articles/20130103-NEWS-301030416; http://doenetwork.bravepages.com/979dfca.html

Keywords: **Eyewitness, Codefendant testimony**

Case 291

Defendant: **Naraine "Cyril" Ramsammy**

Victim: Annette Rabino

Trial: December 2006/March 2008 Jurisdiction: Broward County, Florida

Murder: January 2000

Evidence: Victim was defendant's common-law wife. Before her disappearance, defendant found out that victim was having an affair and was pregnant. Witnesses stated that defendant threatened to kill her and her boyfriend. The couple's son, 6 years old at the time, later testified that he witnessed defendant choking his mother the day before she disappeared. Defendant did not report victim missing for two months, and told witnesses several different explanations for her disappearance (that she had gone to Trinidad for an abortion, that she had been hospitalized for a suicide attempt, or that she had left). Five months after the disappearance, victim's mother received a typewritten letter supposedly from victim, stating that she had wronged defendant. The return address on the letter had the same zip code as the defendant's residence. A body was located in the Everglades swamp in 2004, and though DNA testing was inconclusive, the genetic profile was similar enough to victim's mother that authorities determined they must be biologically related. Defendant was convicted of second-degree murder. The conviction was reversed in August 2010, however, due to insufficient evidence. The appellate court judge was primarily concerned with witness testimony constituting extrinsic evidence and hearsay that was presented at trial without predicate. The testimony of defendant's childhood friend regarding statements from defendant's son was deemed unusable as substantive evidence.

Sources: Charley Project; *Naraine Ramsammy v. Florida*, Number 4D08-2028, District Court of Appeal, Fourth District, August 11, 2010

Keywords: **Forensic evidence: Other, Life, Eyewitness**

Case 292

Defendant: **Gary Lee Rawlings**

Victim: Sally Brown

Trial: Jurisdiction: Oklahoma City, Oklahoma

Murder: May 26, 1982

Evidence: Victim was defendant's ex-wife. In victim's petition for divorce, she stated that defendant beat her severely. In an affidavit signed in

March 1982, defendant acknowledged that he had an "uncontrollable temper" and pledged not to visit the couple's 2-year-old daughter for six months. Victim disappeared after leaving her daughter at a daycare center. Defendant picked the child up from daycare with a typewritten letter allegedly signed by victim. Witnesses close to victim stated she would not willingly leave her child with defendant. In the days leading to victim's disappearance, defendant leased a plane, rented a car, and purchased a handgun. There were bloodstains in the trunk and on the driver's side of the rental car, and blood was found in the cargo area of the plane. Defendants' cellmates testified that he discussed the gun used to kill victim, and described how to transfer the body from the cargo area of the plane to the front seat so it could be thrown out. The letter to the daycare center and a letter of resignation allegedly written by victim were typed on an IBM typewriter in the office of defendant's airline. Defendant's mother and experts testified that victim's alleged signatures on the letters were actually written by defendant. Investigators believe victim's body was dumped out of the plane over the Gulf of Mexico. Defendant convicted of first-degree murder and sentenced to life in prison.

Sources: http://newsok.com/without-body-proving-murder-more-difficult/article/2613699; *Rawlings v. Oklahoma*, 740 P.2d 153 (1987)

Keywords: **Informant, Forensic evidence: Other, Life**

Case 293

Defendant: **Arthur Nelson Ream**

Victim: Cindy Zarzycki

Trial: June 2008 Jurisdiction: Macomb, Michigan

Murder: April 1986

Evidence: Victim was a 13-year-old girl who was friends with defendant's son. Defendant lured victim to a Dairy Queen on the pretense of taking her to his son's birthday party. (In fact, defendant's son's birthday was in January, not April.) Friends of victim testified that victim told them she was meeting defendant the morning of her disappearance. One of these witnesses also testified that she saw a white van, similar to defendant's, in the Dairy Queen parking lot that morning. Defendant had prior convictions for the sexual assault and rape of young girls, and admitted in police interviews that he had a fetish for 13-, 14-, and 15-year-old girls. Defendant came under suspicion around 2004 and was incarcerated on a rape conviction. Defendant made many incriminating statements that led to his trial, but they were later ruled inadmissible. He also claimed he was shopping with his wife at the time of the murder, but she refuted this. There was no physical evidence, but a missing persons flier for victim was found among defendant's belongings. After his arrest in 2008, defendant claimed that victim died from an accidental fall in his warehouse. After his conviction, defendant led police to victim's body and claimed victim had died from an elevator accident at his carpet warehouse. Defendant convicted of first-degree murder and sentenced to life in prison without parole.

Sources: *Michigan v. Ream*, Court of Appeals, No. 288256, April 22, 2010; http://www.macombdaily.com/article/20080713/NEWS01/307139995&template = printart
Keywords: **Life, Eyewitness, Confession to police**

Case 294

Defendant: **Rudy Matthew Rebeterano**
Victim: Michael Guy Johnston
Trial: 1982 Jurisdiction: Box Elder County, Utah
Murder: July 22, 1981
Evidence: Victim was last seen at defendant's ex-wife's apartment. Victim had met defendant's ex-wife at a bar the previous night, and defendant became jealous when he saw the two of them talking and playing pool. Defendant had history of violence and jealousy, and had tried to run over a man who was helping his ex-wife move furniture. When victim and defendant's ex-wife returned to her apartment, defendant was waiting for them. Defendant and victim began shouting. Defendant's ex-wife left, but heard scuffling noises and a loud groan. Defendant's ex-wife hid across the street and watched defendant exit the apartment and load a large white bundle into trunk of victim's Ford Torino. That morning, police found fresh blood spatter that matched victim's blood type, and defendant's ex-wife stated that a bed sheet and several kitchen knives were missing. One of these missing knives was later recovered from the roof of her building. Victim's car was recovered, and the same blood type was found on the bumper and soaked into the trunk mat. The blood belonged to victim. Defendant failed a polygraph examination. Defendant was convicted of second-degree felony homicide and was released from custody after five years.
Sources: *State v. Rebeterano*, Supreme Court of Utah, No. 18428, April 30, 1984; Charley Project; Bradford, K., "Ex-wife testifies in murder trial of Rebeterano," *The Deseret News*, March 16, 1982
Keywords: **Forensic evidence: Other, Eyewitness**

Case 295

Defendant: **Charles Reddish**
Victim: Yeda Sharon "Dede" Rosenthal
Trial: June 2002 Jurisdiction: Cherry Hill, New Jersey
Murder: February 23, 1991
Evidence: Defendant was a maintenance worker in victim's apartment complex. He broke into her apartment, stole $80, and then smothered her to death. While under arrest for the 1995 murder of his girlfriend, defendant confessed to breaking into victim's apartment in 1991 and killing her so she could not identify him. Days later, he returned and dumped her body in a remote area of Salem County. Defendant led investigators to the site, but no body was recovered. Defendant was originally sentenced to death, but the conviction was reversed because prosecutor told jury that defendant was incarcerated when he

confessed to police. Defendant then pleaded guilty to manslaughter and was sentenced to life.

Sources: *State v. Reddish*, Supreme Court of New Jersey, 859 A.2d 1173(2004); http://articles.philly.com/2002-06-27/news/25350205_1_death-verdict-inmates-on-death-row-police-search; http://articles.philly.com/2005-07-30/news/25433001_1_suffocation-sentencing-body

Keywords: **Confession to police, Life**

Case 296

Defendant: **Hans Reiser**

Victim: Nina Reiser

Trial: April 2008 Jurisdiction: Oakland, California

Murder: September 2006

Evidence: Victim was a Russian national who married defendant, a U.S. citizen, and the inventor of Linux, a computer operating system. Victim and defendant separated in May 2004 but never completed divorce proceedings. During this time, she was also granted a temporary restraining order after allegations of abuse. Victim accused defendant of failing to pay medical and child-care expenses, for which defendant was scheduled to face trial. Victim disappeared after dropping their children off at defendant's home. Her vehicle was found several days later with groceries inside. Before authorities were alerted that victim was missing, defendant started picking his children up from school on days when victim would ordinarily have picked them up. Days after the disappearance, witnesses saw him washing his driveway and wearing heavy clothes despite the heat. Investigators found victim's blood on a sleeping bag cover in defendant's car. The car also contained trash bags, masking tape, murder books, a siphon pump, and absorbent towels. The car's front passenger seat was discovered to be missing (a traffic citation showed that it had not been missing three months earlier), and there was an inch of standing water on the floor. Blood containing DNA from both the defendant and victim was found on a pillar in the entryway of the defendant's home, but a forensic specialist later testified that the sample might have been contaminated. Defendant made attempts to evade police surveillance, which was used as evidence of "guilty conscience." Defendant convicted of first-degree murder, but agreed to plead guilty to second-degree murder in exchange for revealing the location of victim's body. He admitted to strangling victim, and her remains were discovered and positively identified. He was sentenced to 15 years to life.

Sources: http://www.sfgate.com/bayarea/article/OAKLAND-Man-s-home-searched-wife-is-missing-2469643.php; http://www.sfgate.com/bayarea/article/OAKLAND-DNA-match-of-bloodstains-in-case-of-2542328.php; http://www.sfgate.com/bayarea/article/Reiser-deal-ultimately-hinges-on-judge-s-OK-3205315.php; http://www.wired.com/threatlevel/2008/01/scientist-now-n/

Keywords: **Confession to police, Forensic evidence: DNA, Forensic evidence: Other**

Case 297

Defendant: **Jerry Rice**
Victim: Lindy Rice
Trial: March 1994 Jurisdiction: Wyandotte County, Kansas
Murder: September 14, 1992
Evidence: Victim was defendant's wife. On the night of September 14, 1992, victim telephoned her mother and stated that defendant was acting crazy so she was leaving and bringing the children to her mother's house. Defendant was allegedly demanding $20,000. Victim's mother never heard from her again, though they typically talked daily. Defendant stated that victim had left by car and was reluctant to file a missing persons report. Defendant gave the victim's mother a set of keys that victim had kept in secret at the bottom of her purse. Relatives stated that victim would never leave her children with defendant. Two of the victim's young children (ages 8 and 4 at the time of the murder, 10 and 6 at the time of the trial) later testified that they saw defendant beating her severely. They testified that victim had barricaded herself in an upstairs bathroom the next morning, and that when they tried to look inside, they saw their mother bruised and unresponsive on the floor. They never saw victim after that. Witnesses saw defendant operating a bulldozer near the landfill next to their property two days after victim's disappearance. The defense called several witnesses, who testified that victim had abandoned her children before and that she was seen after the alleged murder. A rebuttal witness, impeaching the first rebuttal witness, testified that defendant's sister told her that she had gone to defendant's house the morning after the murder, saw victim's body, and that defendant admitted to beating victim but that they had also made love afterwards and that she did not wake up the next morning. Defendant convicted of first-degree murder and sentenced to life imprisonment without the chance of parole for 40 years.
Source: *State v. Rice*, Supreme Court of Kansas No. 71971
Keywords: **Life, Confession to friends and family, Eyewitness**

Case 298

Defendant: **Mark Anthony Richardson**
Victim: Shelton Sanders
Trial: April 2008 Jurisdiction: Columbia, South Carolina
Murder: June 19, 2001
Evidence: Victim and defendant were roommates. Victim was last seen and heard from on June 19, 2001, scouting hotel rooms for a friend's bachelor party. His credit cards and cell phone have not been used since that date, and his car was discovered two months later, abandoned in a parking lot. Defendant stated that he and victim were at home alone that night. Witnesses from the neighborhood testified to hearing gunshots. Cell phone records place defendant near where the victim's car was found shortly after June 19, the date he was believed to have been murdered. The defense claimed that there was not sufficient evidence that victim was deceased, and the jury's failure to reach a verdict resulted in a mistrial.

Sources: Charley Project; http://www.nbcnews.com/id/9622250/#.UrjLK6X0BcQ
Keyword: **Forensic evidence: Other**

Case 299

Defendant: **Ronald Rickman**
Victim: Yvonne Rickman
Trial: August 1990 Jurisdiction: Appleton, Wisconsin
Murder: August 14, 1981
Evidence: Victim was defendant's wife. Victim disappeared after she and defendant went on a shopping trip. Defendant told police that she had taken concealed suitcases out of the car and left. The victim's sister reported her missing and stated that she would never have abandoned her daughter. Defendant had killed two people in 1962 but was found not guilty by reason of insanity. Victim had a handgun registered in her name, which defendant kept under the front seat of his car. Defendant was making sexual advances toward teenaged members of a youth group he was involved in and confided that he had marital problems. Defendant gave police, friends, and relatives conflicting accounts about victim's whereabouts and the circumstances of her disappearance. While incarcerated on separate charges, defendant told his cellmate that he had lied about his wife's disappearance, that he did not know if he killed his wife, and compared it to the deaths of the men he had killed in 1962. He noted that it would be hard to charge him because nobody had the gun or the body. The court noted striking similarities between the two murders, where defendant was alone with the victim(s), used a gun, was provoked to anger, and had no recollection of what happened after he became angry. Defendant convicted of first-degree murder and died in prison of natural causes in 2004.
Sources: *State v. Rickman*, Court of Appeals of Wisconsin No. 92-1744-CR; http://www.examiner.com/article/the-disappearance-of-vonnie-true-story-of-yvonne-rickman-ron-rickman
Keyword: **Confession to friends and family, informant**

Case 300

Defendant: **Paul Riggins**
Victim: Nancy Riggins
Trial: July 2001 Jurisdiction: Howard County, Maryland
Murder: July 1996
Evidence: Victim was defendant's wife. Defendant was in the midst of a four-year-long affair with the family's underage babysitter when his wife disappeared. He was later convicted of child abuse for having sex with the babysitter when she was 14 years old, and the babysitter later testified that he had asked her to marry him shortly after his wife's disappearance. She also testified that he said he would take care of victim after she threatened to reveal affair to babysitter's mother. Friends and relatives stated that victim would not have abandoned her daughter. Defendant was convicted of first-degree murder and sentenced to life imprisonment with the possibility of parole after

15 years. Prosecutors chose not to seek life without the possibility of parole so that defendant would have a reason to reveal the location of the body. Six years later, defendant told police where he had dumped his wife's remains.

Sources: *State v. Riggins*, Circuit Court of Maryland, No. 13K00039672, September 21, 2000; http://www.washingtonpost.com/wp-dyn/content/article/2007/10/22/AR2007102202179.html; http://articles.baltimoresun.com/2001-11-30/news/0111300354_1_riggins-anger-nancy; http://ww2.gazette.net/stories/112107/burtnew205030_32360.shtml; http://articles.baltimoresun.com/2004-02-27/news/0402270186_1_riggins-nancy-murder-conviction

Keywords: **Life, Confession to friends and family**

Case 301

Defendant: **Michael Rimmer**

Victim: Ricci Ellsworth

Trial: November 1998/2004 Jurisdiction: Shelby County, Tennessee

Murder: February 1997

Evidence: Victim lived with defendant while she was temporarily separated from her husband. In 1989, defendant was convicted of the aggravated assault and rape of victim. Victim disappeared from her workplace, the Memphis Inn, around 3 a.m. on February 8, 1997. A guest entered the inn and found the front desk empty and the bathroom covered with blood. The hotel manager inspected the scene along with investigators, and stated that it looked as though there had been a fight. She noted $600 missing in addition to towels, sheets, and bath mats. Victim's husband directed investigators to defendant. Defendant had been released from prison a few months prior to the murder, and immediately afterward he left Memphis, abandoning most of his personal belongings as well as his job, and failing to pick up his last paycheck. Investigators sent samples of the hotel towels and fabric from defendant's car for forensic examination, which revealed DNA types from the same individual present on all samples. DNA samples from victim's mother matched these same DNA profiles. During defendant's previous incarceration, he told fellow inmates that he would kill victim because she stopped sending him money. Defendant's brother testified that defendant came to his house the morning of February 8 with a shovel in the backseat, asking about how to get blood out of the seat. At his first trial in 1997, defendant was convicted of premeditated first-degree murder and sentenced to death. The death sentence was thrown out for procedural violations concerning irregularities in the jury verdict. The resentencing hearing in 2004 also resulted in the death penalty. The case has been plagued with allegations of prosecutorial misconduct and improper suppression of evidence favorable to defendant (eyewitness testimony placing another man at the scene). There are also allegations that a detective provided false testimony and that the prosecutor was aware this testimony was false. In October 2012, the conviction was overturned because the defense failed to adequately investigate case and because the lead prosecutor made false statements about the existence of the evidence. A retrial was set for July 2014.

Sources: *State v. Rimmer*, Court of Criminal Appeals of Tennessee, No. W2004-02240-CCA-R3-DD, August 13, 2007; http://usatoday30.usatoday.com/news/nation/2011-08-25-tennessee-prosecutor-misconduct-case_n.htm; http://californiainnocenceproject.org/blog/2012/10/17/tn-death-row-inmate-michael-dale-rimmer-released-prosecutorial-misconduct-or-ineffective-counsel/
Keywords: **Forensic evidence: DNA, Forensic evidence: Other**

Case 302

Defendant: **Robert Rivera**
Victim: Katelyn Rivera-Helton
Trial: March 2000 Jurisdiction: Delaware County, Pennsylvania
Murder: August 10, 1999
Evidence: Victim was defendant's 1-year-old daughter. Defendant was abusive to victim's mother while she was pregnant and after she gave birth in December 1997. In July 1999, victim's mother escaped with victim and filed assault charges against defendant. She gained sole custody of victim. On August 10, 1999, defendant attacked victim's mother at a convenience store, beating her, and dragging her by the hair and throat. When a passerby intervened, defendant fled and went to victim's daycare. He broke into the caregiver's house and forcibly removed victim. For the next several hours, he called victim's mother, threatening that she would never see victim again. Defendant and victim were last seen in his car at a gas station at 7 p.m. Defendant returned to the same station two hours later, and victim was no longer in the car. After his arrest, defendant told police that he had given victim to another woman. A friend of defendant's testified that defendant visited him the night of the kidnapping and that his spade went missing during that time. Defendant told a fellow inmate that he had suffocated victim, discarded her clothing, and asked the inmate to tell his lawyer that his friend committed the crime. The clothes and the spade were recovered, but not the body. Investigators testified that defendant continually insinuated that he murdered victim, but not overtly. Defendant convicted of second-degree (felony) murder and sentenced to life in prison.
Sources: *Com v. Rivera*, Superior Court of Pennsylvania, No. 411-00, August 18, 2003; Charley Project
Keywords: **Confession to friends and family, Informant, Eyewitness, Life**

Case 303

Defendant: **Ulysses Roberson**
Victim: Alexander Olive
Trial: December 2009 Jurisdiction: South Lake Tahoe, Utah
Murder: December 1985
Evidence: Victim was defendant's 4-year-old son. Defendant was angry that victim was mixed race and called him a "bad seed." Defendant was allegedly in a quasi-polygamist cult, and the victim's mother was one of his girlfriends whom he kept in a separate residence in

Sacramento. Victim lived primarily with defendant, who beat and tortured him in an apparent attempt to rid him of a demon. In the first week of January, defendant told victim's mother that he had sent victim to a Muslim school. One of defendant's other girlfriends came forward in 1997 and told investigators that she saw defendant holding victim in the air and beating him with firewood the night he disappeared. In 2001, investigators convinced another girlfriend to come forward. She testified that at the end of December, she saw defendant punching victim in the stomach in the garage. Soon after, defendant woke her from a nap and told her that victim was dead. Defendant carried the body in the house with a blanket and told others that he was sleeping, then placed the body in the tub with running water. She believed that defendant later loaded the body into a U-Haul van and then drove around with her in the passenger seat for several hours, stopping in two remote locations. DNA testing of a blanket recovered in a U-Haul at defendant's house showed that blood on the blanket originated from the offspring of defendant and the victim's mother. Defendant was charged with murder in 2001, and the case went to trial in 2009, resulting in a conviction of second-degree murder. He was sentenced to 15 years to life.

Sources: *People v. Roberson*, Court of Appeal, Third District, California, No. C064027, August 9, 2012; Charley Project

Keywords: **Eyewitness testimony, Forensic evidence: DNA**

Case 304

Defendant: **Wayne Clifford Roberts**

Victim: Surette Clark

Trial: 1996 Jurisdiction: Tempe, Arizona

Murder: 1970

Evidence: Victim was defendant's 4-year-old stepdaughter. Victim was killed in 1970, but she was not reported missing until 1994 when the defendant's sister told police that defendant admitted the murder to his brothers in 1971, claiming it was an accident. Defendant apparently shook the victim to punish her, and she became sick. Defendant panicked and buried her, possibly alive. Defendant and the victim's mother moved to Canada, from where he was later extradited. Victim's mother and the defendant's siblings testified against him at trial. Defendant convicted of second-degree murder and served 12 years in prison before being released on parole. Skeletal remains had been recovered in Tempe in 1979, but positive identification was not made until DNA analysis in 2010, after defendant had been released on parole.

Sources: http://www.azcentral.com/community/tempe/articles/2010/08/05/20100805tempe-child-197-cold-case-Identity-abrk.html; http://www.ottawacitizen.com/news/Case+murdered+girl+closed+after+years/3383494/story.html; http://www.upi.com/Top_News/US/2010/08/05/DNA-closes-case-of-1970-Arizona-murder/UPI-30901281039300/

Keyword: **Confession to family and friends**

Case 305

Defendant: **Buddy Robinson**
Victim: Christiana Fesmire
Trial: 2012 Jurisdiction: Androscoggin County, Maine
Murder: July 1, 2011
Evidence: Victim lived in the apartment below defendant, defendant's twin sister, and defendant's nephew. Defendant's sister had previously hired victim to work as an escort as part of her online prostitution ring. Defendant got into an argument with victim while she was moving out and beat her until she hit her head against the bathtub. Then he drowned her in the tub. He wrapped the body in a comforter, placed it in the trunk of his sister's car, and later buried her in a swamp. He used victim's cell phone to call his sister to tell her he had fought with victim. Defendant's sister testified at trial that he had admitted the details of the murder to her. Her statements to police were initially inconsistent, but she agreed to tell the truth because the defense tried to make her an alternative suspect. Witnesses at the apartment that day overheard defendant referencing the body in the trunk, and defendant's sister confided to others that her brother murdered victim. Defendant also confessed to other witnesses, in person and via text message. These witnesses were granted immunity in exchange for their testimony. Victim's blood, identified through DNA analysis, was found in her home and in the car used to transport her body. Defendant later confessed to police as well, stating that he did not remember where he dumped the body. Defendant convicted of murder and sentenced to 55 years in prison.
Sources: http://bangordailynews.com/2012/11/09/news/lewiston-auburn/witness-says-brother-confessed-to-drowning-disposing-of-victim/?ref=relatedBox; http://bangordailynews.com/2012/11/10/news/lewiston-auburn/witness-says-murder-suspect-talked-of-body-in-trunk/?ref=relatedBox; http://host-38.242.54.159.gannett.com/news/article/222217/2/Buddy-Robinson-found-guilty-in-Fesmire-murder
Keywords: **Confession to family and friends; Confession to police, Forensic evidence: DNA**

Case 306

Defendant: **Gary Lee Robinson**
Victim: Tammi "T. J." Campbell
Trial: April 2010 Jurisdiction: Franklin County, Ohio
Murder: June 12, 1999
Evidence: Victim was defendant's ex-girlfriend. Defendant was allegedly abusive toward victim. She left Kentucky a year before her disappearance to escape defendant, but then later invited him to live with her in her new Ohio apartment. Victim was last seen on June 12, 1999, dropping her 12-year-old son off with a friend. She was planning to break up with defendant. She failed to meet her drug dealer at 3 a.m. and failed to show up at work the next morning. Victim's friend went to her apartment to look for her and found defendant there alone. Victim's personal belongings were there, and her car was parked across the street at a Dairy Queen. He claimed she was probably

out using drugs. Neighbors testified to hearing sounds of a struggle around 3:30 a.m. the night victim disappeared, and some of victim's jewelry was found buried in the backyard of defendant's parents. Defendant admitted the murder to another ex-girlfriend, stating that he had choked victim to death inside their apartment and disposed of the body in a local landfill. Defendant was convicted of murder and tampering with evidence and sentenced to 20 years to life in prison.

Sources: http://www.dispatch.com/content/stories/local/2010/04/10/despite-lack-of-body-jury-convicts-man-of-murder.html; http://www.dispatch.com/content/stories/local/2010/06/11/killer-sentenced-still-no-body.html; Charley Project

Keywords: **Confession to friends and family, Eyewitness**

Case 307

Defendant: **Tamara Robinson**
Victim: Tiana Martin
Trial: March 2006 Jurisdiction: Fresno, California
Murder: July–August 2003

Evidence: Victim was defendant's 10-year-old niece. Victim and her two sisters had been living with defendant a year before the murder. The defendant severely abused her three nieces, and ultimately beat victim to death. Victim's sister witnessed defendant confine victim to a hot garage without water, then beat her with a baseball bat, a meat tenderizer, and a curtain rod until victim collapsed. Defendant attempted CPR, but when she could not revive her she stuffed the body into a sleeping bag and left it in the apartment for several days before forcing victim's sisters to dispose of the body in a dumpster and clean the bloodstains. Victim was not reported missing until September 9, after family members began inquiring about the girl's disappearance. Defendant initially claimed that victim had run away, then claimed that victim's sisters had beaten her to death months earlier. Victim did not start school along with her sisters and had missed several important doctors' appointments in the months since her disappearance. One of victim's sisters confided to her vice principal that victim was dead. Both sisters testified against defendant at trial. Defendant was convicted of second-degree murder and felony child abuse and was sentenced to 15 years to life.

Sources: http://www.fresnobee.com/local/story/11975857p-12738050c.html; Charley Project; http://abclocal.go.com/kfsn/story?section=news/local&id=4308223

Keyword: **Eyewitness**

Case 308

Defendant: **Jesus Rodriguez**
Victim: Isabel Rodriguez
Trial: 2004/2005/November 2007 Jurisdiction: Miami, Florida
Murder: November 13, 2001

Evidence: Victim was defendant's wife. Victim petitioned for divorce in October 2001, and then obtained a restraining order against defendant when he threatened to kill her. Victim disappeared on November 13, 2001. The night before, defendant called a tenant on the victim's property and asked whether she would be going to work the next morning. On November 13, defendant's daughter drove to his farm and saw a fire burning on his property. She testified that defendant had scratches on his nose and was pressure cleaning his car, which had been seen at victim's house a few hours earlier. Defendant's girlfriend testified that defendant left the house that morning without scratches, but returned covered in them. Two days later, investigators transported defendant's car to the medical examiner's office and noticed substantial efforts had been made to clean the trunk. When detectives went to defendant's home, defendant stated that they didn't need to worry about the restraining order because victim would never come back. At his arrest in April 2002, defendant told officers that he had killed victim for money, not out of jealousy. Fellow inmates later testified that defendant confessed to killing victim with a baseball bat. The first trial was declared a mistrial due to witness tampering, and the second trial resulted in a mistrial when defendant hired someone to kill the prosecutor. At the third trial in 2007, defendant was convicted of first-degree murder as well as kidnapping and aggravated stalking and was sentenced to life in prison.

Sources: *Rodriguez v. State*, Court of Appeal of Florida, Third District, No. 3D08-182, February 10, 2010; Charley Project

Keywords: **Life, Informant, Confession to police, Confession to friends and family**

Case 309

Defendant: **Michele Roger**

Victim: David A. Richmond

Trial: August 1994 Jurisdiction: Sanford, Florida

Murder: September 6, 1992

Evidence: Victim was defendant's live-in boyfriend. Victim's daily phone calls to his parents stopped in September 1992. His parents reported him missing in October after defendant claimed that victim left their condo for Homestead, Florida. Defendant had stabbed victim to death then drove to her parents' house for help. Her father and brother rolled the body up in carpet and then carried it back to their car. The body was burned on a vacant lot, then possibly put through a wood chipper. The remains were then mixed with concrete in three separate boxes and dumped in the ocean. Investigators only found a small amount of blood at the couple's condo. Defendant described the disposal of the body to coworkers, who later testified against her. Defendant admitted at trial to stabbing victim, but claimed that she suffered from battered-spouse syndrome and that she only stabbed victim once after he tried to push her face onto a hot stove. Witnesses stated that both defendant and victim were extremely violent toward one another. Defendant had been treated for severe injuries in the past, and her defense attorney believes she was convicted based solely on her family's disposal of the body. Defendant convicted of second-degree murder and sentenced to 17 years in prison, which was later commuted to probation.

Sources: http://articles.orlandosentinel.com/1999-01-05/news/9901050218_1_clemency-mortham-roger; http://articles.orlandosentinel.com/1998-09-18/news/9809180418_1_roger-family-michele-abused; http://articles.orlandosentinel.com/1993-09-23/news/9309230548_1_jim-richmond-roger-co-workers; http://articles.orlandosentinel.com/1994-08-17/news/9408170048_1_david-richmond-jim-richmond-omara; *Roger v. State*, Court of Appeal of Florida, Fifth District, No. 94-2548, March 22, 1996

Keywords: **Confession to family and friends, Confession to police**

Case 310

Defendant: **Joseph Romano**

Victim: Katherine Romano

Trial: May 2002 Jurisdiction: Quincy, Massachusetts

Murder: September 26–27, 1998

Evidence: Victim was defendant's wife. Victim had decided to leave defendant and move out but changed her mind and stayed to stop the house from being foreclosed. She told defendant that he had until October 1 to move out. Defendant likely beat victim to death in their home, possibly with a baseball bat. He then chopped her up with a neighbor's chainsaw in front of their toddler son. After he returned the power saw, the neighbor's wife became suspicious because the blade had been replaced and contacted the police. Pieces of victim's bone, muscle, and tissue were found on the handle of the saw, and heavy blood spatter and deep human tissue were found in the home. Defendant claimed that victim had run away or that drug dealers had killed her, but his statements to police were inconsistent and victim had a history of notifying family members about planned trips. Defendant convicted of second-degree murder and sentenced to life in prison. Conviction upheld in August 2006.

Sources: http://www.dailynewstranscript.com/news/x253543419?zc_p=0; http://www.boston.com/news/daily/31/romano.htm

Keywords: **Life, Forensic evidence: DNA, Forensic evidence: Other**

Case 311

Defendant: **Robert Ruff**

Victim: Patsy Gaisior

Trial: November 1984 Jurisdiction: Washington, DC

Murder: December 3, 1980

Evidence: Victim left work on her lunch break on December 3, 1980, in Harrisburg, Pennsylvania. Defendant and his companion, Frank Johnson, both recently released from juvenile detention, abducted victim, a stranger to them both, on her lunch break and stole her car. Victim was last seen at the drive-up window of a bank a few hours later, accompanied by two black males who stayed with her while she withdrew $250. Defendant and Johnson arrived in Washington, DC, around 7 p.m. that evening, driving victim's car. Johnson was carrying a gun and victim's checkbook, and asked his mother and his sister to forge victim's signature on the checks. Both refused, and defendant threatened Johnson's mother, saying he would do to her what he had done to that girl. He then told Johnson's sister's roommate that he had stolen the car, killed the owner, and dumped her body in the Anacostia River. Johnson also told his sister that he had shot a white girl and thrown her body in the river. The next day, defendant left with Johnson's gun, victim's car, and victim's personal effects. He was arrested days later for a separate armed robbery and was still carrying these items. During this time, Johnson recounted their crime against victim to several family members. In May 1982, defendant was convicted in Pennsylvania of kidnapping, transportation of stolen vehicle, and conspiracy to kidnap. In 1984, defendant and Johnson were charged with murder, to which Johnson pleaded guilty. Defendant was convicted, largely based on Johnson's testimony.

Sources: *United States v. Ruff*, United States Court of Appeals, Third Circuit, No. 83-3100, September 23, 1983; Charley Project; Thomas A. (Tad) DiBiase

Keywords: **Codefendant testimony, Confession to family and friends**

Case 312

Defendant: **Edward Rulloff**

Victims: Harriet and Priscilla Ruloff

Trial: October 1856 Jurisdiction: Tioga County, New York

Murder: June 23, 1845

Evidence: Victims were defendant's wife and infant daughter, respectively. Defendant was a noted philologist, one who studies ancient languages, and he purportedly has the second largest brain ever recorded. Victims were last seen on June 24, 1845, and then were likely beaten to death by defendant. The next day, defendant borrowed a horse and wagon from a neighbor, apparently to transport a chest of tools. The neighbor helped defendant load a large, heavy wooden chest into the wagon. When defendant returned, he was seen lifting the box out of the wagon, suggesting it was substantially lighter. It was believed that the bodies were dumped in Cayuga Lake, but the lake was dragged without success. Defendant told victims' relatives that his wife had left him and had gone "between the lakes." Victim's brother arrested him, and defendant was convicted of his wife's abduction. After he had completed his 10-year sentence, he was arrested for her murder. Defendant claimed double jeopardy, so he was tried for the murder of his child instead. Defendant convicted of murder and sentenced to hang but escaped from jail in 1857. He was recaptured in 1860 and sentenced to hang again, but successfully appealed his conviction. It was determined that circumstantial evidence may be legally sufficient to convict someone of murder, even without a body, but that there must be unequivocal proof. Defendant was implicated in several other murders, and was finally convicted of the first-degree murder of a store clerk and was publicly hanged in 1871. Before his execution, he confessed to killing his wife by smashing her skull with the pestle he used to grind medicine, but did not confess to the murder of his daughter.

Sources: *Rulloff: The Great Criminal and Philologist,* 1905, Halliday, Samuel D., http://digital.library.cornell.edu/cgi/t/text/text-idx?c=cdl;cc=cdl;

idno=cdl140;view=toc;node=cdl140%3A7; http://www.murderbygaslight.com/2010/08/man-of-two-lives.html; http://www.trutv.com/library/crime/serial_killers/history/john_rulloff/11.html

Keyword: **N/A**

Case 313

Defendant: **Robert Peter Russell**

Victim: Shirley Gibbs Russell

Trial: May 1991 Jurisdiction: Quantico, Virginia

Murder: March 4, 1989

Evidence: Victim was defendant's wife and an officer in the U.S. Marine Corps. Defendant was formerly a member of the Marine Corps as well, but was discharged for disciplinary reasons. Witnesses stated that defendant was abusive toward victim and unfaithful. Victim consulted with a marriage counselor and ultimately decided to separate from defendant. They moved out from the married officer's quarters, and defendant purchased a Raven .25 caliber semi-automatic pistol. Victim arranged to meet defendant at the married officer's quarters at the Quantico military base on March 4 to prepare for a mandatory inspection. Victim disappeared sometime during the day. She has not been seen since, and all her bank accounts have been inactive. Throughout March 4, defendant began contacting her friends asking about her whereabouts, and alternately told other officers on the base that victim had gone to buy paint. That night, defendant borrowed his new girlfriend's car to drive to Pennsylvania to visit his parents, although he owned his own pickup truck. When he returned the car, it had been cleaned, waxed, vacuumed, and had a deodorizer hanging from the rearview mirror. Defendant then asked his girlfriend's father-in-law how to remove bloodstains from concrete. In the days after the murder, victim's commanding officer noted a rust-colored stain at the married officer's quarters, but the stain was removed by the time investigators came. The government's theory was that defendant shot his wife behind the ear while they were in a storage shed adjacent to their quarters and then dumped her body in a Pennsylvania mineshaft. Investigators uncovered a computer disk belonging to defendant that contained a file named "murder" with a 26-step guide to committing murder. Defendant's girlfriend, among other witnesses, testified that defendant had threatened to kill victim before, had showed his girlfriend a homemade silencer, and had discussed the best ways to kill a person. Defendant's ex-wife testified that defendant had previously threatened to kill her and dump her body in a Pennsylvania mineshaft. Defendant convicted of the federal offense of first-degree murder of an officer in the Marine Corps and sentenced to life. The conviction was upheld in August 1992.

Sources: *United States v. Russell*, United States Court of Appeals, Fourth Circuit, No. 91-5110, August 12, 1992; http://articles.mcall.com/1991-05-04/news/2801106_1_russell-s-family-verdict-four-women-and-eight

Keywords: **Life, Forensic evidence: Other**

Case 314

Defendant: **Katherine Rutan**
Victim: Logan Tucker
Trial: August 2007 Jurisdiction: Woodward, Oklahoma
Murder: June 23, 2002
Evidence: Victim was defendant's 6-year-old son. A former boyfriend and an ex-husband both testified that defendant was extremely abusive toward her two sons and especially toward victim. One former boyfriend testified that defendant said she wished there was some way she could kill her kids and get away with it. Two months before the murder, defendant's children were taken into protective custody when defendant told Tulsa police she was afraid she was going to hurt her children. Defendant also asked her parents to take custody of victim, but they declined and her children were returned to her. Defendant accused victim of trying to burn their house down and alternately tried to have him arrested or placed in inpatient psychiatric care at a hospital. Defendant and her two sons were sharing a home with Melody Lennington, defendant's boyfriend's coworker, at the time of the murder. On June 23, 2002, Lennington awoke to the sound of victim screaming. A short while later, she found defendant awake at the computer. Defendant told Lennington that victim was sick so she put him in a back bedroom. When Lennington left for work at 6 a.m. the next morning, defendant was still at the computer and told Lennington that she had moved victim to the basement. Victim was never seen again, and defendant told witnesses conflicting stories about where victim was, (including that the Department of Human Services had taken victim, that he had gone camping with her brother, or that he had been killed by a drunken driver), and that she was going to treat it as if victim were dead and tried to give away victim's clothes and toys. Defendant's brother called police the next week, asking them to check on defendant's sons. Defendant tried to evade police and told them that victim was with her brother. Defendant approached a stranger and asked him to leave a phone message, posing as her brother and stating that victim was OK. Investigators found a wad of masking tape in defendant's basement that contained clumps of victim's hair and blood. Drain cleaner, rope, and plastic were found in her car. Victim's younger brother, 4 years old at the time of the murder, testified that the last time he saw victim he was in the back seat of the car, that he was very white, and was not moving or speaking. The car stopped, and defendant carried the victim out toward a house blocked by trees, then returned without him. Victim's brother also testified that defendant borrowed a shovel to "bury Logan" and put dirt on Logan. Lennington noted her suitcase had gone missing, and a sanitation worker testified to seeing the same suitcase on the curb wrapped in plastic. Defendant convicted of first-degree murder and sentenced to life imprisonment without the possibility of parole. Conviction upheld in 2009.
Sources: *Rutan v. State*, Court of Criminal Appeals of Oklahoma, No. F-2007-1022, February 13, 2009; Charley Project; http://www.woodwardnews.net/x1155999849/Arrest-made-in-Tucker-case
Keywords: **Life, Eyewitness, Forensic evidence: DNA**

Case 315

Defendant: **Exondia Jaye Salado**
Victim: Manuel Salado
Trial: March 2011 Jurisdiction: Oklahoma County, Oklahoma
Murder: October 8, 2007
Evidence: Victim was defendant's husband. Witnesses claimed that the marriage was unstable, that both victim and defendant had had affairs, and victim wanted a divorce. The night before his disappearance, victim went to a friend's house and asked to stay the night because he was afraid defendant would kill him. He changed his mind after speaking with defendant over the phone. Victim was reported missing after failing to show up for a weekend of military drills as part of his Army Reserve basic training. Defendant claimed that victim left on his own, but his cell phone, credit cards, passport, and all his identification were left behind, along with his young daughter. A box of bullets was discovered at the home, with six bullets missing. Defendant's computer showed online searches for how to dismember a body, cannibalism recipes, how to build a barbecue pit, and how a body decomposes. Defendant told her lover and one other friend that she had shot victim in his sleep, cut his body into pieces, and stored it in a footlocker for several days before cooking the pieces in a grill. After the murder, defendant and her daughter moved in with her lover in Chicago. Then she moved to Florida, where she was arrested and charged in December 2008. Defendant convicted of first-degree murder and sentenced to life without parole. Appeal denied in October 2012.
Sources: http://newsok.com/former-lover-testified-exondia-salado-confessed-to-killing-husband-in-oklahoma-city/article/3551263; http://www.newson6.com/story/14344779/oklahoma-city-woman-convicted-of-fatally-shooting-husband-in-2007; http://www.blackchronicle.com/news/Archives/March-31.pdf
Keywords: **Life, Confession to friends and family**

Case 316

Defendant: **Jeffrey Salas**
Victim: Tony Epps
Trial: April 2009 Jurisdiction: Sedgwick County, Kansas
Murder: March 2007
Evidence: Victim and defendant had previously engaged in criminal activity together. Victim was last seen in Wichita on March 21, 2007, when he left to see a friend but never returned home. Two days later, his car was found parked at a restaurant with his cell phone locked inside. The state's theory is that defendant killed victim over an $18,000 drug debt. Shortly after victim's disappearance, defendant asked to keep his SUV in a friend's garage. The friend suspected the vehicle was stolen and contacted authorities. Small amounts of victim's blood was found in the garage and in the SUV. Defendant also allegedly told an ex-girlfriend "I did it" in reference to victim, but did not elaborate. Defendant acquitted of first-degree murder.

Sources: Charley Project; http://www.examiner.com/article/salas-murder-trial-ends-with-acquittal; http://cjonline.com/news/state/2009-04-15/bodiless_murder_trial_begins

Keywords: **Forensic evidence: DNA, Confession to friends and family**

Case 317

Defendant: **Tony Sandoval**

Victim: Kristina Tournai-Sandoval

Trial: August 2010 Jurisdiction: Greeley, Colorado

Murder: October 19, 1995

Evidence: Victim was defendant's wife, and she had left defendant three years prior to her disappearance because she found out he was suspected of using her car to stalk a woman. Defendant had a lengthy history of stalking, assault, and voyeurism prior to his marriage to victim. Victim was last seen on October 19, 1995, when she completed her night shift as a registered nurse. She notified friends that she was going to meet defendant to discuss financial issues and the divorce papers she had filed weeks earlier. She told witnesses that she was afraid to meet him, so she promised to call her sister no later than 12:30 p.m., but never made the call. Victim's car was found later, and a police dog traced her scent from her car to defendant's house a few blocks away. A neighbor across the street heard a single gunshot around 9 a.m. that morning. Authorities staked out defendant's home the day after the disappearance, and witnessed him return at 5:45 a.m. In his muddy car they saw a large bucket, muddy gloves, rope, a flashlight, a loaded 9 mm handgun, and a mud-caked shovel. When police knocked on the door, defendant's aunt answered and initially said he was not home. Then she allowed one of the officers inside while defendant was in the shower. He was caught a few minutes later climbing out of the bathroom window. Three of victim's credit cards were found in the bathroom and bedroom, and defendant had fresh scratches on his face and body. Investigators did not think they had enough physical evidence to charge defendant at that time. Defendant was not charged until 14 years later, mainly because the time lapse made it increasingly unlikely that victim was still alive and had disappeared of her own volition. Defendant convicted of first-degree murder and sentenced to life without the possibility of parole.

Sources: Charley Project; http://blogs.denverpost.com/coldcases/2008/03/02/new-profile-husband-mum-about-wifes-disappearance/22/2/; http://www.thedenverchannel.com/news/husband-charged-with-murder-14-years-after-wife-disappears

Keyword: **Eyewitness**

Case 318

Defendant: **Thomas Sax**

Victim: Matthew Pettersen

Trial: March 2003 Jurisdiction: Florida

Murder: September 2000

Evidence: Defendant, who murdered the victim with Tommy Ray Daigle, blamed victim for the drunken-driving arrest of their friend. The two men beat and strangled victim and put his body in a dumpster. Daigle testified at the trial that Sax had committed the murder by punching, stomping, and strangling the victim and that he, Daigle, had stabbed victim with a knife to put him out of his suffering. Defendant argued that Daigle had committed the murder. A friend of victim's also witnessed part of the attack. Sax's home was a bloody crime scene, and victim's baseball cap was recovered from a trash bin. Defendant obtained a license in his brother's name, fled to Colorado, and was seen with a bag full of bloody clothes. An inmate testified that defendant bragged he was going to get away with murder because he had taken care of "that kid" and he would not be found. Defendant also confessed to a friend of his brother's that he was a "murderer."

Sources: Stapley, G., "No-body murder cases often reach jury, some win," *Modesto Bee*, July 17, 2003; http://articles.sun-sentinel.com/2003-03-05/news/0303050169_1_matthew-pettersen-abbey-road-murder

Keywords: **Confession to friends and family, Codefendant testimony, Informant**

Case 319

Defendant: **Glyn Scharf**
Victim: Jan Scharf
Trial: September 2004 Jurisdiction: Placerville, California
Murder: May 14, 2002

Evidence: Victim was defendant's soon-to-be-ex-wife, who had initiated divorce proceedings in October 2001. Victim and defendant continued to live together throughout the divorce proceedings, though defendant was very opposed to the divorce. He told victim and victim's daughter that if he could not have her, no one could. In the month before she disappeared, victim claimed that defendant was poisoning her and tested positive for a heart medication that she had not been prescribed but which defendant had access to as a paramedic. Victim also reported a gun missing from their home. Victim was last heard from on May 14, 2002, when, while she drove home from work, she spoke by phone with a man she was dating. Around 8 p.m. that night, victim's next-door neighbor heard a woman screaming, followed by a woman saying "No, no, don't, don't," more screaming, and then a car driving off quickly. When the neighbor looked outside, defendant's car was gone. Victim's mother and daughter reported her missing four days later. Her car was found the next day in the parking lot of a health club she had frequented. There was evidence that victim did not voluntarily disappear: she was planning her daughter's wedding, had just been promoted, and was dating someone with whom she had made plans to meet two days after she disappeared. Her personal belongings had been left behind, and she had not told anyone she was planning to go somewhere, which was uncharacteristic for her. Defendant had made plans to visit his girlfriend the night of the murder, but canceled that afternoon because he had to do laundry. Two days later, he laundered his clothes at his girlfriend's house, which he had never done before, and investigators uncovered some of victim's jewelry buried in the same girlfriend's yard. Seventy-six witnesses testified at the trial. Defendant convicted of first-degree murder and sentenced to 25 years to life in prison. The conviction was upheld in 2006, and defendant committed suicide in prison in May 2007.

Sources: *People v. Scharf*, Court of Appeal, Third District, California, No. C048480, April 24, 2006; http://www.sacbee.com/2007/05/09/173625/scharf-guilty-of-murder.html; Charley Project

Keyword: **Eyewitness**

Case 320

Defendant: **Dennis Schermerhorn**

Victim: Logan Nathaniel Bowman

Trial: May 2004 Jurisdiction: Galax, Virginia

Murder: January 2003

Evidence: Victim was defendant's girlfriend's 5-year-old son. Defendant and victim's mother were both very abusive toward the victim, and witnesses frequently saw bruises on his body. Before his disappearance, victim was scalded on his legs, feet, groin, and buttocks. Victim was last seen at home on January 8, 2003, but his mother did not report him missing until January 23. The victim's father last saw victim at Christmas, but was told thereafter that he could not see victim because he was ill. In April 2003, defendant and his girlfriend were indicted for child neglect for failing to seek medical attention for victim's burns and for failing to report him missing for two weeks. A few months later, they were also charged with felony murder, arguing that victim's death was a result of defendants' failure to report him missing. Defendant's girlfriend entered an Alford plea and then testified against him, claiming that victim was scalded in the bathtub and defendant wouldn't allow her to take him to the hospital. When victim disappeared, defendant told her that he had taken victim to his mother, a nurse, but he was never seen again. Defendant's girlfriend claims he was probably sold, but has since told conflicting stories about her son's disappearance. Defendant claims that his girlfriend drove off with victim after he was burned and returned a day later without victim, claiming that he was with his father. In May 2004, the murder charge against defendant was dismissed based on a lack of evidence, and defendant was convicted only of child neglect and sentenced to one year.

Sources: http://www.roanoke.com/roatimes/news/story147363.html; http://www.roanoke.com/roatimes/news/story165423.html; Charley Project

Keyword: **Codefendant testimony**

Case 321

Defendant: **David Schubert**

Victim: Juliana Schubert

Trial: September 2002 Jurisdiction: Arlington, Washington

Murder: June 30, 1989

Evidence: Victim was defendant's soon-to-be-ex-wife, as divorce proceedings between the two were nearly complete. Prosecutors contended that, as an outcome of the divorce, victim would have likely been awarded full custody of their two children and the majority of their financial holdings. Defendant, a reserve police officer, told at least one witness that he wanted to kill victim to find peace for himself. Victim disappeared from her rural home, leaving behind all her personal belongings, her children, and her vehicle. Defendant claimed victim left voluntarily, but provided conflicting stories about where she had gone and from where she was calling him. He picked up her belongings from work and attempted to collect her last paycheck. He also claimed to have hired a private investigator to find her and told various people she was in Chicago, New York, and Arizona. He also admitted to a friend he would kill victim in order to get peace of mind. Defendant was first charged with second-degree murder in 1994, but the case was dismissed when the lead detective, a key witness, became too ill to testify and later died of leukemia. In October 2001, defendant was charged with first-degree murder, but the trial resulted in a jury deadlock. A third trial commenced in September 2002. Defendant convicted of second-degree murder and sentenced to 13½ years in prison. In 1998, victim's parents won a settlement against defendant when he was found to be victim's slayer.

Sources: http://www.seattlepi.com/news/article/13-1-2-year-sentence-for-1989-murder-1098836.php; Charley Project; *Nelson v. Schubert*, 994 P.2d 225 (Wash. App. 2000)

Keyword: **Confession to friends and family**

Case 322

Defendant: **Albert Raymond Scott**

Victim: Christine Gill Scott

Trial: January 1968 Jurisdiction: Piru Creek, California

Murder: March 13, 1965

Evidence: Victim was defendant's common-law wife and mother of their two daughters. Neighbors testified to hearing victim and defendant arguing frequently. Victim disappeared on March 13, 1965. Her regular letters to her mother stopped, and neighbors no longer saw her walking her daughters to school, as had been her daily habit. The night she disappeared, defendant and his stepson carried a heavy cardboard box from defendant's bedroom to the car. Defendant and the children drove to an area of Piru Creek and buried the box. A week later, defendant sold victim's clothing and sold his stepson a .22 caliber rifle he had purchased only a few weeks earlier. Defendant instructed his daughters to tell people that victim had left, and on the day of the burial, stated, "I got rid of her." Defendant also told his stepson that he had shot victim in the back of the head with the rifle. Defendant's calendar had the date of victim's disappearance circled. Underneath was written, "Chris left us." Defendant convicted of first-degree murder in a nonjury trial and sentenced to life imprisonment. Conviction was upheld in 1969.

Source: *People v. Scott*, Court of Appeal, Second District, Division 2, California, Cr. 14999, July 22, 1969
Keywords: **Life, Confession to friends and family, Eyewitness**

Case 323

Defendant: **Robert Leonard Ewing Scott**
Victim: Evelyn Scott
Trial: December 1957 Jurisdiction: Los Angeles, California
Murder: May 16, 1955
Evidence: Victim was defendant's wife of five years. Victim was older than defendant and substantially wealthier, with approximately $1 million in assets. Victim disappeared on May 16, 1955. Defendant provided conflicting stories regarding the disappearance, alternatively stating that she had run away or that she had been hospitalized. Two months later, defendant began a relationship with another woman. Victim's brother reported her missing in March 1956. By then, defendant had withdrawn large sums from victim's safe deposit boxes, deposited it into his own accounts, and replaced the missing funds with envelopes of sand. Victim's dentures, eyeglasses, and other belongings were found among buried ashes near the incinerator at the couple's home. Defendant fled to Canada after he was indicted for forgery and theft. While he was gone, he was indicted for murder and then arrested at the Canadian border. Defendant convicted of first-degree murder and sentenced to life imprisonment. Defendant rejected parole twice because it would have been a tacit admission of guilt, but after his release in 1978, defendant admitted to the murder to an author who had written a book on his case. He told her, on tape, that he hit victim in the head with a hard rubber mallet, wrapped her body in a tarpaulin, and then buried her body in the desert outside Las Vegas.
Sources: http://content.time.com/time/magazine/article/0,9171,868087,00.html; http://articles.latimes.com/1986-02-23/news/vw-11270_1_evelyn-scott; In re Scott's Estate, District Court of Appeal, Second District, Division 1, California, Civ. 23693
Keyword: **N/A**

Case 324

Defendant: **Rocky Seaman**
Victim: Loreese "Loree" Hennagin
Trial: 2000 Jurisdiction: Kenai Peninsula, Alaska
Murder: October 10, 1996
Evidence: Victim was defendant's brother's girlfriend. Victim and defendant's brother robbed defendant's mother of cocaine, jewelry, and cash. Defendant's brother and victim's mother testified that defendant and his mother made threats against victim after the robbery. Defendant and his mother planned to kill victim in retaliation, recruiting a drug dealer to assist them. The drug dealer later pleaded guilty to second-degree murder and testified against defendant, stating that he lured victim to a beach before paging defendant. Defendant arrived and started beating victim when the witness fled.

While under arrest for a separate charge, the witness confessed to a cellmate his role in victim's disappearance. Defense provided evidence that victim had voluntarily disappeared before, and suggested that her disappearance may have had something to do with her drug involvement. Defendant and his mother acquitted of murder but convicted of conspiracy and sentenced to 90 years in prison.

Sources: Charley Project; http://peninsulaclarion.com/stories/102600/new_1026000006.shtml; http://peninsulaclarion.com/stories/102500/new_1025000009.shtml; http://peninsulaclarion.com/stories/041501/new_0415010003.shtml

Keyword: **Codefendant testimony**

Case 325

Defendant: **Bryan Sedlak**
Victim: Patrick Kenney
Trial: February 2009 Jurisdiction: Homestead, Pennsylvania
Murder: February 2005

Evidence: Defendant and victim were allegedly using cocaine together at the back of a tanning salon at the time of the murder. Defendant claimed he killed victim in self-defense when victim ran out of cocaine and tried to rob him of money and drugs. Defendant testified that victim shot at him three times with a pistol before defendant returned fire with a .22 caliber rifle. He also claimed that a friend disposed of the corpse and would not reveal its location, but the friend later testified that he saw the body and did not move it. He stated that defendant bragged about the killing and claimed to have skinned victim. Witnesses testified that defendant admitted to killing victim and asked for help moving the body. Defendant convicted of third-degree murder. After his conviction, defendant led investigators to part of victim's remains in a failed attempt to reduce his sentence. Only nine bones were recovered, showing evidence of dismemberment by table saw. Defendant sentenced to 19 to 38 years in prison.

Sources: http://www.wpxi.com/news/news/classless-killer-gets-19-38-years-in-hidden-body-m/nGdx3/; http://www.post-gazette.com/frontpage/2009/02/19/Body-still-missing-but-man-convicted-in-killing/stories/200902190324; http://www.post-gazette.com/neighborhoods-city/2009/08/11/Sedlak-sawed-apart-corpse-sentenced-adamant-it-was-self-defense/stories/200908110106

Keywords: **Eyewitness, Confession to friends and family**

Case 326

Defendant: **William Seifert**
Victim: Mark Seifert
Trial: 1987 Jurisdiction: Cattaraugus County, New York
Murder: February 13, 1987

Evidence: Victim was defendant's brother. Defendant asked an acquaintance to pose as a secretary for Tri-State Developers, call victim on the phone, and read from a letter he had written. The letter indicated that victim was recommended for a contracting job and gave him detailed directions to a meeting site. Victim told several witnesses about the meeting, planned for February 13. Victim was last seen on this day at a restaurant near the proposed meeting place, where he told another witness about the meeting and verified the directions to the site, which was on a rural road. Witnesses in the vicinity of the meeting spot heard a single rifle shot that morning. At 10:45 a.m., victim's car was found at the proposed meeting site engulfed in flames. At the scene, investigators found pools of blood that matched victim's blood type and also contained bone fragments and brain tissue, but no human remains were found in the burnt vehicle. Defendant had not gone to work the morning of the murder. After being contacted by police, defendant left home and did not return for six days. Defendant's wife reported defendant missing along with two vans and one gun. One vehicle was recovered with identification markers removed. Fibers from the vehicle's carpet matched those recovered at the scene of the car fire. Human blood was found in the car containing a semi-rare enzyme found at the scene as well. When police found defendant, he claimed that Tri-State Developers had contacted him and had asked him to contact victim. Defendant was caught lying about his alibi and about his knowledge of the area where victim disappeared. Defendant convicted of second-degree murder. Conviction upheld in 1989.

Source: *People v. Seifert*, 152 A.D.2d 433 (N.Y. 1989)

Keywords: **Eyewitness, Forensic evidence: Other**

Case 327

Defendant: **Gary Shawkey**

Victim: Robert Lee Vendrick

Trial: May 2011 Jurisdiction: Orange County, California

Murder: February 15, 2008

Evidence: Victim was a 71-year-old retiree from Phoenix who made several failed investments, largely with defendant, whom he considered a friend and business partner since 2002. Several e-mails from defendant to victim involved pleas for cash, promising substantial returns. After investing nearly $1 million with defendant, victim became financially strained. Victim's wife began stopping money transfers to defendant and convinced victim to hire an attorney to recoup some of the lost finances. Defendant convinced victim that he had a secret computer deal and that they needed to travel by boat to a remote island south of Catalina in California. The deal also required victim to open a $100,000 bank account, and he was to net him $1.2 million in the next few weeks. Victim asked his brother for a personal loan to set up the account then flew to California. Defendant purchased a sailboat two days before victim's disappearance, and the seller demonstrated how to use the boat. The night before his disappearance, a woman with whom victim was having affair stayed with him in his hotel room. The next morning, victim told her to stay in the hotel and he would return later that day. He left behind his diabetes medication and computer. Defendant and victim both boarded defendant's sailboat, as recorded by surveillance cameras, in Dana Point Harbor bound for Catalina Island on the morning of February 15, 2008. En route to Catalina, defendant left victim several voicemails commenting that he hoped victim had already made it on the ferry. Defendant arrived on Catalina later that afternoon without victim. Defendant remained on Catalina and left more voicemails with victim. On February 19, he attempted to access the funds set up in the new bank account. Victim's wife reported him missing when he missed his return flight to Phoenix. In victim's rental car, investigators found a distribution directive calling for a disbursement to victim's brother, who had loaned him the money for the bank account. Defendant's DNA was on the directive, but it was unsigned. Defendant told investigators that victim was uncomfortable on the boat and so defendant dropped him back off on the dock. Defendant told several contradicting stories to investigators about the circumstances of the disappearance and about victim wanting to leave the country because of an illness or to be with his mistress. Defendant convicted of special circumstances murder for financial gain. Conviction upheld on September 3, 2013.

Source: *People v. Shawkey*, Court of Appeal, Fourth District, Division 3, California, G045698, September 6, 2013

Keywords: **Eyewitness, Life, Forensic evidence: DNA**

Case 328

Defendant: **Timothy Wayne Shepherd**

Victim: Tynesha Stewart

Trial: October 2008 Jurisdiction: Houston, Texas

Murder: March 2007

Evidence: Victim was the defendant's ex-girlfriend. Victim was a freshman at Texas A&M. Defendant killed her in his apartment when she came home for spring break because she had started dating someone else. Defendant disposed of the body by burning it on his two barbecue grills on his balcony apartment over the course of two to three days. The fire department was called, and one firefighter testified to seeing meat and bone floating in the bathtub. A neighbor testified that he had been burning something on the grills for days and then threw both grills in the dumpster. Defendant remained silent when questioned by police, but confessed to Quanell X, leader of Houston's New Black Panther party. He led investigators to the trash can where he left her body. Victim's teeth were found in the disposal. Defendant convicted of murder and sentenced to 99 years in prison. After his conviction, defendant confessed that he and victim fought about her new relationship and that victim grabbed a knife. Defendant stated that he grabbed her around the neck to disarm her but choked her to death out of anger then dismembered her with a jigsaw and barbecued the remains.

Sources: *Shepherd v. State*, Court of Appeals of Texas, Houston (14th Dist.), No. 14-08-00970-CR, January 11, 2011; http://www.khou.com/news/local/crime/stories/khou081003_tnt_shepherd_trial_quanellx.d88d95a8.html; http://www.chron.com/news/houston-texas/article/Harris-County-man-takes-stand-tells-of-killing-1777412.php

Keywords: **Confession to police, Confession to friends and family, Eyewitness, Forensic evidence: Other**

Case 329

Defendant: **Steven Sherer**
Victim: Jami Sherer
Trial: June 2000 Jurisdiction: Seattle, Washington
Murder: September 30, 1990
Evidence: Victim was defendant's wife and mother of their 2-year-old son. Witnesses stated that defendant was very controlling about victim's appearance and behaviors. He coerced her into dying her hair, enlarging her breasts, and losing weight. He also coerced her into performing three-way sexual encounters, having sex with other men, and was physically abusive. Police responded to several 911 calls stemming from violent fights at their home. On September 28, 1990, victim told a witness she planned to leave defendant and would live at her parents' house. The next day, defendant was upset when he could not find victim. He accused her of cheating on him with one of the men he had arranged for her to have sex with and threatened to kill her. The next day, victim told defendant over the phone that she wanted a divorce. Defendant convinced victim to meet him at a club, where defendant grabbed her purse and left. Victim went back to her home to collect her purse and some clothing. She admitted to defendant that she had spent the previous night in a motel with another man. She called her mother, saying she was on her way, but never arrived. Later that night, defendant told his sister that victim was missing and spent the next several days with victims' parents because he did not want to go home. One witness noticed a shovel in defendant's car and was told by defendant that the Northwest was a dumping ground for missing persons. Defendant had his car cleaned and detailed after the disappearance, and had the carpets at his house professionally cleaned. One witness noted that his behavior was inconsistent from other times victim had left him, and another found victim's missing persons posters crumpled in his glove box. Two months later, defendant began dating other women and told inconsistent stories about what had happened to his wife. A few months later, defendant replaced a section of carpet in his garage, and a year later, he gave away some of victim's clothes. Defendant convicted of first-degree murder and sentenced to 60 years in prison. A year after the trial, defendant attempted to hire a fellow inmate to kill victim's mother and the prosecutor from his case. Conviction upheld in 2002.
Sources: *State v. Sherer*, Court of Appeals of Washington, Division 1, No. 47074-4-I, Aug 19, 2002; http://www.seattlepi.com/news/article/Bizarre-revenge-plot-is-alleged-1112454.php
Keyword: **Eyewitness**

Case 330

Defendant: **Richard Skaggs**
Victim: Mark Berumen
Trial: February 2004 Jurisdiction: Phoenix, Arizona
Murder: July 2002
Evidence: Victim was last seen on July 28, 2002, at a nightclub. Three defendants were implicated in the victim's murder, including

defendant. Victim was likely shot to death in the apartment of one of the killers, near the nightclub. Neighbors testified to hearing a gunshot that night, and records indicate that a bathtub was replaced because of gunshot damage. The owner of the apartment pleaded guilty to manslaughter in October 2004, but defendant was charged only with crimes that followed victim's death, including theft, and was sentenced to 46 years in prison. Defendant remains a suspect in murder.

Sources: http://www.azcentral.com/specials/special14/articles/1008coldcase08.html; Charley Project

Keywords: **Eyewitness, Forensic evidence: Other**

Case 331

Defendant: **Billy D. Smith**

Victims: Harold Enzler, Nancy Bellamy

Trial: February 2003 Jurisdiction: Kenai Peninsula, Alaska

Murder: 1994

Evidence: Defendant murdered his girlfriend's estranged husband and the estranged husband's new girlfriend. Defendant's girlfriend and victim were in the middle of a child custody dispute. Defendant had previously threatened victim with a gun during an argument between victim and his estranged wife. Victims disappeared on March 27, 1994. Defendant was interviewed, but there was insufficient evidence to charge him. Three years later, defendant was arrested on drug charges and offered information about victims. Defendant claimed that he had a friend arrange a drug transaction with victims, and instructed victims to park their car on Marathon Road and pop the hood. Defendant reached into vehicle and shot victims. He and two companions dismantled the vehicle and disposed of the bodies and gun in nearby bodies of water. Defendant confessed to murdering the victims, then later appealed, claiming that he only confessed because police agreed to hire him as an undercover drug informant and that he was interrogated after requesting a lawyer. Appeal denied because there was no such agreement and request for a lawyer was ambiguous. Defendant convicted of two counts of first-degree murder and tampering with physical evidence. He was sentenced to 129 years in prison.

Source: *Smith v. State*, Court of Appeals of Alaska, No. A-8735, March 25, 2009

Keyword: **Confession to police**

Case 332

Defendant: **Eugene Marvin Smith**

Victim: Cindy Booth

Trial: September 1997 Jurisdiction: Delta County, Colorado

Murder: August 4, 1993

Evidence: Defendant was a family friend of 14-year-old victim. Victim disappeared riding her bicycle in August 1993 on her way to visit defendant after school. Defendant refused to speak to police, and was serving a prison sentence for unrelated charges of child molestation during the course of the investigation into victim's disappearance. Defendant convicted of second-degree murder and child abuse, sentenced to 48 years. Conviction upheld in September 2013. Victim's skeletal remains were found by hikers in 2004 and positively identified through dental records and mitochondrial DNA testing. Some have suggested that serial killer David Middleton, whom defendant knew through his construction work, may have also been responsible for victim's death.

Sources: http://www.upi.com/Top_News/2004/12/05/Bones-identified-as-missing-teen/UPI-29341102289694/; http://articles.latimes.com/1998/jun/14/local/me-59742/2; Kaye, Jeff, *Beware of the Cable Guy: From Cop to Serial Killer*

Keyword: **N/A**

Case 333

Defendant: **Jay C. Smith, William Bradfield**

Victims: Susan Reinert, Michael Reinert, Karen Reinert

Trial: October 1983 (Bradfield) and 1986 (Smith) Jurisdiction: Upper Merion, Pennsylvania

Murder: June 22, 1979

Evidence: Bradfield was engaged to Susan Reinert, a single mother of two. Bradfield and Susan Reinert were both teachers at a school where Smith was principal. Susan Reinert did not know Bradfield was seeing other women, and made him the sole beneficiary of her estate and her $730,000 life insurance policies. Defendants allegedly conspired to murder Susan Reinert to recover the proceeds from her life insurance and her estate. Susan Reinert and her children, Michael and Karen, disappeared on June 22, 1979, on their way to meet defendant. Susan Reinert's body was discovered in the trunk of her car the next morning, parked at a hotel parking lot. She had been beaten and then killed with a morphine injection, but her two children were never found. Bradfield was initially convicted with misappropriating Susan Reinert's money. After his release two years later, Bradfield was convicted of conspiring to murder all three victims and received three life sentences. Several witnesses testified that Bradfield was with them in New Jersey at the time of the murder, so investigators believed that Bradfield orchestrated the murders while Smith carried them out in the basement of his home in exchange for a portion of the life insurance proceeds. Smith had previously been arrested for robbery. During one arrest, police found in his vehicle loaded handguns, a mask, and a syringe filled with a tranquilizing drug. Bradfield had previously told witnesses he was afraid that Smith might kill him. Physical evidence found in the defendants' homes and vehicles linked them together. Smith was convicted of three counts of first-degree murder and sentenced to death. Case was initially remanded for retrial in 1992 because of the impermissible use of hearsay evidence and prosecutorial misconduct. Prosecution intentionally withheld exculpatory material and suppressed evidence while arguing for the death penalty. Conviction reversed because the prosecutorial misconduct was found to violate the double jeopardy clause, prohibiting the retrial. Both defendants died proclaiming their innocence.

Sources: *Pennsylvania v. Smith*, 568 A.2d 600 (Pa. 1989); http://www.cnn.com/2009/CRIME/06/30/pennsylvania.reinert.murders/index.html?eref=rss_crime&utm_source=feedburner&utm_medium=feed&utm_campaign=Feed%3A+rss%2Fcnn_crime+(RSS%3A+Crime; http://www.mainlinemedianews.com/articles/2011/06/23/main_line_times/life/doc4e035c1cc05c7662222473.txt

Keyword: **Forensic evidence: Other**

Case 334

Defendant: **Jerry T. Smith**

Victim: Edna Blodgett

Trial: December 1996 Jurisdiction: Post, Texas

Murder: June 3, 1993

Evidence: Defendant was victim's abusive, live-in boyfriend. Victim was 76 years old, almost 30 years older than defendant, when she disappeared on June 3, 1993. Victim had a protection order against defendant, but witnesses stated that he had continued to see her. Defendant initially charged with forgery after trying to cash a check from victim's bank account a few weeks after disappearance. Prosecution presented evidence that defendant had committed assault against his father, ex-wife, and victim, and had also beaten victim's dog to death. Defendant's cellmate also testified that defendant confessed to murdering victim, placing the body in a 55-gallon drum, and lighting it on fire. Defendant convicted of murder and sentenced to life imprisonment. The conviction was vacated and remanded on the grounds that the trial court erred in admitting evidence of the prior assaults. Defendant was convicted again on remand, and second conviction was upheld in 2000.

Sources: *Smith v. State*, Court of Criminal Appeals of Texas, No. 996-98, June 23, 1999; *Smith v. State*, Court of Appeals of Texas, Amarillo, No. 07-97-0032, September 19, 2000; http://lubbockonline.com/news/120496/witness.htm; Charley Project

Keywords: **Life, Informant**

Case 335

Defendant: **Larry David Smith**

Victim: Carolyn Maryann Bealer

Trial: 1979 Jurisdiction: Garden Grove, California

Murder: 1979

Evidence: Victim and defendant were friends. In 1979, defendant called victim's family, demanding $100,000. Victim was never seen after that time. Thirty witnesses testified at trial about victim's life and daily routine in order to convince the jury she was unlikely to have left on her own. One witness saw defendant arguing with a young woman before boarding a boat in Dana Point Harbor and claimed that the boat later returned without victim and without the anchor. Small bloodstains were found on defendant's shirt that matched victim's blood type. Defendant convicted of first-degree murder and sentenced to life in prison without parole.

Sources: http://articles.latimes.com/1997/oct/26/news/mn-46912; Charley Project

Keywords: **Eyewitness, Life, Forensic evidence: Other**

Case 336

Defendant: **Dennis Sochor**

Victim: Patricia Gifford

Trial: October 1987 Jurisdiction: Broward County, Florida

Murder: December 31, 1981

Evidence: Victim, 18 years old, was celebrating New Year's Eve at a lounge with a friend in 1981. Defendant and his brother were there as well, and helped escort victim's friend to her car when she became ill. Victim's friend awoke in her car the next morning and reported victim missing. Defendant's picture was broadcast on television, and defendant's roommates said that after seeing his picture on TV he left suddenly. Police interviewed defendant's brother, who implicated defendant in victim's disappearance. Defendant's brother stated that defendant and victim were kissing in the parking lot and victim agreed to go with them. Defendant drove to a secluded area where defendant climbed on top of victim and pinned her hands to the ground. Victim was screaming for help, and defendant's brother tried to intervene. Defendant ordered his brother back into the truck while he assaulted victim. Defendant reentered the truck without victim, and the next morning defendant's brother found woman's clothing in the car along with a set of keys. Defendant also confessed to police, stating that he wanted to have sex with victim and choked her when she fought back. Defendant claimed his brother was not with him, and did not remember clearly because he had been drinking. Defendant convicted of first-degree murder and kidnapping, sentenced to death, but the Supreme Court vacated the judgment because the trial judge violated the Eighth Amendment by weighing a "coldness" factor in his sentencing. On remand, defendant again sentenced to death. Defendant's motion for post-conviction relief was denied in 2004.

Sources: *Sochor v. State*, Supreme Court of Florida, No. 71407, May 6, 1993; http://articles.sun-sentinel.com/1987-11-03/news/8702030422_1_death-sentence-life-sentence-seay

Keywords: **Death penalty, Confession to police, Eyewitness**

Case 337

Defendant: **David Wayne Srout**

Victim: Christopher Robert Marcus

Trial: February 2008 Jurisdiction: Mohave County, Arizona

Murder: August 4, 2005

Evidence: Defendant and three others killed 18-year-old victim as part of a plan to rob him of several thousand dollars he had recently received from an insurance settlement. Victim was lured to a house under the pretense of signing and paying for a vehicle. While incarcerated, one of the defendants wrote a letter to his mother disclosing the involvement of his three companions in the murder. All defendants admitted the murder to investigators but told conflicting stories about what happened. Victim was apparently taken to a back shed where one of codefendants struck him in the face with a crowbar. Another codefendant then slit victim's throat, and then two defendants buried the body in a shallow grave in the desert. Some of the defendants were paid for their involvement. Blood was found on the floor of the shed and in the trunk of the car used to transport the body. Two of the codefendants pleaded guilty for their roles in the killing and testified against defendant. The fourth codefendant, tried after defendant, pleaded guilty as well. Defendant convicted of first-degree murder and sentenced to life with no possibility of release for 25 years.

Sources: *State v. Srout*, Court of Appeals of Arizona, Division 2, Department B, October 2, 2012; http://www.kingmandailyminer.com/main.asp?SectionID=13&SubSectionID=18&ArticleID=14391

Keywords: **Codefendant testimony, Eyewitness, Life, Confession to police**

Case 338

Defendants: **Thomas St. Clair, Herman Sparf, Hans Hansen**
Victim: Maurice Fitzgerald
Trial: 1893 Jurisdiction: "High seas" off California coast
Murder: January 13, 1893

Evidence: Defendants and victim were all seamen working onboard an American vessel, *The Hesper*, off the coast of California, and were all part of the starboard watch on the night when victim disappeared. While searching for victim, the captain found blood on the deck. The next morning, they discovered a strip of scalp that matched the victim's hair. A broom and another wooden bludgeon were found covered in blood, and a greasy hatchet was found under St. Clair's bunk. The captain isolated the starboard watch and spotted blood on Sparf's cheek. Defendants denied knowledge about the blood and the victim's whereabouts. Other witnesses on the boat heard men shouting and a dog barking that night, and St. Clair told another crewmember that victim had been thrown overboard. St. Clair changed his clothes the next day and threw another bundle of clothes overboard. Witnesses saw that his hands were bloody. Once the captain ordered defendants to be placed in irons, the defendants instructed other seamen not to say anything about what happened. Defendants all pleaded not guilty and were tried separately. Defendants were convicted of murder and sentenced to death. St. Clair appealed, and his conviction was upheld in 1894.

Source: *St. Clair v. United States*, Supreme Court of the United States, No. 1,062, May 26, 1894

Keywords: **Eyewitness, Death penalty, Forensic evidence: Other, Confession to family and friends**

Case 339

Defendant: **Raymond Louis Stabler**
Victim: Dennis Kenton Thomas
Trial: 1973 Jurisdiction: Macy, Nebraska
Murder: September 18, 1972
Evidence: Defendant and victim were both members of the Omaha Indian tribe of Nebraska. On September 18, 1972, victim was drinking heavily and driving around with friends when he passed out in the car, which was left parked near a Mormon church. Defendant, 18 years old, was also drinking with another group of friends and was walking to his sister's house when they saw the parked car where victim had passed out. Testimony shows that there was an occupant in the back seat of the car when defendant opened the car door, possibly to search the occupant's pockets. The car was set on fire several hours later and a body was discovered inside, too severely burned for positive identification. A few days later, while under arrest for an unrelated charge, defendant admitted to killing victim and setting fire to the car. At trial, defendant disavowed the content of his confessions at trial and stated that they were not voluntary. Witnesses testified to seeing defendant's footprints near the burning car. Defendant's bloodstained jacket was presented at trial, but all the blood was consumed in government tests and defendant was unable to show whether the blood was even human. Defendant convicted of second-degree murder on Indian reservation, but judgment was reversed by the Eighth Circuit because testimony about the footprints and exhibition of the jacket was in error. The case was remanded.
Source: *United States v. Stabler*, United States Court of Appeals, Eighth Circuit, No. 73-1261, January 8, 1974
Keywords: **Confession to police, Forensic evidence: Other**

Case 340

Defendant: **Joseph Allen Stanley**
Victim: Martin Alan Gentry
Trial: 1990 Jurisdiction: Sacramento, California
Murder: July 1986
Evidence: Victim was defendant's best friend. Victim left home on July 20, 1986, to meet a woman and purchase marijuana but never returned. Police received an anonymous tip that defendant threatened to shoot victim, believing that victim was pursuing a woman that defendant was interested in. When police interviewed defendant, defendant claimed he was forced at gunpoint to lure victim from his home. He claimed that he witnessed an unknown gunman shoot victim. Defendant's girlfriend initially told police she knew nothing about victim's disappearance then later said that defendant had confessed to shooting victim himself. Defendant tried twice, and both trials resulted in hung juries.
Sources: Charley Project; Doe Network
Keywords: **Confession to police, Confession to friends and family**

Case 341

Defendant: **Jack Stephenson**
Victim: Melissa Yon
Trial: August 1998 Jurisdiction: Lexington County, South Carolina
Murder: November 15, 1995
Evidence: Victim was defendant's common-law wife. The couple was having problems, and defendant found love letters victim had written to another man, along with motel receipts. Victim was diagnosed with chlamydia the day of her disappearance. When victim's family could not contact her, defendant repeatedly told them that she was working around the clock, though her boss had not seen her either. Defendant contacted victim's coworker at the same time and told her that victim was too ill to go to work. Victim's family contacted police, and defendant provided inconsistent statements about victim's whereabouts. Defendant later abandoned his half-brother's car, and police found spots of blood likely belonging to victim. Defendant's half-brother told police that defendant had confessed to killing victim and hiding the body under their mobile home but that defendant immediately retracted the statement and said it was a joke. Defendant spent a year on the run, telling his half-brother that it was for delinquent child support payments. Defendant's half-brother claims police tricked him into signing an arrest warrant for defendant. Defendant claimed that victim ran away after he accused her of having an affair. Defendant convicted of murder and sentenced to life imprisonment.
Sources: Murderpedia; http://news.google.com/newspapers?nid=1876&dat=19980811&id=tz8fAAAAIBAJ&sjid=r88EAAAAIBAJ&pg=6041,2176607
Keywords: **Forensic evidence: DNA, Confession to friends and family, Life**

Case 342

Defendant: **Bryan Stewart (a.k.a. Rick Valentini)**
Victim: Jamie Laiaddee
Trial: November 2011 Jurisdiction: Chandler, Arizona
Murder: March 18, 2010
Evidence: Victim was defendant's girlfriend and the primary source of the couple's income. Defendant lied about his age and his education level. "Bryan Stewart" was one of his several aliases. Victim lost her employment shortly before disappearing and was both physically and verbally abused by defendant. The day before victim's disappearance, she wrote an e-mail to a friend stating that she was afraid of defendant and that police couldn't protect her. Defendant told at least two witnesses that he had killed victim with a sawed-off shotgun. Investigators found a weapon matching this description among other weapons in defendant's storage unit. Defendant told friends that he and victim broke up the day before she disappeared, and that victim had gone to Denver for a job. Victim's credit cards, identification, and cars were left behind, and victim had just gotten a job in Chandler. After her disappearance, victim ceased all communication as well as Internet and credit card activity. Defendant was caught using victim's

car and credit cards the day after her disappearance. Defendant told fellow inmates that he had disposed of the body so well that it would never be found, alternately telling witnesses that he had fed the body to pigs or that he had cut it up and put it into bags. Defendant convicted of second-degree murder and related fraud and weapons charges, and he was sentenced to 54 years collectively.

Sources: http://blogs.phoenixnewtimes.com/valleyfever/2011/12/bryan_stewart_aka_rick_valenti_1.php; http://www.azcentral.com/news/articles/2011/11/23/20111123chandler-man-guilty-murdering-girlfriend.html

Keywords: **Confession to friends and family, Informant**

Case 343

Defendant: **Doug Stewart**
Victim: Venus Stewart
Trial: February 2011 Jurisdiction: St. Joseph's County, Michigan
Murder: April 2010

Evidence: Victim was defendant's wife and mother of their two daughters. Victim and her daughters were living with her parents in Michigan at the time of the murder, while defendant lived in Virginia. Defendant told a friend he met over X-Box Live that he could get away with murdering victim and asked the friend to be his alibi by living in his apartment and pretending to be him. The friend agreed and posed as defendant until defendant called him on April 26 and said, "OK, dude, it's done." Defendant told him that he had posed as a mailman with a package and placed victim in a headlock when she came outside to open the front gate. GPS data from defendant's accomplice were entered into evidence at trial, and phone records showed defendant in Michigan on the day of the disappearance. Defendant's pinky fingerprint was found on a tarp package at the scene where victim disappeared. Defendant convicted of first-degree murder and sentenced to life without parole. Conviction upheld in 2012

Sources: *People v. Stewart*, Court of Appeals of Michigan, Docket No. 303879, September 11, 2012; http://www.mlive.com/news/kalamazoo/index.ssf/2012/09/doug_stewarts_murder_convictio.html; http://www.woodtv.com/news/local/sw-mich/doug-stewart-murder-trial-march-11-2011

Keywords: **Codefendant testimony, Forensic evidence: Other, Life**

Case 344

Defendant: **Charles Stobaugh**
Victim: Kathy Stobaugh
Trial: February 2011 Jurisdiction: Denton, Texas
Murder: December 29, 2004

Evidence: Victim was defendant's estranged wife and mother of their two children. Victim was afraid of defendant, hiding all potential weapons in the house and developing a safety plan for herself and her children when she initiated divorce proceedings Defendant would have lost half his farm in the divorce. Victim's teenage daughters told investigators that victim disappeared after meeting with defendant at his secluded farmhouse, the day before the divorce would be finalized. Defendant claimed that victim had left after their meeting, but her car was still parked in the driveway the next morning with the keys in the ignition. Since that day, she had not accessed her bank accounts or tried to contact anyone and left behind all personal identification. Prosecution focused on disproving other explanations for victim's disappearance and on the fact that defendant was the last person to see victim alive and was the only person with motive to kill her. Defendant's daughter testified on behalf of defendant, and her testimony at trial contradicted statements and sentiments she had expressed during initial interviews at the time of victim's disappearance. Prosecutors believed that in the seven years it took to go to trial, defendant convinced her that victim had abandoned them. Defendant convicted and sentenced to 25 years. Conviction was overturned in January 2014 based on insufficient evidence to convict.

Sources: http://www.dallasnews.com/news/community-news/denton-county/20110217-denton-county-jury-finds-charles-stobaugh-guilty-of-murdering-estranged-wife-as-final-divorce-decree-neared-in-2004.ece; http://www.tdcaa.com/journal/vanished-without-trace; http://www.nbcdfw.com/news/local/Punishment-Phase-Starts-in-Stobaugh-Trial-116417229.html; http://www.wfaa.com/news/local/Brother-of-2001-murder-victim-says-overturned-conviction-for-alleged-killer-a-slap-in-the-face-250400981.html

Keyword: **N/A**

Case 345

Defendants: **Thomas Suleski, Roxanne Suleski**

Victim: Alexandria Christine Suleski

Trial: October 1994 Jurisdiction: Lexington, Kentucky

Murder: August 1989

Evidence: Victim was the 5-year-old daughter of Thomas and stepdaughter of Roxanne. In October 1989, defendants began telling neighbors that victim was missing. Law enforcement conducted extensive searches for victim, but found nothing. Defendants moved back to California the next year with their other two daughters. In August 1993, the eldest daughter contacted the FBI and stated that the defendants had sealed victim in two layers of plastic garbage bags as punishment for wetting the bed and left her in the bag overnight. She stated that Thomas returned from work early the next day and carried a heavy box out of the bedroom, in which she believed he had placed victim's body. At the FBI's behest, defendants' eldest daughter tape-recorded a conversation with Thomas, where he admitted to disposing of victim's body in October 1989 and later returning to Kentucky to destroy the remains. Defendants convicted of first-degree murder in addition to kidnapping, child abuse, and tampering with physical evidence. Both were sentenced to life imprisonment. Thomas's conviction was upheld in 1999, and his motion to vacate his sentence was denied in 2004.

Source: *Suleski v. Com*, Court of Appeals of Kentucky, No. 2001-CA-000457-MR, January 30, 2004

Keywords: **Life, Eyewitness, Confession to friends and family**

Case 346

Defendants: **Sean "Rico" Thomas Sullivan, Kenneth Campbell**
Victims: Toby Jermele Bing, El Shawndrae Jones
Trial: April 2003 Jurisdiction: Hilton Head Island, South Carolina
Murder: February 1999
Evidence: The victims were friends. Campbell was the leader of a crack cocaine trafficking ring, and Sullivan was his associate. On February 18, 1999, Bing received a phone call requesting that he drive to Bluffton. The victims were last seen in Bluffton later that afternoon, and the car they were driving was found abandoned in Savannah, Georgia, six days later. Some time afterward, a large pool of blood was found under the back porch at the residence of Sullivan's mother, and DNA matched it to Bing. The amount of blood indicated that Bing could not have survived his wounds. Slugs and bullet holes were also found on the property. Phone records placed victims in vicinity where defendants ran their drug operation, and defendants made incriminating statements to cooperating witnesses. Testimony suggested that defendants lured victims to their deaths because they were rival drug dealers. Campbell was convicted of conspiracy and sentenced to life. Sullivan was convicted of conspiracy, distribution, possession with intent, and firearms conspiracy and was also sentenced to life. During sentencing proceedings, the district court found that defendants had participated in victims' murders so applied the first-degree murder enhancement. The Fourth Circuit vacated the life sentences because the jury did not consider the murders. On remand for resentencing, Sullivan was sentenced to 480 months, which was affirmed in August 2007.
Sources: *United States v. Sullivan*, United States Court of Appeals, Fourth Circuit, Nos. 03-4601, 03-4610, July 11, 2006; http://www.lowcountrynewspapers.net/archive/node/71604; *United States v. Sullivan*, United States Court of Appeals, Fourth Circuit, Nos. 06-5186, 06-5206, August 3, 2007
Keywords: **Life, Forensic evidence: DNA, Confession to friends and family, Forensic evidence: Other**

Case 347

Defendant: **Angelica Swartout**
Victim: Newborn baby
Trial: February 2012/May 2012 Jurisdiction: Lane County, Oregon
Murder: October 2010
Evidence: Victim was defendant's newborn son. In December 2010, defendant told police that she delivered the baby in the bathroom at work, suffocated it, and put it in a garbage container, and then told her family that she had given birth to a stillborn at the hospital. Defendant's sisters called police when they could neither retrieve the body from the hospital nor find a record of birth. At trial, defendant disavowed the content of her confession and claimed she had never been pregnant, that she had faked the pregnancy to get attention from her family, and that she had confessed only because she was stressed and sleep-deprived and did not want to expose her lie. At

trial, defense presented photos showing defendant's stomach smaller in September 2010 than in July 2010. Defendant also presented a negative pregnancy test from Planned Parenthood in March 2010, seven months before the alleged birth. The first trial resulted in a hung jury (11–1 for conviction) after doctors performed pelvic examinations and provided conflicting opinions on whether defendant had given birth. Defendant acquitted at second trial.

Sources: http://projects.registerguard.com/web/news/28158356-57/jury-swartout-lane-murder-fate.html.csp; http://www.huffingtonpost.com/2012/02/09/angelica-swartout_n_1265372.html

Keyword: **Confession to police**

Case 348

Defendant: **Johnnie Sweet**

Victim: Latisha Frazier

Trial: April 2013 Jurisdiction: Washington, DC

Murder: August 2, 2010

Evidence: Victim, 18 years old, was a friend of 18-year-old defendant. Defendant planned and coordinated victim's beating because he believed she had stolen $900 from him. He recruited six other friends to assist him in the beating. Victim was lured into defendant's house, and then cornered in a bedroom where she was beaten, stomped, bound with duct tape, gagged, choked, and thrown in a closet where she died from her injuries. After a failed attempt at dismemberment, her body was dragged to a dumpster. One codefendant testified that he went to defendant's house when a friend asked for help getting rid of a body, but did not know who had been killed until he saw news reports and missing persons posters and decided to go to the police. All six codefendants pleaded guilty, and two of them testifyed against defendant. Defendant convicted of first-degree felony murder, kidnapping, and evidence tampering, and he was sentenced to 52 years.

Sources: http://homicidewatch.org/2013/08/01/i-was-wrong-johnnie-sweet-says-at-sentencing-for-latisha-frazier-death/; http://homicidewatch.org/2013/04/24/johnnie-sweets-attorney-advises-client-to-accept-plea-offer-in-latisha-frazier-murder/; http://www.washingtonpost.com/local/prosecutors-say-johnnie-sweet-orchestrated-the-murder-of-latisha-frazier/2013/04/23/6a8b5e5a-ac25-11e2-a8b9-2a63d75b5459_story.html

Keywords: **Codefendant testimony, Eyewitness**

Case 349

Defendant: **Tory Teigen**

Victim: Troy Klug

Trial: 2004 Jurisdiction: Rapid City, South Dakota

Murder: July 2004

Evidence: Victim allegedly owed defendant a $300 drug debt. On July 12, 2004, victim went to purchase methamphetamine from defendant's friend and disappeared shortly thereafter. Defendant and his friend later visited victim's girlfriend and began rummaging through victim's belongings. When victim's girlfriend expressed concern about his whereabouts, defendant and his friend said he was no longer a problem. Two days later, defendant drove to meet another friend in Belle Fourche and showed him a bound, gagged man in the trunk of his car—likely still alive at the time. The next day, when the friend inquired about the man in the trunk, defendant said he had left the man in a toolbox all day. When the friend expressed concern about the heat, defendant stated it was too late, that he had been beating him and had felt the bones crush and that "that's what did him in." A few days later, another witness helped defendant clean his car and noted that it had been stripped to the metal and bleached, and that maggots were floating in the bleach. While incarcerated, defendant wrote to a fellow inmate incriminating notes that were presented at trial. The two owners of the residence where victim was kept in the tool shed pleaded guilty for their roles in the killing. Defendant convicted of kidnapping and sentenced to 100 years in prison. The conviction was upheld in 2008. In 2009, defendant pleaded guilty to felony murder and led investigators to the site where victim was buried. He was sentenced to life without the possibility of parole.

Sources: *State v. Tiegen*, Supreme Court of South Dakota, No. 23759, October 3, 2007; http://rapidcityjournal.com/news/local/tory-teigen-admits-to-murder-gets-life-without-possibility-of/article_c534ea52-a624-5fe6-849c-884e1e4bdf04.html; http://rapidcityjournal.com/news/local/top-stories/officials-certain-troy-klug-s-body-found/article_75d712be-234c-5ddf-b2d6-a4852a26dfd7.html

Keywords: **Eyewitness, Confession to friends and family, Life**

Case 350

Defendant: **Dennis Tetso**

Victim: Tracey Leigh Gardner

Trial: October 2010 Jurisdiction: Baltimore, Maryland

Murder: March 6, 2005

Evidence: Victim was defendant's wife. Witnesses stated that victim was having an affair and had seen a divorce attorney, that defendant was very controlling, and that defendant was moving his stuff into storage. Defendant knew about victim's affair and had confronted both victim and victim's boyfriend about it. Victim failed to meet her boyfriend at a Motley Crue concert on March 6, 2005, and had not been seen since. Video footage from a hotel near where victim's vehicle was abandoned showed someone locking the vehicle with a keyless remote. After the disappearance, defendant was found to be carrying the sole keyless remote to the vehicle. Victim's vehicle was found abandoned almost two weeks later. Victim's grandmother visited defendant and victim's home after the disappearance and noted a comforter missing, and defendant was moving his stuff back in from storage. Defendant did not participate in any of the searches for victim. Defendant also expressed a desire to purchase an expensive boat, and claimed to be the beneficiary of victim's life insurance policy. Defendant convicted of second-degree murder and sentenced to 30 years in prison. Conviction upheld in 2012.

Source: *Tetso v. State*, Court of Special Appeals of Maryland, No. 2219, June 4, 2012
Keyword: **Forensic evidence: Other**

Case 351

Defendant: **Leonard Bryce Thomas**
Victim: Lisa Seabolt
Trial: Jurisdiction: Kern County, California
Murder: August 1996
Evidence: Victim was defendant's soon-to-be-ex-wife. They were in the middle of an apparently amicable divorce, despite victim's infidelity and defendant's controlling habits. Victim left her children with her twin sister one weekend so she could find her own apartment, but failed to pick her children up again. Defendant came to get the children several days later and said that victim's boyfriend had just been released from jail so they were probably celebrating. Victim's sister called the jail, but victim's boyfriend was still there and hadn't heard from victim. When police could not get a search warrant for defendant and victim's apartment, victim's twin broke in and found the mattress soaked in blood, which was later matched to the victim's DNA. Investigators later found blood spatters on the wall and furniture, consistent with blunt force trauma, which defendant claims were from a nosebleed. Victim led an unpredictable lifestyle, and was using crystal meth. Victim's twin went undercover as victim because witnesses from the drug world were unwilling to talk to police. Victim's twin found out that a prominent drug dealer and his girlfriend had visited victim and defendant the night of victim's disappearance. The dealer testified that defendant was carrying a gun, and that they all got high on crystal meth but that victim was acting unusually groggy. At trial, witnesses stated that defendant made threats against victim and tried to pay a friend $5,000 to kill victim's boyfriend. Defendant worked in oil fields, and investigators believe he may have dumped the body into an oil well. Defendant convicted of second-degree murder and sentenced to 15 years. A mistrial was almost declared after allegations of jury misconduct, and defendant tried to hire an undercover officer to kill victim's twin in anticipation of a new trial. He was convicted and sentenced to an additional 12 years.
Sources: http://www.nbcnews.com/id/12580458/#.Usgm6qX0BcQ; http://www.people.com/people/article/0,,20128262,00.html
Keywords: **Forensic evidence: DNA, Informant**

Case 352

Defendant: **William Thomas**
Victim: Rachel Thomas
Trial: March 1994 Jurisdiction: Duval County, Florida
Murder: September 12, 1991
Evidence: Victim was defendant's soon-to-be-ex-wife, and they were living separately at the time of her disappearance. Defendant and his friend went to victim's house under the pretense of delivering papers,

where defendant beat victim, taped her up, and placed her in the trunk of her car. Later in the day, defendant's girlfriend witnessed him park and abandon victim's car at a mall after wiping it down with a towel. Blood in the trunk later matched victim's blood type. Defendant told his girlfriend that his secret mafia family had taken victim and instructed her to tell others that she had gone with him to victim's home but that they had not seen her. Defendant told his mother that he had gone to victim's house, but she wasn't there. There were signs of a struggle at victim's home, including blood on baseboards and a vent in the foyer. Tennis shoe prints were found in the garage. When questioned by investigators, defendant claimed he did not own any tennis shoes, though witnesses saw him wearing tennis shoes the day of victim's disappearance and defendant was later seen throwing his tennis shoes away. Defendant told at least four witnesses varying stories about victim's disappearance and murder. Defendant made several incriminating statements to police, and then killed his mother in order to prevent her from implicating him in victim's murder. At a police interview, defendant's friend who assisted in the initial abduction admitted his involvement and agreed to inform on defendant. Defendant convicted of first-degree murder and sentenced to death. Defendant pleaded guilty to murdering his mother and was sentenced to life imprisonment.

Sources: http://www.floridacapitalcases.state.fl.us/case_updates/Htm/311509.htm; http://www.law.fsu.edu/library/flsupct/84256/84256brief.pdf; http://www.floridasupremecourt.org/pub_info/summaries/briefs/01/01-1439/01-1439_ans.pdf

Keywords: **Death penalty, Eyewitness, Codefendant testimony, Forensic evidence: DNA**

Case 353

Defendant: **Aaron Thompson**
Victim: Aaroné Thompson
Trial: August 2009 Jurisdiction: Arapahoe County, Colorado
Murder: 2002–2004

Evidence: Victim was defendant's 6-year-old daughter. Defendant claimed victim ran away after a family fight. Investigators found the mattress in her bedroom missing. Defendant claimed she ran away in November 2005. Based on testimony from victim's siblings, and because victim had never been enrolled in school and her parents could not provide a recent picture of her, investigators believe she may have been killed two years earlier. Defendant's seven other children testified that he regularly abused them with belts, wires, and baseball bats. They also testified that victim was severely beaten for bedwetting, locked in a closet, and denied proper nourishment or medical attention. Defendant's girlfriend eventually told police that victim had died suddenly, and defendant concealed her body out of fear their other children would be removed. A friend of defendant's girlfriend tape-recorded their conversations, where defendant's girlfriend repeated this version of events. In 2003, defendant's girlfriend contacted her aunt and asked what to do if a child stops breathing. After defendant's girlfriend died of heart problems, defendant told police she was responsible for victim's death but did not testify at trial. Defendant convicted of 31 counts of child abuse, including child abuse resulting in death. Sentenced to 114 years imprisonment.

Sources: *People v. Thompson*, 181 P.3d 1143 (Colo. 2008); http://www.thedenverchannel.com/news/father-indicted-in-aarone-thompson-case-60-counts; http://www.denverpost.com/news/ci_13759035

Keyword: **Confession to family and friends**

Case 354

Defendant: **Drew Thompson**
Victim: Rita Bartschot
Trial: August 1991 Jurisdiction: King County, Washington
Murder: August 1990

Evidence: Victim was staying at her deceased mother's house in Seattle when her friend was suddenly unable to reach her by phone. Victim had a very consistent, predictable daily routine, and her absence was highly unusual. Victim's friend contacted a next-door neighbor who had keys to the house. The neighbor had seen victim doing yardwork on August 24, 1990, but said her car had been missing since then. When neighbor entered house, she noticed that the TV was on, the cat had not been fed or watered, and the coffee pot was starting to mold. She reported victim missing, and police began investigating on September 1, 1990, and found that her ATM card had been used every day since her disappearance to withdraw the maximum allowable amount of cash. The user had been photographed by hidden cameras at the ATM, and police recognized defendant, who lived in the same neighborhood where victim was staying. Police staked out the machine and arrested defendant as he was making a withdrawal. Victim's car was later found abandoned with defendant's fingerprints and bloodstains matching victim's blood type in the back seat. Witnesses saw defendant driving victim's car at the time of her disappearance. Defendant told a cellmate that he threatened victim to get the PIN number, and that he "had kept her until he verified that the numbers were good" and that cops would never find the body. Defendant convicted of first-degree murder. Conviction upheld in 1994.

Sources: *Wisconsin v. Thompson*, 870 P.2d 1022 (1994); http://www.seattlepi.com/local/article/Brothers-twisted-tale-One-a-rapist-accused-1303568.php

Keywords: **Forensic evidence: Other, Informant, Forensic evidence: DNA**

Case 355

Defendant: **Raymond "Ray" or "Little Ray" Michael Thompson**
Victim: James "Jimmy" Savoy
Trial: June 1986 Jurisdiction: Broward County, Florida
Murder: March 1982

Evidence: Victim was a self-employed carpenter who became involved in a marijuana smuggling enterprise run by defendant in 1979. Defendant hired victim to construct special cabinets for two smuggling boats, where bales of marijuana could be hidden. Victim also built a safe in the concrete floor of his carpentry shop, where he kept $500,000 to $600,000 of the enterprise's proceeds at defendant's behest. Victim disappeared with the money in autumn of 1981, and was pursued by defendant and others from the marijuana enterprise, which put an open contract on his life. Victim was found by defendant and codefendants in March 1982 and kidnapped. His hands and feet were taped, and defendant questioned victim about missing money. Victim claimed that a hooker stole it. Defendant and codefendants took victim out on a boat, beat and shot him, and threw him overboard. Several codefendants testified pursuant to plea agreements. Several were implicated in victim's murder as part of racketeer influenced and corrupt organizations (RICO) conspiracy charges. Defendant convicted of first-degree murder and sentenced to death despite the jury's recommendation of a life sentence. The death sentence was upheld on appeal in October 1989.

Sources: *Thompson v. State*, Supreme Court of Florida, No. 69352, October 19, 1989; *United States v. Finestone*, United States Court of Appeals, Eleventh Circuit, No. 86-5224, May 7, 1987

Keywords: **Death penalty, Codefendant testimony**

Case 356

Defendant: **Craig Thrift**

Victim: Terry Eugene Ross

Trial: April 2014 Jurisdiction: Ware County, Georgia

Murder: May 11, 1991

Evidence: Victim was defendant's cousin and best friend. Defendant bragged to one of his ex-wives and friends that he had shot and killed the victim. He also claimed to have dumped the body in a swamp where no one would find it. Another of defendant's ex-wives provided an alibi for defendant, claiming they had gone to a party and defendant was too drunk to do anything after but sleep it off. Defense was allowed to reopen its case to have detective testify about a man who allegedly saw victim in January 1992. Defendant was found guilty of felony murder.

Sources: http://jacksonville.com/news/crime/2014-04-16/story/craig-thrifts-ex-wife-provides-alibi-his-murder-trial-presumed-death-his; http://jacksonville.com/news/crime/2014-04-17/story/jury-finds-craig-thrift-guilty-felony-murder-cousins-death

Keyword: **Confession to friends and family**

Case 357

Defendant: **Matthew Tjeltveit**

Victim: James Weishahn

Trial: March 2007 Jurisdiction: Washoe County, Nevada

Murder: June 2002

Evidence: Victim and defendant were partners in a failed check-cashing scam. Victim was missing for three years when a witness told police that defendant had been telling his friends that he had killed victim.

Defendant confessed to the killing and to dumping the body in a trash bin. Defendant claimed he had been on a methamphetamine binge and that victim had threatened to kill his toddler during an argument about the failed check-cashing scam. Defendant convicted of first-degree murder and sentenced life imprisonment with the possibility for parole after 40 years.

Sources: http://www.rgj.com/article/20070322/NEWS01/703220332/Jury-convicts-man-murder-despite-absence-body; http://www.tahoedailytribune.com/article/20070608/REGION/106080086

Keywords: **Confession to friends and family, Life, Confession to police**

Case 358

Defendant: **Bradley Hugh Tocker**
Victim: William McGrath
Trial: April 2011 Jurisdiction: Maricopa County, Arizona
Murder: August 2009

Evidence: Victim hired defendant to help renovate his home and gave defendant keys to his house. Defendant was financially strained and fell behind on two mortgages after moving his mother into a care facility. On August 18 and 19, defendant called victim several times on his cell phone, the last of which was a 28-minute call on the night of August 19. A few hours later, victim's neighbor awoke to the sound of two gunshots. After that date, friends and relatives were unable to contact victim. Some received strange e-mails from victim saying he had left Phoenix. Someone posing as victim left phone messages to cancel appointments, but witnesses stated that the voice obviously did not belong to victim. Defendant was photographed making large cash withdrawals from victim's bank account. Police entered victim's house and found victim, victim's dog, and victim's car missing. Over the next few days, someone changed the contact information on victim's investment accounts, large transfers were made to defendant and defendant's mother, and defendant sold victim's stripped car. Inside defendant's car police found a.45 caliber bullet, bank receipts documenting deposits into defendant's account, and a receipt documenting a trash deposit at a solid waste disposal site. In one of victim's residences, police found a shipping box addressed to defendant's mother. The box contained a Glock .45 with blood evidence matching DNA on victim's razor, documentation about victim's financial records, and victim's personal calendar. Defendant convicted of first-degree murder and sentenced to life imprisonment. Victim's body discovered buried under a house in Phoenix after the trial.

Sources: *State v. Tocker*, Court of Appeals of Arizona, Division 1, Department C, October 2, 2012; http://www.abc15.com/dpp/news/region_phoenix_metro/central_phoenix/police-recover-body-of-man-missing-since-2009

Keywords: **Forensic evidence: DNA, Forensic evidence: Other, Life**

Case 359

Defendant: **Jenaro Torres**
Victim: Ruben Gallegos

Trial: March 2007 Jurisdiction: Honolulu, Hawaii
Murder: May 1, 1992
Evidence: Victim and defendant both worked at the Pearl Harbor Naval Base. Victim was a cashier assigned to cash paychecks in a satellite cashier's cage on May 1, 1992, the day of his disappearance. Defendant was a PHNB police officer. Though defendant was off duty, he approached victim in uniform at the satellite cashier's cage. Witnesses saw defendant and victim leave together; victim was carrying a canvas bag containing approximately $80,000 in cash. Later that day, federal officials searched defendant's car on the base and found a canvas cashier's bag with $78,000, a revolver with three spent cartridges, a stun gun, and victim's personal belongings (including personal identification and wallet). Victim and defendant initially charged with theft, but after 10 days the charges against victim were dropped. A few years later, a witness told police that defendant had admitted to robbing a bank and putting his accomplice "out of commission" when he started to back out. Defendant was charged with murder 13 years later. Defendant convicted of second-degree murder and sentenced to life imprisonment, but case reversed on appeal due to technical error. On remand, defendant pleaded no contest to assault and was sentenced to 10 years. By the second trial, three witnesses had died.
Sources: *State v. Torres*, Intermediate Court of Appeals of Hawai'i, No. 28583, December 15, 2009; http://www.hawaiinewsnow.com/story/22800206/exclusive-suspect-in-92-disappearance-speaks-out; *State v. Torres*, Supreme Court of Hawai'i, No. 28583, August 9, 2011; http://archives.starbulletin.com/2007/03/22/news/story02.html
Keywords: **Life, Eyewitness; Confession to friends and family**

Case 360

Defendant: **Richard Tovar**
Victim: Janette Espeleta
Trial: September 2000 Jurisdiction: Orange County, California
Murder: July 1998
Evidence: Victim was eight months pregnant with defendant's child, and she had recently named him the father in a form she submitted to initiate child support payments. Defendant did not want to pay child support, so he shot victim twice in the chest and then recruited two accomplices to help him dispose of the body in the ocean. Defendant's accomplice testified against him at trial. The day before the murder, defendant and accomplice rented a boat. Victim's friend stated that the day of her disappearance, victim saw defendant drive by on the street and became frightened. Phone records showed extensive communication between defendant and accomplices that afternoon. One accomplice testified that defendant came to his house driving victim's car and that victim's body was inside. After disposing of the body in the ocean, defendant told accomplice he was taking victim's car to Tijuana to be burned. One accomplice's girlfriend told police that defendant and accomplices had expressed concern about being caught for the murder, and prosecution presented evidence to contradict defendant's alibi. Defendant convicted of two counts of

first-degree murder and one count of conspiracy and sentenced to life imprisonment. Conviction upheld in 2003.

Source: *People v. Tovar*, Court of Appeal, Fourth District, Division 3, California, No. G028242, June 30, 2003

Keywords: **Life, Codefendant testimony, Forensic evidence: Other**

Case 361

Defendants: **Brenda Vanessa, Frank Jose Trejos**

Victim: Maria Guadalupe Barrientos

Trial: February 2005/May 2005 Jurisdiction: Fort Bend County, Texas

Murder: June 1994

Evidence: Victim was mother and mother-in-law to respective defendants. Defendants were unemployed and living at victim's residence, but victim was going to throw them out because they did not help with household chores, so defendants strangled her and dumped the body in a remote field. Defendants reported victim missing in June. Traces of blood were found in the residence. Victim's car was recovered in Houston weeks later with personal identification and keys still inside. Case remained unsolved until the Department of Public Safety formed a cold-case missing persons unit in 2001 and reopened the case. Police reinterviewed Frank, who confessed to the murder. Brenda also confessed, but pleaded not guilty at trial. Defendants' attempts to help investigators find the body failed. Defendants tried separately, both convicted. Brenda sentenced to 80 years, Frank to 45 years.

Sources: http://www.texnews.com/1998/2003/texas/texas_Daughter_14.html; http://www.chron.com/news/houston-texas/article/Woman-gets-80-years-for-killing-mom-over-chores-1936278.php

Keywords: **Confession to police, Forensic evidence: Other**

Case 362

Defendant: **Jerry Wayne Trussell**

Victim: Franklin "Punkie" Harrod, Jr.

Trial: October 2006/June 2007 Jurisdiction: Sedgwick County, Kansas

Murder: July 29, 1997

Evidence: Victim and victim's wife were friends with defendant and defendant's wife. Victim and defendant jointly owned a car they raced at a local speedway. Victim's wife testified that victim was abusive and that she left him in January 1997, taking their two daughters to Arkansas. Victim filed for divorce and was awarded temporary custody but dismissed the divorce action when his wife discovered she was pregnant. Victim's wife told defendant's wife she wanted to get rid of victim but that she would be a suspect. She then suggested that defendant and defendant's wife could kill victim instead. Defendant told victim's wife he would kill victim in exchange for sex. The three began having weekly conversations about murdering victim. Defendant tried to borrow a gun from a neighbor, stating it was to kill victim. After the murder, the neighbor reported this information anonymously. Defendant and wife were evicted in July 1997 and moved in with victim and wife. The night of the murder, defendant told his wife that he couldn't find anyone to kill victim so they would have to do it themselves. The next morning, defendant told victim's wife to stay in the house. Defendant and victim began fighting outside and defendant told his wife to get the gun and shoot victim, which she did. Defendant and wife buried victim in a remote location, and victim's wife filed a missing persons report. One witness testified that defendant had asked her husband for help in disposing of victim's body. Several years later, defendant's wife started offering inconsistent versions of the murder that implicated defendant and victim's wife. In 2004, defendant's wife and victim's wife both confessed and agreed to testify against defendant as part of plea agreements. First trial resulted in a hung jury after defendant's statement was ruled inadmissible because of a Miranda violation. The statement was ruled admissible in the second trial. Defendant convicted of aiding and abetting first-degree murder and conspiracy to commit first-degree murder. He was sentenced to 25 to life and 146 months, respectively. Conviction upheld in 2009.

Source: *State v. Trussell*, Supreme Court of Kansas, No. 99,411, August 21, 2009

Keywords: **Codefendant testimony, Confession to police, Confession to friends and family, Life**

Case 363

Defendant: **Gregory Mung Sen Tu**

Victim: Lisa Tu

Trial: 1991 Jurisdiction: Montgomery County, Maryland

Murder: July 13, 1988

Evidence: Victim was defendant's wife of 10 years when she disappeared. All victim's communications and financial transactions ceased after July 13, 1998, and all her personal possessions were left behind. Defendant was having financial difficulties and was the beneficiary of victim's life insurance policy. Defendant also knew that victim was having an affair. Defendant had also purchased a handgun before the disappearance. Blood likely belonging to victim was found in the basement and on the couch cover where she slept. Three days after victim's disappearance, defendant had a trash collector haul away the couch where victim slept, though it was in good condition. Investigators believe victim's body may have been hidden in the couch. Defendant told conflicting stories about victim's whereabouts. When defendant learned he was a suspect, he briefly flew to Taiwan before returning to Maryland and then going to Las Vegas, where he claimed to be looking for victim. In Vegas, he gambled, looked for a job, solicited a prostitute, and used false names in various transactions. Defendant convicted of first-degree murder, but conviction overturned on appeal because court erred in denying defendant's motion to suppress evidence taken from his hotel room in Vegas. On remand, defendant convicted of second-degree murder. Conviction upheld in 1993.

Source: *Tu v. State*, Court of Appeals of Maryland, No. 147, Sept. Term, 1993, October 25, 1994

Keyword: **Forensic evidence: Other**

Case 364

Defendant: **Judy Diane Valot**
Victim: Peter Theriault
Trial: June 2005 Jurisdiction: Santa Ana, California
Murder: December 1998
Evidence: Victim was defendant's boyfriend and coworker. Defendant and her 13-year-old daughter moved in with victim in June 1998. Defendant was becoming increasingly jealous and accused victim of having an affair with a coworker, voicing her suspicions to several witnesses and telling one that she would kill victim if he were cheating on her. Victim taught defendant how to shoot and, as a Vietnam veteran, was very meticulous in handling and storing his gun. Victim disappeared on December 2, 1998. Defendant and victim missed work for the next several days. Defendant claimed she and victim were breaking up and he agreed to stay away until she had moved out. One neighbor saw defendant riding into the desert alone on her ATV for about an hour. She told one witness that she had thrown her bedding away because the cat urinated and then that she had always been worried that victim would get carjacked. Investigators found bloodstains in victim's residence and defendant's truck, and the DNA matched a sample taken from victim's mouthwash bottle. They also found victim's guns in defendant's trailer. Police activated the LoJack device on victim's missing vehicle and found it three miles from his residence. Defendant denied moving vehicle until police claimed that they had surveillance footage; then she changed her story to say that victim had left on foot rather than in his car. A photograph at the time of arrest showed blisters between victims' fingers. Defendant's first conviction in 2002 reversed because the record did not show the requisite "demonstrable reality" that a dismissed juror shirked her duty to deliberate. The second trial resulted in a hung jury. At third trial, defendant convicted of second-degree murder and sentenced to 15 years to life. Conviction upheld in 2006.
Sources: *People v. Valot*, Court of Appeal, Fourth District, Division 3, California, No. G035830, December 22, 2006; http://articles.latimes.com/2005/jul/23/local/me-valot23
Keywords: **Forensic evidence: DNA, Forensic evidence: Other**

Case 365

Defendant: **Orlando Cruz Vasquez**
Victim: Joaquin Coelho Estevez
Trial: 1990/1991 Jurisdiction: San Jose, California
Murder: December 13, 1988
Evidence: Victim was a relatively well-known public figure who had programs on Portuguese-language radio and television in San Jose. Victim was last seen driving away from his real estate office the morning of December 13, 1988, for an appointment. He never made the appointment and was never heard from again. Victim left the office door unlocked with his wallet, money, and personal identification inside. Victim was very consistent and reliable and was not likely to abandon his wife and six children. Victim's car was recovered a month

later, driven by defendant. Defendant claimed to have purchased it from an unidentified person a few days earlier for $150, but neighbors testified that defendant had had the car for several weeks. Victim's personal belongings were found in defendant's house, including the sweater and wristwatch he had been wearing when he disappeared. Defendant was wearing victim's ring. In the trunk, investigators found scratch marks and signs that someone had tried to pry open the trunk lock from the inside. Investigators believed defendant had an accomplice, but a second suspect committed suicide during the investigation. First trial resulted in hung jury. At second trial, defendant convicted and sentenced to 30 years.

Sources: Charley Project; Doe Network

Keyword: **Forensic evidence: Other**

Case 366

Defendant: **Anita Vega**

Victim: Anna Marie Arguello

Trial: July 1994 Jurisdiction: Clinton County, Indiana

Murder: 1969–1970

Evidence: Victim was defendant's 3-year-old daughter. On the day of the murder, defendant kept her 9-year old-daughter home from school. Victim had wet the bed the previous night, and as punishment she had been beaten, deprived of food, and kept in a cold room without clothing. Throughout the course of the day, defendant's daughter witnessed defendant brutally beat victim and forced her to lie down in a tub filled with cold water. After several hours in the tub, victim was placed out on the cold porch. Victim may have died from drowning, beating, starvation, or hypothermia. Defendant told her daughter, "If you ever tell, I will kill you, and you've seen me do it." Defendant's boyfriend brought a box into the house. Defendant's daughter saw that the blanket she had used to cover victim was sticking out of the box when defendant's boyfriend carried it away. Defendant kept saying they would be in trouble if a policeman saw, and defendant's boyfriend stated that it wasn't easy to bury a body in frozen ground. When defendant's daughter asked about the victim in 1985, defendant gave her a brown sack and said it was a surprise. Inside the sack was a bone on top of dirt. Defendant's daughter approached police in September 1992. Investigators could only find victim's birth certificate and no other record of her. When police confronted defendant, defendant initially denied victim's existence, but when confronted with the birth certificate, she claimed that she had found victim unconscious and that her boyfriend buried her. Defendant convicted of involuntary manslaughter. Conviction upheld in 1995.

Sources: *Vega v. State*, Court of Appeals of Indiana, No. 12A04-9411-CR-465, October 17, 1995; http://articles.baltimoresun.com/1994-11-09/features/1994313206_1_anna-marie-booth-child

Keywords: **Eyewitness, Confession to police**

Case 367

Defendant: **John Allen Vickery**
Victim: Pablo Ortega
Trial: March 2001 Jurisdiction: San Bernardino County, California
Murder: November 23, 1998
Evidence: Victim and defendant got into an argument during a failed methamphetamine transaction, each accusing the other of depriving him of expected profits from manufacturing the meth. Victim punched defendant during the argument, and defendant drew his .25 caliber gun. Two days later, defendant approached victim with a sawed-off shotgun, which he then exchanged for a .25 caliber semiautomatic pistol. Defendant attempted to hit victim with the butt of the pistol, then stepped back and fired two shots. Victim was still alive, so defendant fired four or five additional shots and then enlisted two accomplices to help bury victim and dispose of victim's car. At least one witness was present during the shooting who later testified. Shortly after a police interview, defendant confessed the murder to an officer while smoking a cigarette outside. Defendant convicted of murder and sentenced to 50 years to life. Conviction upheld in 2002.
Sources: *People v. Vickery*, Court of Appeal, Fourth District, Division 2, California, No. E029689, May 13, 2002; http://www.vvdailypress.com/articles/-1695—.html
Keywords: **Confession to police, Life, Eyewitness**

Case 368

Defendant: **Charles Anthony Walker**
Victim: Elmon Tito Davidson, Jr.
Trial: 1995 Jurisdiction: Greensboro, North Carolina
Murder: August 11, 1992
Evidence: Defendant decided to kill victim after neighbors told him that victim tried to steal money and drugs from his girlfriend's apartment. Defendant told his girlfriend to lure victim to the apartment and keep him there. Defendant and accomplices then entered the apartment armed with pistols, announced they were going to kill victim, and instructed victim's girlfriend to leave. Defendant and accomplice bound victim with tape and beat him. Accomplice cut victim's throat and shot him in the finger and arm through a pillow. Defendant fired the final shot to victim's neck. Defendant and an accomplice went to a hardware store to purchase cleaning supplies, then dumped victim's body into a dumpster. Defendant's girlfriend wrote him a series of letters stating that she had lied to police about his involvement in the murder. Defendant's girlfriend later testified against him as well as all his other accomplices except for one. Defendant convicted of first-degree murder and conspiracy and sentenced to death. Defendant was nearly executed in 2004 when he was granted a stay. In 2006, his conviction was overturned when a court determined that police had concealed evidence. In 2007, he pleaded no contest to being an accessory to murder and to conspiracy, and was sentenced to 30 years in prison with credit for time served. Defendant was released in 2009,

then rearrested for shooting at the girlfriend who had testified against him at trial.

Sources: *State v. Walker*, Supreme Court of North Carolina, No. 76A95, May 10, 1996; Walker v. Lee, United States Court of Appeals, Fourth Circuit, No. 03-11, January 22, 2004; http://www.indyweek.com/indyweek/new-evidence-in-charles-walker-murder-trial/Content?oid=1197728; http://truthinjustice.org/charles-walker.htm; http://www.newsobserver.com/2010/10/28/764515/zahra-bakers-searchers-find-prosthetic.html

Keywords: **Codefendant testimony, Eyewitness, Death penalty**

Case 369

Defendant: **Leslie Walker**

Victim: Eugene "Bud" Branton

Trial: June 1985 Jurisdiction: Reno County, Kansas

Murder: August 6, 1984

Evidence: Victim and defendant were coworkers. Defendant told a friend that victim always carried large amounts of cash and that he had a plan to rob and murder victim. Defendant and his friend practiced firing two 12-gauge sawed-off shotguns in a secluded area of a nearby county, where investigators later found spent shell casings and shotgun shell boxes. On August 6, 1984, after defendant saw that victim had cashed his paycheck, defendant and his friend drove to victim's home and lured him into their car by offering to sell him a horse. They drove to an isolated country road where defendant and friend both shot victim to death then dragged his body to a ditch. They took victim's wallet and threw the shotgun shells out the window on their drive back to town. They went to victim's home and removed any items that might have their fingerprints. Defendant later told friend that he had moved the body and disposed of his shotgun. Defendant's friend contacted police in January 1985 and confessed his role in the murder. He agreed to wear a wire and discussed the murder with defendant. Defendant convicted of first-degree murder and sentenced to life imprisonment. Conviction upheld in 1986.

Source: *State v. Walker*, Supreme Court of Kansas, No. 58690, July 18, 1986

Keywords: **Codefendant testimony, Confession to friends and family**

Case 370

Defendant: **John Wallace**

Victim: William Turner

Trial: November 1949 Jurisdiction: Coweta County, Georgia

Murder: April 20, 1948

Evidence: Victim was tenant farmer on wealthy defendant's land, and defendant stated he was manufacturing illicit liquor on his property. Victim was white and defendant did not like his influence on the "colored" tenants, so he asked him to leave. Victim was arrested for stealing defendant's cow, and defendant arranged for his early release from the jail. Witnesses saw defendant and accomplice chase victim and then beat him with a pump shotgun, so hard that the gun fired, and another unknown blunt instrument. Victim was then placed in the back of the car, and was still being beaten in the back seat when the car drove away, though witnesses stated victim had stopped moving. A physician testified that, based on witnesses' description of the beating, a man defendant's size would likely have killed a man victim's size. Defendant forced two black field workers to help pull victim's body out of a bloodstained well, and they saw that victim was missing the back of his head. The workers later led investigators to the site, where bone fragments and ruptured brain tissue were recovered. Defendant burned the body and shoveled the ashes into a creek. Defendant claims that victim died when defendant's shotgun accidentally fired. Defendant convicted of murder and sentenced to death, the first white man in Georgia to be condemned to death based on the testimony of two black men. He was executed by electric chair in 1950.

Sources: *Wallace v. State*, Supreme Court of Georgia, No. 16450, January 11, 1949; http://www.academia.edu/1592835/Notable_Georgia_Criminal_Trials

Keywords: **Eyewitness, Forensic evidence: Other**

Case 371

Defendant: **Jesse Iva Pate Warmke**

Victim: infant

Trial: 1943 Jurisdiction: Davies County, Kentucky

Murder: July 8, 1943

Evidence: Victim was defendant's illegitimate infant child. Victim left her village in Utica to deliver the child in Louisville a few weeks before the murder. On the night of July 8, 1943, a witness saw defendant traveling alone with victim and then saw her again a few hours later without victim. The next morning, police interviewed defendant about missing victim. Defendant claimed that she accidentally dropped victim while crossing a railroad trestle. Investigators searched the creek beneath the trestle and found a baby cap on the bank, which defendant identified. After further questioning, defendant admitted to throwing the baby because she was humiliated by victim's illegitimacy. Defendant repudiated her confession at trial and stated that she dropped victim by accident and vaguely remembers wandering around barefoot thereafter. Defendant convicted of manslaughter and sentenced to nine years' imprisonment. Conviction upheld in 1944.

Source: *Warmke v. Commonwealth*, Court of Appeals of Kentucky, 297 Ky. 649, May 26, 1944

Keyword: **Confession to police**

Case 372

Defendant: **Jesse Elwood Watkins**

Victim: Craig Lee White

Trial: September 2008 Jurisdiction: Cape May County, New Jersey

Murder: February 23, 1990

Evidence: Victim was defendant's cousin. In 1989, victim began a sexual relationship with defendant's live-in girlfriend. In the next few months, relatives testified that victim and defendant's relationship became strained and they fought. When defendant proposed to his girlfriend, she admitted her relationship with victim. Witnesses testified that defendant expressed extreme animosity toward victim thereafter and threatened him. Relatives were afraid victim would be hurt. Defendant asked a friend how he would get rid of a dead body. On February 23, 1990, victim told relatives he was going to cut down trees with defendant that evening and said he would be right back. He was never seen again and left behind all his personal belongings. The next day, defendant asked relatives if they had seen victim and told conflicting stories about his last encounter with victim. He also asked a friend to lie about seeing victim. A few years later, defendant told two girlfriends that he murdered victim but told conflicting stories about how the murder was carried out. In March 2007, defendant was living with his brother and, during an argument, threatened to do him like he did victim. Defendant's brother reported the threat to the police, but at trial stated he did not know what the threat meant. Defendant convicted of first-degree murder and sentenced to 45 years in prison. Conviction upheld in 2011.

Sources: *State v. Watkins*, Superior Court of New Jersey, Appellate Division, No. 07-04-0240, November 17, 2011; http://www.pressofatlanticcity.com/news/top_three/article_e08b89f6-3c38-11de-8587-001cc4c03286.html

Keyword: **Confession to family and friends**

Case 373

Defendant: **John Matthus Watson**

Victim: Everilda "Evie" Watson

Trial: June 2010 Jurisdiction: Clark County, Nevada

Murder: July 2006

Evidence: Victim was defendant's wife, but she was planning to leave him. Defendant knew of victim's plan and did not want to lose half of his assets, so he lured victim to Las Vegas in July 2006 on the pretense of celebrating her birthday. When defendant returned from vacation without victim, her adult children reported her missing. Defendant rented a room at the Circus Circus Hotel in his own name but also rented a second room at the Tuscany under a fake name. Victim's DNA was found in the shower drain in the Tuscany room. Investigators believe victim was shot and dismembered with a band saw in the Tuscany room. Blood was found in the couple's vehicle, and defendant was seen on surveillance video purchasing an electric saw, bleach, and trash bags. In letters from jail, defendant admitted to cooking and eating part of the body. Defendant convicted of first-degree murder and sentenced to death at his own request.

Sources: http://www.reviewjournal.com/news/retired-teacher-gets-death-penalty-wifes-murder; http://vegasmurderwatch.com/nvdr.html

Keywords: **Death penalty, Forensic evidence: DNA, confession to friends and family**

Case 374

Defendant: **George Watters**
Victim: Myrtle Watters
Trial: 1927 Jurisdiction: Sacramento, California
Murder: January 27, 1926
Evidence: Victim was defendant's wife. Defendant shot his wife. Defendant's 10-year-old daughter witnessed the murder and was the prosecution's primary witness. She testified that defendant shot and dismembered victim in front of her and then threatened to cut her throat if she ever told anyone. Defendant told inconsistent stories about victim's whereabouts. Defendant convicted of first-degree murder.
Source: *People v. Watters*, Supreme Court of California, Cr. 2955, September 22, 1927
Keyword: **Eyewitness**

Case 375

Defendant: **Jeffrey Weston**
Victim: Frances Franchey
Trial: 2003 Jurisdiction: Richland County, South Carolina
Murder: August 6, 1998
Evidence: Victim was defendant's mother. Defendant was 38 and living with victim in her apartment. Witnesses said that victim did not want defendant to live with her and was terrified of him. She was talking about asking defendant to move out when she disappeared on August 6, 1998. The same day, a witness saw the trunk to victim's car was open and lined with plastic. Same witness saw defendant driving victim's car, which he had never done before. Another witness saw defendant loading garbage bags into the trunk of the car. Another witness saw plants turned over on victim's porch and an empty bottle of bleach. Police went to the apartment, and defendant told them that victim had run off with a man and left a note. When police came a second time, defendant said victim's purse and keys were missing though witnesses saw them in the apartment before and after the interview. Defendant also changed the shower curtain in the bathroom. Defendant vacated the apartment, and police found that linoleum in the kitchen and a section of carpet had been torn out. Bloody drag marks were found matching victim's blood. Defendant convicted of murder and sentenced to 40 years imprisonment. Defendant later confessed at posttrial hearing to murdering and dismembering victim, stating he had been off medication for schizophrenia and that victim had been hitting him when he pushed her and she hit her head. He led investigators to her remains, buried near the apartment, in 2008.
Sources: *State v. Weston*, Supreme Court of South Carolina, No. 26099, January 17, 2006; *Weston v. Warden*, Perry Correctional Inst., United States District Court, D. South Carolina, Florence Division, No. 4:10-0107-JMC-TER, January 26, 2011; http://www.wistv.com/story/7797434/son-admits-to-10-year-old-murder-leads-police-to-body
Keywords: **Forensic evidence: DNA, Eyewitnesses**

Case 376

Defendant: **Charles Thomas White**
Victim: Randal "Randy" Beck
Trial: June 1992 Jurisdiction: Gwinnett County, Georgia
Murder: January 23, 1992
Evidence: Defendant claimed he was a prospective employee at victim's bakery business and was staying in victim's condominium for a few days. When victim's family couldn't contact victim, they went to his condo and saw defendant driving victim's car with victim's dog. Victim's wallet was in the trunk. Police found several bloodstains in victim's condominium, primarily in the living room and on the sofa. The blood matched victim's blood group, and an expert testified that victim likely died from that amount of blood loss unless he received immediate medical treatment. The night of victim's disappearance, defendant told a witness that he had just slit the throat of a man who had made a homosexual advance. He claimed they got into a fight and defendant had killed victim in self-defense. Two hours later, he told another witness about the murder, and then the next day told his father that he had cut victim across the neck and killed him. At trial, defendant testified that victim had drugged him and he had awoken to find victim sexually assaulting him. A fight ensued, and defendant wrestled a knife away from victim, accidentally cutting his neck. They continued fighting and defendant kicked victim in the head. Defendant then cleaned up, put victim's body into victim's vehicle, and dumped the body in the woods. Defendant claimed that most of the fight was in the kitchen, but there was no blood evidence in the kitchen and substantial blood evidence in other rooms. Defendant convicted of murder. Conviction upheld in 1993.
Sources: *White v. State*, Supreme Court of Georgia, No. S93A0102, May 3, 1993; http://archives.savannahnow.com/sav_pdf_archive/text/fr245/C_2343106.pdf
Keywords: **Confession to family and friends, Forensic evidence: Other**

Case 377

Defendant: **Steven Wayne White (a.k.a. Jane Golden)**
Victim: James Albert Boyd
Trial: December 1987 Jurisdiction: Tampa Bay, Florida
Murder: February 6, 1987
Evidence: Defendant was victim's boyfriend. Victim was last seen at a bank prior to leaving on a scheduled trip for South Africa. Bank employees called police when defendant posed as victim and tried to withdraw money from victim's bank accounts. At victim's residence, police found bloodstains, bullet holes, and spent cartridges. Valuable items were missing from the residence. Defendant and victim's former girlfriend were driving victim's car and had several hundred thousand dollars worth of victim's belongings. Victim was a bisexual transvestite, and defense argued that he voluntarily disappeared so he could start a new life as a woman. Defendant convicted of first-degree murder and sentenced to life imprisonment.

Sources: http://www.stpete.org/police/publicinterest/missing-persons.html; Doe Network; Charley Project
Keywords: **Life, Forensic evidence: Other**

Case 378

Defendant: **Jonathan Whitesides**
Victim: Eric Humbert
Trial: 1993 Jurisdiction: New Albany, Indiana
Murder: January 15, 1992
Evidence: Defendant and victim were friends and coworkers. Victim disappeared on his way home from work. Victim's car was later found abandoned in Louisville with a bullet hole in the windshield, blood evidence in the hatchback, and brain tissue behind the radiator. Investigators exhumed victim's father in order to match DNA to blood and tissue evidence. Police also discovered a possible affair between defendant and victim's wife. At first, defendant claimed he and victim played basketball after work the day of his disappearance. After police found 9 mm cartridge cases and blood in defendant's garage, defendant claimed that he and victim fought when victim accused him of "hosing" his wife, and victim accidentally stabbed himself in the neck. Defendant's story was inconsistent with blood spatter analysis of the garage, which suggested a gunshot wound. Defendant convicted of murder and sentenced to 40 years imprisonment.
Sources: http://livedash.ark.com/transcript/body_of_evidence__from_the_case_files_of_dayle_hinman/5100/HLN/Saturday_April_02_2011/578608/; http://www.nwafs.org/abstracts/spring98.htm
Keywords: **Forensic evidence: DNA, Forensic evidence: Other, Confession to police**

Case 379

Defendant: **Cornelius Wilhelms**
Victims: Unknown
Trial: June 1839 Jurisdiction: New York County, New York
Murder: March 1839
Evidence: Defendant and two others convicted of throwing the master and officers of a ship, *Braganza*, overboard during a mutiny. There were two women on board who were also murdered. The mutineers were caught by a German vessel and returned to the United States for trial. All three men were sentenced to death. Believed to be first no-body murder trial in the United States.
Sources: *United States v. Brown*, Case No. 14,656a; http://www.nytimes.com/1860/07/14/news/execution-hicks-pirate-twelve-thousand-people-bedloe-s-island-scenes-tombs-bay.html
Keywords: **Death penalty, Codefendant testimony**

Case 380

Defendant: **Augustus Williams**
Victim: Mary Perrine

Trial: Fall 1985 Jurisdiction: Montgomery County, Ohio
Murder: February 1985
Evidence: Victim disappeared while shopping at a mall in Dayton. Witnesses in the mall parking lot that night testified to hearing the muffled screams of a woman and gunshots. Two witnesses saw a black male with a gun near a vehicle matching the description of victim's vehicle. Witnesses saw defendant spray painting a vehicle, later identified as victim's, to change the color from blue to white. Another witness testified that defendant had offered to pay him to drive the vehicle to Chicago and abandon it there, and another testified that defendant had tried to pay him to paint it. Blood matching victim's blood type was found in the vehicle's carpeting. While under arrest for theft of the vehicle, defendant stated, "I hope this isn't about that white lady" and "I bought the car, but I did not kill this lady" before police had mentioned a killing or murder. Defendant's juvenile accomplice testified against him, stating that he and defendant went to the mall the day of the murder and defendant was carrying a gun. They followed victim to her car, planning to rob her, and began to physically assault her. Defendant threw victim into the back seat and shot her in the chest. Victim was still alive when they carried her into the woods, and defendant instructed accomplice to shoot her. Defendant was convicted of aggravated murder and kidnapping. In 2004, defendant filed a motion for a new trial after defendant's accomplice recanted his trial testimony but was denied.
Sources: *State v. Williams*, Court of Appeals of Ohio, Second District, Montgomery County, Nos. 9597, 9815; *State v. Williams*, Court of Appeals of Ohio, Second District, Montgomery County, No. 19854, June 18, 2004
Keywords: **Codefendant testimony, Forensic evidence: Other; Confession to police**

Case 381

Defendant: **Daniel Norman Williams**
Victim: Alma Nesbitt
Trial: 1904 Jurisdiction: Portland, Oregon
Murder: March 1900
Evidence: Victim was defendant's wife, who moved with him to Oregon shortly after their engagement in May 1899 so they could set up two homesteads and then consolidate them upon their marriage. Victim disappeared along with her mother, who was staying on her homestead at the time. On June 23, defendant forged victim's signature to amend his homestead entry to include part of victim's homestead. Victim later moved to Washington State with a woman posing as victim. Defendant provided investigators with inconsistent statements regarding the whereabouts of victim and victim's mother and wrote letters discouraging victim's family from searching for her. Victim's family came to defendant's homestead to investigate and found, buried on the property, gunnysacks soaked in blood and two tufts of hair also soaked in blood. Relatives testified that one of the sets of hair belonged to victim's mother. Defendant may have burned vic-

tim and her mother's bodies after they were discovered to be missing. Defendant convicted of murder.

Source: *State v. Williams*, Supreme Court of Oregon, 46 Or. 287, April 28, 1905

Keyword: **Forensic evidence: Other**

Case 382

Defendant: **Jimmy Russell Williams**

Victim: John McGraw

Trial: April 1980 Jurisdiction: Dallas County, Texas

Murder: December 2, 1978

Evidence: Defendant was taking drugs and drinking beer with a friend when victim knocked on his door. When defendant did not respond, he walked around and knocked on a window before returning to the front door, where defendant shot him in the stomach with a shotgun in front of three witnesses. Defendant and two friends tried to drive victim to hospital, but he died en route. Defendant and friends then abandoned the body in a remote location. Witnesses in the neighborhood saw victim's body being placed in an automobile, and one witness called police to report it. Witnesses and defendants' friends testified against him. Defendant convicted of first-degree murder and sentenced to 30 years imprisonment. Conviction upheld in 1981.

Source: *Williams v. State*, Court of Appeals of Texas, Dallas, No. 05-81-00288-CR, December 30, 1981

Keywords: **Eyewitness, Codefendant testimony**

Case 383

Defendant: **Robert T. Williams**

Victim: Peggy Hilton (a.k.a. Peggy Isly)

Trial: June 1860 Jurisdiction: Rockingham County, North Carolina

Murder: December 1, 1859

Evidence: Victim and defendant were in a sexual relationship for a year or two prior to her murder. A few days after victim's disappearance, a search party found burned wood near defendant's house. Among the ashes were bone fragments. Defendant had his slave dig up the burn site when another search party was called. When a nearby creek was dragged, searchers recovered bone, hairpins, buttons, and a black substance similar to that found in the fire pit. Defendant suggested that victim's stepfather or brothers had killed her and burned her on his land. Defendant convicted of murder.

Source: *State v. Williams*, Supreme Court of North Carolina, 7 Jones (NC) 446, June 1860

Keyword: **Forensic evidence: Other**

Case 384

Defendant: **Christopher Andaryl Wills (a.k.a. "Ed Short," a.k.a. "Michael Wills")**

Victim: Zabiullah Alam

Trial: 2001 Jurisdiction: Groveton, Virginia
Murder: June 1998
Evidence: Victim caught defendant burglarizing his apartment on April 4, 1998. Defendant was arrested and charged with burglary. Victim appeared as the sole witness at defendant's preliminary hearing on June 15, 1998, and positively identified him. The case was bound over to the state grand jury. That night, defendant spoke to his incarcerated brother over the phone; the conversation was recorded by the Augusta Correctional Facility. Defendant discussed victim's testimony and suggested he would stop the victim from testifying against him. Two days later, defendant purchased a cell phone under a fake name. A handwritten note was left on victim's doorstep advertising jobs and listing the cell phone number defendant had just acquired. Throughout the course of his plan, defendant continually called his brother to update him, and the conversations were all recorded by the prison. Prior to disappearing, victim told his family he had called the number on the handwritten flier and had an interview scheduled for June 25 with "Mr. Felliece's" secretary in Washington DC. Victim's family reported him missing when he didn't return. That day, defendant told his brother that everything was taken care of and referenced disposal of the body. While in court for his superseding indictment, defendant told other prisoners that he could not be executed because the body would never be found. Defendant's cell phone, purchased under the fake name, showed outgoing calls to victim's home number and pager. Defendant convicted of kidnapping resulting in death and interstate stalking resulting in death, and was sentenced to life imprisonment without the possibility of parole. Conviction upheld in 2003.
Source: *United States v. Wills*, United States Court of Appeals, Fourth Circuit, Nos. 01-4630, 01-4813, 01-4964, October 7, 2003
Keywords: **Life, Forensic evidence: Other, Informant, Confession to friends and family**

Case 385

Defendant: **Stephen Michael Wilson**
Victim: Brian Bleyl
Trial: 1989 Jurisdiction: Maricopa County, Arizona
Murder: February 28, 1981
Evidence: Victim was a 12-year-old paperboy who disappeared on his newspaper route on the afternoon of February 28, 1981. Defendant was openly homosexual, and victim and other youths allegedly made homophobic remarks to him. Victim's bike was found behind defendant's apartment, and a witness testified to seeing victim at defendant's door around the time of his disappearance. Defendant also allegedly confessed to two acquaintances and a doctor, saying he became enraged after victim made homophobic insults. A three-week recess was declared in the middle of the trial so that the trial judge could go on vacation. Defendant acquitted and later died of AIDS-related causes in December 1994 but continued to maintain his innocence.

Sources: http://www.phoenixnewtimes.com/1994-01-05/news/end-of-an-ordeal/; Charley Project; http://www.debbiemilke.com/en/mjplay/hendrix.shtml#.UsshlKX0BcQ

Keywords: **Eyewitnesses, Confession to friends and family**

Case 386

Defendant: **Seth Lawton Winder**

Victim: Richard Hernandez

Trial: November 2011 Jurisdiction: Denton County, Texas

Murder: September 2008

Evidence: Defendant was a homeless man who murdered victim during a sexual encounter in victim's apartment. Large amounts of blood were found in victim's apartment, and tissue from internal organs in the bathtub where they believed the body was dismembered. Defendant was caught using victim's debit card after his disappearance, and was found walking along a road with his clothing and backpack covered in victim's blood. Investigators later found pornographic images of defendant, taken in victim's apartment, on a camera recovered from defendant's father's garage. At defendant's campsite, they found more of victim's blood and a sword. Defendant was diagnosed with paranoid schizophrenia and was deemed unfit to stand trial in April 2009. After several months in a state hospital and two years of delays, defendant was tried again in November 2011. A mistrial was declared when the judge learned defendant had stopped taking his anti-psychotic medication, and defendant was ordered to a state hospital.

Sources: http://www.dallasobserver.com/2012-01-12/news/can-accused-killer-seth-winder-stay-sane-long-enough-to-stand-trial/full/; http://www.dallasvoice.com/gay-dallas-man-murdered-dismembered-1038702.html

Keyword: **Forensic evidence: DNA**

Case 387

Defendants: **Eric Witte, John Witte, Hilma Marie Witte**

Victim: Elaine Witte

Trial: November 1985 Jurisdiction: Laporte County, Indiana

Murder: January 8, 1984

Evidence: Victim was mother-in-law to defendant Marie and grandmother to defendants Eric and John. In 1981, Marie instructed 16-year-old Eric to shoot his father while he slept on a sofa. In 1982, defendants moved in with victim, and Marie began discussing ways to kill victim and made attempts to poison her. On January 8, 1984, Marie ordered 15-year-old John to shoot victim in the ribcage with a crossbow. Defendants and several friends spent the next several months disposing of victim's body with knives, a chainsaw, a trash compactor, a garbage disposal, and acid. The remains that were not destroyed were stored in the freezer then discarded across several states. Eric and John's friends helped dispose of the body, and later testified against defendants. John testified against his mother as part of his plea agreement, and all three defendants confessed to planning the murder beforehand, and Eric testified against her as well. Marie convicted of murder and conspiracy and received a collective sentence of 90 years imprisonment.

Sources: *Witte v. State*, Supreme Court of Indiana, No. 46S00-8810-CR-887, February 12, 1990; http://articles.chicagotribune.com/1985-11-13/news/8503180389_1_crossbow-killing-john-witte

Keywords: **Eyewitness, Codefendant testimony**

Case 388

Defendant: **Johnny Wright (a.k.a "Errol Edwards")**

Victim: Rebecca Doisy

Trial: February 2011 Jurisdiction: Boone County, Missouri

Murder: August 1976

Evidence: Victim met defendant through her work as a waitress and agreed to go out with him after repeated requests. Victim disappeared in August 1976 after last being seen with defendant, and she was reported missing when she did not show up for work. Defendant was questioned by police and released. In 1985, defendant confessed to an acquaintance at a methadone clinic, and the acquaintance contacted police. A warrant was issued for defendant's arrest, but he was not arrested until September 2009 when he went to pick up a background check on a prospective employee. He had been living in various states under the name "Errol Edwards." At trial, a second witness came forward, saying that defendant had confessed to him. Defendant convicted of second-degree murder and sentenced to 30 years imprisonment.

Sources: http://www.ajc.com/news/news/local/georgia-grandfather-convicted-of-murder-three-deca/nQp9M/; http://www.connectmidmissouri.com/news/story.aspx?id=571814#.Ussj9KX0BcQ; http://www.missourinet.com/2011/04/11/wright-to-serve-30-years-for-murder-of-rebecca-doisy-in-columbia/

Keyword: **Confession to friends and family**

Case 389

Defendant: **Myron Wynn**

Victim: Robert Wykel

Trial: December 2010/April 2011 Jurisdiction: King County, Washington

Murder: February 1996

Evidence: Victim was last seen accompanying defendant to a remote wooded area. Victim had previously given defendant a $1,000 deposit for a car that defendant was unable to produce. Victim expressed frustration with defendant to several witnesses and a desire to get his money back. Defendant was having financial difficulties and living on his girlfriend's income. Defendant provided inconsistent and evasive statements regarding victim's disappearance, and tried to incriminate a friend. In 2000, defendant's sister contacted authorities with information that defendant had a diamond with him when he moved back to Texas in late 1997, matching the unique description of the diamond on the ring victim always wore. Based on a verbal description from victim's daughter, a jeweler made a drawing of the ring that matched the diamond defendant brought to Texas. Defendant's former girlfriend testified that he tried to give her a diamond ring in the days following victim's disappearance. The first trial in December 2010 resulted in a hung jury, but a second jury convicted defendant of first-degree murder and robbery. Defendant sentenced to 20 years imprisonment. Defendant appealed his conviction for robbery but not murder. Conviction upheld in 2013.

Source: *State v. Wynn*, Court of Appeals of Washington, Division 1, No. 67227-4-I, June 3, 2013

Keyword: **Forensic evidence: Other**

Case 390

Defendant: **Dmitriy Yakovlev**

Victim: Irina Malezhik

Trial: March 2011 Jurisdiction: Kings County, New York

Murder: October 15, 2007

Evidence: Irina Malezhik left her apartment building on October 15, 2007, which was the last time anyone saw her. She was carrying a makeup bag when she left her apartment lobby in Brooklyn. She was reported missing on November 8 by a personal friend. At the time of her disappearance, she worked as a court translator and was working with delicate information related to fraud and organized crime; however, the police did not feel her work had anything to do with her disappearance. The day after her disappearance, there were deposits made into the account of Julia and Dmitry Yakovlev from the Malezhik checking account. There were four checks, all signed with her name, which was found to be forged. The defendant was a native of Russia and had been a surgeon there. On November 10, the Yakvolevs got a credit card in her name. In July 2009, the Yakovlevs were charged with identity theft equaling more the $37,000. The Yakvolevs used these ill-gotten gains to go shopping and purchase many expensive items, which included matching wristwatches. Before she disappeared, Malezhik expressed fear that she would be receiving a phone call from someone she knew only as Dmitry. The Yakvolevs still maintain their innocence, they stated that they did not even know her, and they suggested that Malezhik returned to Ukraine, her home country. Her family was also from Ukraine, and she had no relations living within the United States. Upon further investigation, there was nothing to suggest she had in fact left the country, and Dmitry admitted knowing her. He confessed she had given him instruction in English and that she had borrowed money from him to purchase furniture. Dmitry was subsequently charged with the murder of Malezhik in March 2010. When police were searching his home in 2009, they dug up the basement looking for Malezhik's remains, which were not located. However, there were several personal items belonging to her, including her Social Security card, cell phone, and underwear, which contained her DNA. During this search, they also located several personal items belonging to another man believed to have been murdered by the defendant and his wife. A third victim was tied to the defendant through the defendant's use of his credit cards. At trial, the government established that Dmitry knew all three victims; he was, in fact, the last person to have seen them alive, and subsequently had personal items belonging to each of them, which included their personal identifications. It was also shown that the manner in which one victim's body was dismembered would take a level of surgical skill that Dmitry possessed. Julia Yakovlev pleaded guilty to credit card fraud and identity theft in February 2011 prior to her trial. Dmitry was convicted of all 15 charges he was facing, which included the deaths of Malezhik and the two other men. He received a 30-year prison sentence.

Sources: Charley Project; http://www.fbi.gov/newyork/press-releases/2011/dmitriy-yakovlev-sentenced-to-30-years-in-prison-for-identity-theft-involving-three-missing-or-murdered-persons; http://www.fbi.gov/newyork/press-releases/2011/dmitriy-yakovlev-sentenced-to-30-years-in-prison-for-identity-theft-involving-three-missing-or-murdered-persons

Keywords: **Forensic evidence: DNA, Confession to police**

Case 391

Defendant: **Justin Yoshikawa**

Victim: Carlee Morse

Trial: November 2011 Jurisdiction: Wayne County, Michigan

Murder: August 20, 2010

Evidence: In a statement to police, and upon question by the court on a plea bargain after three days of trial, the codefendant, Nicholas Cottrell, claimed he met defendant at a drug house early in 2010 and hatched the murder plan. The motive was unclear, but possibly due to victim's stomping on defendant's face while he was sleeping. Codefendant confirmed that the victim, 16, was lured from her family's Westland apartment on the 7000 block of West Bonnie. At about 12:30 a.m., victim stepped outside to make a call and was barefoot and in her pajamas. Victim was lured into codefendant's 1998 Ford Escort to smoke marijuana. Defendant hid underneath some clothes and cardboard in the back seat of a car, and victim sat in the front. After driving around for a while, at some point, a requested song came on the radio, and defendant strangled victim with a dog leash until she was dead, while codefendant held her legs. They hid the car in a garage. The next night, defendant placed her body in trash bags. Defendants then drove around randomly while smoking marijuana, and placed the victim's body in a dumpster outside a red brick church about an hour or two away. When codefendant refused to testify at trial, his earlier testimony was read into the record. Defendant then pleaded guilty to second-degree murder and was sentenced to 25 to 65 years. Codefendant was sentenced to 25 to 50 years for second-degree murder.

Sources: http://www.zimbio.com/Crime/articles/-3Aksekda8P/Carlee+Morse; http://www.thenewsherald.com/articles/2011/01/17/news/doc4d30b978cf37a531030928.txt; http://www.tv20detroit.com/news/local/Man-Sentenced-in-Choking-Death-of-Ex-Girlfriend-135751593.html; http://www.myfoxdetroit.com/story/18485191/suspects-mother-charged-in-carlee-morse-murder; http://prisons.einnews.com/news/saginaw-correctional-facility-michigan

Keyword: **Codefendant testimony**

Case 392

Defendant: **Evans York**
Victim: Michael Azzarro
Trial: March 22, 1994 Jurisdiction: Van Nuys, California
Murder: February 13, 1993
Evidence: Azzaro, 16 years old, and York, 19 years old, were seen together in victim's new red Isuzu Rodeo in the Van Nuys area. Defendant told police he went with victim to Los Angeles, and they were both abducted at gunpoint. Defendant said he escaped but that victim was still being held. Family members reported victim missing the next day. Phone company records during that same time listed calls from the victim's car phone to the defendant's guardian. The victim's car was found on Imperial Highway in Lennox. April Cotton told the police that 10 days after victim disappeared, she overheard defendant admit the crime. She said defendant said, "Blood, I can't go back to the Valley.... I snatched the blood up out of the car and I pulled out the strap on him, and when I busted, I just jumped in the car and boned out." The police translated this as street slang for pulling someone out of a car, shooting him, and then jumping in the car and leaving. However, she changed her testimony at the trial, saying she heard it from a third party. Defendant was acquitted of murder, as the evidence was deemed too circumstantial and unreliable.
Sources: http://articles.latimes.com/1994-02-23/local/me-26243_1_evans-york; http://articles.latimes.com/1994-09-10/local/me-36816_1_circumstantial-evidence
Keyword: **Confession to friends and family**

Case 393

Defendants: **William Younger, Ross Younger, three others**
Victim: Connie Franklin
Trial: December 17, 1929 Jurisdiction: Stone County, Arkansas
Murder: March 9, 1929
Evidence: This was a bizarre case where it is alleged that victim testified at his own trial. In March 1929 victim Connie Franklin disappeared. He was betrothed to Tillie Ruminer, and she and a witness named Bertha Burns reported him missing. Burns found victim's bloody hat and later led police to an ash pit where bone fragments and teeth were found. Sheriff Sam Johnson testified that these bone fragments were found near Burns's home. Dr. C. W. Garrison, the state medical officer, determined that the bone fragments came from a human skull. (At trial, however, he could not swear to this, as the temple piece was mislaid.) Ruminer, victim's fiancée, reported that she and victim were attacked by defendants Hubert Hester, Herman Greenway, Joe White, and William Younger. (Alex Fulks was also indicted as the ringleader.) Ruminer alleged that Hester and Greenway took her into the woods and raped her, while the others tortured, mutilated, and then burned Franklin alive. (At the trial, she said that she only saw victim beaten unconscious.) Ruminer said she had remained quiet initially about what had happened due to threats to her and her family. A grand jury indicted the defendants, and the case was set for

trial. In early December, just before trial, Marion Franklin Rogers came forward and testified that he was the same man as Connie Franklin. It came out that Rogers had a wife and children and had been in a mental hospital, from which he escaped in 1926. Ruminer and her father testified that they were not the same man. The defense presented witnesses from the community, including Rogers, that they were the same man. A deaf mute witness corroborated Ruminer's story of the attack. In addition to not being able to swear now that the skull fragment was human, the doctor and another witnesses testified that the teeth found were not human. The "victim" testified that he left town when Ruminer said she would not marry him and returned only because he heard men were on trial for his murder. After the jury initially deadlocked, the court told them that the government had spent $8,000 on the case, and they needed to reach a verdict. All the defendants were then acquitted.

Sources: https://en.wikipedia.org/wiki/Connie_Franklin_murder_case; http://www.encyclopediaofarkansas.net/encyclopedia/entry-detail.aspx?entryID=5929

Keyword: **Eyewitness**

Case 394

Defendant: **Eugene Zapata**

Victim: Jeanette Zapata

Trial: September 2007/February 2008 Jurisdiction: Dane County, Wisconsin

Murder October 11, 1976

Evidence: Thirty years after the murder, in an investigation that had been reopened, defendant confessed during a plea bargain that he went to his wife's house and had a divorce- and custody-related argument, which made him wild with anger. He repeatedly hit his wife from behind at the top of the head with a draftsman's tool. He then pushed her down and strangled her until his hands hurt. He wrapped a cord about her neck, but by that time she was dead. He cleaned up the blood, wrapped her body in a tent, and drove it to a plot near Highway 151 and Reiner Road and hid it in underbrush. He later took the body to a piece of land he owned in Juneau County, and it remained there 24 years. After selling the land, he took the body to Sun Prairie storage locker, where he cut the body into pieces and disposed of in numerous dumpsters in Mauston landfill. There was no way to recover the body. Corpse-smelling dogs did indicate human remains at the two locations, but this evidence was excluded in the first trial. At the trial, the prosecution showed that victim was a reliable and punctual person. Her purse and other personal items were found shortly after her disappearance. The prosecution also showed that the defendant had left work early the morning of her disappearance, was out of work the next day, and came into work late the following day. He told police he had to care for their children on the day he missed, but the children were actually in school. In the trial, defendant did not testify in his own defense, and the jury deadlocked 10–1–1 for conviction. The defendant then pleaded guilty to reckless homicide and received a sentence of 5 years in prison. Case was notable because there was no physical evidence.

Sources: http://socyberty.com/crime/eugene-zapata/; http://www.620wtmj.com/shows/jeffwagner/45156067.html; http://www.nbc15.com/news/headlines/9784647.html; http://dogsdontlie.com/main/2008/12/cadaver-dogs-how-reliable-are-they-at-detecting-death/comment-page-1/

Keyword: **Confession to police**

Case 395

Defendant: **Guillermo Zarabozo**

Victims: Jake Branham, Kelley Branham, Scott Gamble, Samuel Kairy

Trial: July 2008/February 2009 Jurisdiction: Dade County, Florida

Murder: September 23, 2007

Evidence: The victims were charter boat captain Jake Branham, his wife, Kelley, and crew members Gamble and Kairy. Trial testimony showed that Zarabozo and codefendant Kirby Archer paid $4,000 cash to hire the boat *Joe Cool* in September 2007 for a purported trip to Bimini, Bahamas. Prosecutors alleged that Archer hijacked the boat and headed for Cuba to escape a child molestation and theft investigation in Arkansas. Archer pleaded guilty to first-degree murder, robbery, kidnapping, and hijacking. Archer testified that as the boat reached Bimini, he retrieved his loaded semiautomatic pistol and took position on the fly bridge. Archer heard a shot on the lower deck and shot the captain and his wife, whose bodies tumbled over the railing. Archer was sentenced to five consecutive life sentences. Zarabozo was tried on charges of murder, robbery, kidnapping, hijacking, and weapons charges. Zarabozo claimed he was on a secret CIA mission to Cuba when, without his knowledge and intention, Archer hijacked the boat, and he claimed that he was allowed to live because he agreed to throw the bodies overboard. At the first trial, the jury deadlocked on the nonweapons counts, believing Zarabozo's claims that the hijacking and murders had been planned and initiated by Archer, without Zarabozo's knowledge. Zarabozo owned the gun that was the murder weapon. At the initial trial, Zarabozo was found guilty on the weapons charges. At his retrial, Zarabozo was found guilty on four murder charges and given five consecutive life sentences plus 85 years.

Sources: https://en.wikipedia.org/wiki/Guillermo_Zarabozo; http://www.mahalo.com/guillermo-zarabozo/; http://www.theledger.com/article/20090506/NEWS/905065077/1410?Title=Man-Gets-Life-Plus-85-Years-for-Joe-Cool-Boat-Killings&tc=ar; http://www.theledger.com/article/20090506/NEWS/905065077/1410?p=2&tc=pg; http://mikeb302000.blogspot.com/2009/05/guillermo-zarabozo-gets-5-life.html; http://articles.sun-sentinel.com/keyword/guillermo-zarabozo/recent/2

Keywords: **Confession to police, Codefendant testimony, Life**

Case 396

Defendant: **Hasson Zarif**

Victim: Zaheerah Zarif

Trial: March 9, 2000, Jurisdiction: New York County, New York
Murder: Spring 1996
Evidence: Three years after murder, defendant confessed to having shot his wife several times in the head and chest at close range with a 9 mm Glock, and there was corroboration by his repeated display of a consciousness of guilt and an admission of homicidal intent. There was evidence of defendant's motive to kill his wife, with limited admission into evidence of prior threats. Defendant led the police to an abandoned lot in Brooklyn, where human bone fragments were found. There was a $100,000 policy on her life. "The victim's disappearance strongly suggested a homicide, because the evidence was wholly inconsistent with the possibility that she abandoned her possessions and departed without ever contacting any of her relatives." Defendant found guilty of second-degree murder and given 22 years to life.
Sources: http://caselaw.findlaw.com/ny-supreme-court-appellate-division/1397961.html; Newman, A., "Police Say Husband Confesses to Killing his Wife Three Years Ago," *New York Times*, February 17, 1999
Keywords: **Confession to police, Life**

Case 397

Defendant: **Robert Zarinsky**
Victim: Rosemary Calandriello
Trial April 1975 Jurisdiction: Monmouth County, New Jersey
Murder: August 25, 1969
Evidence: The victim, 17 years old, was walking to the corner store for milk, and four eyewitnesses saw the victim in the defendant's car, which was later found with the door handles and windows missing. The defendant's wife said that a pair of blue panties recovered from the defendant's car belonged to her and gave her husband an alibi for the time of the murder. Police found a ballpeen hammer in the car that had hair on it from someone other than victim. In 1988, defendant admitted to the police that he had accidentally killed her and buried her body in a grave in northwest New Jersey. He also stated to another investigator that he had thrown her body in the ocean. Defendant bragged to others that he could not be prosecuted without a body. The defendant was convicted of first-degree murder and sentenced to life in prison.
Sources: https://en.wikipedia.org/wiki/Robert_Zarinsky; http://www.murderpedia.org/male.Z/z/zarinsky-robert.htm
Keywords: **Eyewitnesses, Confession to police, Confession to friends and family, Life**

Case 398

Defendant: **Reuben Zavala**
Victim: Nicholas Andrew Plaza
Trial July 2007 Jurisdiction: Bexar County, Texas
Murder: October 23, 2001
Evidence: The victim was the 5-year-old son of the defendant's girlfriend, Priscilla Plaza, who testified that the defendant sexually and

physically abused the victim. She stated that the last time she saw him he could not walk due to an ankle injury, and he had injuries to other parts to his body. Defendant confessed in a television interview that the victim stopped breathing, and his body was dumped in trash bin behind a bank. The girlfriend eventually pleaded guilty and testified against the defendant, telling the jury of his physical and sexual abuse of the victim. She testified to the extreme injuries her son had when she last saw him, including an ankle injury, emaciated with his hair falling out, and red spots all over his body. Defendant was convicted of injury to child and sentenced to 67 years.

Sources: Charley Project; http://www.411gina.org/nicholasplaza.htm

Keywords: **Confession to friends, Codefendant testimony**

Case 399

Defendant: **Marek Zochowski**

Victim: Lisa Zochowski

Trial: 1998 Jurisdiction: Maricopa County, Arizona

Murder: December 27, 1990

Evidence: Defendant and victim were married. In December 1990, they went to Christown Mall. Defendant claimed that victim left with two other people and never returned. A deliberate disappearance was ruled out because the victim had a young child. Since the defendant was the husband, the motive was presumed to be marital related. Blood was found in a car, and it appeared victim put up a vigorous resistance. Defendant was convicted of first-degree manslaughter and sentenced to 20 years.

Source: http://www.azfamily.com/news/Exclusive-Photos-Reveal-What-Happened-to-Missing-Mother-172670901.html

Keyword: **Forensic evidence: Other**

Index

C

D

I

J

K

M

N

Q

R

T

U

V

Z

Milton Keynes UK
Ingram Content Group UK Ltd.
UKHW021627071024
449327UK00020BA/1214